Collected Thoughts

on Teaching and Learning, Creativity, and Horn Performance

DOUGLAS HILL

Alfred Publishing Co., Inc.
16320 Roscoe Blvd., Suite 100
P.O. Box 10003
Van Nuys, CA 91410-0003
alfred.com

ISBN-10: 0-7579-0159-X
ISBN-13: 978-0-7579-0159-1

Collected Thoughts on Teaching and Learning, Creativity, and Horn Performance
By Douglas Hill

ISBN-10: 0-7579-0159-X
ISBN-13: 978-0-7579-0159-1

Project Manager: Thom Proctor
Production Coordinator: Sharon Marlow
Art Design and Layout: Thais Yanes
Layout: Susan Gershman

Photographs of French Horns in chapter headings courtesy of G. LeBlanc Corporation.
Photographs on pages 3, 4, 5, 7, and 8 used by permission of Ed Harris, GIA Publications, photos by Bruce Benward.
Back cover photograph of Douglas Hill by Katrin Talbot.

[1] *Method for Cor Alto and Cor Basse*, Duprat, English Translation by Viola Roth, © 1994 Viola Roth, Published by Birdalone Music, 1994, All Rights Reserved, Used by Permission, p. 37.

[2] "The Urge to Achieve," *Classics of Organizational Behavior*, David McClelland, © 1978, Moore Publishing Co., 75.

[3] *The Marriage of Sense and Soul, Integrating Science and Religion*, Ken Wilbur, © by Ken Wilbur, Reprinted by Permission of Random House, Inc., All Rights Reserved, p. 75.

[4] *The Art of Study*, by Edmond Bordeaux Szekely, © I.B.S. International, All Rights Reserved, Used by Permission. To obtain other books by Edmond Bordeaux Szekely, please write to I.B.S. International, P.O. Box 849, Nelson, B.C., Canada, V1L 6A5, p. 90.

[5] *Freedom to Learn*, Carl Rogers © 1994, Reprinted by Permission of Pearson Education, Inc., Upper Saddle River, NJ 07458, p. 90.

[6] *Motion/Stillnes* (SN 1067), Recorded by the Tom Varner Quartet, Liner Notes Written by Nat Hentoff, © 1983 Soul Notes Records, All Rights Reserved, Used by Permission, p. 103.

[7] *Musings: The Musical Worlds of Gunther Schuller: A Collection of Writings*, Gunther Schuller, © 1986 Oxford University Press, Inc., Used by Permission of Oxford University Press, p. 105.

This book is dedicated to all of the wondrous students who have chosen me
to be part of their growth. I have learned so much from all of them.
And I wish to continue my dedication to all of those
who might find guidance and inspiration from these collected thoughts.

Douglas Hill
December 31, 2000
Madison, Wisconsin

Forethoughts

After more than 30 years of teaching at the college level, with the award of a partial sabbatical from the University of Wisconsin, I can, at long last, share these collected thoughts on the rewarding art of teaching, the remarkable act of performance, and the intellectual and spiritual wonders of musical creativity.

So many fine learning and playing opportunities have come my way. My student years included such effective teachers as Kenneth Freese, Duane Schulz, Jack Snider, Philip Farkas, Rudolph Puletz, Abe Kniaz, and Paul Ingraham. Later as a performer, I attended Tanglewood and Aspen and performed with Henry Mancini, Andy Williams, the Rochester Philharmonic, the New York City Ballet Orchestra, the Martha Graham Dance Co., the Alvin Ailey Dance Co., Mostly Mozart at Carnegie Hall, the Contemporary Chamber Ensembles of New York and Chicago, the New York Brass Quintet, the Spoleto Festival Brass Quintet, the Aspen Festival Orchestra and the St. Louis, Indianapolis, and Grand Rapids Symphonies. Since arriving in Madison, I have performed with the Wingra Woodwind Quintet, and I presently perform with the Wisconsin Brass Quintet and the Madison Symphony Orchestra. A long-term affiliation with the International Horn Society as a soloist and clinician at numerous regional, national, and international workshops and as president from 1977 to 1980 has provided me with important exposure to and contact with celebrated contemporary artists, pedagogues, authors, and composers.

I have enjoyed many teaching opportunities during the past twenty-five years at the University of Wisconsin in Madison, and over the last thirty-two years on the campuses of Indiana University, Wilkes College, the University of Connecticut, the University of South Florida, Oberlin College Conservatory, the Sarasota Music Festival, and the Aspen Music School. Scores of invitations to serve as a clinician have taken me to campuses around the country and to conservatories in China, Europe, and Canada. All of these enlightening experiences have provided me with a perspective on many varied learning environments and on the astounding abilities of the growing number of talented horn students.

In the early 1970s, Robert Weast invited me to be an Associate Editor of Music Reviews for the *Brass World Magazine*. Later, Paul Mansur, then editor of *The Horn Call: Journal of the International Horn Society*, asked for reviews for that periodical as well. These editorships provided the opportunity to study and learn from the multitudes of materials being published for horn students, teachers, and performers. Numerous chances to teach have provided contact with hundreds of talented students and their technical and musical problems, which has, consequently, allowed me to make practical use of the best of these review materials. Observing these students and sharing in their learning has stimulated an intense interest in education as an art form and in the varied subtleties of the learning process.

It was as early as junior high school that lifelong interests in composing, jazz, and improvisation began. These important creative activities have enhanced understanding of many things musical and have become important aspects of many things educational. Original composition and improvisation have added significantly to my maturation as an interpretive performer.

As an outgrowth of these wonderful experiences and fortunate opportunities, I wrote more than thirty articles that were published in numerous periodicals. An equal number of outlines and notes-for-discussion were created and shared at various clinics and workshops and with private students as tutorial handouts.

In 1986 it was an honor to be invited to produce the educational video *Hill on Horn*.* This 105-minute teaching tool includes performance demonstrations on early and modern instruments, an extensive master-class segment with a young student, discussions and demonstrations on warm-ups and practice procedures, and many other technical and psychological considerations spanning the informational needs from beginning to advanced levels of ability.

---

* *Hill on Horn* is available from the Department of Continuing Education in the Arts, Lowell Hall,
   610 Langdon Street, Madison, WI 53703, and would serve well as a supplement to this text,
   providing sound and sight to these many ideas and attitudes.

Thus, it was from the compilation of all of these materials and related experiences that this book began. After collecting and reviewing these materials, I selected, revised, and rewrote the most interesting and helpful. Next, I added an extensive amount of new materials and perspectives that would help to create a more complete text. The result is this compendium of information, hints, instructions, ideas, opinions, perspectives, and enthusiastic admonitions for those things that help one to grow and enjoy the world of music and the many wonders of music-making.

This book is strongly founded on the patience of my supportive wife Karen, wonderful daughter Emily, and the horn students at the University of Wisconsin who graciously understood why I had to take so much time to consolidate and solidify these uncollected thoughts. As it turns out, the process lasted longer than a semester, but the knowledge that this long-awaited project is complete brings glee to my heart. It is my sincere hope that it will also bring service to its readers.

There are many to thank for their interest and efforts in this book becoming a reality. The two who must receive a very special thank-you are Norman Schweikert and Jeffrey Snedeker. Both of these remarkable men spent hours and hours concerning themselves with its every detail. I cannot possibly thank them enough!

My wife Karen and good friends Nancy Becknell, Jean Rife, Frøydis Ree Wekre, and Jeffrey Agrell helped in spotting typographical errors and inconsistencies and gave concerned advice regarding its content. Steve Salemson contributed valuable thoughts regarding its publication. Johnny Pherigo and Paul Mansur, as past editors of *The Horn Call*, contributed significant advice and suggestions regarding many of the original articles. For all of that help I give my sincerest thanks.

The University of Wisconsin horn students, during the past fall semester, began using this text as a reference, and I wish to thank them all for their comments, suggestions, input, and support, especially Kevin Frey, Abigail Pack, Daren Robbins, Lin Foulk, Christian Johanson, Ellie Jenkins, and Jeff Suarez, all members of the Teacher Talk seminars.

Thanks also must be extended to Jeffrey Snedeker, editor of the International Horn Society's *Horn Call*, and to Robert Weast, past publisher and copyright owner of *The Brass World Magazine*, for their unconditional permission to use the materials that originally appeared in those two fine periodicals. Further gratitude is extended to Ed Harris of GIA Publications for the unconditional use of the photographs that were taken by Bruce Benward and first used in my earlier elementary teaching text *Introducing the French Horn*. The pre-publication perspectives and endorsements from Barry Tuckwell, Norman Schweikert, Verne Reynolds, Frøydis Ree Wekre, A. David Krehbiel, Nancy Becknell, Jeffrey Agrell, Randy C. Gardner, Johnny Pherigo, Michael Hatfield, Kristin Thelander, Jean Rife, Paul Mansur, and Jeffrey L. Snedeker are all deeply appreciated.

And finally, Thom Proctor, who saved my earlier book *Extended Techniques for the Horn* from total oblivion through his interest and fine editorial talents, deserves additional gratitude for his support of this new project. I deeply appreciate his concern and expertise in the preparation of this book as well.

Contents

The Craft and Techniques of Performance

1. Getting the Good Start

What follows is a primer for starting well on the horn. If followed carefully and thoughtfully, a student (with help from a teacher) should be able to create a very substantial beginning. The details discussed would also be of assistance to any student who has perhaps made a few unsuccessful choices along the way. These are the basic details of our craft.

The horn, which is often called the French horn in North America and England, and also among jazz aficionados (to distinguish it from all of the other horns), is a popular instrument with the audiences of the world. Its mellow tone quality, smooth articulations, and true vocal character charm the listeners, while its ability to sound muscular and aggressive demands the attention and respect given to other powerful voices. The horn is an instrument of great beauty! We must never lose sight of this fact as we discuss and work with all of the little details which go into successful performances on the horn.

The horn is basically a metallic loudspeaker that is gently placed in contact with the player's lips. It is the player who produces and controls the sound, not the horn. The horn simply amplifies and enhances the player's sound. So, let's look first at what the player must do.

Relax! Relax as much as possible while you learn the following steps. Relaxation is the key to all successful development. You can identify relaxation through the physical sensations of warmth (in the hands and the face) and heaviness (throughout the body, especially the shoulders and the face). It is true that it takes the actions of many muscles working together to produce a tone. You must learn to use only the muscles needed and no others; all other muscles should remain relaxed and uninvolved. As often as possible, allow for the sensations of relaxation to enter all that you do while practicing and performing.

POSTURE

Let's work first on posture. Good posture is not just about looking good; it affects all that you do on your instrument. You must first learn to hold your body in an upright and balanced position. It is your bones that should ultimately do this job, not your muscles. Let your carriage carry you. You should avoid leaning on the backs of chairs because they differ drastically one from another and are almost never well aligned with the human body. (Most chairs are designed primarily to stack, not to support all possible body shapes.) While sitting on the edge of your chair in eager anticipation, with both feet flat on the floor creating a tripod with your torso, allow your body to feel a bit taller than normal by letting it follow your forehead as it points gently toward the stars. With such a lofty thought in mind, allow your shoulders to feel broader while not allowing them to raise. Imagine that your shoulders are very heavy. Your backbone should feel straight, not arched. Add to all of this a relaxed face starting at the top with sleepy eyes and on down to a loosened jaw. With all of the above in place, if you feel stiffness or tension anywhere in your body, especially in your face or hands, try to shake it out. Imagine the tension seeping out through the pores of your skin. Or better yet, tighten the tension even more, hold it for two seconds, and then let it all out, feeling the chills and warmth of the blood rush, while returning your full body to a well-balanced, ascending posture.

HAND POSITIONS

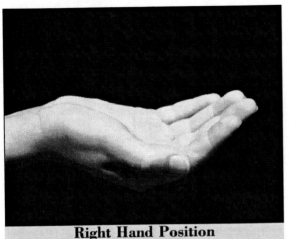

Right Hand Position

Your hands should always feel relaxed and warm. Using your mind to warm your hands is actually quite easy. It is a primary practice in the field of biofeedback training and is often used to alleviate headaches. Simply *will* it to be. Suggest to yourself the feeling of warm liquid gradually moving down through your inner arms, eventually filling your hands with warmth. Let them both hang to your sides and observe their natural curve. Your left hand should retain this general shape with a slightly increased spread of the fingers as if gently holding on to a tennis ball. The right hand will also retain its naturally curved shape with a slight pulling back of the thumb and a gradual straightening of the fingers, much like a cupped hand for swimming. When both hands are relaxed and loose, feeling the warmth of a rapid blood flow, it is a near certainty that your arms and shoulders will also be relaxed, feeling heavy yet ready for work. This is important. (A readiness for tennis on the one hand, and swimming on the other, with thoughts pointing toward the stars, should provide you with a great deal of enthusiasm!)

THE HORN

I would recommend that all young students start with a single F horn or a full double F/B♭. F is the notated key for most horn music, and the sound of an F instrument is more easily made full and rich by the younger player, establishing a better concept of this special quality of the horn.

Now, remove the horn from its case to check these important new ideas about posture. As you remove the horn, always be careful to hold on to a solid piece of tubing, not a sliding one. Using both hands is a good idea. This will help to avoid possible dents. If a horn becomes dented, you have weakened the metal, and it may not reproduce your fine playing as well as it could. It is important to treat your horn with great care. The mouthpiece should be inserted firmly with a slight twist in a clockwise direction so that it will not fall out and become severely scratched or dented. To remove it, simply twist in a counterclockwise direction and pull gently.

FRONT VIEW

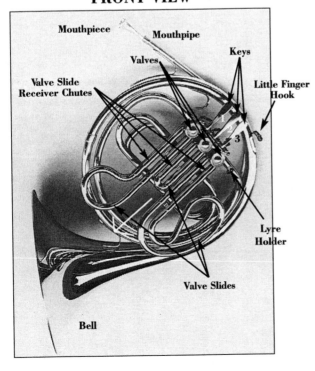

Mouthpiece
Mouthpipe
Valves
Keys
Valve Slide Receiver Chutes
Little Finger Hook
3
Lyre Holder
Valve Slides
Bell

BACK VIEW

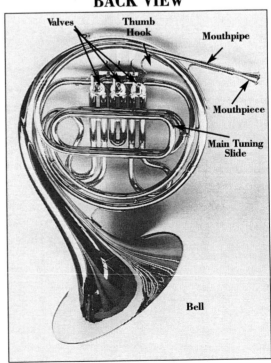

Valves
Thumb Hook
Mouthpipe
Mouthpiece
Main Tuning Slide
Bell

POSITIONING THE HORN

Most horns are designed for an average body size, which often makes them too large for a younger player. While learning such preliminary techniques as posture, it is important to remember that you are establishing the foundation for a potentially lifelong vocation or hobby. So do it correctly—right from the beginning. While getting your horn ready to play, bring the horn to you—to your size and to your shape—while in your perfect posture. Always do this no matter how you grow or change over the years! If you are still small, or simply short through the torso, turning your head slightly to the left while twisting your leg or legs to the right might be necessary while resting the horn on your leg. As you grow, you may need to raise the bell off your leg entirely to retain your all-important posture. It is never acceptable to wrap your body around your horn. Bring the horn to you and to your own body. Your body is what you have to work with, so work with it.

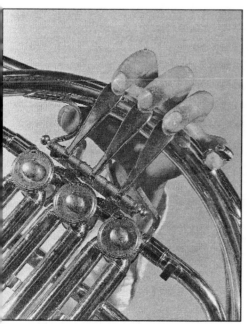

Hold the horn balanced between your left hand and somewhere on your right leg, allowing the right hand to be freely placed within the bell. Most of the time, your right hand should rest with the outstretched fingers against the lower outside of the bell and the palm pointing up toward your chest. Rest the middle finger of the right hand at the four-o'clock position within the circle of the bell.

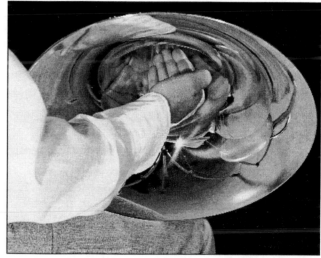

The left hand should remain curved with the fingertips resting on the keys. The thumb and little finger should gently grip the fixed hooks, or the little-finger hook and thumb valve on a double horn. If you are already tall through the torso, or choose to play off the leg, the right hand becomes the other point of balance for the horn. The right hand with the same cupped shape is best placed at the two-o'clock position, with the palm facing down toward your hips. It is vitally important that you hold the horn with your hands and not allow the lips to become a point of balance for the horn. Such pressure to the lips will interfere with the vibrations and will cause a player to tire very rapidly!

BREATHING

Now that you know how best to position your body, you are ready for the most important element in the playing of a wind or brass instrument: air and all of its uses. To bring in the large volume of air necessary for the long phrases, and for the full and vibrant sound that is so characteristic of the horn, you must first use your entire mouth as the main route to an open throat and a relaxed and expandable abdominal area. Allow additional air to come in through the nose. Remember, the more air the better! An excellent and simple way to fill with air is to inhale deeply while producing the actual sound of the whispered word "how." "HOW." As you do this, feel air rushing across the bottom of your mouth. You will also notice that your lower stomach or abdominal area will expand both down and somewhat forward. As you reach the end of your inhalation, your lower-back area and the middle area of your chest will also expand outward a little. Encourage this feeling of "getting fat," for it will help you to pull in even more air. This is all good, but only if the shoulders remain motionless and the throat does not ever feel constricted or tightened in any way.

When your lungs fill with so much air, it is easy to imagine that you should close off a valve somewhere in order not to experience an uncontrolled release. The logical place for such a valve would be your throat, but (trust me) that is simply not necessary. Take a breath in the manner just described with the throat open and relaxed. Simply suspend the air and imagine that it is a warm pool resting undisturbed just below the cavern of the mouth. Now release just a little air without making a sound. Now suspend it again. Now gradually release the remaining warm air. One soon learns that there is no need to hold the air back at the throat. There is never a need for that manner of extreme throat tension.

As you have noticed by now after having breathed for so many years, air in the lungs naturally wants to be released or exhaled and will be if simply allowed to, especially at the beginning of the exhalation. This is also true when you play the horn, with just a few refinements. You do not really need to push out the first part of this air, since it is naturally supported by all of the air compressed within the lungs and from the natural elasticity of the rib cage, which simply wishes to relax back to normal. After the initial release of this internal air pressure from within the chest area, you must gradually begin to use your abdominal area to push gently against the underside of the lungs. It is important to realize that this movement within the stomach area is not a flexing of muscles, but is a directional movement of a large area of the body. This is more like dancing than like lifting weights. You simply begin to "get skinny." It is the exact opposite movement you felt so naturally during the inhalation when you "got fat." Think only about the muscles of the sides that relax as you inhale and contract as you complete your exhale.

The muscles at the front surface of the abdomen (the so-called abs) need not tighten under normal playing conditions. If you start to intentionally tense these abdominal muscles, as if bracing to be hit in the stomach or lifting a heavy weight, you will find an almost uncontrollable tension forming at the throat. Try to sing a warm, relaxed tone while your stomach is tense. The sound of your voice will be naturally quite constricted. It is possible to learn to open your throat with all those tensions going on, but why waste all that energy if it is not necessary and so unnatural? You will need that energy for more important matters.

So, to inhale, simply pull the air across the bottom of the mouth, and drop the abdominal area down and forward while producing the sound of a whispered "HOW." Suspend the air within an open throat and allow the air to release quietly. Always blow "warm air" into your horn and allow the abdominal area to both follow and support the air from below the lungs by gradually receding in and upward. The use of "warm air" is very important for the development of an overall relaxed approach to playing.

THE APERTURE/EMBOUCHURE

Next, the discussion turns to the vibrating, pitch-making device that is called your aperture. The aperture is the central portion of the lips that the air comes through, carefully positioned to respond by vibrating various air speeds. A well-formed aperture exists entirely within the rim of the mouthpiece. This vibrating membrane is aided in its formation by the embouchure. Much like the tuning of a string on a violin or guitar, the embouchure is a tuning of the facial muscles to conform to your own face. You must find a relaxed, yet firm positioning of the muscles of the cheeks, chin, and lips to allow for a flexible and appropriate aperture. Like a well-tuned string, the embouchure, once formed, should not go through any excessive changes (at least not in normal, middle, and high range playing).

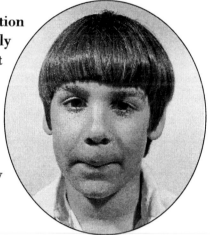

To form the embouchure, begin by humming the sound *emmm*. Feel the position of your jaw. Notice how the teeth are separated, yet the jaw is relaxed. Now simply tuck the corners of the mouth (firm but not flexed) in toward your teeth. This is not a full smile but is just enough of a smile to inhibit the formation of air pockets in the cheeks and top lip while blowing. This firm tucking should also cause the chin muscles to be pointing downward set in a flattened or concave position. Thus, the lower lip will never fill with air, and the chin will remain stable and never bunch upward. Before, during, and after the formation of an embouchure, attempt to feel heaviness in the face, especially around the eyes. Look tired like a basset hound. (Try to imagine that.)

From this relaxed positioning of the facial muscles, it is simply a matter of forming a very slight pucker at the center of the lips, as if the letter "p" is about to be pronounced. With the release of a steady airstream through an oval-shaped aperture, you should be able to produce a vibration. If your teeth form a natural overbite, then your top lip will probably also protrude farther than your bottom lip. Allow your embouchure and aperture to conform to your natural facial formation as much as possible. This point is very important in finding your best embouchure.

Practicing this buzz without a mouthpiece or with a mouthpiece rim is very beneficial in small doses. It is not possible to buzz well and have an extremely faulty embouchure. While buzzing you can also learn a great deal about the proper embouchure muscles needed and about the important balances between the air pressure and the aperture opening. A large range is not necessary. Simply try for a clear and open sound with an obvious pitch center.

MOUTHPIECE PLACEMENT

It is now time to place the mouthpiece on your ready and willing embouchure. Remove the mouthpiece from your horn and position the rim of your mouthpiece to rest with two-thirds to three-fourths of its circle on the top lip. The exact proportions depend upon the shape of your own particular lips and the exact formation of your teeth. Wiggle the mouthpiece around within those proportions and find the most comfortable position. Once you get somewhat comfortable, remember that feeling and memorize what it looks like through the consistent use of a mirror. With the mouthpiece ready near the lips, form and create that clear and open buzz at the aperture. Hold that feeling and replace the mouthpiece on the lips while allowing the texture of the lips to relax just enough to absorb the rim of the mouthpiece. The pressure of the mouthpiece against the lips should be only enough to seal the leakage of air through the sides of the mouth. Now create a resonant, clear buzz through the mouthpiece with a solid, constant air stream.

MOUTHPIECE MOISTURE

You should always lick your lips and moisten the rim of the mouthpiece before playing. This helps to seal in the air, aids in a more fluid vibration at the aperture opening, and allows for greater all-around fluency and endurance as you develop your technique to perform more difficult passages. Try the above process again with your lips and the mouthpiece rim nice and wet. A slippery feeling is good. Without lubrication, moving parts will freeze up, but you should want a warm and fluid sound at all times. Inhale a full breath through the corners of the mouth, keeping the mouthpiece close to the lips while inhaling. Moist lips allow this action to be much smoother.

MOUTHPIPE ANGLE

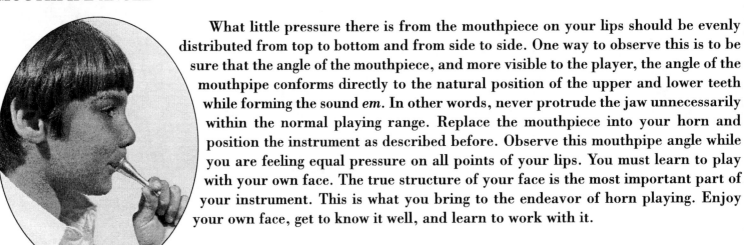

What little pressure there is from the mouthpiece on your lips should be evenly distributed from top to bottom and from side to side. One way to observe this is to be sure that the angle of the mouthpiece, and more visible to the player, the angle of the mouthpipe conforms directly to the natural position of the upper and lower teeth while forming the sound *em*. In other words, never protrude the jaw unnecessarily within the normal playing range. Replace the mouthpiece into your horn and position the instrument as described before. Observe this mouthpipe angle while you are feeling equal pressure on all points of your lips. You must learn to play with your own face. The true structure of your face is the most important part of your instrument. This is what you bring to the endeavor of horn playing. Enjoy your own face, get to know it well, and learn to work with it.

ARTICULATION

With all of the preceding information understood and in place, you are ready to release a full column of warm air past a vibrant aperture into your horn. To make this release precise, use the tongue in much the same manner as you would to say the sound "tahhh." The tip of the tongue very briefly touches the gum line near the top teeth. At the release of the warm air, the tip of the tongue drops quickly down and slightly back, resting near the bottom of the mouth. Let the air flow with a constant speed as described above. To stop this tone, you simply suspend the air. Let the air motion cease.

It is almost never necessary to stop the air with a constriction at the throat or with a placement of the tongue up to the gum. When these methods are used, you are performing an extended technique for a particular type of extraordinary sound only asked for by a modern composer. (There is plenty of time for that later.) Regarding articulation, the air does most of the work. The tongue helps only to establish a type of beginning to each sound. This is just like normal speech. The softer the tongue touches the gum line, the less compression for the air release, and the more mellow, smooth, or legato the note will sound. There are many transient qualities, or consonants, possible, with "t" and "d" being the most commonly used by brass players. After the air is released, the sound of the note is only as good as the air stream that follows, which includes the vowel quality of the tone, such as *tah, dah, toh,* or *doh.* You should not overemphasize the importance of the tongue or work it too hard. Simply understand its function as it primarily clarifies the release of the air. Some say that you must *attack* a note, but the whole idea suggests an image of your tongue as a large and dangerous knife. Think of the tongue more as a door that opens new vistas.

RANGE OF PITCHES

The number of pitches required for a professional horn player is approximately four octaves, or 48 different pitches. These can be divided into five ranges from the top down: high (high C down to third space C♯), middle (third space C down to middle C♯), middle low (middle C down to fourth space G♯ bass clef), low (fourth space G down to low F♯), and extreme low (low F down to the pedal C). Each of these ranges has its own sets of concerns, and each blends into the other, depending on the strengths and weaknesses of the player. You should first and foremost be concerned with the middle range, since all good technical habits will focus on how you produce these notes.

FINGERING CHART

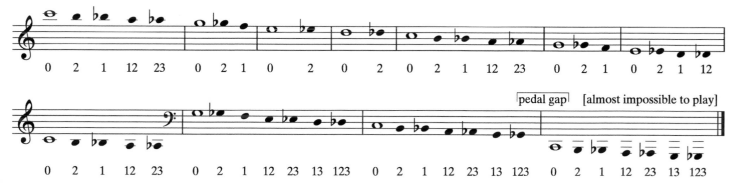

This fingering chart is designed to help you understand the horn in F and how it works in relationship to a series of pitches called the overtone series. This series is nature's scale. All of music is based on these notes. For the horn player, the actual fingerings you need to learn first are the notes marked Open or 0 (no fingers down), shown at the first of each measure. This includes all Cs, all Gs, most Es, and one D. These are the primary notes of the overtone series. Each of these open notes is then lowered a half step by using the second valve and a whole step by depressing the first valve. When another open note appears, the sequence starts again. In the bass clef, you can see the entire sequence. Learn this sequence of fingerings: 0, 2, 1, 12, 23, 13, 123. The reason this works can be seen by looking at the slides that are attached to the valves on your horn. You see that the shortest is attached to the second valve, the next is the first, and the longest is the third. In pushing a valve key, you add the tubing of that slide. The second valve lowers the horn by a half step, the first valve by a whole step, and the third valve by a step and a half. You will notice that valves 1–2 are used in this sequence for a step and a half rather than valve 3. Valve 3 is usually built to be a little too long so that when it is used with valve 2 or valve 1 it will be more in tune. Look again at the fingering sequence, and you will see that the math is quite easy to understand. Memorize these patterns while learning why they work. (Go to the end of this chapter and find how the B-flat horn, the thumb valve side of your double horn, relates to the F horn fingering patterns. It's all quite simple.)

FINDING THE NOTES

You should begin by finding the written second line G on your horn. First, go to a piano and play the piano's middle C. That is the horn player's written second line G. Learn that relationship. The horn in F sounds a perfect fifth (seven half-steps) below its written pitch. This can be confusing, but only if you don't learn it! (That's the funny thing about confusion.)

With the piano's middle C in your ear, go to the horn and try to buzz that written G, first without the mouthpiece, then with the mouthpiece, and then with the horn. As soon as you are able to control that pitch, think often about how it feels on your lips and with your air. Begin to memorize that sensation. While sounding your written G, begin to relax the aperture slightly and allow the note to pop down to the E. Relax a bit more and allow it to slip down to the C. Go back to the piano and play a middle C, down to an A, and then down to an F. This should sound like the same pitches you were playing. Play them many times on both instruments and learn this melody. Does it sound like "The Star-Spangled Banner" (sol-mi-do)? Whenever you pick up your horn, go for the G and see if you can find that melody. If the melody is different, figure out which of the three notes you are on by finding its neighboring open note. Learn to feel what is right at the lip and hear what is right with your inner ear, the ear you use to sing. The horn has many pitches quite close to each other that use the same fingerings, especially in the higher register. Horn fingerings do not help to find the pitch very much. To play horn well, you must learn to hear notes well. It's not hard; it just takes time, concentration, and a good memory for sounds and sensations. Hearing all of the other notes will come soon. You could begin by doing all of the above with either the second or the first valve down. Experiment. Be inquisitive. Make up games or melodies for yourself. The sooner you learn, the more fun you will have.

HIGHER AND LOWER PITCHES

To move into the upper register from this very relaxed middle range, you must begin to make the aperture opening even smaller, though not tighter, while you increase the speed of the air. Do only as much as you need to of each. It is also an aid to shift the vowel formation position of the tongue from *ah* toward an *eh*. In other words, as you ascend in pitch, the tongue gently arches upward for its basic position within the mouth. Don't force anything. Let this ascent into the upper range be as gradual as it has to be. (If you can run a mile in six minutes, how long will you have to practice to run it in five minutes and fifty-five seconds?) It all takes time. There are shortcuts that you might discover, but chances are they will cause you to tense up and force. If you chose to use tension or force as a means of playing your high notes, it will take much more time in the future to undo such habits than it would to have learned it correctly in the early stages.

To play lower pitches from the normal middle-range setting, you simply allow the oval-shaped aperture to relax into a bigger opening while expanding inside the mouth to simulate the vowel formation of *awe*. The speed of the air stream may feel a little bit slower as you descend, but you should always feel a solid stream of air flowing through the entire length of your horn and beyond.

Somewhere near the written G below middle C, most horn players must undergo a shift of jaw position. Here is where a protruding and dropped jaw often becomes necessary (as if you are singing your lowest possible pitch). It is also similar to the shift to another string for a violinist or, in this case, to another tuning of the embouchure. Along with this shift of jaw (made as slight as possible), you will also notice, or need to create, an even larger vowel formation inside your mouth, moving from *awe* toward *oh* or *uh* as you descend into the lowest octave. These shifts will also require a visible ascending movement of the mouthpiece and mouthpipe. This will be necessary and quite natural because you must keep equal pressure on the lips that have shifted along with the jaw.

CONTROLLING VOLUME

Dynamic ranges from soft to loud have some basic similarities to pitches from the high to low ranges. Soft playing is similar to the high range in the need for a smaller, though not tighter, aperture and the use of a smaller vowel-sound formation. To play very softly you must develop super-sensitive control of a tiny aperture with a slower, solid, and steady airstream. Do not let the gentle, mellow quality of the softer sounds mislead you into being too physically passive with your airstream. Think of the air as if it were a laser beam projected through the horn.

Loud playing is similar to the low range in the need for a larger aperture and a larger vowel-sound formation than normal. To play loudly you must allow the aperture to relax as it becomes larger, while the airflow increases in both size and speed. Though the sound of a loud horn is very powerful and bold, you must not get misled into believing that this muscular sound requires a great deal of body tension. It only requires a greater volume of air and an aperture that is relaxed and open enough to respond. (Let the horn be the loudspeaker; that is why it is attached to your face.)

PRACTICING

All of this information, exciting as it must seem, is only information. None of these ideas belongs to you until you have experienced them or something similar. If you wish to improve (which I'm certain you do since you are reading this), you must take what has been presented as if it were a seed, only a suggestion of what it might become. You must plant it, water it, water it some more (without expecting any instant results), and enjoy watching it grow. You must practice: that means putting in consistent time almost every day, always aware of what you are experiencing, with your mind actively listening and memorizing how your best efforts feel. Study carefully what works for you. You must constantly pay attention, listen, feel, and think. As the opera star Beverly Sills has said:

"There are no shortcuts to any place worth going."

Practicing should be well planned and diverse, as well as very regular. It is more important that you practice a little every day than a lot now and then. You should, at whatever level you now play, develop a warm-up session that you play every day. As with any athlete, muscles need to be carefully stretched. The blood flow after a night's sleep needs to be reawakened gradually. You might wish to include medium-long tones, tongued and slurred scales or scale patterns, and arpeggios in order of increasing difficulty. As you advance, add in some lip trills, multiple tonguing, and larger intervals—all of the things that are basic to your particular capacity and playing needs. This warm-up should ideally be of your own design and based on your present level of performance ability. Asking for guidance from your teacher is a great idea. Gain the basic principles and a few pitch patterns, and then create your own workout.

Each day you should divide your practice between technical studies, melodic etudes, solos or songs, a little sight reading, your ensemble music and, when you are ready, transposition studies and orchestral excerpts.

Your best teacher is your own experiences and your own awareness of what you are now doing. Every thoughtful experience seems to tell you what you need to do next. If you include an additional person, you will be able to develop many exciting goals for yourself. Make good use of that additional person, that special teacher. It always helps to have four ears and four eyes working on the same solutions. The horn is an instrument of great beauty. You owe it your best at all times!

B♭ Horn Fingering Chart

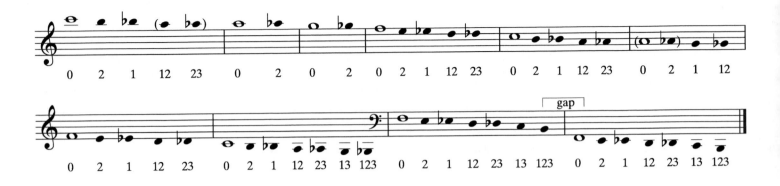

F Horn/B♭ Horn Parallel Comparison

B♭ Horn
F Horn

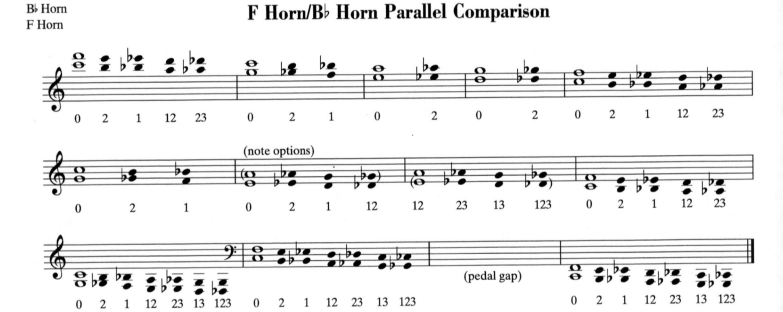

2. The Warm-Up as a Complete Session

The original version of the following appeared as an article in The Horn Call *and was written in response to an earlier published article in which the author considered most substantial warm-ups as paranoid head-trips and a waste of one's time and endurance. My experience as a performer and teacher has taught me that such an attitude can be quite misleading, especially for the younger, developing student of the horn. We must take charge of our development as players, use our heads, and accept the physical reality that constantly requires great power and enormous subtleties from our muscles. There are no athletes or dancers who, after using their heads, would regularly perform without a workout or maintenance session. Such neglect would ruin their strength and their flexibility in a very short time. As performers, we are using our facial muscles in a way that is quite contrary to what they were initially designed to do. These muscles of the face and their relationship with an exceptionally coordinated air supply require more than just inherent skill and a good attitude. They require exercise–intelligent, progressive, consistent exercise. When you have learned that through your own hard work you have created a strong, dependable, and flexible set of muscles, the best of all head-trips will occur. You will have confidence, and it will be based on personal achievement.*

A warm-up can serve many functions depending on its length, organizational plan, and completeness. If its only purpose is to circulate the blood and reacquaint the embouchure with the contact of the mouthpiece and the phenomenon of various vibrational demands, then a short (10–15 minute) warm-up could suffice. Perhaps some medium-long tones and a few scales and arpeggios organized with increasing difficulty would serve this very important initial function of a warm-up. However, for truly serious students, especially during their most formative years, a warm-up session should involve much more than just this initial function. It should cover all of the basic technical needs of horn playing, thus providing the student with the following:

1. A physical workout that will greatly contribute to overall strength and increased endurance.

2. A test and recalibration of the entire coordination process.

3. An aid in developing and maintaining a consistency of responses in all physical aspects of performance.

4. An overview through which any developing bad habits can be detected long before they become major problems.

5. The confidence gained from experiencing the techniques which are going well.

If carefully planned and executed, such a session could take from 45 minutes to an hour, and would serve as a daily foundation for the consistencies and strengths demanded of today's performers, as well as a source of development towards greater endurance and other long-range goals.

There are as many ways to formulate such sessions as there are mouthpieces and mind-sets, but a few valid guidelines could be suggested:

1. Each section of the session should have a specific purpose for its inclusion.

2. The session should begin with simplicity in all aspects and increase very gradually in range, dynamics, and all other included complexities.

3. The first few sections should be designed so as to fulfill the initial function of a warm-up as discussed above.

4. The technical aspects of playing to be exercised should include posture, breathing considerations, tonal control, slurring, tonguing (staccato, legato, etc.), register changes, intervals (slurred and tongued) of increasing dimensions, full dynamic spectrum, scale and arpeggio patterns, lip trills, multiple tonguing, and stopped horn.

Some additional equipment could be of benefit during such a session: a mirror, a metronome, a chromatic tuner, a B.E.R.P.* attachment for initial buzzing exercises, and occasionally a recording device. The mirror can serve the double function of showing what you are doing correctly as you gain the desired results and what faults might be creeping into your embouchure. The metronome is useful for consistency, for the measurement of improvement, and for simply keeping the session moving. The chromatic tuner is a must for a continual check of intonation throughout the entire session. Having the tuner off to the side is best, so that it is used as a reference after you have decided that what you are hearing and feeling is correct. (You must learn to hear the horn, not to play the tuner.) The relatively new attachment called the B.E.R.P. is inserted into the leadpipe or onto the mouthpipe and receives the mouthpiece. It allows the player to buzz naturally with a resistance that simulates the horn's at the normal angle of contact without actually resonating the instrument. Such an exercise is useful for air and blood flow at the initial stages of a maintenance session. A high-quality recording device should also be used now and then to check intonation and to serve as a third ear for a more objective appraisal of your overall performance and growth.

If all of the above ideas and tools are sincerely applied to one's initial practice session virtually every day, such a complete warm-up session would, I strongly believe, be the single most important passage to strength and consistency in performance. However, one must be willing to take the time to formulate truly thoughtful exercises, to allow them to grow and change as needs and desires grow and change, and then to conscientiously perform each exercise each day with focused concentration and a burning desire to grow.

Rather than share my own personal warm-up (which has gradually evolved around my strengths and weaknesses and from my belief in the Farkas Warm-up since 1963), I have included two levels of outline to be applied toward the development of your own personal maintenance session. The first outline is rather general but includes the basic format that I know has worked for me and many of my most successful students. The second is far more detailed and includes some annotations to explain the purposes for each inclusion.

Create your own warm-up/maintenance session. There are no magic notes that will work for everyone. If there were, we would all know them by now. We have to take this trip on our own, use our heads, learn from the patterns of others, and quickly establish some patterns based on our own successes. As you age in this profession, you will need consistent patterns to depend upon for maintenance. You will also find that the earliest patterns may need to be gradually modified as you gradually change. What is suggested here will serve many a purpose if applied thoughtfully. Good luck, use your head, and enjoy the trip.

*B.E.R.P. contact info.
   Musical Enterprises, P.O. Box 1041,
   Larkspur, CA 94977-1041
   1-888-927-2448
   www.berp.com

General Outline for a Basic Maintenance Session

A. Preliminary Preparations

1. Relaxation routine (loosening up)
2. Buzzing lips alone (increase blood flow)
3. Buzzing mouthpiece alone (contact with lips)

B. Warm-Up

1. First tones (centered, warm sound)
2. Slurred scales (air follow-through, line)
3. Tongued arpeggios (louder flexibility)
4. Slurred, arpeggiated patterns (softer flexibility)
5. Aggressive scales (louder, articulated response)

C. Maintenance and Development

1. Trills (relaxed flexibility)
2. Multiple tonguing (light, quick agility)
3. Other techniques (stopped, mute, gliss., etc.)
4. Larger intervals (slurred, legato, staccato)

D. Winding Down

1. Accuracy (isolated attacks, long tones)
2. Low-range relaxation (pedal notes, sustained)

Secondary Warm-Up (re-warm-up)

A. Relaxation, loosening up, air movement, warm tone production

B. Slurred arpeggios, gradual range expansion, flexibility exercise

C. Tongued scales and interval patterns, dynamic expansion

A Suggested Detailed Outline for Designing a Thorough Warm-Up/Maintenance Session

A. **Relaxation Routine**

1. Posture and position of balance

2. Loosen and stretch

3. Increase blood flow throughout body

4. Deep breathing (See Chapter 3, Air section.)

B. **Lip Buzzing (without the mouthpiece)**

1. Single mid-range notes, clarity and focus

2. Gradually expanding outward (scale patterns)

3. Control intonation

C. **Mouthpiece Buzzing (without the horn)**

1. Focused, clear, supported sound, medium dynamic

2. Scale-like patterns, melodic and resonant

3. Expand tessitura without excess pressure

D. **First Beautiful Tones**

1. Limited activity, mid-range expanding outward

2. Finding absolute pitch centers, resonate, medium dynamics

3. Isolated medium to long tones (avoid extreme physical effort), use "full bows" (like a cellist)

E. **Melodic Scale Patterns (slurred)**

1. Major or minor patterns

2. Covering from 6 to 12 keys (circle of 4ths or chromatic)

3. Enjoyable melodic pattern at medium dynamic (well-supported vocal character)

F. **Articulated Arpeggios (louder)**

1. Choosing from major, minor, or dominant 7th patterns (expanding outwardly to extremes)

2. Covering from 6 to 12 keys (circle of 4ths or chromatic)

3. Exciting activity at forte with full sound

G. **Slurred Arpeggios (softer)**

1. Choosing from major, minor, augmented, or fully diminished patterns (to extremes)

2. Choosing from 6 to all keys depending on modes and patterns chosen

3. Larger intervals, quicker tempo, effortless flexibility (like the woodwinds)

H. Aggressive Scale Patterns (very loud and full)

1. Choosing from major, minor, whole-tone, chromatic; or Dorian, Lydian, Phrygian modes

2. Cover all "keys/modes" and full range of the horn

3. Orchestral brass section sound, heavily articulated (or slurred aggressively, at times)

I. Trills (lip/tongue trills primarily)

1. Fullest possible range (e' to c''' or above)

2. - with use of crescendo and decrescendo

3. Building from short flips to extended trill patterns

J. Multiple-Tongue Studies

1. Double-tongue, varied tempos, dynamics, and range

2. Triple-tongue—*tuh-kuh-tuh* and *tuh-tuh-kuh*, varied tempos, dynamics, and range

3. Cross-double tongue (triplet pattern—*tuh-kuh-tuh, kuh-tuh-kuh, tuh-kuh-tuh*)

4. Kuh alone (repeated notes and scales)

5. Flutter tongue—varied dynamics and range

6. Varied consonant exercises *(y, z, th, d, t, d, th, z, y)* (see Articulation Variety in Chapter 3)

K. Other Useful Techniques (based on own needs)

1. Stopped horn—varied attacks, range, dynamics

2. 3/4 stopped/echo horn—varied attacks, range, dynamics

3. Mute practice—varied melodic and articulated

4. Glissandi, half-valve, vocalizations, circular breathing, vibrato, quarter-tones, etc.

L. Large Intervals (slurred and tongued)

1. 5ths and 4ths, ascending and descending (varied articulations and dynamics)

2. One- to two-octave leaps ascending and descending (varied articulations and dynamics)

M. Accuracy Study (hearing and feeling initial attacks)

1. Isolated, unrelated attacks (medium length, full air)

2. Alternating dynamic extremes

3. Relaxed approach, winding-down effect

N. Low Range (warm-down)

1. Warm descending patterns, melodic (and in tune)

2. Sustained pedal notes, controlled medium dynamics

3. Extending Techniques

During the middle to late 1970s, it became obvious to me that the majority of contemporary composers were ignoring the horn with all of its potentials in favor of the other brass instruments.

That prompted me to design and administer a composition contest and composition-commissioning project through the International Horn Society shortly after being elected to its Advisory Council. Subsequent communications with some of the great composers of that time made obvious the problems they were having with the horn as a possible means of expression. It seems that many of them had been told by their horn-playing acquaintances and colleagues not to do this or that technique, which they had initially thought would be possible after having successfully written it for a trumpet or tuba. There was also nowhere for the composers to go for instruction or advice within the written literature. One of this country's most esteemed avant-garde composers asked me to clarify what he had gleaned from his only source at that time, *The Harvard Dictionary of Music*, which is a wonderful but general reference.

These experiences, along with my own interests at that time as a dabbling composer, prompted me to author the book *Extended Techniques for the Horn: A Practical Handbook for Students, Performers, and Composers*, now published (reissued in 1996) by Studio 224, Warner Bros. Publications. Since its first publication in 1983, the book has remained the only text of its kind. A number of younger and many not-so-young composers have referred to it for their own compositions, and some have used it for instructional purposes. Horn players have also been challenged, or at least rudely awakened, by what was compiled from the 300 scores and books available at that time. A performance CD consisting of 30 minutes of aural examples was included to demonstrate the practicality of the extended techniques requested of horn performers.

During these past 15 years, many huge strides have been made by young and exceptionally talented performers. The music of the past is being played better and better all of the time. The expectations have been raised for us all. There are even composers who are taking chances writing for the horn, expecting us to have grown with the new standards being set. Mark Schultz (JOMAR Publications) from Austin, Texas, is a perfect example of such a composer. He has had his good friend and colleague Thomas Bacon perform his works for him, which is probably part of the reason that his compositions are so musically effective and creatively virtuosic. I believe it is possible for all of us to stretch out toward an extension of our basic techniques. It may take some time to learn and to physically develop many of the specifics, to know and love this newer music, and to eventually feel free and confident to administer some of the extraordinary demands, but its worth it. The margin attained will serve as the cushion that makes all other more conservative performance demands sound effortless.

I would like to share a few insights and exercises that have helped my students and myself over the years regarding the extension of some basic and not-so-basic techniques. It is my hope to develop many of these ideas into some practical exercises and etudes in the future; but for now, allow my suggestions to stimulate your creativity and cause you to create your own detailed exercises.

AIR

Let's begin with the single most important technical consideration for any wind player—air! There is only one technique that we need to think about all of the time, and that is the acquisition and utilization of the air. Everything else we do is rather unique to the experience of horn playing, so when we are not practicing or performing, we are not doing anything which might actually undo our well-developed skills. The lips, for instance, are at rest when we aren't playing, but inhaling and exhaling air continues in a shallow manner. We spend the vast majority of each day practicing shallow breathing. Therefore, the efficient and sufficient breathing necessary to play the horn cannot easily become a habit, at least not to the extremes found in a few of our compositions.

Since the specifics of breathing and blowing well are thoroughly explained elsewhere in this book, what can be done to make it even better? I will describe here a progressive breathing exercise that grew out of basic yoga breathing processes, Aston Patternings, Alexander Techniques, and common sense.

First, find a balanced, relaxed posture, away from the back of the chair.

1. Flex your lower back muscles by slowly rocking them back toward the tailbone creating a letter *C* with your spine, neck, and lowered head, releasing air. Feel the stretch in your lower back muscles.

2. Slowly shift your weight forward projecting your chest outward, inhaling air while your head, neck, and extremely arched back reverse the letter *C* formation. Feel the abdominal muscles stretch.

3. Assume a position of neutrality midway between these stretching positions, feeling all of your weight in balance on your bones, not held up by your muscles. Focus your attention forward while allowing your head to raise slightly upward.

4. Shake your shoulders, arms, and hands loosely and freely, releasing any residual tension. Feel the blood rushing through the fingers.

Then start a metronome at 60 b.p.m., and follow the pattern below, breathing fully and correctly with a smooth and circular reverse at the ends of each inhalation and each exhalation:

1. Inhale for 3 beats, exhale for 6 beats, repeat.

2. Inhale for 4 beats, exhale for 8 beats, repeat.

3. Inhale for 5 beats, exhale for 10 beats, repeat.

4. Inhale for 6 beats, exhale for 12 beats, repeat.

5. Inhale for 3 beats, exhale for 15 beats, repeat.

6. Inhale for 2 beats, exhale for 18 beats, repeat.

7. Inhale for 1 beat, exhale for 21 beats, repeat.

8. Inhale for 1 beat, exhale for as long as you can without pain, repeat.

This exercise can, and perhaps should, be modified (at least at first) to accommodate your present capacity, but soon you will realize that it is the timing of the inhalation and exhalation that causes much of the sensation of a lesser capacity. Over time, this exercise will help to extend your ability to relax, focus, concentrate, and move your air with greater control.

Here is another air-related exercise that helps a great deal. I first encountered a version of it in Gunther Schuller's book, *Horn Technique*, where he credited it with a very long history.

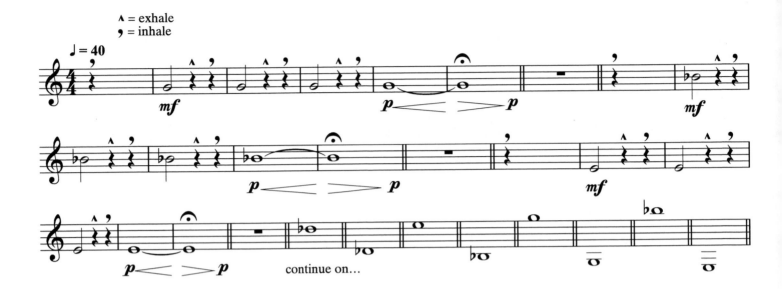

1. Set the metronome to 40 b.p.m.

2. Inhale fully on beat 4 (in 4/4 time).

3. Play a solid, second line G for two beats at .

4. Exhale fully all of the residual air on beat 3.

5. Inhale fully on beat 4.

6. Continue this sequence two more times.

7. Play a second line G for 8 (or more) beats, beginning , crescendo for 4 beats, diminuendo (as long as possible) into silence.

8. Rest for at least 8 seconds.

9. Repeat the full exercise on third line B♭.

10. Continue full repetitions on first line E, fourth line D♭, bottom space D♭, fourth space E, ledger line (below) B♭, etc.

If each sounded half-note is full and solid, and each long-tone is controlled regarding pitch and dynamics, this simple exercise can reap many technical benefits. The pitch choice pattern being suggested is obviously an expanding diminished arpeggio, which allows for progressively lower, less stressful notes to follow the progressively higher ones, providing some relief for the aperture/embouchure. Exercises which ebb and flow often provide greater results. Doing this exercise through only one such arpeggio is enough, extending as high and as low as possible each day. Begin with first space F♯ on the following day and first space F the day after that.

LONG TONES

There is no one single type of exercise that receives more praise from one group of players and more disdain from the other than long tones. "Long tones are boring!" "Long tones solved all of my problems!" Extremes perhaps, but both are true to an extent.

To solve the boredom issue, I suggest that the player have a plan to follow that provides a maximum result from the minimum amount of time. Beyond that, the bored student should become more focused on the results of the exercise. Focus on the future results not the boredom of the moment.

The following pattern has done wonders for the students who have tried it over an extended period of time. I have noticed significant results almost immediately, every time I come back to it.

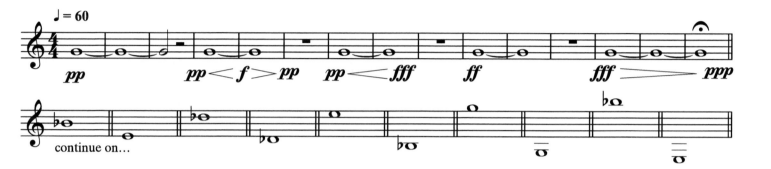

1. Set the metronome at 60 b.p.m.

2. Play a second line G, ø, for 10 beats, rest for 2 beats.

3. Play G beginning at ø, crescendo to f and back to ø in 8 beats, rest 4 beats.

4. Play G beginning at ø, crescendo to μ in 8 beats, rest 4 beats, play   for 8 beats, rest 4 beats, attack μ diminuendo for 12 beats (or more) to ¬, relax awhile.

5. Repeat the above pattern following the diminished arpeggio pitch design suggested for the second breathing study (up to B♭, down to E, etc.) Begin with first space F♯ on the following day and first space F the day after that.

This exercise extends endurance, range, dynamic control, pitch control, centering, and usually improves one's overall sound. The number of beats should be flexible depending on the range and level of fatigue, but do try to extend yourself toward a greater length as you get stronger and learn to pace the air better. *Long tones forever!*

TRILLS

The trill is a technique that has been required of horn players since the pre-Baroque period. This rapid fluctuation between neighboring pitches can be accomplished with the valves, especially at the half-step, or with a coordinated action including the lip, air, and tongue between two pitches of the same harmonic series and, consequently, the same fingering.

The valve trills need to be practiced, especially when awkward fingerings are the only choice. They also need to be very well-controlled for those times when the composer asks for flexible speeds or irregular fluctuations, or when a valved trill must match a lip trill stylistically.

Create your own studies that require valve combination trills and tremolos, such as 1 to 2, 1 to 23, 12 to 23, 13 to 2, etc. Have a fingering chart available which lists all possible fingerings for every note on your F/B♭, or B♭/high F horn. With this information, you could create a trill chart using normal and optional fingerings for effective half-step finger trills, where the second valve is the only valve moving to lower and raise the pitch. Some of these options will, unfortunately, be out of tune, or require that you perform on weaker harmonics, but knowing them and practicing them may help present important and sometimes necessary options.

In a technical sense, lip trills are another story. For some reason, this particular technique causes a great deal of grief for many students. I learned it before anyone told me that it was difficult to do. That, I believe, is an important point. To believe something is difficult causes one to try too hard. I believe that lip trills are some of the most relaxing physical gestures that we do, or at least they should be.

A key component in understanding how they need to work should involve a rethinking and renaming. They should be thought of as "lip/tongue/air" trills. The procedure involves all three aspects of your playing in coordination with each other, so that none of them have to work too hard. The biggest problem is usually when the student exerts extreme lip-flexing between two neighboring notes. Notes which are usually a breeze to administer when slurred during a scale passage. Begin to solve this over-flexed approach by trying the following:

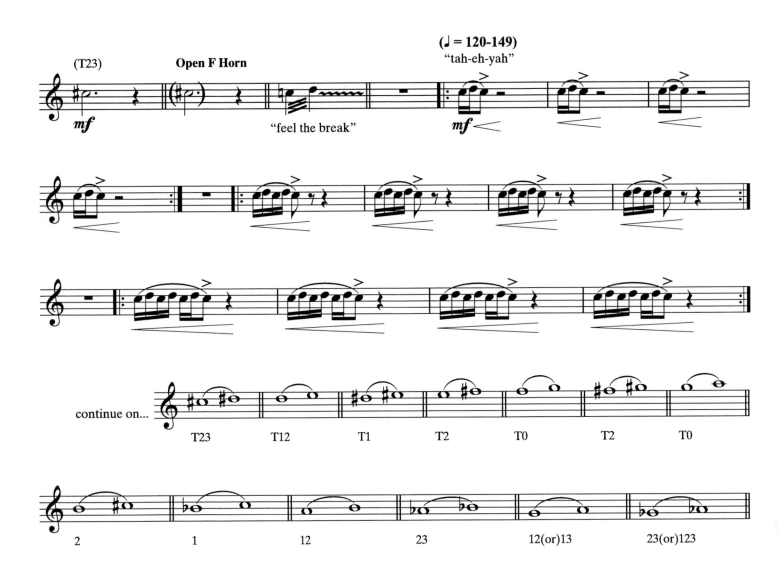

1. Play a third space C♯ on your horn.

2. Try to play it again, open on the F horn.

3. This being impossible, allow the pitch to slide back and forth between a sharp C and a flat D, feeling the break between notes.

4. Flip across this break by allowing the tongue to gesture the motion needed to produce tah-eh-yah (two sixteenths and an eighth note) while crescendoing slightly into the third note *(yah)*.

5. Repeat this flip many times on these two pitches learning to feel it as a single gesture.

6. Increase the gesture to a tah-eh-yah-eh-yah (four sixteenths and an eighth), always crescendoing slightly but surely into the last note.

7. Repeat this amount of flipping many times until it feels like a single gesture.

8. Continue to add one more group of sixteenths to the flips until you have a trill that feels like a floating gesture and that is more like a long tone than a strenuous flexibility study.

Repeat this exercise up a half-step, then down a half-step, and so on, noticing that the tongue gesture becomes an increasingly important factor as you go higher, to the point that above the staff the tongue does most of the work, and below the second space A the lip does more, but not all, of the work. However, in all of the ranges, the air follow-through is mandatory! So many students attack a trill and stop blowing. This flipping feeling comes from responses to the air of the lip and tongue. Without the air, they can only wiggle around with no sound! We could reconsider the new name, "lip/tongue/air trills," and simply call them "flip trills."

MULTIPLE TONGUING

To multiple tongue, you must become comfortable using the middle of the tongue in tandem with the tip of the tongue to create a rapid duple or triple pattern of air pulsations. The tip of the tongue (as if enunciating the consonant *t*) should gently strike the front of the upper gums near the top of the teeth and quickly be drawn downward, rather than backward, into the oral cavity. That is important for single-tonguing, but even more important for multiple-tonguing. The middle of the tongue is best used if it too can be placed as far forward in the mouth as possible (as if enunciating the consonant *k*).

The most common problem with these procedures is the movement of the tongue in a somewhat horizontal fashion. The tongue going back and forth, rather than up and down, causes the *k* syllable to be too far back in the throat, while the *t* strikes far in the front. This slows down the action and separates the articulations, which causes an uneven air pulsation at the aperture with the guttural *k* sound usually much less precise than the *t*. The internal motion becomes similar to that used in pronouncing *tug-gut-tug-gut*, which produces a slow and labored sound and soon causes a tension in the tongue and jaw.

The main reason for multiple-tonguing is to allow us to pulsate the air quite rapidly. We must find a way to make the motions as effortless as possible. The following exercise might help:

1. Call the cat, "Here kitty, kitty, kitty, kitty."

2. Assume the cat's name is Tihkih, and call her again, "Here Tihkih, Tihkih, Tihkih, Tihkih."

This may sound quite silly, I agree, but that is double-tonguing with the tongue being placed as far forward as possible for each stroke. To practice that first without the horn and later with the horn helps to lighten up the tongue strokes. The use of the *h* in the call is to remind you to use lots of air as you work on multiple-tonguing. Without air follow-through, there is nothing for the lip to respond to. The tongue makes no sound but interrupts the air. It is the air that plays the horn.

Triple-tonguing can be done in three different configurations. Each has its own advantages and should be developed to the point of competency and comfort. The most appropriate, in my opinion, is the use of the consonants *t-k-t, t-k-t*, for two important reasons. When a composer writes a grouping of three pulses, they are weighted with the strongest emphasis on the first and the weakest weight on the second of the three notes. The *k* for most of us is the weaker sound.

Another reason comes from my experiences hearing students who use the *t-t-k, t-t-k* pattern. This pattern, for some reason, periodically evolves into a less-than-even triplet becoming almost an eighth and two sixteenths. However, I recommend that both of these orderings be practiced and perfected. At the professional level, the hornist in a brass quintet, or in an extremely exacting brass section, may need to be able to do either or both patterns to match the other players.

The third triple-tongue pattern is what I call cross double-tonguing. This is a wonderfully effective way of creating a very even repetition of notes (such as near the end of Dukas' *Villanelle*). The idea is to use a double-tongue pattern, shifting the natural accent to every third note (if not with your air, at least within your mental sense of subdivision): *t-k-t, k-t-k, t-k-t, k-t-k*.

To become effective at any of the above, it helps to practice simple tongued etudes and exercises using only the consonant *k* instead of *t*. When the tongue starts to become stiff or tired, stop and rest. Return with a less forced positioning of the tongue against the roof of the mouth, keeping the tongue as far forward as possible.

The quality of sound is all important, even on the short, fast notes; so after you are sure you have the tongue comfortably forward in the mouth (via the *tih-kih-tih, tih-kih-tih* formation), gradually open up the vowel sound placement during the released-tongue position: *tah-kah, tah-kah*. Know also that the ability to administer varied consonant tongue placements, the most obvious being the more legato *dah-gah* and *dah-gah-dah*, should be considered and practice with equal enthusiasm. Practice the following exercises and expand on these ideas to help you create a flexible and versatile multiple-tongue.

1. Repeat a single mid-range pitch 16 times at a moderate tempo forming *kih* alone, feeling the placement of the tongue.

2. Repeat the same pitch 16 times using *keh* alone, retaining the tongue's placement on the roof of the mouth.

3. Repeat the above using *kah* alone, retaining the tongues original placement.

4. Run a scale or scales using only *kah* into the various ranges, retaining the forward placement of the tongue.

5. Using *kah* alone, administer some arpeggiated patterns into various ranges.

6. Repeat Numbers 1-5 using the various double-tongue patterns, starting with the consonants *t, k, d*, and *g*.

7. Repeat Numbers 1-5 using each of the triple-tongue patterns of the consonants *t, k, d* and *g*.

ARTICULATION VARIETY

The depth of our verbal communication skills is dependent upon the depth and substance of the available vocabulary to express ourselves. As we advance as performers, we develop as communicators of music. Music is an abstract language, the meaning of which is conceived in the mind as an abstract thought, then conveyed through the horn using the vocabulary of the craft. One of the aspects of brass performance practice that I believe needs a great deal more attention is the immense variety of articulations that are available. The full compliment of attacks (transients) and releases (decays) can and should become major aspects of the vocabulary. These aspects of sound need as much detailed attention as is given to concepts of basic tone quality. In fact, the transients actually define the basic identities of our sounds to the listener. If the attack is removed from the recorded sounds of a horn and a flute, for example, the distinction as to which is which becomes quite unclear. Thus, the specific qualities of the initial articulations are just as important as the follow-through regarding the evaluation and creation of a beautiful tone.

In most learning situations, we are told to tongue the normal notes with a *t* stroke and the more legato notes with a *d* stroke. If not using these manners of air release, then the notes are simply slurred as smoothly as possible. That would assume that we can use only two consonants and the one vowel quality to imitate a note (*tah, dah,* and *yah*). This is an oversimplification perhaps, but my experience shows that for many students, and a striking number of professionals, little thought and little practice has gone into all of the other useful options.

The consonant sound *t* can be administered with a wide variety of compression or pressure against the gum. As it becomes more relaxed, it blends into a hardened *d*, which can also gradually be relaxed to cover a variety of decreasing compressions, blending into *l*'s and eventually *y*'s, which become the sound of a timbral vibrato. This articulation continuum can and should be practiced. Try the following exercise on a repeated mid-range note (at first), at   without any crescendo or diminuendo.

1. Set the metronome at 100 b.p.m.

2. Take a very full breath, release it all, and breathe in again.

3. Play eighth notes starting with the most compressed *tut* possible.

4. Continue very gradually relaxing the compression of the tongue away from the roof of the mouth.

5. After reaching the vaguest audible tongue movement possible (less than a *yah*), gradually pulsate the air back toward a more deliberate sound.

6. Return to the extreme *tut* staccato position of the tongue by the end of the exhale.

Keep track of how many different degrees of consonant sounds you can administer during a complete exhalation. Listen to hear that each is different from the last, and that they don't fall into distinct groupings of four of one sound, four of another. This exercise takes control but teaches you how vast the vocabulary can be, on only one note at one dynamic! These variations are quite natural for jazz instrumentalists who generally try to imitate the sounds of singers who, of course, have all of the consonants possible at their disposal. The Baroque style can also be greatly enhanced by articulation variety as the performer needs to group the melodic patterns without producing an inappropriate legato sound. The hand horn player must develop various degrees of tonguing to unify the motion between the wide variety of hand position changes. It is also simply more fun to have discovered and perfected these choices, while it provides a much more interesting listening experience for your audiences and performance colleagues.

FLUTTER-TONGUE

This particular sound-effect technique is probably the most difficult to teach and to learn. Some say that either you can flutter (roll) your tongue or you can't. However, it can be learned. The actual procedure requires that the player curl a flattened tongue upward in a relaxed yet firm manner against the roof of the mouth near the front. The sides of the tongue should feel the upper back teeth and stay in contact with them through the flutter. With a consistent, normal stream of air, the front portion of the tongue will tend to alternately resist and allow the air through in a rapid fluttering motion. The spot where the air escapes might be off to one side or the other. Let it happen how it wants to happen. Each person's tongue is unique.

The most common misconception seems to be the positioning of the tongue either too high in the mouth or too far back against the roof of the mouth. Other false impressions include positioning the tip of the tongue on the teeth or creating a tongue shape that is pointed rather than flat. The frontal contact points should, in most cases, be on the ridge of the gum nearest the front teeth. Also, the tongue is often flexed by the player thinking there is a need for an extreme effort. The tongue for this technique must be relatively relaxed and allowed to respond to the air much like the aperture always does. Both are merely positioned to respond to the flow of the air in the production of a desired vibration.

1. Position the tongue as described above.

2. Pronounce loudly the words "taught her" so that it sounds like *taugh trrrrr*, allowing the entire frontal part of your tongue to sustain a flutter emphasizing the "t" not the "rrr."

3. Repeat the above, whispering the sounds as described.

4. With your horn, repeat the whispering sensations through a vibrating aperture, sustaining the *trrrrrrrrr* as long as possible.

An alternative technique is as follows:

1. Purse your lips into the letter *P*.

2. Build up a firm compression of air behind the lips.

3. Release a small explosion of air while simultaneously pronouncing the letters *P* and *T*, leaving the tongue positioned as described above and creating a loudly whispered purr: *PTrrrrrrrrrrrr*.

If after having given these exercises a great deal of thought and extensive practice you still can't roll or flutter your tongue, the best option is called a growl and is often used in jazz. The technique involves the closing off of the throat, just as you would to gargle when you have a sore throat. Forcing air aggressively through such a constricted opening causes a growling sound that is less easy to control than a flutter and has a dirtier sound, but it often serves the purpose.

VIBRATO

For most of the instruments of the orchestra or band, it is clear whether vibrato is an appropriate component of their sounds. For the horn it is less clear. There are those who think vibrato should never be used because the horn is the pure voice, while the other instruments are the sweet sounds. To some extent that is true. The horn can and does sound beautiful without the additional undulations applied to its sound. However, the string instruments, flutes, oboes, bassoons, and saxophones sound quite dull without vibrato. Clarinets and the other brasses seem to fluctuate between the sweet and the pure as needed. Why not the horns?

Actually, in some countries such as Russia and the Czech Republic, and among many soloists and some orchestral players from around the world, vibrato is used a great deal and to great musical advantage. Vibrato should be thought of as an enhancement to an already beautiful sound or as the intensification of an already excited and flowing musical line. Vibrato does not by itself make an inferior horn tone or a dull musical phrase sound much better.

I recommend the study of three distinct types of vibrato. Each has its own technique and presents its own unique sound. Keeping them separate at first helps one to understand how each works, how each affects the sound, and how each aids in the eventual development of a personalized approach to this special technical enhancement.

1. First, there is an intensity vibrato used to intensify a musical line by pulsating the airstream. Sometimes called a diaphragmatic vibrato, this technique is more successfully controlled at the throat opening. The steady stream of air flows through a rapid partial opening and closing of the throat.

2. Second and least effective, is the timbral vibrato that colors the sound to a subtle degree by changing the vowel formation inside the mouth as the tone is sustained.

3. Third and equally as effective as the first, is the pitch vibrato, which adds a fluctuation slightly above and slightly below the blown pitch through an adjustment at the aperture, often due to the movement of the lower jaw.

There are a few players who have advocated the movement of the right hand in the bell to create a vibrato or to shake the horn in a controlled manner. These methods are not recommended because they can quickly tire the lip due to the fact that both encourage pressure fluctuations at the mouthpiece. These are effects which are applied to the sound after it enters the horn and, consequently, sound much too mechanical. I prefer to project into the horn what I wish for it to resonate and amplify.

To develop these three types of vibrato, begin with the following experiments:

A. **Intensity vibrato**

1. Set a metronome at 80 b.p.m.

2. Without the horn, blow a long stream of sixteenth-note pulsations through your pursed lips, keeping a steady air flow from the source (avoid extreme huffing, but do create a gentle *huh-huh-huh-huh* at the throat).

3. With your horn, play a second line G and produce sixteenth-note pulsations of air, without intentionally altering the pitch centers.

4. Repeat No. 3, gradually increasing and decreasing the speed of the pulsations.

B. **Timbral vibrato**

1. Set a metronome at 80 b.p.m.

2. Without the horn, sing the sounds *ah-ee-ah-ee-ah-ee-ah-ee-ah* and feel the movement of the tongue.

3. With your horn, play a second line G and produce sixteenth-note fluctuations with the tongue over a solid airstream without intentionally altering the pitch.

4. Repeat No. 3, gradually increasing and decreasing the speed of the fluctuations.

C. **Pitch vibrato**

1. Set a metronome at 80 b.p.m.

2. Without the horn, sing the sounds *wa-oo-wa-oo-wa-oo-wa-oo* through partially pursed lips by subtly moving the jaw up and down, allowing the *oo* sound to lower in pitch.

3. With the horn, play a second line G and administer sixteenth-note undulations of pitch over a solid airstream with no fluctuations of the throat or tongue.

4. Repeat No. 3, gradually increasing and decreasing the speed of the undulations.

After each of these three methods of vibrato are understood and are well controlled at many different pitch levels and at varied tempos, it will become obvious that none of them constitute a particularly effective vibrato. The best vibrato for the classical hornist will be a coordinated combination of all three. Redo the above exercise pattern combining all three manners of vibrato, and then apply that sound to a simple and beautiful melody. I recommend that the practice room be where the vibrato should stay for a long time. What happens is that the technique gradually joins your overall musical vocabulary and will eventually enter into your performances naturally and without intentional application.

Appropriate times when vibrato should be used, fortunately for today's horn player, are purely a matter of personal choice. When that musical impulse occurs, enjoy the enhancement that it brings to your musical line. As a technique to be used at other times, I would suggest that you become familiar with the typical vibratos used by the various schools of horn playing throughout history. The most obvious are the Russian and related schools and the French school of generations past. This knowledge is important for the modern player, only to the extent that the application of a controlled and appropriately styled vibrato might come closer to a composer's intentions. (Tchaikovsky was probably expecting to hear a rather obvious Russian vibrato, and Debussy would have assumed he was going to hear that French vibrato so prevalent during the early years of the twentieth century.) Awareness is important; actual imitation is, of course, a matter of personal, artistic choosing.

HAND STOPPING

The most common extended technique requested by composers is for stopped horn. The symbol + is placed over a note, and the player is expected to produce that pitch with a compressed and rather nasal quality. The louder the dynamic, the more nasal and penetrating the quality. This technique has existed since the eighteenth century, but players, acousticians, and teachers are still not in agreement as to what actually happens acoustically.

In the simplest terms, once the right hand finally reaches a complete covering of the bell, and the player compensates adequately by increasing the air pressure against that resistant closure, the pitch seems to pop up one half-step. This is consistently true for the F horn or for the F side of a full double horn. The player then must transpose the fingering to one half-step below the notated pitch (i.e., horn in E). That works fine as far as it goes, which is often as far as it needs to go.

The next level of concern comes when a composer wishes for the sound to slide in and out of stopped and open horn through various glissandi effects. Within modern music, this sound effect is actually fairly common. The performer and the composer must realize that to move the right hand gradually over the bell does not raise the pitch a half step. It lowers the pitch. The interval of change is totally dependent upon the distance to the next lower harmonic of that particular fingering. Try the following experiment.

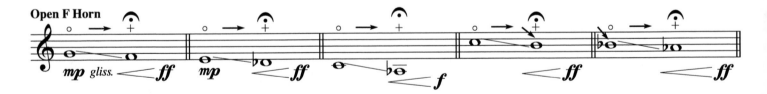

1. Sustain a second line G on the open F horn and gradually cover the bell with an oval-shaped hand, with the thumb pulled back slightly and the fingers gently curved, slightly overlapped, and flush against each other.

2. Relax the aperture enough to allow the vibrations to lower along with the hand's lowering effect. (The movement of the hand actually lengthens the vibrating column of air.)

3. Arrive at the written pitch of F (one step below G and one half-step above E), and sustain that pitch while crescendoing to an   .

4. Play a first line E on the open F horn and follow Nos. 1 and 2 above. After arriving on the D♭ (a minor third below E and a half-step above C), sustain and crescendo to an   .

G, E, and C are the sixth, fifth, and fourth written harmonics on the open F horn. To fully stop a note is to lower it to one half-step above the next lower harmonic, that is if you let the aperture and air go with the results of the right hand's action. The natural tendency, however, is to try to hold on to the pitch of origin. You want to vibrate what is closest to what you see. So you might have noticed with this experiment that the pitch wanted to pop up to the vibration one half-step above the pitch of origin. That's just fine, as long as you (and the composers) are aware that after starting on the G your aperture chooses to vibrate an A♭. You will actually be over-blowing that sixth harmonic and sounding the lowered seventh harmonic (or the flat B♭). You are not actually raising the G. To think of it this way allows for both fully stopped notes and gradual degrees of stopped glissandi to be comprehensible, and it works well for the F horn.

1. Sustain a second line G and gliss in and out of the lower F, covering the bell opening fully with the right hand, in quarter notes over eight beats.

2. Beginning on that G, tongue G open, F stopped in eighth notes over eight beats.

3. Beginning on G, slur eighth-note triplets into and out of the stopped F over eight beats.

4. Tongue sixteenth notes alternating between open G and stopped F over eight beats.

Continue this simple exercise throughout the various ranges of the F horn, always being aware of where you are within the overtone series. Learn to know why this happens by practicing the hand horn (thoroughly discussed in the chapter "The Hand Horn Today, How and Why").

Common problems involving the production of stopped horn include:

1. **Producing a fully closed and compressed sound.** This quite often is caused by an incorrect positioning of the thumb. Be sure your thumb is pulled back alongside the index finger, with the tip pointing towards the middle knuckle of that index finger and a complete seal between the two. The four fingers are closed and slightly bent while overlapping just enough to form an oval-shaped cup that will be able to dissect the bell at a comfortable angle. The cover should be thought of as a door hinged at the middle, simply covering the oval-shaped opening, with little or no force. (Do not try to stuff the bell with your fist, thinking of it as a circular shape.)

2. **Projecting an appropriate volume.** The inside of the mouth should be widened into a larger vowel formation similar to playing lower. The air projection should be more focused and forceful as you blow against the added resistance. It should feel like you are blowing a full   if you wish to project a   volume ($f=$, etc.).

3. **Finding the pitch.** Aim with your ear and the vibrational sensation at the lip for the actual sounding pitch, not the one you are fingering. Thinking one half step too low may cause you to undershoot the pitch, which can be a major problem in the upper range where the harmonics are positioned so close together.

4. **Accuracy in the upper register on the B♭ side of the instrument. The use of the stopped horn hand position is consistent for the F horn.** However, there are flat fingerings which can be used on the B♭ side that can give you a greater security. Most players are secure up to near the written third space C on the F horn. Try using the flattened seventh harmonics on the B♭ side beginning at the written third line B. Thus, B=T(thumb) 13, C=T23, C♯=T12, D=T1, D♯=T2, E=T0. The easiest way to remember these fingerings is to think Horn in F♯ on the B♭ side up to E. Above that it gets less consistent. Try, top line F=T3 (3 alone is designed to be a flat fingering), F♯=T23, G=T3, G♯=T1, A=T2, A♯=T0, B=T1, C=T2. The easiest way to remember these fingerings is to think Horn in G on the B♭ side F♯ to A♯, returning to horn in E from B on upward. All of these B♭ fingerings require a great deal of listening with possible adjusting at the aperture, but they are generally more secure than the F side in the upper octave.

5. **Control or simply production of a stopped sound below written middle C.** Here we run into a varied set of problems. The most common is an inadequate cover with the right hand: too many holes or leaks found most often at the base of the palm or between the fingers. (See No. 1 above.) This range also requires a very forceful air stream through a very wide-open oral cavity. The size of one's hand and the varied sizes of bell-flare openings is another cause for inconsistencies throughout stopped horn requests, but especially in this lower octave. A small, slender hand and a Conn 8D bell flare combine to create a whole set of problems. If your hand has large knuckles and little fat, that too causes serious leaks and much less control in this lower octave. One successful solution involves a rubber kitchen glove for the right hand. Cut off the finger tips down to the second knuckle, the thumb tip down to the first knuckle, and the wrist/palm area up to near the base of the thumb. Wearing such a device does not overly distort the neighboring open notes and does broaden a small hand and fill in the holes between the fingers.

As a teacher who wishes all his students to figure out this stopped horn conundrum through extensive experimentation and practice, I am reluctant to mention a rather successful quick-fix for many of the above problems. The brass mute (sometimes referred to as a stopping mute) closes off the end of the bell in a similar manner and provides a sound that has the basic characteristics of stopped horn. The volume of sound is greater, the actual quality of sound is somewhat less compressed (i.e., more open), and the low range is remarkably easier to produce. Just as with stopped horn, one must transpose down a half-step while using such mutes. The versatile performing hornist must know and be able to perform all aspects of stopped horn for many reasons, such as the above mentioned glissandi and other related effects requested by adventurous, contemporary composers. These effects are not possible with the brass mute. Owning a brass mute is important, however, since some composers request it for its own unique characteristics. They also assume that an advanced performer will own one.

Other less common hand-muting requests that must be understood and practiced include echo horn, half-stopped, and three-quarter-stopped. These three names refer to basically only one technique. The desired and expected sound is usually one of a distant echo or a veiled whisper. To the player, this sound often seems to be an overly muffled or stuffy quality of sound. The symbol used is the + inside a circle, or it is requested through the use of one of its three names. The way this sound is acquired is by covering the written pitch with the right hand just far enough in to lower that pitch one half-step. The player then administers the fingerings for horn in F♯. Practice the following, ideally while watching a chromatic tuner for absolute accuracy.

1. Sustain a normal third space C, gradually bring the right hand inward while relaxing the aperture to allow the pitch to lower one half-step to a B. Make note of how far in the hand must move to produce this change.

2. Sustain a normal second line G, gradually bring the right hand inward while relaxing the aperture down to a G♭. Notice the new right hand position.

3. Repeat the above patterns on E down to E♭ and middle C down to B.

Even within one octave it should become obvious why this effect is called so many names. There is nothing exact about what you must physically do to achieve this change. The cover necessary for the higher notes is greater than for the lower notes. Why does this happen? Refer back to what happens for fully stopped notes. The exact same hand covering activity occurs for all fully stopped notes, but the degree of the phenomenon of change is greater the lower one plays in the overtone series. Thus, the action of covering the bell causes greater change for lower notes and lesser change for higher notes. For echo horn, the action must then be greater to cause the same amount of change (i.e., one half-step) in the upper range than in the lower. After understanding this basic principle, the player must simply aim at the pitch desired, cover with the right hand an appropriate amount, and play as if horn in F♯.

Since the hand remains free-floating in the bell, and the player must learn where the hand should be set for every pitch (based on the ear's close scrutiny), this technique works just as well on the B♭ side of the horn as on the F. It actually works better on the B♭ side in the top octave since the harmonics are farther apart, thus providing a more characteristic echo, rather than a stopped horn sound. Once the overtone series of a given fingering reaches the ninth harmonic, the lowering maneuver for echo horn becomes the same as stopped horn. At this juncture, the sensitive player must try to darken the echo sound by other means in order to distinguish between the two expected sounds. Requests for echo horn in the upper range are, thankfully, very uncommon.

Other hand-muting concerns worth noting include an oscillating wa-wa or extremely distorted vibrato effect through the controlled fluctuation of the right hand; short dips and bends, both up and down from a notated pitch (gestures often used in jazz); and some very infrequent requests for micro-tonal glissandi or micro-tonal pitches, administered with a minute degree of hand cover. Another muting remedy is the use of small patches of felt held in the palm of the right hand to soften the sound and accommodate a conductor's unreasonable desire for ⌐ entrances, or when the members of a woodwind quintet request to obscure the unmatchable resonance of the horn sound.

HIGH RANGE

Performing well in the high range of the horn, though it seems difficult for many, is based on only a few important concepts. Success depends first and foremost on an efficient mid-range mouthpiece placement and pressure, a refined and solid mid-range air control, an appropriately open and relaxed throat position, oral cavity and aperture size in the mid-range, and the setting of cheek and chin muscles just firm enough to avoid air pockets and remain flush with the teeth and gums again in the mid-range. The way one produces the third octave (middle C up to third space C) is the foundation for success in the high range. It is all a 2:1 ratio between the octaves. If the third space C is tense and overblown, there will be no way to double that set of parameters and create the high C successfully.

Compared to the mid-range, the necessary actions for high-range success include:

1. A progressively smaller, more focused aperture opening.

2. A faster, more concentrated airstream.

3. A higher tongue position (more towards the vowel sound eh).

4. A descending airstream (in tandem with No. 3).

5. A slightly descending mouthpipe angle (pressure off the top lip).

6. A focused top lip, with more muscle towards the center (like a beak).

7. Consistently firm (but not tense!) cheek and chin muscles.

8. A bit more mouthpiece pressure anchored on the bottom lip.

Each of these actions should be very gradually developed from the mid-range up, changing only as much as necessary. Less is more! Higher is not harder to do; it is just a difference of degree. It is simply the result of a logical progression of the above physical actions.

An interesting conceptual game that has helped many students is to consider the following:

Where, in front of your body, is high C located?

Think about it, listen for it, and then point at it.

Is it way above your head? Is it out of your reach?

Place it right at your eye level, straight ahead.

Look at it, hear it, and relax as you realize where it is.

Decide where third space C, middle C, and the low range are.

Make sure you can reach them all without bending over.

Dance through the full range with your arms, your ears, and your eyes.

When young students try too hard for too long to force out higher and higher notes before their mid-range is strong, the tensions form, the mouthpiece pressure increases, the lips must then overflex to protect themselves, the sound pinches off, and it becomes obvious that these notes are out of reach. That feeling of desperation then becomes the high range paradigm for those students. Such a scenario is common, unfortunately, and the *undoing* takes more time and energy than the *doing* would if the student had been patient in the beginning. The above conceptual game can help in adjusting to that paradigm.

A few more ideas worth emphasizing that can help to increase one's control in the high range include the hand position in the bell. Try playing your horn above the treble clef staff without your hand in the bell. Near G, the centers start to dissipate, and each note becomes progressively more slippery. This is because the resonating air columns beginning near high G reach a point of nodal demarcation near to where the player's right hand is located. If the hand is not there to support these higher-pitched sound waves, they seem to diffuse and lose their center. Each player should experiment with a hand position that might turn out to be more covered than usual to support these higher notes. I have found that a totally flattened hand pushed somewhat farther into the bell helps support the stability of higher notes without dulling the projection.

Directing the airstream downward as if across the chin, combined with progressively higher vowel formations within the oral cavity, always seems to help. The vowel *ah* may be your desired mid-range setting. Gradually allow the tongue to raise upward but never back towards the throat, into an *eh* moving towards an *ee*. Combined with a rapid air stream through an open throat, this change of vowel formation can help to support and secure a relatively strong high range.

The rapid vibrations that create the actual pitch of a high-range note must come from a strong, focused aperture. It all happens inside the mouthpiece. Learning to buzz without the mouthpiece can help many players discover and improve their high range. Certain lip types, especially the larger, flabbier textured lips, don't always profit as well from lip buzzing. Buzzing, if exercised to an extreme, can also cause a tightened, excessively curled-in, less flexible embouchure. However, learning to create a focused, clear buzz capable of matching pitches extending over two or more octaves and rendering accurate melodies can reap many benefits, especially for the high range. The vowel formation's effect on the high range becomes blatantly obvious with the buzz. Buzzing alone can be overdone. A few minutes at a time should suffice.

Further high-range benefits come from buzzing on the mouthpiece alone, always striving for a focused, wind-filled sound, and through the use of a B.E.R.P. This is a small metal or plastic device, attached to the shank of the mouthpiece with holes to allow the air to escape. It is to be placed into or next to the mouthpipe, allowing the player to retain the natural angle of the leadpipe while experiencing a mouthpiece buzz with a resistance similar to playing the horn. Buzzing in the high range is especially helpful while always feeling the focus and air speed.

The most successful exercises (from many sources, including my students) for extending one's high range on the horn seem to be based on overtone series slurs. Try the following:

1. Begin on a third space C on the open F horn and slur in quarter notes up to D and back to C.

2. Slur again up through D to E, back to C, up to F♯, back to C, up to G, and back to C.

3. Continue this expanding pattern up to the high C or above returning to C, all on the open F horn.

4. Begin again on third line B, second valve on the F horn and repeat the pattern in steps 1, 2, and 3 above.

5. Continue down through first valve, first and second valves, second and third valves, etc.

6. Begin on a third space C♯ on the B♭ side, second and third valves, continuing the pattern. (Repeat with T12, T1, T2, T0 as high as you can go comfortably, and then try a bit farther without forcing.)*

My favorite exercise also involves the overtones but covers a greater range and returns to the lower, more relaxing pitches for the purpose of revitalizing the aperture.

1. Begin on the bottom space, bass clef A♭ (2 and 3 on the F horn), and slur up through the overtones series in eighth notes up three octaves and back.

2. Begin again an octave higher and ascend in eighth-note triplets, up two octaves and back.

3. Begin again an octave higher and ascend in sixteenth notes up one octave and back, twice through.

4. Begin again on that same second space A♭, and glissando four times up and down the octave, ending with a final glissando up to a sustained high A♭.

5. Repeat this exercise on all F horn fingerings and B♭ fingerings as high as comfortably possible and then a bit farther without extreme forcing.

Another exercise that is strongly recommended is on pages 58 and 59 of *The Art of French Horn Playing* by Philip Farkas. Each individual line of that study can be greatly enhanced by alternating dynamics and articulations in the following pattern: tongue the first measure at   , slur the second at *f*, tongue the third at   , and slur the last measure into a sustained final note at *f*. The dynamics should be reversed on alternating days for the best long-term results.

Practicing the cantatas and both Brandenburg Concerti of Bach, excerpts by G. F. Handel, the horn concerti of Telemann, Foerster, Quantz, Neruda, and others of the early to mid-eighteenth century, along with many of the lyrical etudes by Gallay, can greatly enhance one's high register.

*This exercise is notated in *Technical Studies for Solving Special Problems on the Horn* by William Brophy (See Chapter 27).

Throughout all of these recommended exercises and solos, you must remain persistently aware of all that was discussed previously regarding the various techniques and concerns while performing in the high range. Take your time and use your air!

LOW RANGE

A typical verbal exchange that has occurred many times over the years goes like this:

"Why can't I play in the low range as well as I do in the high range?"

"How much do you practice in the low range?"

"Almost never, because it sounds so bad!"

"Oh!"

Most advanced younger students, and even a significant number of professional players, have avoided mastering the low range. The main reason is that historically, the various horn parts within a section were written to emphasize the cor alto or high range on horns 1 and 3, and the cor basso or lower range on horns 2 and 4. This allowed for hornists to specialize. Most of the more advanced players in today's public schools are given the top parts containing most of the solos. Therefore, those who perform these "best" parts are not required to play in the low range as often, if at all. Orchestration manuals have tended to perpetuate this manner of part distribution for a hundred years since the invention of the double horn. Contemporary equipment, however, allows for much greater versatility. Today's professional horn players are expected to be able to musically maneuver through at least three and a half octaves or more, especially at auditions. Every horn player simply needs to take the time and spend the energy to learn the few basic differences between the ranges, while also learning to love the sound of the low horn.

Regarding equipment, however, it must be noted that most horns are built so that the middle and high registers are the easiest to administer. The horn is nearly the longest brass instrument with the smallest leadpipe. It has the deepest mouthpiece with the thinnest rim encircling one of the smallest diameters of all brass instruments. And yet we are expected to perform from within the high range of the trumpet deep into the low range of the tuba. To do all of this on one embouchure is to ask the near impossible.

As mentioned above regarding high range, the low range also requires a relaxed and efficient middle register from which to deviate. From those mid-range settings, these basic deviations include the following:

1. A lessening of the air compression and consequent air projection.

2. An enlarged oral cavity forming lower vowels (*awe* to *oh*).

3. A lowered jaw setting both down and forward.

4. More of the flabby part of the bottom lip involved in the vibration.

5. A more upwardly directed, consistent airstream.

6. Less mouthpiece pressure on the bottom lip (the same as on the top).

7. An ascended angle to the mouthpipe (pivoting upward).

8. Always retaining firm (but not tense) cheek and flattened chin muscles.

The high range grows out of the mid-range quite gradually. The low range, however, requires a greater degree of change, largely because of the size and proportions of the instrument and the mouthpiece. Nos. 2, 3, 4, and 5 above suggest some of the specifics of a "shift," which is necessary for almost all horn players as they enter the low range. Very few students, in my experience, have been able to make this shift through small increments over a large range. Most must find the spot where an upper register setting of the jaw and lips (similar to sounding *ehmmm*) and a useful lower register setting of the jaw and lips (similar to sounding *ohmmm*) converge. Try the following:

1. Set up a mirror on your music stand and observe fully all that happens.

2. Watch your lips and jaw as you descend chromatically from second line G.

3. Do not change anything inside your mouth, but retain the *ehmmm* setting.

4. When a thinning of the sound or a forced quality begins, notice which two pitches that event occurs between, continue downward a few more notes, and then stop.

5. Consider all of the eight steps describing the low range above, produce a solid, second space bass clef low C, and begin to ascend chromatically.

6. Continue upward while changing nothing regarding the lip/jaw setting or the mouthpipe angle.

7. When a flabby, unfocused sound begins to become obvious, notice between which pitches or in what general range this occurs, continue briefly, and then stop.

8. Decide the point between which two pitches that the less desirable sounds and feelings occur. (Though it can differ somewhat depending on the individual, that point is often between fifth line A♭ and G in the bass clef.)

9. Watching the mirror, repeat No. 2; then when reaching your decided point of demarcation (e.g., A♭ perhaps), shift from the normal mid-range setting to the one described in the eight steps above and continue the descending chromatic scale.

10. Begin on a solid low C as above; then ascend with the low setting until you reach the shifting point, suddenly return to the mid-range setting, and continue up to the second line G.

Repeat this exercise many times over a period of days to be sure of the shifting point. Demonstrate this complete process for friends and/or a teacher to get their impressions as well. Different dynamics might also reap new information. Start at first with an   , and repeat it at *f*,   ,   , and   before you decide for sure. After you have decided, practice the shift in larger intervals in melodic contexts, frequently checking a chromatic tuner, while always striving for a consistent and beautiful sound. Give this change adequate time to settle into your technique. *Plan to change as little as possible, but as much as necessary.*

The most common low range problems involve a pooking out of the lips. It is not exactly a pucker, but is more of a rolling out of the lips, based largely on an instinctual need to get to the inside of the bottom lip. That need can more successfully be administered through the lip/jaw shift described previously. Once the lips and cheek muscles lose a firm contact with the teeth and gums, they are literally floating and can no longer be adequately focused or consistently controlled. Always try to retain as much as possible the look and feel of the mid-range regarding the facial muscles and the mouthpiece setting. Pooking out the lips often causes the mouthpiece to slip downward. Recovering from these distortions back into the mid or high range is very awkward and usually causes an audible distortion or break in the sound along with serious intonation problems.

Another problem involves too little or no mouthpipe angle change, which results in too much pressure on the bottom lip as the jaw drops and projects forward. In the mid and upper registers, the top lip is the primary vibrator. In the low range the bottom lip becomes much more active. To exert extra pressure on the bottom lip in the low range is as problematic as too much pressure on the top lip in the high range. These unnecessary stresses against the lip eventually stifle the vibration while overly challenging one's endurance.

There is a strong tendency for horn players to wish to produce a tuba-like quality in the lower two octaves. This is not the best concept of sound to strive for. Using the lowest, and most open vowel formation of *ooh*, especially in the second octave, diffuses the center of the sound and often causes the pitch to be flat. Playing flat in the low range is far too common. The lower second and fourth parts are for the purpose of establishing the pitch base for the section. The air must be directed upward to find the center of where the horn wants to vibrate. The resulting sound, especially to the player's ear, will be brighter than a tuba but warmer than a trombone. Learn to enjoy and accept that sound.

Another important factor is the right-hand position in the low range. It must open gradually as you descend. The lowering effect of a cupped hand on the pitch becomes greater the lower you go in the overtone series. (See the section regarding stopped horn.) This opening of the right hand's cover will add to the player's perception of a brighter and perhaps a bit brassier sound than desired. Rest assured that the sound being heard out front, if it is full of good solid air and accurate pitch, will be rich and full of overtones. Ask others to listen and help.

Exercises and etudes for the development of the low range are readily available. Some are simply transcriptions of tuba etudes or trombone studies, but they help. Others are discussed later in the chapter on etudes. Many teachers advocate the playing of the popular Kopprasch *60 Selected Studies for the French Horn* down an octave at the constant dynamic level of *f* to   . This does work and will help. The most important point is the dynamic level. Philip Farkas mentions in *The Art of French Horn Playing* that these lowest notes have to be actually broken in. Once the ability to make them literally rattle has been accomplished a few times, these notes seem to be acquired permanently. This has proven to be true, as long as one continues to practice them. The low range exercise on pages 60 and 61 in Farkas's book is a very effective study. I have found it to be exceptionally effective when played *f* to   , with the following modifications:

1. Use all normal fingerings, always exercising the harmonics you will be using.

2. Slur the eight eighth notes as notated, add a measure of eight tongued sixteenth notes, and end on the final quarter-note.

3. Add low C♯ and F♯ to the end of the eighth line.

4. Continue the same process down an octave for lines 9 through 14 as far as possible, always playing *f* or   .

5. For lines 15, 16, and 17, return to the notated octave and insert a third measure of three sets of aggressively tongued sixteenth-note arpeggios.

Always try to "rattle" your sound aggressively as you execute the above. That may not be the sound you ultimately wish to produce, but the point is to open up the power. Try to match the sounds among all the notes, whatever that might be, throughout each practice session. The idea is to gain control and balance of the air and the embouchure. Throughout this exercise, relax the aperture. Let the air create the power and allow the lips to respond. Playing aggressively loud is too often accompanied by excessive flexing of the facial muscles. Don't force! Let the horn do the amplifying. After extensive and consistent work on this study, the softer dynamics seem to simply fall into place. (This phenomenon works only in the low register, however.)

Another wonderful low-range study procedure involves pitch bending. In the next chapter on hand horn, factitious tones are discussed. These are the notes acquired through bending the pitch of the second harmonic down as much as a perfect fourth or more through dropping the jaw, opening the aperture, and lowering the vowel formation to an extreme. Such bending was, and still is, a common technique used to correct pitches on the hunting horn, though administered much higher in the horn's tessitura. The interval of change possible through bending gets much smaller the higher you go, but the exercise is always helpful for developing strength and flexibility.

For further development of the low range, try the following:

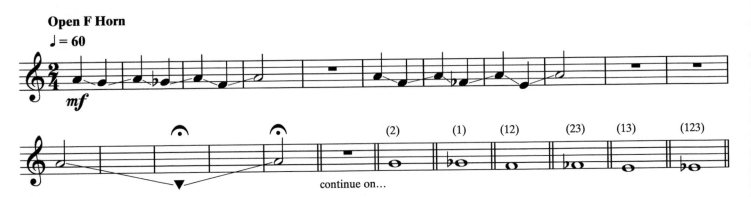

1. Turn on a chromatic tuner and place it within view.

2. Set the metronome at 60 b.p.m.

3. Play a second space bass clef C on the open F horn and bend the pitch down to a B in quarter notes, return to the C, bend to the B♭, come back to the C, then down to the A, return to the C, and then stop.

4. Begin again on C, bend down to A, return to C, come down to A♭, then up to C, down to G, back up to C, and then stop.

5. Begin on C, bend very gradually down as far as you can control, sustain that bent pitch, try to make it as beautiful as possible, return to C, and then stop.

This exercise should be done at a medium dynamic level while always watching the tuner and always trying to make a focused, beautiful sound (but accepting whatever you get). Repeat the above, using each of the descending valve settings on the F horn, then doing it all again on the B♭ side beginning on fourth line F in the bass clef. Create your own exercises bending higher pitches to gain more control of the aperture.

As one gains a greater competency in the low range, the middle register becomes more open and relaxed, which in turn will cause the upper register to become more open allowing for an increase in pitches far above the treble staff. Screech trumpet players in the jazz field practice bass clef factitious tones and pedal notes all of the time. Increasing competency in the low range will reap many rewards, but there are no short cuts—only helpful hints.

VOCALIZATIONS (MULTIPHONICS)

A remarkable quote drawn from Viola Roth's translation of the 1824 *Method for Cor Alto and Cor Basse* by Dauprat reads, "chords that can be made on certain low notes of the horn by singing along with them, in a head tone, sounds which leave through the nostrils. Young students who are shown how to produce these chords pick up the technique almost immediately. Punto, who performed them much better than anyone who has been involved with them since, has himself avowed that they are both easy and silly. Leave, therefore, to the charlatans these bizarre devices which appeal only to mediocrity, astonish only the ignorant, and repel equally both connoisseurs and true artists."[1]

This device has been around for at least 200 years and has always drawn mixed reviews. That has not stopped composers from being interested in the possibilities or kept the players from being intrigued. Thus, we need to know how this works to satisfy the composer's intent (or to repel a few connoisseurs).

The number of effects possible from singing and playing simultaneously have increased through some recent experimentation. One of these, I believe, presents an effective passageway to learning how to coordinate the aperture buzz with the voice.

1. Hum a note within the middle of your vocal range and sustain it while opening your throat as much as possible (with a loud, whispered hum).

2. Play that same pitch on the horn and sustain it while opening in the same way.

3. Hum the note again with the mouthpiece in place and gradually add the vibrating aperture at a unison with the voice and sustain, holding both in tune.

4. Play the note again and gradually include the voice on the same pitch and sustain, holding both in tune.

5. Sound both together and crescendo and diminuendo while holding both in tune.

6. Sound both together and gradually raise the vocal pitch while holding the aperture's vibration steady. (Notice the amplitude modulations, or beats, increase in speed in direct relationship to the change of frequency.)

7. After this becomes somewhat easier to control, play/sing a few simple melodies, in unison within that basic range.

8. Next, try holding a pedal note at the aperture and sing a melody above that pitch and also below that pitch matching volume and timbre.

The original reason for this technique was to produce chords. Hermann Baumann successfully includes this effect on his hand horn recording of the Mozart concerto cadenzas, and it is actually notated in the cadenza of the Weber Concertino. The way these chords occur are most easily defined by figuring the sum and the difference of the pitches played and sung as they lie within a harmonic series. Try the following either as is or up an octave for higher voices:

1. Play a second space, bass clef C

2. Sing the top space, bass clef G.

3. Notice the resultant sounding chord: pedal C, low C, G, first line treble clef E.

4. Simple arithmetic analysis:

The **played** second bass clef	C =	2nd harmonic:	2
The **sung** top space bass clef	G =	3rd harmonic:	+3
The **heard** first line treble clef	E =	5th hamonic:	5

The **heard** first line treble clef E is the *summation* tone.

The **sung** top space bass clef	G =	3rd harmonic:	3
The **played** second space bass clef	C =	2nd harmonic:	-2
The **heard** below the bass clef pedal C	=	1st hamonic:	1

The **heard** pedal C is the *difference* tone.

The same resulting chord will occur for the higher voice an octave higher.

It is the matching of volume and timbre, along with mutually solid pitches, that causes the most successful sensation of chords. The summation and difference tones are audible only when there is a blended and balanced match. That is why a higher voice should, whenever possible, play notes at the higher pitch setting closer to the range and timbre of the voice.

Other important techniques worth extending yourself for include the many different gestures called glissandos, the double horn's unique built-in capacity to perform quarter tones, the numerous half-valve effects, varied air sounds, and combinations of all of the above. Each of these require techniques that are rather self-explanatory once you know the desired effect. To understand them more fully, I refer you again to *Extended Techniques for the Horn: A Practical Handbook for Students, Performers, and Composers* mentioned at the beginning of this chapter.

4. The Hand Horn Today: How and Why

The last 25 years of the twentieth century have seen a remarkable surge of interest in the performance practices of the seventeenth, eighteenth, and early nineteenth centuries. Many years ago, the sudden availability of the Mozart concertos performed on hand horn by the brilliant artist Hermann Baumann caused most of my generation to believe. It was finally obvious that the hand horn was truly an artistic outlet. Many of us began to teach ourselves since there was no available English language tutor at that time; and what we learned was not only how to maneuver about on this new instrument, but also a great deal more about what composers of those periods expected to hear. That changed everything. The Beethoven Sonata Op. 17, the Mozart concertos, Haydn's trio and divertimenti, many classical orchestral excerpts, and even the Brahms Trio Op. 40 required some serious rethinking. In time, such efforts also made it easier to hear the subtleties of pitch, to hear and adjust the varieties of tone color, and to better understand the profound importance of the harmonic series as it relates to our modern horns. Stopped and echo horn also became much more intelligible and much less awkward. To develop the new skills of performance on such a marvelous and unique sounding instrument as the hand horn should be enough reason to devote the time. The bonuses just mentioned should make it a requirement.

What follows is an introductory overview of the basics of hand horn playing for the modern performer. This should serve as a guide to help students get a secure start without stumbling over all of those initial pitfalls experienced by those of us who were self-taught 20 years ago.

THE INSTRUMENT

First, and perhaps most important, locate and acquire an actual hand horn replica if at all possible. The specific problems involved often require different solutions if you are simply learning hand horn techniques on your valved horn. The size of the bell openings alone are often quite different, depending on your type of horn. The weight of the instrument and the consequent vibrancy of an actual hand horn is also an important contributing factor. The next best solution is to have a student line single F horn modified by removing the valve section. It would also help if that particular horn had an additional E♭ crook. Every horn has its own personality, and what is learned on a lesser horn might be significantly different on a better one, causing a reprogramming of those newly developed instincts. In an article by Richard Seraphinoff in the *Historic Brass Society Newsletter* (Summer 1997), he lists and discusses 25 different natural horn makers from around the world. The instruments I have played and recommend as quite good include those made by Richard Seraphinoff, Bloomington, Indiana; Paxman Musical Instrument Ltd., London, England; Gebr. Alexander, Mainz, Germany; Lowell Greer, Toledo, Ohio; and George McCracken, Barhamsville, Virginia.

Throughout history there has been a variety of hand horn configurations. Available instruments and photos from the eighteenth and nineteenth centuries show a remarkable amount of experimentation. There are two configurations which are most common. One is the Orchesterhorn, which has crooks (various lengths of tubing which are used to change the keys of the overtones available) that are inserted at the terminal juncture (the mouthpiece end of the leadpipe) and have a tuning slide located within the body of the instrument. The other is the Inventionshorn with its fixed leadpipe, larger bell, and fewer crooks, which are inserted within the body of the instrument to change keys and serve as the tuning slide. It is the Inventionshorn which is thought to be derived from the Austro-Bohemian style attributed to Joseph Hampel, the credited father of hand horn technique, circa 1740–1750. Either style of instrument is acceptable, with the former producing the brighter, clearer sound and more stable open harmonics, and the latter having the more mellow, resonant timbre with greater room in the bell for hand motions.

THE HARMONIC SERIES

The way the hand horn system works is founded on the harmonic series based on the notated pitch C. Almost (but not) all hand horn parts are based on the written key of C. The crook you use, which will cause the actual pitches available without the hand, is requested on the parts as Horn in E♭, or *Corno en Sol*, etc. This reality is quite convenient for hand horn players, since all we need to learn is one set of hand positions as notated in only one key.

So the first thing the student must do is thoroughly memorize the C harmonic series. These are the pitch levels available to you without any right hand manipulation in the bell. As you notice in Figure 1 below, the seventh, eleventh, thirteenth and fourteenth overtones (also called harmonics or partials and shown as quarter-notes) are out of tune with the tempered scale; they cannot be played with the normal open hand position as can all of the others.

Figure 1

THE "HANDERINGS"

The exact handerings, or right-hand positions in the bell, must be learned gradually and decided upon by each individual player on each individual horn. Your ear is your guide. I've included in Figure 2 the handerings appropriate to my hand on my horn. These may serve as a vague guide for you to begin your search. An interesting set of comparisons can be found on page 99 in *The French Horn* by R. Morley-Pegge, where he graphs the handerings of eight different hornists from 1803 through 1911. They each advocated a surprisingly different set of hand positions. Each is valid, so assume that your conclusions will differ from mine and theirs but will still be valid, at least until you change your horn or your concept of sound. This hand horn experience is definitely not an exact science. Maybe that's why it was and is so much fun.

My handering chart is organized to demonstrate some of the basic principles needed to understand the process being applied. Understanding this process will help the modern student better realize the right hand's many uses in contemporary music. The right hand needs to be partially cupped and perhaps a bit less stiff than usual. As it closes or covers the bell opening and is gradually inserted, the pitch which the horn projects is lowered. The player must let this happen. Avoid compensating with the lip in either direction. Learn to let the hand do the work. This lowering continues until the hand reaches a full cover and ends up sounding one half-step above the next lower harmonic. This fully covered bell opening is what we call stopped horn in today's music. Though it isn't clearly visible through our limited notational system, the distance between each pitch of the harmonic series is progressive. No two pitches are equidistant to any other two. This is "nature's scale" and it is simply perfect. We are not perfect, and our horns are not, so we must devise the compromises. The movement of the right hand, which lowers a given pitch a half-step, is what we call echo horn, or half-stopped or three-quarter-stopped in today's music. (The reason there are so many names for this is because there are so many different hand positions necessary to lower each of these varied harmonics only a half-step.) This can be easily observed through the handering chart. Begin to learn these hand positions for each covered note by working down from the appropriate open harmonics.

Figure 2

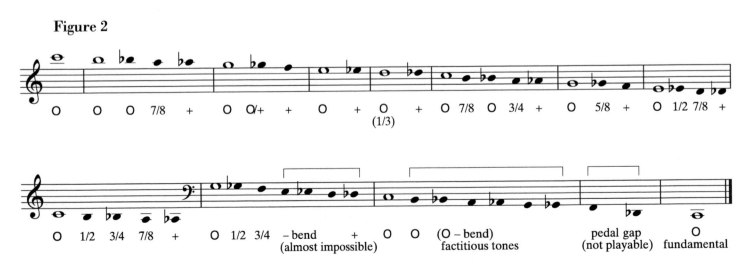

THE CROOKS

As mentioned, the key of the composition usually prescribes the length of crook necessary. The exceptions are usually when multiple horns are designated in differing keys for selective timbral and harmonic effects. The most common keys included Eb, D, F, and E for solo and chamber music works. Other keys, found primarily in the late eighteenth century, included C basso, G, A, Bb basso, Bb alto, C alto, and an occasional B, Ab, F#, and Db. Other keys were requested, but very infrequently, and mostly in opera scores. Since the hand hornist only needs to learn the hand positions for the notated key of C, this should make little difference. However, there are serious differences that require a very versatile and sensitive ear. If what one sees can ultimately sound and feel to the embouchure like any one of 14 different pitches, then the mind's ear must be well trained and always active. Developing such an expertise is quite applicable for the modern performer who experiences similar enigmatic elements of relative pitch when asked to transpose, or even more so when invited to perform a Bb Wagner tuba part.

THE SOUND

One of the wonders of this instrument and technique called hand horn is (and was) its magical, mellow, mystical sound, which seems to be coming from nowhere and everywhere at the same time. Why would Mozart, Beethoven, and Brahms have chosen to feature this instrument and not the trombone, for instance, which was a much more direct, commanding, and harmonically versatile voice back then? It seems obvious why, especially after one hears Hermann Baumann's Mozart concertos. It was the inherent mellow warmth of the tone, the extraordinary legato, and the vocal-like variety of timbres, which were the result of simply producing the notes. These great composers must have been extraordinarily fascinated with the challenge of such idiosyncratic limitations and such consequent potentials. Composers love limitations, and to be faced with such a fascinating and unique set as this must have stimulated their creative energies.

The performer has some serious choices to make regarding the overall sound that will effect every other aspect of their technique. Thus, early and thoughtful decisions are quite important. If you prefer a more open sound, more consistent with today's normal horn sound, the basic right-hand position should be similar to a contemporary hand position. The ultimate limitation to this openness can be deduced by playing the written third line Bb with your hand all the way out of the bell. This is the note that must be in tune because this is the one harmonic over which one has little or no control regarding pitch. I suggest that this be the way to set the tuning slide for the instrument. Tune the mid-line Bb (sounding Eb with the F crook). Then tune the third space C (sounding F with the F crook). This pitch will be found by positioning the right hand to just the right covered position. That hand position will become the basic one for most all of the open notes and will dictate a basically open sound. The covered notes will be learned accordingly, and the overall effect will be one of a fairly well-matched set of timbres between the various settings.

If the performer chooses to have a more covered, distant, mellow quality, then the above tuning process should again begin with the third line Bb (i.e., seventh harmonic). This time leave the fingertips of the right hand touching the inside of the bell with the hand opened flat; then set the tuning slide accordingly. This position of the hand will affect the pitch slightly, and the tone will be less open. Then, find the necessary closure for the written C, and you will notice a more covered basic sound. This quality of sound has a more vocal character but takes some time for most modern hornists to accept as desirable or as a sound that projects. It usually does. This basic hand placement requires less motion between the various hand positions and, thus, a quicker facility. The first approach provides a more open and clear sound with less magic, and the second a less unified sound but with a quicker facility. Each has its strengths, and both methods should be investigated. Somewhere in between these two extremes is where one often finds satisfaction.

INTONATION CONCERNS

Intonation is a constant concern for all horn players on all horns, but for the hand horn player it requires intense concentration, heightened awareness, and immediate adjustability. This aspect of learning to adjust pitches on the hand horn is one of the greatest benefits to the contemporary player upon returning to the lesser problems of valved horn intonation. First, the player must get comfortable with the feel of the seventh, eleventh, and thirteenth partials. Get to know where they are between the usual half-steps and let them lie there. Blow through those centers. These are the harmonics you will have to play, which will be adjusted by the hand to fit the desired chromaticism. Next, find the hand positions that will adjust these three pitches downward to the desired pitch. The seventh, or third line B♭, requires only a shallow cover to bring it down to the pitch A. Blow through that A fully, crescendoing and diminuendoing, while watching a chromatic tuner. (Chromatic tuners are quite helpful and would most surely have been used in the eighteenth century had they only known!) The top line F and the A♭ above the staff are notes that require a full cover but often produce rather insecure feelings similar to the A below them. All three of these pitches descend from flat harmonics. These harmonics have notches with which we are not physically familiar and, thus, all of the covered pitches that develop from them are difficult notes to feel and to tune. Study each as if it were a subject of its own.

Some other pitches that are notoriously difficult to tune are those between the echo horn and the stopped horn positions. The most obvious is the D at the bottom of the treble clef staff. This is a pitch worthy of a great deal of study. If you look at the concerti of Mozart and Haydn and the sonata of Beethoven, among many other compositions, especially earlier classical period works, you will not find this particular pitch notated. It is simply awkward on most horns. However, it became much more common in the early to mid-nineteenth century.

Another less obvious intonation problem is the difficulty distinguishing between the pitch and the timbre of a given note. As the timbres fluctuate among the different hand positions, the ear can easily become confused. We hear from both inside our heads and from the outside. We can't help but hear the immediate and obvious sounds vibrating our skulls, teeth, and eardrums. Simultaneously, we must focus our listening to the sounds emanating from the bell to our right and the rebounded sounds that hit us on all sides. If every sound we produced was similar in tone (as it is for the valved horn), the timbres would quickly become less of an issue, at least regarding our perceptions of pitch. The differences in tone color between the various hand positions are a definite distraction. Pitch perception becomes a difficult issue, but one of major importance. The chromatic tuner can be a helpful tool throughout this learning process but, as always, use it as a point of reference; don't just learn to play the needle. The other obvious tools for self-help would be a cassette, DAT, CD, or other recording device.

ARTICULATION CONCERNS

When the player adjusts a pitch up or down with the hand while vibrating the same harmonic (e.g., third space C down to B, back up to C), the sound of that motion will create a sliding, *do-wa* effect, unless the change of hand position is coordinated with a light tongue. The hand horn player must learn to articulate very inconspicuously to create a legato line, much like the trombone player does between neighboring slide positions. A sound to imitate is the sound of a slur across neighboring harmonics (e.g., third space C up to D, back to C). That slight flick of a sound (similar to the articulation made by a valve interrupting a vibrating air column) can be created through forming a very gentle consonant such as *d* or *l* with the tongue. As long as you are changing harmonics, this will not be necessary, but it might become desirable in many cases for an optional legato sound between notes and for unifying the sound of an extended passage. Here again, the development of a technique necessary for successful hand horn playing will provide the modern hornist with a great new tool for more versatile articulations. Dennis Brain was a master at this type of tonguing. What sounded like a perfect legato was often a tongued passage.

DYNAMIC PROJECTION

To create a dynamically even musical line while administering all of the above techniques requires additional demands and unique challenges for the hand horn player. Coordinated air control is the key. Each degree of cover from the hand will affect the natural projection of any given note. A mid-range dynamic blown into an open third space C will project much better than its neighboring B, which is covered. The player must compensate by varying the air intensity, depending upon the amount of cover required for each note. A third line B♭ (played wide open) down to a neighboring A♭ (which is fully stopped) is an ultimate extreme. The B♭ would need less air (softer), and the A♭ would need much more (louder). The ability to administer such rapid coordinated compensation is absolutely necessary for the hand hornist. If not fully developed, the melodic line projected will not only be of differing timbres, which is inevitable, but will also sound as if alternating first from one level of presence, then from another. When this technique has become well developed, the overall dynamic level of a hand horn performance will be somewhat softer than that of the modern horn. In the early stages of such air coordination, a great deal of practice is necessary, but it eventually becomes nearly as natural as knowing your fingerings. To have attained such control over rapid dynamic shifting is often useful in the performance of certain aspects of modern music. It can also provide the valved horn player with many subtle articulation options in both classical and, especially, jazz contexts.

PROBLEM PITCHES

When the hand horn player is forced to perform a work with particular notes that are obviously of a lesser quality than others, certain nuances should be applied. These problem pitches arise in passages at a tempo that would make absolute clarity through extremely awkward hand changes basically impossible or in passages that include the dreaded top line F or F♯ (which is a major problem on some horns). Nuances to consider include the following:

1. Slightly obscuring the articulation of the problem note.

2. Accenting the stable notes around the problem pitch.

3. Playing the problem note softer in the context.

4. Distorting the rhythm of the problem note.

None of these choices appear to be musically desirable since they favor the manner (technique) over the message of the musical intent. But that may be a distorted thought growing out of our contemporary knowledge of what such a passage could sound like on a valved horn. The composers mentioned before were quite aware of the limitations and potentials of the instrument. One must learn to adjust to the problems and the possibilities. Also, it is often the case that such nuances, when done with artistry and finesse, will be heard by the audience as an obvious, implied pitch or rhythm consistent with the intended musical gesture. This is not a lowering of standards but is just a different set of musical opportunities and requirements. For today's hornist, learning to under-accent, slightly obscure an articulation, and distort a rhythm for gestural purposes has direct applications in jazz and in other forms of aleatoric music.

Another set of problem pitches are those found primarily below the written low C in the bass clef. For example, Beethoven asked for a bottom line G in his Sonata, Opus 17. The hand cover seems not to be the most effective way to perform these notes, and it also tends to disproportionately deaden the sound. These pitches below the C are often called factitious tones. *Factitious* means "artificial or contrived," which is one way to look at it. They are contrived by the opening and relaxing of the aperture, the jaw, and the oral cavity; but to the hand hornist, this is not artifice. The player ideally learns to bend the low C downward to produce a full chromatic set of pitches over an interval of a fourth. (See Weber's Concertino for example.)

Matching the quality of the sound attained throughout the normal range of the hand horn is the next goal. This ability to bend a pitch downward can be applied elsewhere by the hand horn player to correct intonation problems. It was, in fact, a standard method for the hunting horn players when they were called in from the forest to play in tune with the strings and oboes of the time. For the contemporary hornist, this ability to bend pitches is a wonderful tool for many jazz nuances and an effective exercise for gaining flexibility, embouchure strength, and aperture focus throughout all registers of the horn, especially the low range.

TRILLS

Assuming the player has developed a dependable lip/tongue trill, hand horn trills, for the most part, pose few new problems. For whole-step trills between the open harmonics (e.g., written third space C and fourth line D), and neighboring closed harmonics (e.g., third space C♯ and fourth line D♯), the technique is the same. This is also true for half-step trills in the extreme high range (e.g., high B to a high C, in the Brandenburg Concerto No. 1). It is when the neighboring harmonics needed for the trill are not either an exact whole or half-step that the player must learn to finesse an implied set of pitches and hope that the listener will know what is meant harmonically. A common example of such a trill is the notated second space A up to the B. These two pitches require slightly different hand positions to be exactly in tune. The player must begin the trill slowly, accommodating these differences, so that the listener hears what is intended then quickly break into a lip trill with the right hand resting in a compromise position. Another common trill is the top line F♯ to the G. This trill should be started with an in-tune covered position for the F♯ and an open G, quickly sliding into a lip trill between the eleventh and twelfth harmonics with a slightly too open position for the F/F♯ and a slightly too covered position for the G. If the resolutions are scrupulously in tune, the audiences should forgive you.

THE RESULTS

The uniqueness of the hand horn among all of the instruments of the eighteenth and early nineteenth centuries attracted many great composers. Its tone quality was one of veiled magic. Its blending potentials were superior to all other voices, and its limitations, when considered and worked through by the creative minds of genius, became its strengths. When the various qualities of pitches were composed carefully, as in the Mozart concertos, Beethoven's Sonata Op. 17, and Brahms' Trio Op. 40, the aural illusions of light and dark, tension and release, distance and presence became a whole new palette for creativity. The basic essence of this mellow, covered sound separated the horn from the other more forceful brasses and allowed it to become an important, gentle solo voice as well as the substance within the sound of its frequent unison partners. When the right hand was no longer needed in the bell to adjust the pitches, as the valve gradually became the norm, musicians chose to leave it there because of the sound that Mozart, Beethoven, and Brahms loved.

If this is what the great composers of the period were expecting to hear, shouldn't contemporary performers consider these charming idiosyncrasies every time a classical or early romantic work is performed on valved horns? Always consider this veiled and mellow sound; consider the notes that would have been fully covered as projecting a compressed tension soon to be released into an open, more relaxed sound; consider the notes that were slightly covered as if they radiate darkness searching for the lighter opened notes; and consider the humor that would surely have been intended as successive rapid notes alternated between opened and closed. Such considerations should become instinctive to the practitioner of the hand horn upon return to the modern instrument to perform the older music.

How these considerations are applied to contemporary interpretations must be left to the artistic judgment of the individual performer. That is a given. One's judgments, however, can only come from the experiences through which one learns. That is the truth. It is recommended that you experience the hand horn, and through it re-learn the truth of its music.

RECOMMENDED FURTHER READING (In a suggested order of study)

Morley-Pegge, R., *The French Horn*, 2nd Edition, W. W. Norton, NY, 1973.

Fitzpatrick, H., *The Horn and Horn Playing 1680–1830*, Oxford University Press, London, 1970.

Baines, A., *Brass Instruments: Their History and Development*, Faber, London, 1976.

Bruechle, B. and K. Janetzky, *A Pictorial History of the Horn*, Schneider, Tutzing, 1976.

Dauprat, L. F., *Mèthode de Cor-alto et Cor-basse*, 1824, facsimile/translation by Viola Roth, Birdalone Music, Bloomington, IN, 1994.

Austin, Paul, *A Modern Valve Horn Player's Guide to the Natural Horn*, Cincinnati, 1993.

Additional readings and references about the hand horn can be found throughout the journals and newsletters of the International Horn Society and the Historic Brass Society.

RECOMMENDED COMPOSITIONS (At the earlier stages)

Beethoven, L. van, Sonata, Op. 17

Saint-Saëns, C., Romance, Op. 36

Mozart, W. A., Concerto in D, No. 1 (K.412)

Ries, F., Sonata, Op. 34

Haydn, F. J., Concerti in D, Nos. 1 & 2

Haydn, M., Concertino in D

DUETS

Mozart, W. A., 12 Duos (K.487), International Edition (not transposed)

Dauprat, L. F., 20 Duets (in different keys), McCoy Horn Library

Hill, D. (ed.), 27 Rare Horn Duets (Baroque period), McCoy Horn Library

Schubert, F., 5 Duets, Presser Pub. Co.

Rossini, G., 5 Duets, Masters Music Pub.

RECOMMENDED COMPOSITIONS (As you progress)

Brahms, J., Trio, Op. 40

Danzi, F., Sonata in E♭, Sonata in E

Krufft, N. von, Sonata in E

Czerny, C., Andante e Polacca

Gallay, J. F., Caprices, and Concerto in F

Haydn, F. J., Divertimento a tre

Kuhlau, F., Andante e Polacca

Mozart, W. A., Concerti in E♭, No. 2, 3, and 4; Quintet (K.407)

Rossini, G. A., Prelude, Theme and Variation

Rosetti, F. A., Concerti (many)

Weber, C. M. von, Concertino in E

MODERN WORKS FOR HAND HORN (All unaccompanied, in contemporary styles)

Baumann, H., *Elegia für Naturhorn*, Bote & Bock

Pflüger, H. G., *Kaleidoskop für Naturhorn*, Bote & Bock

Snedeker, J., *Goodbye to a Friend*, Birdalone Music

Patterson, R. G., *Four Pieces for Natural Horn* (from composer)

Greer, L., *Het Valkhof* (1991) (composer)

Nicholas, J., *Panachida* (1987), Birdalone Music

Bleuse, M., *Corps a Corps*, Billaudot

See also Paul Austin's article "Contemporary Natural Horn Compositions (1982–1992)" in Volume 24, No. 3 of *The Horn Call: The Journal of the International Horn Society*, for much more information on modern hand horn pieces.

5. Professional Orchestra Auditioning

    If you have the desire to be one of a selected group of individuals who perform in today's professional orchestras, chances are you will have to take a few, or perhaps many, auditions. The typical auditioning procedure is not perfect, but it is fairly consistent in the way it is administered around the world. No better system of selection has yet been devised, aside from the one that costs the orchestra managements more money than they wish to pay.

    Giving every candidate a chance to rehearse and perform on a concert with the desired orchestra is what all auditionees (and orchestra players) would prefer. Instead, you will have to prove your prowess and worth to a small group of orchestra players and a conductor in a matter of minutes—all by yourself. The audition committee members have an even more difficult job. They must select, from scores to hundreds of aspiring candidates, the very best possible colleague, whose playing will enhance and help to improve their orchestra (which is their primary livelihood) with the sounds most needed and desired at every rehearsal and concert for the rest of their lives.

    This is serious business! Getting a job as a performer is not just the logical result of a talented young player coming of age. You must truly want such a result—every day for a number of years. During those years, you will need to learn all you can about orchestral music, orchestral composers, conductors, professional performers, and, most of all, you must learn what is expected from the horn in every important passage found in the basic orchestral repertoire. As you learn to know what is expected, you must also learn how to demonstrate it all through your horn. This is a wonderful challenge. You will be submerging your very being deep into the wonders of some of the greatest artistic achievements of the human race. It is worth the effort but, trust me, it requires sincere and consistent effort!

    Listen to live performances and many varied recordings. Select new and important repertoire each week, works that orchestras often perform and works that contain important horn solos. (See the list of most frequently requested excerpts for auditions at the end of this chapter.) Following excerpt books, complete parts, and, better still, a complete score is the wisest and most wonderful way to supplement your extensive listening. Focused listening to all of the great works of the repertoire is a requirement. Focused listening while studying the score broadens your scope of knowledge and understanding. Focused listening while watching a horn part is a third step that can serve as the bridge back into the practice room with your horn in hand.

    Being accomplished at anything first requires the necessary knowledge and then the experiences acquired while utilizing that knowledge. If you begin to practice excerpts blindly as if they are simply exercises or etudes, you will totally miss the point. You must first listen and listen well. There is no way that a student in a four-year college can cover the vast repertoire in the context of an actual orchestra. But by listening to all of this great music, which is possible, the excerpts will establish their rightful place within your knowledge. That knowledge becomes the foundation for your practice experiences. Tempos, rhythms, timbral relationships, blending needs, musical direction, and the appropriate styles will have their places in your perspective. The solos and the accompanimental patterns you will be learning while you listen will find their places in your memory. An excerpt will become meaningful only when the *music* is known to the performer of that excerpt.

    Young, less experienced performers auditioning for the same positions that older, more experienced performers desire must somehow demonstrate a comparable level of musical awareness. The résumé of your experiences that you will submit to the committee will show what you've done. Your ability to audition will prove what you actually know and what you will be capable of doing in the future if given the chance. Many orchestras hire young players and actually prefer to in some cases. (The young ones are more easily molded.) The truth of the matter is that the players and the conductor are honestly searching for inspired, musical individuals who will match their own abilities and musical tastes and who will become their friends and colleagues.

    To be more specific, the following is a discussion on how to start and continue and complete this long road to becoming an orchestral musician.

RULE: LISTEN FIRST—THEN PLAN YOUR PRACTICE AND WORK CONSISTENTLY.

After you are aware of all of the repertoire you must learn (refer to the lists at the end of this chapter), develop a plan as to how much to do each week. Consider the act of daily listening to be a part of the time allotments. Begin to practice each new excerpt slowly, and don't miss a thing. The eventual tempo should be decided through your listening (with a metronome), asking your teacher's opinion, and then averaging the differences. Mark the part with all tempos and the average for future reference. As you practice, consider what specifics the various audition committees will be listening for, and then make those specifics your goals as you prepare each excerpt.

These are the basic criteria that audition committees use. They are listed from the most objective (facts and realities) to the most subjective (opinions and preferences).

1. *Rhythm*—Absolute rhythm and a consistent pulse is required of an orchestral player, with no exceptions. Any inaccuracies in rhythm are obvious and will cause an immediate elimination!

2. *Accuracy*—Missed notes are obvious and very disconcerting to a listener. Everyone misses notes through human error. No one is hired if the misses sound like a lack of preparation or a lack of skill.

3. *Stability and control*—Consistent control of the sound through all excerpts is obvious to all listeners. Musical conviction is a part of this.

4. *Intonation*—Intonation is a problem in all orchestras, so there is no desire to hire more problems. Exact intonation and blend are sometimes tested by playing with others of the section. Pitch is very important.

5. *Dynamic contrasts*—Appropriate and dramatic dynamic contrasts are required of a performer in an orchestra. A stable control of the sound is expected at all dynamics in all ranges.

6. *Tone color*—Each orchestra section has a basic color of sound into which you must fit if hired. This becomes an issue at the audition to be decided by the committee (who will probably disagree). Perform with your most beautiful, controlled sound and don't go to any extremes to try to please this subjective set of opinions.

7. *Musical communication*—Have a musical message to project for each excerpt based primarily on all that is appropriate to the composer, style, and the specifics of this solo within the piece, but also on how you feel about this particular musical moment. Tell your story. Everyone listening to you is a fine musician, but not all are horn players, so speak to them with the language that is common to us all. Don't exaggerate, but definitely reach out. Boring playing is boring!

8. *General impressions*—This is truly where most of the decisions are made by an auditioner. To think that these men and women who sit through 50 to 200 auditions will focus on the absolute details of each auditionee's performance to the extent of which notes were missed and why, which notes were out of tune and by how much, or which tempo was a little too fast or too slow is to be mistaken. They collect general impressions founded on all of the above. If a rhythm is wrong, you have rhythmic problems; if a few notes are missed, you have an accuracy problem; if you create one very special musical moment that attracts their attention, you are obviously a fine musician.

You must, during each practice session, consider all of the above. You must concern yourself with all of the details of the music and with all of the details of your playing. When an audition occurs, this thorough grounding in the details will be obvious through an overall impression more than through a tabulation of each successful detail. You must be aware of this and prepare to eliminate from your thinking, as soon as possible, all of those detailed distractions. Practice performing these excerpts in such a way as soon as they are thoroughly learned. Each excerpt must become a part of your overall musicianship that you choose to share with others. As you perform an excerpt, think primarily about the musical message that you are certain is consistent with the composer's intent. (All of the details will be there.)

RULE: INTERNALIZE ALL IMPORTANT EXCERPTS—DON'T SIMPLY LEARN THEM.

Etudes are to be used as a means to the various ends they address. You must practice them well until they can be consistently performed with great competence. Then you move on to the next one. Solos are to be learned, and perhaps memorized, to the point that you can stand in front of an audience of adoring public and share your personal interpretations in a relaxed recital or concert format. Excerpts, however, require all of the above (without the adoring public) and more. These moments of musical spotlight become the doorway to a job. They must be learned so completely, and must become so naturally a part of your basic performance vocabulary, that you could render each of them in any order under any possible or sometimes nearly impossible circumstance. This is what is meant by *internalize*.

After all is ready, and you have applied to audition for that great job you know you deserve, there is one secret that appears to be unknown to the many excellent horn players who fall by the wayside each year.

RULE: KNOW WHAT YOU CAN AND MUST DO, AND IGNORE THE REST.

Being a critic while being a performer ruins the performance. When I have asked students how their auditions went, they so often tell me only what the judges must have been thinking when they missed that note. They might also tell of having heard other players performing or warming up and how that affected their own performance. Looking back on a performance and learning from it is simply what we all must do. However, if during the actual audition a performer is preoccupied with what the committee is thinking, or with how much better others will perform than they, then they are being foolish. Know your objectives and take care of all of them. Leave the subjective evaluations to the committee. As was said, the committee's decisions are the most difficult job. Why add all of that to what you are there for when such an opinion will do nothing but distract and confuse? And, in fact, no one will ask you your opinion anyway, so why waste your time and energy having one?

Simply stated, you are there to sell your commodity to the organization. If you have the product they want, they will buy. If you don't, they will buy another's product. That does not mean that your product is inferior. As long as you have devoted your finest efforts to the creation of the product, your fine playing, then someone will buy. If the product needs refinements (and whose product doesn't?), do what you can. Don't take it personally. That distorts the issue and causes negative baggage that will eventually weigh you down. Do what you can. Let the others (those on the committee) do their jobs. Don't waste your time and positive energies doing it for them.

Horn playing is what you do, but it is not who you are. To truly know and totally believe that basic tenet is to free yourself of the baggage that distracts, distorts, and eventually destroys the plans and goals of many talented musicians.

RULE: THINK ABOUT WHY YOU LOVE MUSIC, AND THEN DECIDE TO HAVE FUN.

People who love what they do and are not afraid to show and share their enthusiasm are the type of people most of us wish to be around. From a practical point of view, such aspects of your personality should be made obvious to an audition committee if at all possible. You can't talk from behind the screen, which is the usual preliminary audition procedure, but you do talk to secretaries (never underestimate the importance of their opinions) and personnel managers. Whenever you do have personal contact with these people, realize that they are wanting to like you. They are looking for colleagues. For a young auditionee just out of school, it is difficult to change roles. If you approach the auditioners as if they are your superiors, they will be made uncomfortable. However, if you approach them as if they are darn lucky just to be in your presence, they will be offended. Be your most positive self, while you focus on your appreciation for this opportunity to share what you love to do. Reach out, shake hands, look them in the eye, and be sure to have fun.

A positive attitude about this whole process is the fuel that can feed the fire, if you so choose. Music was a spark somewhere in your past. That fire took hold, and you were ignited into action. Your attitude can take that flame and allow it to either warm your heart or incinerate all of your hard work and worthy plans.

ORCHESTRAL REPERTOIRE, EXCERPTS, PARTS, CDS, AND BOOKS

There are many fine collections of orchestral excerpts available today. Below are listed the collections found to have been useful and enjoyable over the years. Others are listed that fill in the gaps for particular composers or periods. Some are designed for audition preparations focusing on the brief and popular solos. While all are excellent for transposition study, others present more complete parts. In Chapter 24 you will find discussions and reviews of many of these fine collections.

LaBar, Arthur T., *Horn Player's Audition Handbook*, Belwin-Mills Publishing, Warner Bros. Publications.

Moore, Richard, *Anthology of French Horn Music*, Mel Bay Publications.

Chambers, James, *Orchestral Excerpts*, 7 Vols., International Publications.

Chambers, James, *Richard Strauss Orchestral Studies*, International Publications.

Chambers, James, *Richard Wagner Orchestral Studies*, International Publications.

Ritzkowsky/Spach, *Orchester Probespiel - Test Pieces for Orchestral Auditions* (Germany), Peters (Includes CDs of all the excerpts including the orchestral parts!).

LaBar, Arthur T., and Howard, Howard, *Hornist's Opera and Ballet Handbook*, Phoenix Music.

Jones, Mason, *20th Century Orchestra Studies*, G. Schirmer Publications.

Klamand, O., *Mahler, Orchesterstudien 1–5*, Zimmermann.

Schuller/Haunton, F. J. *Haydn: Horn Passages*, Margun Music.

Janetzky, K., *Bach Studies for Waldhorn* (2 vols.), Hofmeister.

Janetzky, K., *Handel Studies for Waldhorn* (2 vols.), Hofmeister.

Klamand, O., *J. S. Bach, Orchesterstudien*, Zimmermann.

Farr, L. A., *Horn Player's Guide to Orchestral Excerpts*, Broad River Press (dated but still useful) (Lists the location of certain excerpts found within older excerpt collections.).

Complete Horn Parts

Thompson, D., *The Orchestral Audition Repertoire for Horn: Comprehensive and Unabridged*, (145 complete parts to 84 compositions, excellent selections totaling 1,043 pages). Thompson Editions, 231 Plantation Road, Rock Hill, SC 29732-9441.

Kalmus Music sells separate first horn parts (through Robert King Music) in collected albums. (Of special interest: Dvorak, Mahler, Prokofiev, Shostakovich, Strauss, Stravinsky, and Wagner), Edwin F. Kalmus & Co., Inc.

TEXTS

Dunkel, Stuart, *The Audition Process, Anxiety Management and Coping Strategies*, Pendragon.

Sharp, Erica, *How to Get an Orchestra Job...and Keep It*, Encinitas Press.

Reid & Weait, *Auditions Are Just the Beginning*, Association of Canadian Orchestras.

RECORDED EXCERPTS

Krehbiel, David, *Orchestra Excerpts for Horn*, with Spoken Commentary, San Francisco Symphony, (20 major excerpts performed and discussed), Summit Records, DCD 141 (taken from *Horn Player's Audition Handbook*, LaBar).

A COMPREHENSIVE ORCHESTRAL EXCERPT LIST FOR THE HORN

What follows is a very comprehensive list of pieces (based upon professional audition lists collected over a 25-year period) from which excerpts have been drawn for auditions into professional organizations, summer festivals, and amateur ensembles, or that have been seen on other lists by reputable compilers and teachers. It begins with the "Top 40," listed in an order of frequency. Next, are 28 more works that were found listed more than just a few times, again in order. In the last section, these 71 orchestral pieces have been seen on lists at least once, but at most only a few times, and are presented in alphabetical order. Also included is a list of the solos and chamber pieces that have been seen either required or suggested for orchestral auditions. This looks like a large amount of music, which it is. But to orchestral musicians, this is their business, their life-blood. Begin listening from the top of the list, and follow it on down. Two and a half to three pieces per week, and you'll be done in one year. Then you can start over again. This is some of the greatness that has brought us into music in the first place. This is a world of magic available to us all. To learn, or better yet to internalize the excerpts from this repertoire, is to get to experience many little bits of that magic.

"TOP 40" MOST COMMONLY REQUESTED
(In approximate order of frequency)

Strauss, *Till Eulenspiegel*

Shostakovich, Symphony No. 5

Tchaikovsky, Symphony No. 5

Beethoven, Symphony No. 7

Beethoven, Symphony No. 3

Brahms, Symphony No. 4

Brahms, Symphony No. 1

Mendelssohn, Nocturne from
   A Midsummer Night's Dream

Strauss, *Don Juan*

Strauss, *Ein Heldenleben*

Beethoven, Symphony No. 9

Brahms, Symphony No. 3

Wagner, Short Call from Siegfried's *Rhine Journey*

Mahler, Symphony No. 1

Dvořák, Symphony No. 9

Brahms, Symphony No. 2

Berlioz, Scherzo from *Queen Mab*

Beethoven, Overture to *Fidelio*

Tchaikovsky, Symphony No. 4

Brahms, Piano Concerto No. 2

Bach, Brandenburg Concerto No. 1

Beethoven, Symphonies Nos. 6 & 8

Wagner, *Das Rheingold*

Strauss, *Don Quixote*

Mahler, Symphony No. 5

Brahms, Piano Concerto No. 1

Bach, Mass in B minor

Haydn, Symphony No. 31

Mendelssohn, Symphony No. 3

Bruckner, Symphony No. 4

Brahms, *Academic Festival Overture*

Mozart, Symphony No. 40

Saint-Saëns, Symphony No. 3

Weber, Overture to *Der Freischütz*

Mahler, Symphony No. 4

Brahms, Variations on a Theme by Haydn

Ravel, Piano Concerto in G

Schumann, Symphony No. 3

Schubert, Symphony No. 9

MORE OFTEN THAN MANY
(In general order of importance)

Debussy, *La Mer*

Beethoven, Piano Concerto No. 5

Rossini, Overture to *Semiramide*

Dvorak, Cello Concerto

Franck, Symphony in D min.

Beethoven, Symphony No. 2

Mahler, Symphony No. 3

Prokofiev, Suites 2 &1 from *Romeo and Juliet*

Wagner, Long Call from the opera *Siegfried*

Mussorgsky/Ravel, *Pictures at an Exhibition*

Stravinsky, Suite from *The Fairy's Kiss*

Stravinsky, Suite from *The Firebird*

Liszt, *Les Préludes*

Ravel, *Daphnis and Chloë*

Rossini, *La Gazza Ladra*

Schoenberg, Chamber Symphony, Op. 9

Strauss, *Death and Transfiguration*

Stravinsky, *The Rite of Spring*

Wagner, Overture to *Die Meistersinger*

Haydn, Symphony No. 45

Strauss, Suite from *Der Rosenkavalier*

Ravel, *Bolero*

Beethoven, Symphony No. 4

Rimsky-Korsakov, *Scheherazade*

Strauss, *Also Sprach Zarathustra*

Ravel, *Pavane for a Dead Princess*

Weber, Overture to *Oberon*

LESS OFTEN THAN OTHERS
(In alphabetical order)

Bartók, Concerto for Orchestra

Beethoven, Aria from *Fidelio*

Beethoven, Concerto for Violin

Beethoven, Symphonies Nos. 1 & 5

Berlioz, *Symphonie Fantastique*

Berlioz, *Roman Carnival Overture*

Bizet, Micaela's Aria from *Carmen*

Borodin, *Polovetsian Dances*

Brahms, *Tragic Overture*

Brahms, Serenades Nos. 1 & 2
Bruckner, Symphony No. 7
Debussy, *Prelude to the Afternoon of a Faun*
Dvořák, Symphonies Nos. 7 & 8
Enesco, *Romanian Rhapsodie*
deFalla, Dances from *The Three Cornered Hat*
Gershwin, Piano Concerto in F
Ginastera, *Variaciones Concertantes*
Haydn, Symphony No. 48
Hindemith, Concert Music for Strings and Brass
Hindemith, *Mathis der Maler*
Hindemith, *Symphonic Metamorphosis*
Humperdinck, *Hänsel und Gretel* Prelude
Kodály, *Háry János* Suite
Mahler, Symphonies Nos. 2, 6, 7, 9
Mendelssohn, Symphony No. 4 "Italian"
Mozart, Piano Concerto No. 27
Mozart, Violin Concerto No. 5
Mozart, Symphonies Nos. 29, 39, 41
Mozart, *Sinfonia Concertante* (for winds)
Prokofiev, *Lieutenant Kije*
Prokofiev, Symphonies Nos. 5 & 6
Puccini, Opening to Act III of *Tosca*
Rachmaninov, Piano Concerto No. 2
Rachmaninov, Symphonic Dances
Rachmaninov, Symphony No. 2
Ravel, *Alborada del Grazioso*
Ravel, *Rhapsodie Espagñol*
Respighi, *Pines of Rome*
Respighi, *Roman Festivals*
Rimsky-Korsakov, *Capriccio Espagnole*
Rossini, Overture to *Barber of Seville*
Rossini, Overture to *Turk in Italy*
Shostakovich, Cello Concerto
Shostakovich, Symphony No. 1
Strauss, Dance from *Salome*
Strauss, *Sinfonia Domestica*
Stravinsky, *Dumbarton Oaks*
Stravinsky, *Fireworks*
Stravinsky, *Jeux de Cartes* ("Game of Cards")

Stravinsky, Suite from *Pulcinella*
Tchaikovsky, *Capriccio Italiene*
Tchaikovsky, *Francesca da Rimini*
Tchaikovsky, Symphonies Nos. 2, 3 & 6
Thomas, Overture to *Mignon*
Wagner, *Ride of the Valkyries*
Wagner, Overture to *Flying Dutchman*
Wagner, *Siegfried Idyll*
Wagner, Prelude to Act III of *Lohengrin*
Wagner, Overture to *Tannhaüser*
Wagner, *Tristan und Isolde* ("Prelude and
   Love Death")

SPECIFIED SOLOS ON AUDITION LISTS
(In general order of frequency)

Mozart, Concertos Nos. 4, 2, & 3
Strauss, Concerto No. 1
Neuling, Bagatelle (low horn auditions in Germany)
Beethoven, Sonata, Op. 17
Strauss, Concerto No. 2

Only One Listing Seen:
Bach, Various movements from Cello Suites
Schumann, Adagio and Allegro, and Konzertstück
Glière, Concerto
Hindemith, Concerto
Mozart, Concerto No. 1

SPECIFIED CHAMBER WORKS ON LISTS

Nielsen, Kvintet for Winds and Horn, Op. 43
Mozart, Serenade for Winds (K.388)
Milhaud, *La Cheminée du Roi René*

Only One Listing Seen:
Beethoven, Octet in E♭, Op. 103
Danzi, Quintet, Op. 68, No. 2
Beethoven, Quintet (transcription from
   Sextet, Op. 71)

6. Relaxation and the Performing Musician

Since early in my teaching, it became obvious that physical and mental tension was the cause of most of my students' (and my own) performance problems. No matter what is known intellectually, it will not be useful if there is a wall of tension in one's way. Many answers were available, but they were found outside of the teaching literature for musical performance. Since the 1970s, many new and wonderful books have been published for performing musicians that address just these concerns. (See the suggested reading list at the end of this chapter.) Over the years, it has been my pleasure to share some of my thoughts on these issues at workshops and clinics. What follows is a realization of my outline used during those sessions.

Assuming that one has the basic physical and mental capacity to perform well and has adequately prepared for such a performing experience, the five major controllable components remaining for the success of that performance are **relaxation, motivation, concentration, imagination,** and **autosuggestion.** Of these, **relaxation** and **autosuggestion** are the framing factors of control. There is much blending between these factors, but it is appropriate to think of relaxation as being the physical affecting the mental, and autosuggestion as being the mental affecting the physical.

Motivation, concentration, and imagination are so much easier to fully realize during an actual performance, when one is thinking positively about oneself and the event, and feeling comfortable and physically at ease. Motivation is what brought the performer to the event in the first place; and without a continued desire to perform, one's enthusiasm wanes, and the mind becomes preoccupied with questions. These constant questions break down the concentration necessary to do what has been planned, and all of that mind chatter and confusion allows no time for the imagination to contribute to the hoped-for magic, which is what motivates one to perform music in the first place. Without physical relaxation and a positive mental outlook, this vicious circle spins around and around until the performer can't tell which way is up.

We have all been there, so what steps can we take to stop that dizzying spin, to solidify the playing field and allow for the performing event to become a controlled outlet for our musical imaginations? Let's investigate the two framing factors. **Relaxation** is frequently defined as the absence of *tension*. Thinking that way immediately sets up an autosuggestion that triggers the body to hear the word tension. Relaxation is in and of itself a sensation that must be positively identified. It is not merely the lack of something. Relaxation can be identified through the physical sensations of warmth (in the hands) and heaviness (in the face, shoulders, and arms) and through the mental sensations of self-confidence and self-trust. It takes quiet practice time to fully recognize these important sensations, then even more time to learn to call upon them quickly while in the act of performance. Once excessive tension enters the body/mind, it is difficult to quickly identify its source or to control its negative effects. Tension, both mental and physical, tends to take the controls and pull us off course. We need to learn to believe in our power to control all of this at the source before it starts. The controls are within us all. Some of us seem more successful learning to focus on the sensations of warmth and heat in our muscles, which calm us down. Others seem to be more readily able to create positive thought patterns, which in turn help us to relax.

Full physical relaxation will not occur without a calm mental attitude.
The mind must be at ease for the body to reach a deep state of relaxation.
The body is the densest part of the mind. They are one. The mind and the body are the same thing!

Herbert Bensen wrote a remarkable book, published in 1975 by Avon Books, which very simply outlined a manner in which one could reach what he called "The Relaxation Response."

1. A quiet place. Shut out external distractions. Closing the eyes can help.

2. A comfortable position and posture.

3. A passive attitude. Letting relaxation happen, knowing it is happening.

4. A mental device. Something to focus on, a sound, a word, a sensation, a visualization.

For centuries, the yoga masters from many world cultures and religious traditions have incorporated such a setting as a place created for meditation. This is also quite similar to the setting for hypnosis or self-hypnosis. Such a place allows us to flush out all of the tensions of the moment. Is this just another one of those dream situations about which performers can only idealize but never truly find to be useful or practical? To some extent, yes, but mostly, no.

During an actual performance, it is often quite difficult to find a quiet place shut off from external distractions. One might also be careful about closing the eyes, especially during an unmemorized performance. However, such a quiet setting could, and perhaps should, be created during those hours and minutes of anticipation preceding the performance. This pre-concert period is often the time when the mind-chatter drifts off into a series of questions that causes one to lose enthusiasm and focus, or even self-trust. One should take the time and find the quiet space. A comfortable position and posture is of great benefit before the performance while in one's quiet place, and it is certainly helpful during the actual performance. A perfect posture, where the muscles are resting on the bones while the bones are aligned upward without force, is a necessity for the air to flow freely in and out of the body and for the music to flow freely from the soul. Extremely good posture is a necessity for all aspects of a successful musical performance. All performing musicians should take the time to study at least the basics of the Alexander Technique and/or the Feldenkrais Method to learn of the subtleties and power of perfect posture.

A few specifics that might help regarding posture include finding a position on the chair or bench that provides you with a sense of balance. Feel as if the bones are holding you up, not your muscles. Twist and stretch around the center of balance to be certain. Feel both feet flat in front and then adjust the hip bones to contain the rest of the weight. Make sure the lower back is neither arched nor slouched. Allow the head to feel as if it were being drawn up and forward. This immediately provides the rest of the upper body with the feeling of being a little taller. The arms and shoulders should remain always heavy and warm, all the way into the hands. Shake out the tension, mentally scan the muscles, and simply require that they be heavy and warm. The shape of the muscles in the hands and arms needed to play all instruments should curve along the smoothest possible physical lines. Avoid all sharp angles: that, along with excess tension, is what causes the blood flow to be restricted, and we need that flow for warmth, relaxation, and full unencumbered movement.

A passive attitude, letting relaxation happen, is both good and not so good during an actual performance. It is, however, just what you should be experiencing during the pre-concert quiet space. During the performance, total passivity may cause complacency and contribute to a boring performance. To be passive is to be inert or lifeless. We don't want that. Nor do we want to have an overactive set of fears and self-judgments controlling our every nuance. Where's the balance? In the field of Tai Chi Chuan there is the saying, "**Be still as a mountain; move like a great river.**"

This phrase and its powerful image are quite appropriate for the performing musician, regarding both a passive attitude and the need to supplement it with an active mental device. With a visualization to focus on, performers need to feel physically and mentally focused, as still as a mountain, while creative imaginations, *chi* (breath), and musical sounds must flow outward, to and beyond audiences, like a great river.

Air is our fuel, air is *chi*, and *chi* is the life-force. For all performers, air is the source of strength and stability. It is the physical necessity that ebbs and flows, as music ebbs and flows. No matter the performance medium, breathing patterns must be studied and made a central part of the communication of musical expression. If one plays a brass or woodwind instrument or sings, the air then takes on an additional level of importance as it serves as the momentum behind and the actual cause of the projected sounds.

Mr. Benson suggests the need to have a sound, a word, a sensation to aid the search for the relaxation response. Air and the ever-necessary process of deep breathing can become just what he suggests. As you inhale deeply, create the sound of the word *how*. This causes many wonderful things to happen, especially for the wind and brass players. The lungs fill from the bottom up, and the lips tend to return to a focused position around or within the mouthpiece. As the air releases, the tongue often forms the consonant *t*, so simply think *to*. *How-to* is easy to remember and it works, so focus on it.

Other specifics regarding breathing suggest that one inhale across the bottom of the mouth, or perhaps imagine the intake to be rushing in through a hole in the lower neck, or even so far down as a hole in the chest. Each of these helps to open the throat and bring in a large volume of air down and deep. As the air rushes in, the abdomen should simultaneously drop down and forward (as if getting fat), later followed by the expansion of the chest, pulling slightly on the pectoral muscles near the armpits. Suspend the air near the open and relaxed throat for that split second when the motion of the air makes its rounded turn back up toward the instrument. Most musicians prefer a warm rather than a cold sound, so at the exhalation create warm air by controlling the release of air through an open, naturally relaxed throat (the same throat opening used to create the sound of the word *how* upon inhalation). As the air is released, the natural elasticity of the chest cavity wishes to return to normal, so allow that to occur first. Only then should the lowered abdominal muscles begin to follow the air upward toward the chest (as if trying to look skinny). Avoid the feeling of flexing the abdominal muscles during the exhalation as much as possible. Let the torso muscles dance with the air, and move sympathetically with the air, not getting involved with excessive pushing and pulling. You are not lifting weights, you are providing *chi* to your sound.

Going toward a more spiritual level, a level at which the true importance of air ultimately belongs, consider the inhalation and the exhalation to be the *inspiration and exaltation* that is felt toward **music**. Let the in and the out of the air become the *ah-ha* of continuous discovery. (One can actually create the sounds and psychic sensation of *ah-ha* while breathing in-out.) These lofty thoughts and actions will certainly provide something quite significant upon which to focus as you perform in a relaxed and confident manner.

Autosuggestion is something you do all day long. Suggestions are made to oneself without even trying. The mind chatters on and on all of the time. The mind seems to need something to fill up the space. Much of this noise is inconsequential. However, some of it is very influential, and the potential for controlled and intelligent thought is ultimately the single most powerful personal tool. *Through the specific use of personally created positive phrases, one can shift one's psychophysiological point of view into a state of being that generates a remarkable sense of power and control.* This remarkable power implies that what you say is what you get and has fascinated great minds for centuries.

"Men are not disturbed by things, but by the views which they take of them." Epictetus (55–135 A.D.)

"People are just about as happy as they make up their minds to be." Abraham Lincoln

"The greatest discovery of my generation is that human beings, by changing the inner attitudes of their mind, can change the outer aspects of their lives." William James

For the performing musician, public speaker, actor, and others who perform, the most devastating problem is fear. Fear breeds worry, and the results of excess worry when applied to a public performance are usually quite unfortunate. The way this happens is actually a very powerful reaction within the body that turns on automatically when there is a perception of an emergency. This reaction is called **"Fight or Flight."** The human body has an alarm system to meet all emergencies. This system produces a super-energy (adrenalin) to use and burn during such a perceived emergency. If the emergency is real, this super-energy will be needed to either fight or depart. However, worry in general, and performance anxiety in particular, are imagined emergencies, and that becomes the problem. From the neck down, one's body cannot tell a real emergency from an imagined one, so it goes into an alarm state and generates an incredible amount of energy. Since the realities of a musical performance do not require such energy, there is no place for all of that power to be spent. Consequently the adrenalin manifests itself as physical tension, shaking, instability, fear, or perhaps even terror. Coexistent with those physical sensations is a consequent lack of confidence and self-trust. Trying to control all of that super-energy is extremely hard work, and it causes great wear and tear on the body and the mind. It leaves one in a "dis-eased" condition.

Since it is never the event but always the attitude toward that event that causes reactions, then one must learn to reinterpret the event of a musical, or of any other public performance, especially if it is found to be uncontrollably frightening. According to Will Schultz, "There is only one fear, un-cope-ability."

So what is there to cope with? Your own personally created perspective of what a performance is. You have control over that perspective. You can change the inner attitudes of your mind.

Autosuggestion is a name given to that power. So how do you do it? Fill the mind with positive thoughts. Be realistic about what one performance really means. Keep focused on why music is important and how performance is simply a way to share these strong and positive feelings with others. Imagine that the audience is there to enjoy the music. The music is the reason. Tell yourself what you want, how you want it, and simply expect it to be that way. Remember, you only have control over your own performance, so create verbal formulas that aim directly at the results you desire from yourself.

Example: "My shoulders are heavy." "My sound is warm."
Comment: Use positive thoughts like these to receive positive results.

Example: "I will not get nervous."
Comment: Avoid the use of all negatives in your verbal formulas. The body's response system will not register the negative. The body will hear that powerful word *nervous* and respond accordingly. (Just to say the word *nervous* ten times without even caring can demonstrate the power of that suggestion.)

Example: "I plan to perform well tomorrow."
Comment: Avoid verbal content that is focusing on the future. Instead it could better be said, "I perform well. I love to perform. I am prepared and ready to perform well."

Autosuggestive phrases can also be called affirmations. That is a good word. You must learn to affirm a belief in your ability to perform. You must take control, take charge of how you want your performances to go. You practice the music over and over again because you want to be technically ready, and you do not want to have any surprises during the performance. That is very affirming. You should also practice over and over again with your mind and with your body as to how you want to feel and what you want to be thinking while you are performing. Affirmations need to be a part of every practice session and a part of every moment of thought about performing.

I wish to share some of my favorite affirmations. These will not necessarily work for everyone. So I suggest that you create your own special way of thinking about relaxation, self-confidence, and the fine art of musical performance.

I'm okay.
I am enthusiastic!
I am relaxed and ready to perform.
I am a strong and competent musician.
I am prepared and eager to share my music.
I love my sound and love to share it with others.
The audience is here because they choose to be, and so am I.
I look forward to my new experiences with quiet confidence.
I am a good person. I have a right to be. I am the best possible me.
I am the leading authority on what I can do. Nobody can be me like I can.
Mistakes are okay. I can learn from mistakes. That is the information I need.
This instant, now, I am calm and at peace with the world.
I am enthusiastic!

What follows is a recommended reading list of some very important books that have been published over the past 25 years. Many of these are now classics in their fields, and each has its own message and its own perspective. I recommend them all. I would especially like to thank the author W. W. Johnston, whose books are listed under Self-Esteem and Personal Growth. Wally Johnston has helped me immeasurably through his books, his recommendations, and our far-too-infrequent personal contacts. He's been a great friend and a terrific uncle.

A RECOMMENDED READING LIST (In a recommended order by category)

Musical Orientation

Lieberman, Julie Lyonn, *You Are Your Instrument: The Definitive Musician's Guide to Practice and Performance*, Huiksi Music, NY, 1991.

Ristad, Eloise, *A Soprano on Her Head*, Real People Press, 1982.

Green, Barry and Timothy Galwey, *The Inner Game of Music*, Anchor Press, 1986.

Kruger, Dr. Irmtraud Tarr, *Performance Power, Transforming Stress into Creative Energy*, Summit Books, AZ, 1993.

Salmon, Paul G. and Robert G. Meyer, *Notes from the Green Room: Coping With Stress and Anxiety in Musical Performance*, Lexington Books, NY, 1992.

Triplett, Robert, *Stage-Fright: Letting It Work for You*, Nelson Hall, Chicago, 1988.

Sibley, Charlotte Whitaker and Donald Ray Tanner, *But I Played It Perfectly in the Practice Room!* (includes two relaxation tapes), 1987, University Press of America.

Kaslow, David M., *Living Dangerously With the Horn: Thoughts on Life and Art*, Birdalone Books, Bloomington, IN, 1996.

Severson, Paul and Mark McDunn, *Brass Wind Artistry*, Accura Music, 1983.

Psychophysiology, Autogenic Training, Health

Borysenko, Joan, *Minding the Body, Mending the Mind*, Addison, Welsley, 1987.

Pelletier, Kenneth, *Mind as Healer, Mind as Slayer*, Delta, 1977.

Relaxation, Meditation

Bensen, Herbert, *The Relaxation Response*, Avon Books, 1975.

Mason, L. John, *Guide to Stress Reduction*, Peace Press, 1980.

Inner Game Concepts

Herrigel, Eugen, *Zen in the Art of Archery*, Vintage Books, 1971.

Galwey, Timothy, *The Inner Game of Tennis*, Random House 1974.

Visualization

Samuels, Mike and Nancy, *Seeing With the Mind's Eye*, Random House, 1977.

Gawain, Shakti, *Creative Visualization*, Bantam Books, 1982.

Biofeedback

Brown, Barbara, *Stress and the Art of Biofeedback*, Bantam, 1978.

Green, Elmer and Alyce, *Beyond Biofeedback*, Delta Books, 1977.

Alexander Technique

Jones, Frank Pierce, *Body Awareness in Action*, Schoken, 1979.

Feldenkrais Method

Feldenkrais, Moshe, *Awareness Through Movement*, Harper, Row, 1977.

Self-Esteem and Personal Growth

Johnston, W. W., *Take Charge: A Guide to Feeling Good* and *Self-Esteem or Self-Abuse, Where Do You Stand?*, Acorn Endeavors, 1918 NE 143 Avenue, Portland, OR 97230.

7. Horn Playing: A Balancing Act

The original version of the following chapter was my first attempt to share some of my opinions about the complex act of performance. You will find some of these ideas repeated in other chapters, couched in different words or as observed from different perspectives. These balancing factors in performance, the fascinating dualities of daily life, and the compensations felt or imagined at the spiritual level all continue to fascinate and stimulate my thinking and I hope continue to add to my learning and teaching.

To perform well requires a finely tuned sense of balances. Too much of one muscle (embouchure) and not enough of another (air control) causes muscular stress. Too much of one thought (fear of inadequacy) and not enough of another (confidence) causes mental stress. Too great a concern for the manner of presentation (technique) and not enough for the message (the music, the art) and you have failed to communicate.

You must learn to understand the importance of these balances before you can release yourself from the excessive accumulation of overlapping techniques acquired during many years of intense and sometimes confusing private study. You must learn to understand the importance of all of these balances before you can undo detrimental attitudes toward yourself as a performer or toward music as an art form worthy of communicating to others.

Regarding some of the main points to be discussed, the *Macmillan Contemporary Dictionary* defines balance as "equality between forces and elements."

Balance, as it relates to the craft of playing, is "physical equilibrium." Balance, as it relates to the act of performing, is "mental and emotional stability."

Balance, as it relates to the art of music, is "an aesthetically pleasing integration of elements, proportion, and harmony."

Your goal as an artist is to strive for an exact balance of necessary forces and elements so that you might, at many levels, communicate your message, your understanding, your enthusiasm, your manner or style, and your awareness of the composer's intentions. During your pursuit of this ideal goal, you should learn to enjoy your place along the continuum of development. You must fully experience where you are, where you've been, and where you are going. Without this pursuit, there is no goal. *Pursuit* and *goal* need always remain in *balance*.

CRAFT IN BALANCE

A relaxed body requires good posture. You must find a position on the chair where your full weight is resting on the bones. Feel the heaviness of your shoulders and upper body at the hipbones as if gently pushing into the chair. While retaining this relaxed heaviness, allow your head to elevate slightly as if being gently pulled by a string attached to the top of your forehead. While standing, the same feelings are needed, with the body weight resting on the bones balanced near the balls of the feet so that you can raise to your toes without leaning forward.

Bring the horn to your body shape and best posture. Don't allow the shape or size of the horn to be the cause of your bending out of balance. The instrument's weight should be distributed equally between the palm of your left hand and your right leg. If you hold it off of your leg, balance it between the two hands. Avoid the lips as a means of support for the horn at all times. Both hands should retain a relaxed and natural curve, and the shoulders and arms should rest downward and remain heavy without tension.

A versatile embouchure requires a well-balanced set of facial muscles. The best way to discover this balance is to simply begin with your own natural jaw position while pronouncing and sustaining the sound *emmm*. The chin and cheek muscles, as well as those of the lower forehead and all around the eyes, should feel heavy and drawn downward. From this relaxed and quite natural foundation, the corners of the mouth should then be evenly tucked inward to allow for one consistent setting. With a proper stimulation from the player's air, such a setting should respond with an even and clear buzz at the aperture.

The placement of the mouthpiece requires only the small amount of pressure necessary to seal off air leakage (under ideal conditions). A balanced pressure on top, bottom, and both sides of the lip requires an appropriate angle of the mouthpiece in relation to your own bite. Angle your horn in an exact relationship to your own natural teeth formation. This is also necessary for equal action from all facial muscles. When placing the mouthpiece high upon your moistened lips, allow the muscles themselves to accept or absorb the rim surface evenly.

A free-flowing sound requires a relaxed balance between the force of the air flow and the size and texture of the aperture. Regarding the act of breathing, you must balance accurately your inhalation with a complete and unencumbered exhalation. While inhaling through the mouth, make the sound of the word *how*, and then exhale, through an open throat, a relaxed stream of "warm air." To aid in this circle of air motion, you must allow the abdominal region to drop downward and forward. Next, allow for a slight stretch at the pectoral muscles near the armpits while rounding the top of a full inhalation. To follow through the exhalation smoothly and completely, the exact reversal is needed. The chest must relax (deflate) first before the abdomen returns to its normal position en route to an upward flow in toward the lower rib cage. These are the simple motions of "looking fat" and "looking skinny."

Flexing of the abdominal muscles, which is quite common among brass players, is not a natural action in successful deep breathing and should be avoided, or at least held to a minimum. It drains one of needed energy, forces one to endure internal isometrics, and often causes the sensation of a completed exhalation before all of the air has been expelled. You must learn to relax your movements in order to accurately feel and control the circle of air as it fills your body, fills your horn, and fills the room with free-flowing sounds.

The aperture is simply a tool formed to respond to the motion of the air by vibrating. A relaxed yet firm and consistent positioning of the lip center within the rim of the mouthpiece, balanced with a fast, flowing, warm air column, allows for a free-flowing sound. Too much lip tension, sometimes necessary because of too slow an air stream, sounds constricted, limits flexibility and the high register, and soon cuts down on endurance. The aperture itself should be as opened and relaxed as possible, not serving as a point of excessive resistance but as a freely responding vibrator. A controlled balance is needed, and that usually requires a feeling of a quicker, fuller airflow for most players. A good way to visualize it is that one must *waste air!* Let it all out through the horn. Don't hold any of it back. The result of such a positively balanced sensation usually proves to be anything but wasteful.

PERFORMANCE IN BALANCE

A relaxed and confident mind is so necessary for successful performances. For that to occur requires the relaxed body that has just been discussed. By consistently practicing and developing your "craft in balance," you gain a confidence in your body's ability to do the job required. By consistently being mentally confident and enthusiastic about your performance abilities and growth along that continuum of development, the body does a better job.

The separation of the "mind" and the "body" is only a convenient concept for the sake of conversation and is not a reality. The body is the densest part of the mind. The mind should perhaps be thought of as the most inconspicuous part of the body. To comfortably believe this relationship is to free the critical mind from over-punishing the sometimes cumbersome and inadequate body. It just might be the mental punishment itself that is causing the demonstrated physical inadequacy. What many believe is that the craft of playing or the technique is the primary reason for successful performances. This often happens without a balanced belief in mental power—the power to know that one is a worthy performer with something important and worthwhile to share with others. If such a dichotomy is the case, then one is out of balance.

Worry and fear are in balance with failure. Trust and enthusiasm are in balance with success. You must prepare positively and enthusiastically for your performances, and perform without excessive self-judgment but with self-trust if you expect all of those intricate balances so far discussed to be displayed as desired and deserved. Autosuggestive phrases, or the use of positive self-talk, has done wonders for many performers. It simply involves the use of such phrases as "I am enthusiastic," "I love this music and want very much to share it with others," "I am prepared and ready to perform well," rather than the negative mind-chatter that often occupies thoughts before a performance. Such phrases should be of your creation utilizing only positive, believable, self-supportive language and thoughts, while avoiding such phrases as "I am not nervous" or "This time maybe I'll get it right."

ART IN BALANCE

For an aesthetically successful musical performance to occur, one must produce a pleasing integration of appropriate stylistic proportions that are then technically and spiritually communicated to a receptive listener. How does one develop a capacity for such a lofty ideal? *Experiences!* Diverse experiences within all forms of music will be of great help, starting as soon as now. An open-minded exposure to all forms of sincere and lasting music through extensive listening and active participation will be a necessity for you to reach the necessary levels of understanding and sustain this performance ideal at a refined and professional level. As a performer, it is the multiple skills combined with an artistic adroitness that are ultimately shared with audiences. Art is the goal!

This all goes back to the practice room. Resourceful performers with a strong understanding of appropriate stylistic proportions can create such a balance for themselves daily within their practice routines. Plan to balance the content of work between exercises, etudes, solos, chamber music, excerpts, and large ensemble repertoire. Within each of these categories, diversify the content between periods of music (i.e., Baroque, Classical, Romantic, Contemporary, etc.), styles of music (i.e., classical, jazz, avant-garde, popular, folk, ethnic, etc.), manners of playing (i.e., loud and soft, high and low, aggressive and passive, etc.), and manners of performance (i.e., reading, memorization, improvising, etc.). By opening the mind and heart to all forms and manners of sincere and lasting music, one prepares for greater goals, more substantial growth, and more mature, artistic performances.

THE BALANCING ACT

According to Yehudi Menuhin, "The task for the performer consists in establishing an equilibrium between the composition and his own conscience." When the craft and positive mental attitude and the devotion to the artistic wonders of music are not integrated or balanced, when one issue distracts from the other (e.g., becoming obsessed with one's own performance skills to the detriment of the music), the performance suffers. The audience experiences disappointment, and the performer feels the frustrations. Learning to balance the resounding joys of music with the periodic frustrations of performance is quite demanding, but it is necessary for all to confront. Frustrations bring valuable information, and successes bring joy. The mix is the reality!

Simply stated, this is the ultimate challenge for performers: to have the skills and the knowledge to be the presenter and the dreamer who communicates the wonders of the music through our medium to our audiences.

8. Practicing Full Circle

The following discussion about practicing is somewhat abstract and philosophical. This is as it should be. Practicing a musical instrument is so often relegated to the level of mundane drudgery. I wish to take a look at how enjoyment can become the focus of practice. If we practice enjoyment, we can enjoy our performances more easily. If we practice in a state such as frantic desperation, then that is what our music will sound like. To raise our practice skills to an artistic level will allow us to perform in an artistic manner more easily.

Your attitudes toward what you do tend to control how well you accomplish your goals. You control your attitudes, and you control your goals. Such important and powerful controls are available to those musicians with enthusiasm, direction, perseverance, intelligence, and an open mind ready for change and growth.

Practice is where you spend the bulk of your growth as a performer. You literally spend the vast majority of your musical life alone practicing for concerts, rehearsals, auditions, and competitions. What can you do to control this time and to make it the most beneficial and enjoyable? What can you do to make these practice sessions into artistic experiences for yourself?

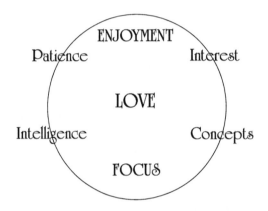

With **love** as the central force anchored by both the obvious **enjoyment** of the music and the medium, and by the controlled efforts to **focus** abilities and awareness, you can soon develop full use of this circle of growth. Through the identification of your interests, the development of your concepts, the full use of your intelligence, and the patience necessary to allow all of this to happen at its own required pace, practicing will become desirable and surprisingly exciting. If you expect your performances to evolve to new heights, you need to begin the process by perfecting your own personal practice skills.

LOVE

Just as children are drawn to the mystery of their reflection in the clear surface of a pond, and to the joyful wonder as it dissolves with the action of a falling drop of rain, we are drawn to that which is a reflection of ourselves and to that over which we have some, but not full, control. Gravity pulls the airborne drop of rain downward just as love pulls us with a force both controlled and mysteriously uncontrolled deep into the world of music. While practicing, keep in the front of your thoughts why you love to perform and wish to improve. It may be the love of your sound, the modulations of tone from deep within your instrument, the love of the sensorial activity of simply playing your instrument, the love of doing well at an important and difficult task, or the all-consuming wonder that you feel for the phenomenon of music. With these personal and important feelings as your focus, such love will cause outward-flowing ripples that will touch all elements of your practice and ultimately your performances. And the stronger those initial ripples are, the stronger will be those that rebound to stimulate the center of your musical being.

INTEREST

One of the most exciting sensations is to be so interested and involved in what you are doing that you lose all track of time and place. Imagine that your mind is like a mirror (or the surface of a clear pool) that simply reflects what it sees. Your mind is always busy thinking of something just as a mirror is always reflecting something. The mirror, however, cannot look back upon itself and reflect. It can only look outward with clarity, absorbing what it sees while having no interest in itself. Try to think like a mirror. If you can become so interested and involved in your music, what you are practicing, what is being experienced and learned, and how enjoyable (even exciting) music can be, you will then lose track of time and place and have no space left for the distracting and often meaningless mind-clutter that confuses your focus.

CONCEPTS

The wish to reflect the simple beauties and profound character of the best music possible requires that you first know and understand what is possible. The initial steps in concept development begin in one's open and absorbing mind and then work their way through the instrument of expression. You must imitate at first, just as a baby does an adult or as a foreigner does in a new culture. Soon, however, you begin to modify these concepts, allowing them to evolve and to be more compatible with your own special abilities, desires, and personal musical messages. A primary function of substantive practice is to implant new concepts, to absorb and internalize their true potential, to improve in that direction through experimentation, and then to hear and enjoy the full growth of new and fertile ideas.

FOCUS

Each successful practice session needs a solid and well-conceived plan—an intelligently designed goal or set of goals. This is, however, only a lofty ideal and will remain unrealized if you fail to fully develop the art of concentration and the ability to attain and retain a focus in the single-minded direction of that goal. Keep your ideal concept in focus at all times. For instance:

Legato . . . a smooth motion from note to note . . .
flowing up then down with the line . . . feel the
gliding of your canoe upon a glass-smooth pond . . .
move only the muscles needed for a forward motion . . .
hear the liquid flow . . . sing this love-filled line . . .
enjoy the gentle movement from moment to moment,
actively expect nothing less than your focused concept
while you passively accept what is being sounded
with a positive interest. As you then rest and review
your performance, plan modifications if necessary
toward your goals with the excitement of the process
as your reward.

INTELLIGENCE

Trust in your own abilities to improve and to know what is best for yourself. No one knows you as well as you do. Believe in your own ideas while you continue to absorb other information from **all** possible sources. Be **interested** in your problems, not intimidated by them. Without problems or mistakes there are no answers, and without answers there is no learning and no growth. While you experiment with solutions, keep track of what works for you. Quickly move on from that which doesn't work. Keep searching. Trust in your acquired knowledge drawn from thoughtful experiences while you continue to collect information from teachers, books, peers, recordings, magazine articles, educational videos, and of course from live performances. Knowledge is experience—the digested information within an intelligent person that nurtures health and well-being and that causes well-doing.

PATIENCE

To fully digest the many forms of information made available to an open and intelligent mind takes time. All true growth seems to work at its own pace and often in an erratic manner. Until you have experienced such erratic learning for yourself, you cannot possibly know how that pacing will work. The fun is in observing and enjoying the process—the journey towards your goal. In most cases, concepts and goals should be thought of as directions rather than actual destinations. For example, you may wish to develop that perfect legato; however, you soon realize that even though you apply your intelligence based on your experiences, you may still never actually produce such a perfect legato sound, at least not all of the time. Should that then invalidate the goal? Not at all. Not if you can fully experience that wonderful movement toward improvement. To be overly impatient is to be living (thinking) in the future, which will inevitably cause you to miss out on all that is happening right now in your potentially productive and possibly enjoyable practice session.

ENJOYMENT

If you have decided to devote such a great deal of time, effort, concentration, dedication, persistence, and even sacrifice toward your artistic endeavors, why not enjoy the whole process, including practice. Enjoyment is a state of mind generated from within yourself and fed by powerful forces: a love for what you are doing; a deep interest in what is happening at the moment; a strong belief in the importance of the event; an ability to retain a focus on that event; an ample understanding of the components of the activity; and an ability to require nothing from the event. Although you expect great results, accept with great interest whatever happens.

One should not expect happiness or satisfaction from each and every practice session. These two states of mind are often granted far too much value and importance. They are at best momentary emotions, usually based on getting what you think you want while not always knowing what that is. Remember, it is often dissatisfaction that becomes the primary force for higher levels of motivation. The true substance of real enjoyment comes with the full awareness of the processes of learning and the acceptance of the inevitabilities of change.

The way in which you practice is the direction toward which you will improve. If you practice in a haphazard fashion, you will have little consistency or control. If you work in a mood of anger, it will soon become impossible to demonstrate your love for the music. You will simply not have developed the abilities to perform well if you haven't consistently practiced equally as well.

Our performances reflect clearly how we practice.

Think on these thoughts, apply them as directly as you can, and enjoy completing this full circle. Allow these ideas to wash through your mind and clean away the accumulated debris of negative attitudes and unproductive methods that have cluttered your past practice sessions. What might develop from such a change is a new clarity of thought and consistency of action, causing a very positive ripple effect for all that you perform and to all for whom you perform.

The Process of Teaching and Learning

9. High Expectations

This chapter is primarily directed at public school teachers, conductors, and those giving lessons to young horn students in hopes of discouraging that dominant belief in the one label so often granted the horn. High expectations are needed of us all for dreams to be realized.

Have you ever heard it spoken, "The horn is the most difficult of all instruments to play"? Have you ever noticed how most published composers and arrangers are always extremely careful not to write anything too high, too low, too fast, too extended, or too exposed for the horn? Have you ever gone to a band or orchestra concert and heard the horn players sound as if they too believed that such ideas are accurate assumptions?

Based on their beliefs of the limitations of the horn's capabilities, many music teachers expect less from horn players than other instrumentalists. They pass this attitude on to their students, some of whom go on to become professional performers. In turn these performers, along with overly cautious composers and professional conductors conditioned to ignore the horn section, transmit this lowered set of expectations to the audience.

To be realistic, the primary problem is ultimately inherent in the horn itself. The quality of its sound and attack make it virtually impossible to hide a missed note. For a string player, the near miss simply sounds out of tune, and for many other instruments it might be a wrong note with the right sound. However, for the horn player, the sound of a miss is an obvious calamity (often referred to as a "clam"). All performers miss notes, but with the horn there is often that minor explosion, a miss that admittedly destroys the musical line. This causes tentativeness or even fear in the performer, a cautious and frequently undemanding attitude from the conductor, and a general sense of uneasiness from an audience listening to an exposed horn solo. I contend that in most cases, it is this factor and this factor alone that has perpetuated the difficulty of the horn attitude. This mindset of fear then turns in on itself and becomes a greater problem than the inherent idiosyncrasies of the horn.

However, when teachers and conductors expect as much from their horn players as they do from the other instrumentalists, these horn players are often much more successful and usually more accurate. They feel more a part of the group, much less ignored, and no longer feared. No one can succeed where success is not expected. A number of years ago, I was teaching a near beginner. He was quite intelligent and learned quickly. Near the end of one lesson he asked, "How high can the horn go?" It was then that I realized my answer to that important question could have quite an effect on his perception and potentially his high range. My answer could make that potentially slippery register a problem for him for some time to come, or I could mislead him (just a little) into a comfortable, free-blowing high range. I answered, "The written F to G (above high C) are good notes to work toward," and I played them for him. (The embouchure I used to produce these notes was drastically curled inward producing a rather pinched sound, but he was unable to evaluate such a lack of tone quality at his age.) He took it all in stride and returned after a few weeks with a very secure high C.

My first teacher also kept his attitudes about the difficulties of the horn to himself. While in high school, I was learning a Mozart concerto and needed to know how to play a lip trill. He demonstrated one with very little fanfare, and I returned the next week performing lip trills with ease, which is the only way they can be produced.

Over the years, I've had a few students who had been told that they had a natural set of high chops but that their low ranges would be difficult for them. Such a judgment became a prediction, which in turn became true, at least until these powerful, negative labels were discarded. Students have been told that trills are impossible, that stopped horn below middle C is not possible to produce on the horn, and so on. In almost all cases these negative attitudes, fed to them by others in authority, have developed into walls that block out the joy of making music.

> *"Men are not disturbed by things, but by the views which they take of them."*
> **Epictetus (55–135 A.D.)**

Many aspects of horn playing can be made into impossible dreams by the views one takes of them. Quite often the view a student takes of a specific technique has been instilled by a teacher the first time the challenge presented itself. Do not pass on your prejudices or your own problems to your students. Try to discard such pessimistic attitudes and, as a result, raise expectations of these students. Sure, the horn has its difficulties, maybe even a few more problems than some other instruments, but why should that become the focus? That is the challenge, and meeting challenges is what it is all about. I believe strongly that students learn as much from teachers' attitudes as they do from the well-chosen words. By expecting positive results perhaps we can help eliminate that pervasive aura of difficulty surrounding this challenging yet beautiful musical instrument.

SUPPLEMENTING THE HORN PLAYER'S REPERTOIRE

Many directors have found that a great deal of the middle school and high school band and orchestra repertoire has boring horn parts, apparently the result of the belief that the horn is a difficult instrument and that students should not be challenged for fear of a musical disaster. Directors and private teachers can and should challenge their horn students with duet, trio, and quartet literature. This particular small ensemble repertoire is not flooded with masterworks, but all of those in the following list are quite good. Such an opportunity will allow young hornists to play melodic material, to work toward an improved section sound, and to develop the techniques necessary for more advanced levels of playing. Horn ensembles are also a lot of fun because multiple horns sound good together, and most horn players seem to enjoy each other. Other forms of chamber music are also encouraged but not to the exclusion of horn duets, trios, and quartets.

At the time of publication of this text, some of these selections were unavailable from the respective publishers. However, they may be available in school, university, or teachers' personal libraries.

MIDDLE SCHOOL LEVEL

Horn Duets

Hoss, Wendell (ed.), *60 Selected Duets*, Los Angeles Horn Club, Southern.

Howe, Marvin (ed.), *Seventeen Horn Duets*, The Hornist's Nest.

Lasso, Orlando di, *Twelve Duets*, Ms Publications.

Mayer, Rudolph, *Twelve Bicinia*, Shawnee.

Mönkmeyer, Helmut, *Masters of the 16th and 17th Centuries*, Pelikan Musikverlag.

Niggli, Friedrich, *Acht Jagdlieder*, C. F. Peters.

Pottag, Max (ed.), *60 Horn Duets*, Belwin.

Voxman, H. (ed.), *Selected Duets for French Horn*, Rubank.

Williams, Clifton, *24 Duo Studies*, Southern.

Horn Trios

Butts, Carrol, *Ode for Horns*, Pro Art.

Conley, Lloyd, *Lento and Lilt (Trio With Piano)*, Kendor.

Kling, H. and Wm. Teague (ed.), *30 Selected Pieces*, AMP.

Racusen, David, *Canonic Etudes*, Shawnee.

Rosenthal, Irving (ed.), *Four Classical Transcriptions for Three Horns*, Western.

Schaeffer, Don (ed.), *Ancient Fugue (16th Century)*, Pro Art.

Schaeffer, Don (ed.), *Horn Trio Album*, Pro Art.

Stoutamire, Albert and Kenneth Henderson, *Trios for All*, Belwin.

Horn Quartets

Bacon, Thomas (ed.), 88 *German Quartets*, Southern.

Beethoven, Ludwig van, *Three Equali*, Robert King (alternate horn parts published with the original trombone quartet version).

Da Victoria, T. L., Donfray (ed.), *Ave Maria*, Studio P/R.

Di Lasso, Orlando and Marvin Howe (eds.), *Exandi Deus*, Southern.

Handel, G. F., d'Areses (ed.), *Largo*, Carl Fischer.

Howe, Marvin (ed.), *Madrigals*, Volumes 1 & 2, The Hornist's Nest.

Mayer, Rudolph, *Four Little Pieces*, Southern.

McCoy, Marvin (ed.), *Three Hunting Songs*, McCoy.

Mozart, W. A., Ostrander (ed.), *Alleluja*, Editions Musicus.

Mueller, B. F., *29 Quartets* (4 books), Southern.

Neuling, Otto, *Jagd Quartett*, Pro Musica Verlag.

Palestrina, G. P., *Christe Lux Vera*, Kendor.

Pottag, Max (ed.), *Quartet Album*, Belwin.

Rossini, G., *Fanfare de Chasse*, Benjamin.

Stout, L. and C. Leuba (eds.), *Folk Song Suite*, Southern.

Voxman, Himie (ed.), *Quartet Repertoire*, Rubank.

Wagner, Richard, *Pilgrim's Chorus*, Sam Fox.

Wagner/Pottag, Max, *Tannhaüser*, Belwin.

Wagner/Shaw, Lowell, *King's Prayer from Lohengrin*, Belwin.

Winter, James, *Suite for a Quartet of Young Horns*, The Hornist's Nest.

HIGH SCHOOL LEVEL

Horn Duets

Bach, J. S./Ramm, E., *9 Duets*, Medici.

Heiden, Bernhard, *Five Canons*, AMP.

Hill, Douglas, *Ten Pieces for Two Horns*, The Hornist's Nest.

Hill, Douglas, *27 Rare Horn Duets* (hunting horn), McCoy.

Janetzky, Kurt (ed.), *Waldhorn Duette—18th and 19th Centuries*, Hofmeister.

Kopprasch, Wilhelm, *Eight Duets*, International.

Moenkemeyer, *Masters of the 16th and 17th Centuries*, Pelikan.

Mozart, W. A., *12 Duos*, MacGinnis & Marx.

Nicolai, Otto, *Duets Nos. 1–6*, Musica Rara.

Schenk/Reynolds, Verne, *Six Sonatas*, MCA.

Wilder, Alec, *22 Duets*, Margun.

Horn Trios

Bach, J. S./Shaw, Lowell, *Five Bach Trios* and *Bach Trios*, Vols. 2 & 3, The Hornist's Nest.

Barrows, John, *La Chasse*, The Hornist's Nest.

Beethoven, Ludwig van, *Trio, Op. 87*, Cor.

Boismortier, *Sonata*, The Hornist's Nest.

Dauprat, *Grand Trio No. 1 & 2*, Billaudot.

Dauprat, *Grand Trio No. 3*, Carl Fischer (Boismortier/Shaw).

Fritchie, W. P., *Jazz Stylings*, Vols. 1 & 2, McCoy.

Hill, Douglas, *Five Pieces for Three Horns*, The Hornist's Nest.

Mozart/Walshe, Robert, *Divertimento No. 2*, The Hornist's Nest.

Shaw, Lowell, *Tripperies*, The Hornist's Nest.

Reicha, Anton, *10 Trios, Op. 82*, KaWe.

Horn Quartets

Bozza, Eugene, *Suite*, Leduc.

Heiden, Bernhard, *Quartet for Horns*, AMP.

Hill, Douglas, *Shared Reflections*, Manduca.

Hill, Douglas, *Americana Variations*, www.reallygoodmusic.com.

LeClaire, Dennis, *Quartet*, Southern.

LoPresti, Ronald, *Second Suite*, Shawnee.

Mitushin, A., *Concertino*, Southern.

Reynolds, Verne, *Short Suite*, Robert King.

Shaw, Lowell, *Fripperies*, (eight volumes of four quartets each), The Hornist's Nest.

Stanhope, David, *Cortettes* (humorous), The Hornist's Nest.

Tcherepnine, A., *6 Pieces*, Editions Musicus.

(Please see the Key to Publishers in the back of this book for more information.)

10. The Horn Section: Bringing the Sound Around

One of the most serious performance problems for the hornist from the middle school band to the professional orchestra is projecting the best possible sound. The horn sound should not be direct like the other instruments, but the horn players should not have to force their sounds simply to be heard. Below are some thoughts on what can be done by school teachers, conductors, and players to solve some of these problems.

The horn is a very special instrument. Its sound has a magical presence that seems to be coming from nowhere and everywhere at the same time. Its timbre is both warm and resonant, heavy and gentle. Its sound is loved by audiences around the world, yet it is pointed in the wrong direction. This elusive and indirect sound is partially the cause of its magic, but it also creates many problems. All other instruments in the orchestra and band project their sounds out toward the audience or, in some cases, up or across the stage. Only the horn projects backward and down. The solutions are not all that complicated. The real problem is that solutions are often not even considered by those in charge of the ensemble seating arrangements. The players are often reluctant to ask or are simply unaware of how well they are projecting in the first place.

Balance between sections within a large group is certainly one of the most important problems. Then there is the projection among the horns between ranges, the matching of certain types of articulation, the matching of timbres as controlled by the right hand positions in the bell, and simply the problem of hearing each other. Here are some solutions that I hope will help.

POSITIONING THE HORN SECTION

1. The first horn player should always play with the bell facing down the section. This allows all of the other hornists to hear one leading player set a standard. First is also usually the highest part and the one with the greatest melodic interest. Another consideration is that the other players will not be as audible to the first horn so as not to negatively influence him or her. The assistant first, if used, is usually placed to the left of the solo first so that the first and second players will be side by side.

2. Provide each player, not just each part, with a separate stand for reasons of visual directness and to allow the players to all have their bells facing in the same direction. This is truly worth the extra effort involved.

3. Ample space (ideally two feet) is necessary between players to allow their full sounds to be free-flowing and not absorbed by their neighbors' clothing. (Can you imagine a curtain draped less than two feet in front of the trumpet sound?)

4. Position all players the same distance from the rebound surface behind them.

5. Whenever possible, use a wood backdrop approximately six feet behind your row of horn players. Avoid cloth or curtain backdrops whenever possible but never any closer than six feet. Avoid putting the horns in front of other sections due to the absorption of their clothing.

6. Lucite, plastic, brick, and concrete are less desirable rebound surfaces than wood but better than curtains or clothing.

7. Never put the horns in front of the percussion, especially the timpani and bass drum. The intense vibrations projected by these larger drums literally become a concentrated, focused blast of air pressure that enters the bells and can affect the aperture's control of a note. It will also negatively affect endurance.

It is normal that most ensembles rehearse in one space and then, after only one dress rehearsal or two, perform in a much larger concert setting. The horn players are greatly affected by these differences, and the conductors are often equally confused by what they should ask and expect from their horn sections. In a smaller more confined rehearsal space, the horns often sound much more present than they will in the larger concert hall. One must be empathetic and help the hornists to prepare for the concert hall requirements. The volume necessary should be encouraged and rehearsed, even in a loud or more present rehearsal space.

Another important placement consideration involves the frequent positioning of the horns in front of the other brass instruments. What happens in that situation is that when the trumpets and trombones hear the direct sound of the horns, they play louder to compensate. This increase is heard directly by the hornists who then increase their output, and the result is that the brass players all start over-blowing their instruments, often causing distorted sounds. It is always best to place the horn section all in a row in the back of the ensemble.

BALANCING THE HORN SECTION

1. With all the bells facing the same direction and equally distanced from the rebound surface, each member of the section should match a basic right hand position within the bell. I often recommend that it rest, cupped, with fingers straight, at the four o'clock position if resting on the leg, or the two o'clock position if held off the leg. The depth of the hands should also be very similar, considering the different sizes and shapes of hands and bells. I usually suggest a position in as far as the thumb knuckle.

2. The various ranges of the horn project quite differently. Thus, the players must compensate. The top octave-and-a-half projects quite well from a   dynamic and louder; thus, it does not need to be very aggressive until   or more. From the first space F down an octave and a half, a frequent range for second and fourth horn parts, the natural projection is much less; thus, the players need to play a bit louder than the higher parts. The low range needs full volume, a clear sound, and solid intonation. Avoid distorting or making it too brassy, however.

3. All players on second, third, and fourth parts should adjust to the player on their left for both intonation and the matching of tone colors. (Play in tune and in tone.) Exact intonation projects well.

4. Similar vowel formations formed inside the mouth while playing, such as *ah* or *awe*, help to create a blended section sound.

5. Matching the beginnings and endings of all chords, or matching articulations, creates a greatly enhanced blend.

6. Breathing together aggressively, like a team, causes all of the above to work even better.

OTHER IMPORTANT CONSIDERATIONS

1. No part is any more important than any other part in a horn section. Each has a job. The first horn sets the style for the section and must learn to tune and to adjust to the articulations of all the other instruments. The second horn must tune to, adjust articulations, and support the sound of the first horn, usually playing a bit louder. The third horn must match, often note for note, the first horn, at times taking a leadership role when the first is not playing. The fourth horn must tune to, adjust articulations, and support the sound of the third horn, usually playing a bit louder. The assistant horn must be prepared to fade in and support the first horn, being ready to lead the section at any time.

2. High range unisons require the strongest players using similar fingerings and equal air support.

3. Common intonation problems include all first and second valve combinations (always sharp), fifth partials being low (i.e., first line E down to C♯ on the F side), B♭ side and F side of the horn not being in tune with each other (usually the B♭ side is sharp), extreme high range going sharp for stronger players and flat for less strong players, the low range being often flat and flabby sounding.

4. Mutes should be of the same brand or have very similar sounds. Those of black fiber-board with wooden ends are the most common for professionals. The section must practice together alone with the mutes to hear and match the mute placement within the bell. The corks do not need always to be in contact with the bell flare.

5. Stopped horn must be learned by every player, and an attempt should be made to match sounds. Be sure the right thumb is pulled outward and the hand is dissecting the bell at an angle with an oval shape. The air pressure must be intense and constant.

6. Never mix muted and stopped sounds together unless asked for by the composer. These two sounds are actually quite different. The stopped sound eliminates the lower frequencies, and the mute suppresses the upper frequencies.

7. Sections improve quickly when allowed to perform in duos, trios, and horn quartets. There is extensive literature at all levels for such chamber music. (See Chapter 9.)

The horn is a beautiful and mysterious instrument whose players are often left alone to fend for themselves in the larger ensembles, never knowing what is being heard out front. It sounds rather loud to the player; however, since most conductors have been encouraged to leave the hornists alone (they are all such sensitive creatures!), it is never known for sure what is being heard. If you are a conductor, tell them and help them to create an acoustical environment that will enhance the entire ensemble by allowing the hornists to blow with a similar intensity to that of the other brass players. If you are a player, ask for many other ears to listen for you, take their word for it, and adjust accordingly.

11. Stages of Musical Development

According to David McClelland, a Harvard psychologist and author of the chapter "The Urge to Achieve" in the book *Classics of Organizational Behavior*[2], the population of the world could basically be divided into two groupings. The minority 10% enjoy challenges and opportunities and are willing to work to achieve their goals. The majority 90% don't seem to care much at all.

In my experience as a teacher of exceptionally talented and motivated young horn students, the above statement seems totally out of proportion. To most teachers of music, these proportions will also seem askew. Perhaps that is because the majority who choose the challenges of musical performance fit at least to some degree into the definition given by Fred Luthans regarding the above-mentioned approximate 10% of people: "They assume personal responsibility through self-initiation, set moderately high goals—challenging yet attainable—and demand immediate and precise feedback."

One can assume then that the people who choose to participate and grow through the many disciplines of music are exceptional in the greater scheme of things. As a teacher, one should never lose sight of that fact. Teachers are fortunate to have such talent to work with. Within that good fortune, however, there is a need to provide the best direction and insightful support. So if these exceptional people are setting "moderately high goals" and "demand immediate and precise feedback" from their mentors and teachers, they are owed a thorough and thoughtful perspective as to where they are in their patterns of growth and what they should expect to do next. Teachers need to know about basic learning patterns and need to be aware of how that knowledge can be used to help direct and motivate students.

When students set moderately high goals that are both challenging and attainable, they have set the stage for potential dissatisfaction. This is not dissatisfaction to the levels of extreme stress or unhappiness but is more an attitude that serves as a necessary and primary force for *motivation* and *growth*. Without this feeling of wanting or needing more from their music, the students might as well join those who don't care all that much. Motivation could be defined as the desire to maximize pleasure and minimize pain, or it could be thought of as the drive within that results from unfulfilled needs. Teachers can help to create some of those needs through assignments and expectations. Motivated students as they progress will instinctively create some of those musical assignments as well. In addition to the self-assigned goals and patterns along this path of development, there are more general needs that present themselves as basic patterns for growth. All students and teachers of music should observe these patterns.

I have found it quite interesting to consider Abraham H. Maslow's research relating to human motivation and parallel it with appropriate levels of musical growth. Through his synthesis of many earlier studies on the biological factors and the energies which sustain human behavior, he arrived at a hierarchy of needs. The first level begins with the simple physiological needs, then moves on to the need to feel safe and secure. The third level involves "belongingness" and love, after which comes the need for self-esteem and personal achievement. The fifth level at the top of this pyramid involves the need for greater knowledge, aesthetic awareness, and self-actualization.

In theory, each of these levels of need requires the realization of the preceding one before it becomes necessary or even appropriate to progress upward to the next. In simple terms, if one has no food, there is nothing else that seems important. If one is simply not hungry, then shelter from the elements and other danger is the single most necessary need. Next, one finds a desire for companionship and a feeling of belonging, followed by a desire for personal self-worth and the external acknowledgment of achievements, and eventually evolving to the highest level of internally generated self-worth and personal satisfaction.

This remarkable pyramid of needs can be further reinforced and enhanced by what Ken Wilber in his book *The Marriage of Sense and Soul: Integrating Science and Religion* calls "The Great Nest of Being."[3] These nests are more commonly referred to as the "Great Chain of Being" by such writers as Huston Smith, whom many consider to be the world's primary authority on comparative religion. This manner of explaining human reality constitutes a philosophical consensus spanning the centuries and, to a large degree, most all of the world's religions. As with Maslow's hierarchy of needs, each level of reality is a nest or a part of a chain progressing toward the next, and all are, thus, ultimately interrelated and dependant.

The terms used by Wilber to describe "The Great Nest of Being" through the disciplines of religion and science include:

1. Matter / Physics

2. Life / Biology

3. Mind / Psychology

4. Soul / Theology

5. Spirit / Mysticism

The similarities with Maslow are striking and quite a stimulation for thought. They have, in fact, provided substance and meaning to what I will simply call "Stages of Musical Development." In relating these profound sequences to the patterns of which teachers and students should be aware, one can use these sequences as basic perspectives to motivate students and oneself through the many levels of growth.

1. Beginning with the basic material needs, one must be sure that the student has an instrument that works well and a physical space in which to practice. They will also need musical materials from which to work, including printed music and recordings and, ideally, some low-pressure, appropriate instruction.

2. Safety or comfort needs and biological requirements include the basic physical attributes necessary to perform and possibly excel on their chosen instruments and the freedom from excessively negative parental or peer pressures. Hostility or unreasonable demands from a teacher can also cause young students to feel unsafe and overly anxious, greatly hampering physical abilities to improve on their instruments. Support and encouragement can help alleviate these fears.

3. Love, a sense of belonging, deals with the mind's ability to find comfort and support among others. For the developing music student, this need can be readily filled through positive group participation. The bands, orchestras, and choral ensembles will provide much of this if the teacher or director openly values each player. Mutual cooperation, rather than excessive competition, can help. Switching the parts around and encouraging chamber music ensembles also helps. Challenge everyone without hostility; they must continue to feel safe. The groups might not sound as accomplished at first, but it is not until the students feel like valued contributors to the group that they will be ready to move on to the next level. Without that next level, the ensembles will never sound great.

4. Self-esteem, a sense of achievement, status among their colleagues, and the deeper awareness of their own personal feelings and beliefs come to the students who have experienced the first three levels, have devoted themselves to their own personal development and, thus, have decided that music must continue to be a large part of their lives. This decision comes at first from the mind, but it must ultimately be felt from deep within the soul. These students will have experienced many successful performances; will have had a great deal of positive support from peers, parents, and teachers; and will feel great joy in the act of music-making.

5. The joy of music can be experienced at so many stations along the way. When it finally arises to the level of the spirit and the student is capable of truly feeling this, then the journey through self-actualization as a musician takes on a significance somewhere beyond the ego. Enthusiasm for the art, periodic levels of heightened awareness, and peak experiences within one's musical activities becomes the reward. Music, in all of its manifestations, eventually becomes the primary focus for further discoveries. The individual retains his or her identity, but it is not this identity that drives the individual; it is the music.

To be specific, from the student's perspective, these five levels or nests can be used to describe more specific activities that will most likely occur and, in many cases, be necessary for music students as they grow.

1. In the beginning, a youngster may choose to start an instrument simply as a novelty or as a form of play. A fancy looking instrument, like a horn, can make a young child seem rather unique with a great new toy.

2. Soon the child desires to join a group. It is important that the other kids want to play instruments too. The extra adult attention and recognition along with low-level competition may even stimulate the desire to improve a little.

3. The need to be admired within their peer groups, to receive special attention from their teachers and family, to be part of successful ensembles, and even to compete for grades or awards will add to their developing egos and to each student's need for more than simple acceptance.

4. By this level, formal musical training becomes both a desire and a necessity. The student now needs the challenges presented through contact with peers of similar abilities and interests and with respected specialists. The full palate of music becomes of greater importance at this stage. Composition, music theory, history, teaching, conducting, and advanced performance problems gradually become part of the student's daily concerns. Becoming a musician is more the goal, with the performance medium as the most important pathway or means but not necessarily the end in itself.

5. By this stage, sharing what one can do and what one knows becomes a way of life. This is the stage for the fine teachers, exceptional professional performers, effective conductors, compassionate coaches, and advanced amateurs who have chosen to continue to grow and learn about music, not for those individuals who remain stuck between levels three and four, preoccupied with their own egos, self-esteem, and personal fame. This is when one searches for deeper meanings and pure aesthetic enjoyment. Music is a spiritual goal available to all of us—eventually.

Why might students practice at these five levels?

1. At first, it is for the fun of it, for the novelty, and for the desire to play with their fancy new toy.

2. If they practice a little, they might not be noticed, but they will still be part of the game.

3. If they practice more than the others, they might be noticed and admired for it.

4. If they practice a lot, they will achieve levels of self-worth and possible employment.

5. They desire to maintain, continue to learn, and experience the joys of performing music.

What do they practice at these various levels of development?

1. Students must focus on simple melodies and on the physical acts of the fingers, the lips, the bow arms, or controlling the vocal cords.

2. The music of their ensembles becomes most important, but a few scales are also essential, along with a song or two to play for the folks at home.

3. Solos are added to the ensemble music, perhaps for contests, along with the fundamentals of scales and arpeggios, and a few etudes. Preparing for and taking private lessons becomes the norm.

4. Basic repertoire for the instrument, technical studies, important etudes, orchestral excerpts, chamber music, ensemble music, and personal warm-ups are all mixed together with the preparation materials for auditions, contests, juries, and recitals.

5. If employed, they will practice whatever is scheduled next for a performance. After that, anything is fair game, including new repertoire, improvisation, extended techniques, early performance practice concerns, and run-throughs of the old repertoire of importance.

This exercise could be continued into other aspects of musical growth, but the point has been made that everyone has had to or will have to go through each of these basic stages, one at a time, before he or she can get to the higher levels of understanding and awareness and, if one perseveres, to the level of the spiritual. Students must feel comfortable and confident in level one before they can move on to level two. A common problem is the teacher who might expect a level three of dedication, direction, and drive from level-one students, simply because of their demonstrable talent. The students are not ready for that. The students themselves must become dissatisfied with where they are before they can move on to the next stage.

It is also important to know that these levels or nests are only suggested stages that cannot possibly describe any one student. These categories will overlap, and students may appear to be in more than one level at any one time. They might even find themselves back in an earlier level for so many different reasons. All of this, and the thoughts stimulated in the reader, is simply an exercise in perspective. Teachers must use this information to be aware of the unique placement of students along their own continuum of development. Teachers must learn to be aware of where the student is at any one time in order to motivate him or her to fulfill the proper sequence of needs.

To shift the focus now from the teacher's concern for the student's developmental patterns to the teacher's own hierarchy of needs, one must assume that there is a basic desire driving these teachers toward excellence.

1. Teachers must possess the tools, the instruments, the knowledge, and the degrees, all of the physical materials that will allow them the right to set up shop as a knowing and caring facilitator.

2. Teachers need to have personal confidence in what they plan to do based on their life skills, their people skills, their street smarts, the desire to help others, their knowledge that others will believe in them, the self-assurance that they are safe and comfortable, and the certainty that they will succeed and prosper professionally.

3. Teachers need to feel part of a larger group of similar-thinking, supportive colleagues, whether in a job environment, an organization of music teachers, or both. Their situations must be mentally stimulating and allow for the application and sharing of their love, concern, and knowledge with others.

4. Most highly motivated teachers need to know that they are doing a very special job, that they are helping their students as much as is humanly possible, and that the results are obvious and appreciated by their students, the parents, their colleagues, and their administrators. Their self-esteem is somewhat dependent on these outward signs of approval, but the consequences are often extraordinary soul-filled teaching and learning.

5. After years of working within the realms of Nos. 3 and 4, it is the ultimate hope that a teacher may enter into a stage of pure enjoyment and renewed love for the subject. The wonders of music, the success of their students, and their own learning become what is ultimately important, not primarily the noteworthiness of their teaching. The joy of music can then be shared at a spiritual and mystical level. These mentors, these gurus, these remarkable teachers are few but not rare.

Teachers are only human, and so are the students. All must traverse similar stages of development, but in their own ways and at their own rates. Maybe the reason why it is so interesting to be a teacher is because these levels, these nests, this chain of being is so universal and necessary, but it can never be experienced the same way twice. To observe and help others maneuver through these passages is one of the ultimate joys of teaching.

12. In Preparation for College and a Career in Music

Before spending the vast amounts of necessary time and effort trying to become a professional horn player or teacher, students should contemplate whether this is the career they truly want. Students who cannot imagine doing anything more important with their lives, who actually enjoy the rewards of long hours of solitary practice, who wish often to share their music with others, and who simply cannot fit enough great music into their days are the ones who will have the best chance to eventually find their place in the music profession.

If you can commit positively to music with the deepest conviction, then ask yourself to commit positively again tomorrow morning and each day after that! Commitment, focus, dedication, and self-discipline make up the foundation for a successful career in music. Only students who have well-defined goals and can remain focused and are determined each and every day to reach those goals will have a chance to find a life with music at its center. You must want it, or it will never happen. When it does happen, all of the hard work will have been worth it.

When you are deciding during middle school or high school to go to college and pursue a major in music, you should seriously consider some preliminary and specific goals. First, locate the best private horn teacher in your area. Ask your band or orchestra director for suggestions. Check out the local or nearby colleges or conservatories, talk to other students (more than two), and don't just settle for the most convenient or the least expensive teacher available. Ask questions and actually audition your teacher. This is a very important decision. How you learn to work and what materials you work on can have a major effect on your later success. Compatibility and respect are also important components in a teacher/student relationship. Make certain that you are compatible and that you feel respect for and from your teacher. Again, do not underestimate your chances of studying under the best possible teacher available. Just ask.

Own your own double horn. Ask about brands of horns from all of your music teachers, and talk to more advanced students who have searched for and decided on a particular instrument. There are so many fine horns available. Go to music stores, try out all that you can, borrow other students' horns, and make sure that the machine is good—that all the valves work quietly, all of the slides move smoothly, the metal is in sturdy condition, and that you can get all of the notes (within your present technique) with similar ease. After making such judgments, trust yourself to pick out the one that seems somehow to call to you. Before you buy, it is also a good idea to take the horn to a local professional or advanced horn player (ideally your teacher) and have it evaluated.

Play your horn! Play whenever you possibly can. Make it a priority. Private play is called practice, which can and should be a joyful experience. (See Chapter 8, "Practicing Full Circle.") Other play includes both your large ensembles and the small ensembles you create for yourself from groupings of your like-minded musical friends. Find places to perform together—often. Playing basketball or soccer or tennis is a lot of work, but it is still play. Practicing is also a lot of concentrated work that brings the rewards of growth and the results of having more fun. The better you play, the greater the fun.

If all of the above is already part of your daily and weekly life, then you are on your way. If not, begin immediately! Do what you have decided to want.

During the high school and college years is when most serious horn students spend vast amounts of time and energy focusing on their musical, technical, professional, and personal growth. This is when you come in contact with many others who have similar goals for themselves. These people, or people very much like them, will be your colleagues for the rest of your musical life. Learn to get along, listen to them, support their successes, and grow together through your mutual love of music. The music world/business is a very close-knit group. We all need each other, and we all need great music. This is a beautiful bond. Enjoy being a positive part of it.

Before your college years, you are in most cases told by your local government or by your parents where you are to go to school, who your teachers will be, and what subjects you should study. Then all of a sudden at the age of 17, you are asked to decide what to do next. That is an incredible responsibility. What an important sequence of changes such a decision will make on the rest of your life. How do you know what to do? What steps should you take first?

To begin with, ask professionals (i.e., those who are doing what you have decided you want to be doing after college) the many important questions racing through your mind. Prepare these questions over a period of time, and write them down when they come to you. Also, prepare a wish-list and a list of personal musical preferences as they seem appropriate to you at your present level of development. For example:

I am a horn player who wishes to be an orchestral musician.

My favorite orchestras are _____, and the horn players I enjoy listening to the most are _____.

I do enjoy studying other subjects and would love to have peers with other interests, but I do plan and desire to focus on all aspects of music.

I already practice _____ hours a day and plan to work even harder.

I want to be in a school with lots of fine horn players so I can learn from and with them.

I seem to respond best to a teacher who will guide me toward my goals and not prescribe a specific set of requirements and rules.

Where should I go?

Such statements are well designed, thoughtful, and personal. They tell a lot about you and will require thoughtful answers from those professionals you approach.

Ask similar questions of all of your school music teachers and counselors. Keep a notebook. Go to libraries and ask for catalogues for the schools that become interesting to you. Write to those schools and ask for all available materials, or locate their Web sites and download what you need. Consider the differences between small colleges and universities, larger universities, conservatories, and both private and public institutions. Talk to older students who you have known that have similar goals and abilities and who have done such research and made their decisions. There is so much to consider, so do all of this research during your junior year. By the fall of your senior year, you will be very busy arranging for and practicing for the all-important (return) visits and auditions at your chosen schools.

Plan to visit every school that interests you. This should definitely be in conjunction with your official playing audition and, if at all possible, during your junior year. Invest in these trips. You must know how you feel being there. Try to attend rehearsals, concerts, and recitals, and find some horn students and ask them thoughtful questions that might help you get a feel for what it might be like for you. These students are just as interested in you as you might be in them. Your coming to this particular school will add to their lives as well. These students are the people who can answer the specific questions that the professors may find awkward or that you might find awkward asking professors. Come prepared to interview students and plan to listen carefully. Choose more than one student if possible.

Meet with as many teachers as possible and interview them openly and honestly. Be sure to meet the specific horn teacher with whom you would study. Take a lesson with this person and get a feel for your mutual compatibility and for his or her teaching style. Look over the facilities, the campus, the housing possibilities, and even the city itself. Remember that this may be the very place where your professional life will find its foundation and where your personal life will flower into adulthood. Try not to be overly influenced by the hype that some schools may display more than others. Once you are a student on a campus, it is the feel of the environment, the attitudes of your peers and teachers, and the content of the work that will constitute your daily life.

The actual audition should definitely involve a personal appearance and extended visit whenever possible. Sending a tape for an audition puts you in a much less favorable position for acceptance. You will have no control over how or when the tape is played, for whom it is played, whether it is played in its entirety, or whether the equipment used is worthy of your sound. You will not be there to sightread or respond as a human being to the professors of the auditioning committee. Professors are simply older people who have dedicated their lives to teaching younger people. There is a very strong tendency for professors to select students with whom they have conversed in person. Auditioners who have been introduced only through application forms, phone calls, or recorded sounds will be selected less often.

Each institution will have its own specifics regarding the content and procedures for the actual audition, but some generalities are a safe guess. You will probably be given ten to twenty minutes to play for the professor(s) of horn and perhaps the other brass faculty. In smaller schools you might also perform for the woodwind faculty and conductors as well. While preparing for these events, please realize that these professors are quite experienced at listening to young students at all stages of their development. They can hear where you are (having been there themselves), and they deal with these issues all of the time. Your job is to simply represent yourself and your playing as comfortably as possible on that day. Show where you are along your own path of growth. Be prepared! Be very well prepared to demonstrate what you have done up until then on your horn. Be yourself, and let them see who you are. Share your personality. That should be simple. That's what you do everyday. It is their job to decide acceptability. Don't take on that job for yourself at any audition. It is impossible to be the defendant and the jury at the same time, and to try will cause you to lose your focus—to lose your self.

Content requests for the various schools will vary, so be sure you know the specifics down to the last detail long before you go. It is quite safe to assume that the committees will want to hear one or two solos from the basic repertoire, ideally in contrasting styles. Sight-reading is commonly requested, so be prepared for treble clef and both octaves of bass clef (including old notation, which is read up an octave from the notated pitch). A few transpositions in the more common keys of E, E♭, D, C, B♭, and G may be a part of the sight-reading, so be ready. Scales are often requested. Be prepared for all major, melodic, harmonic, and natural minor scales for two octaves. Also be prepared to demonstrate your full range through a chromatic scale. Orchestral excerpts may be requested at certain conservatories and universities, so having the basic excerpt repertoire prepared would add favorably to the depth of preparation that you might wish to demonstrate.

Taken in its entirety, these audition materials could never be presented in an average 15-minute audition. However, your commitment, dedication, and discipline would be noticed and respected by the committee. Such a depth of preparation can be heard in all that you play, so you wouldn't have to play it all. A very special gesture that is not required at most auditions but that would be a wonderful way to represent your hard work and attract special attention to your organizational skills would be to prepare a printed list of everything you have ready for the audition. Make multiple copies for each member of the audition committee and hand these out upon entering the room. List only those solos, excerpts, or etudes that you have ready to perform in a suggested order, being prepared to perform it in any order requested. This will make a very strong impression on the members of the faculty and will guarantee that they will know how serious you are and how complete your preparation has been.

To reiterate, be ready to ask questions of the committee—thoughtful questions that need answers. Be prepared to talk and show your enthusiasm for the art of performance, your love for the horn, and your ambition to learn. Don't overdo it; just be yourself. Also, take notice of the questions, reactions, and interest you feel from the faculty. These may be your mentors. They may be the ones who help to mold your professional life. After each audition is over, make notes about how you felt at the time, and then later write down how your feelings have grown regarding each experience.

Most music schools and conservatories will also expect you to demonstrate a certain level of understanding in music theory. You will probably be asked to take a test covering the rudiments of music, such as scales, intervals, key signatures, triads, and so on. A few high schools do offer such a course. If so, take that course. If not, I recommend that you work with a private tutor, perhaps in collaboration with a piano teacher. Learning piano skills is also very important for all musicians since you will have to pass piano exams for your college music degree; so you might as well start now. Whether or not such opportunities exist for you, a recommended basic book of music theory fundamentals is *Scales, Intervals, Keys, Triads, Rhythm, and Meter*, 3rd Edition, Norton Press, 1998 (includes a CD). There are also a number of computer programs that cover the same basic materials.

Now imagine that you have auditioned at four wonderful music schools and have been accepted at each of them. Congratulations! What do you do to decide? Check your notes. After having traveled to each of the campuses, you must have developed some gut feelings about how comfortable you were or would be at each of them. That is one of the most important considerations, but not the only one. Know that gut feelings can tell you "no" more easily than "yes." Think long and hard about your desires and goals and about your past experiences as a musician. Sometimes what is the most comfortable is simply what is the most familiar. If you are from a high school where you are a big fish in a small pond, "comfortable" might mean that you eliminate a larger situation where you will be initially challenged to swim in a larger pond with lots of big fish. Is eliminating that challenge right for you? Many students are attracted to the schools where they will get into the best organizations right away, and many schools use that as a point for recruitment. Consider all that could mean to your ultimate goals and to the importance of having an inspirational peer group from which you can learn and grow. Challenge yourself. Change is inevitable, so take chances. The chances you take, however, should seem sensible and inspiring to you.

Another very important and very confusing part of the process of choosing a music school is the scholarship "raffle," which is played by many young students and their parents each year. The decision of choosing a school is full of subjectivity. Opinions, conjectures, gut feelings, reputations, recruitment hype, and hearsay all enter in. When the schools being considered all look similar, or are all acceptable, how does a family decide? The one objective element that can so easily tip the scale is the ever-present bottom line. Of course, money is important, especially if you don't have enough or must go too deeply in debt. The concern is with the deceptions that this process can convey to impressionable young students and their tired parents who are looking for the clearest, easiest answer.

To an aspiring young student, the following questions often occur:

How much money are they going to give me to go there?

Is my playing worth only that much money to that school and this much to the other?

The school that gives me the most money wants me the most, right?

To the parents, the following concerns and beliefs are quite natural:

If the tuition is extremely high, the school has better faculty and is a better school.

The package being given my child is so impressive, it can't help but raise his or her self-esteem.

All schools are pretty much the same, so let's go for the sale item.

All of this appears rather simplistic. Of course, everyone wants to do what's right for the student. However, what must always be remembered is that colleges, universities, and conservatories are all big businesses. They are full of great people who are doing wonderful things, but they are still big businesses that also want to do what's right for their own perpetuation and growth.

For students and their families to step back and see why and how scholarships are offered from each institution is important. All institutions are funded primarily from private donations, research money derived from private and/or government sources, tuition payments, and (if a state university) from tax dollars. The private schools charge the most, in part because they do not receive as much, if any, government money. State institutions, for the most part, charge about what it costs to educate the students and can charge no more than mandated by their state legislatures.

Thus, the private schools can and do tend to charge far more than it costs to educate each student. This extra revenue can then be used to offer huge scholarships while having some left over to create a strong public image through attractive brochures and effective use of the media. For example, many private schools that charge large amounts for tuition are also able to offer large scholarships rather freely. The main reason they can do this is that costs for running any educational institution are rather similar among campuses, and faculty salaries differ far less than the difference in tuitions. It has also been well documented that certain schools charge a great deal more than necessary to create the image of quality. We all are led to believe that "we get what we pay for."

Most of these institutions offer financial packages that look very supportive, especially when they come close to covering tuition. What you must know and receive in writing from each institution before money becomes a reason for your decision is the exact description of the complete contents of that package for each of the four years—not just for the first year. It is not unusual that an institution will provide a package that includes scholarships, grants, work-study, and loans, where the first year is heavy on the scholarships and light on the loans. Year by year, however, the allocations can change so that by the senior year the financial aid is made up primarily of loans and very little in the way of scholarships or grants. This technique uses huge initial scholarships for the purpose of recruiting talented young players. The package stays the same, but the contents differ. Once students have become part of a particular institution, they infrequently want to leave their friends, teachers, and familiar surroundings just because of money. Many institutions know this and profit well from it. Be sure to find the real bottom line before you get too caught up in the numbers themselves.

It should also be noted that very large scholarships are also offered by almost any school that is in dire need for certain instruments to fill the ranks of the organizations and, thus, allow for a particular program, such as the band or orchestra, to exist for all of the other students in attendance. You should always take that issue into account. Do you want to be one of the only horn players at your new school or even one of the most advanced going in as a freshman? You might or might not, but you should always feel comfortable asking why you have received a particular scholarship.

The above discussion about the scholarship "raffle" is full of generalizations, but they are based on personal experience. Suffice it to say that you the student should choose the best situation. Choose the place that you found to be the most interesting, stimulating, attractive, challenging, and ultimately appropriate for your own personal goals and needs. After that decision has been made, try to strike the best financial deal possible from that chosen school. (If more than one school is completely appropriate, all the better.) Once you have finally enrolled and begun your lessons, studies, and ensembles, all of these tedious considerations will have faded out of your thoughts. That's when the fun of being a musician occupies each and every day, and the joy of learning makes it all worthwhile.

With such an exciting life ahead of you, take a few long, deep breaths and recommit yourself to your goals. Get back into that practice space and lose yourself in that gorgeous sound you love. On the next page is a short list of some very basic repertoire that will help you get ready for a college audition, college career, and eventually a professional career as a musician who loves to play the horn well.

SUGGESTED SOLOS FOR COLLEGE AUDITIONS

Mozart, W. A., Concertos Nos. 3, 2, 4, 1, and Concert Rondo

Strauss, R., Concerto No. 1, Op. 11

Saint-Saëns, C., *Morceau de Concert*, Op. 94

Strauss, F., Concerto, Op. 8

Krol, B., *Laudatio* (unaccompanied)

SOMEWHAT MORE DEMANDING SOLOS

Haydn, F., Concerto No. 1

Schumann, R., *Adagio and Allegro*, Op. 70

Dukas, P., *Villanelle*

Bozza, E., *En Forêt*

Jacob, G., Concerto

Weber, C. M. von, Concertino, Op. 45

SUGGESTED EXCERPTS FOR COLLEGE AUDITIONS (from *Horn Players Audition Handbook*, compiled by Arthur T. LaBar [Belwin Mills/Warner Bros. Publications] and other sources listed in Chapter 24)

Tchaikovsky, P. I., Symphony No. 5 (solo from *Andante Cantabile*)

Strauss, R., *Til Eulenspiegel* (opening solo)

Shostakovich, D., Symphony No. 5 (1st movement, unison low passage)

Strauss, R., *Don Juan* (unison horn call)

Beethoven, L. van, Symphony No. 3 (3rd movement, trio, 1st or 2nd part)
  Symphony No. 9 (slow movement, extended 4th horn solo)

Brahms, J., Symphony No. 3 (3rd movement solo)

Wagner, R., *Rhine Journey* (Siegfried's short call)

SUGGESTED READING

Farkas, Philip, *The Art of French Horn Playing*, Summy-Birchard/Warner Bros. Publications.

Tuckwell, Barry, *The Horn*, MacDonald and Co., London.
  (Presently available only through the International Horn Society)

The Horn Call: Journal of the International Horn Society (journals issued four times a year)

13. Recitals Are a Good Thing

What follows is directed at the ambitious high school student, all college-level students, and those special adults who have the desire to advance as performers through the experience of public solo and/or chamber music performances. Recitals take a great deal of dedication but serve a major role in one's growth as an artistic individual, and that's a good thing.

An intelligently planned, thoroughly prepared, and ultimately well-performed recital can do more for a student's personal musical development than any other single event. Now, that's a strong statement and potentially a good thing. Recitals provide an opportunity for performers to focus on a conscientiously selected group of compositions for an extended period of time, after which they get to share their best playing in a formal setting with friends and family. Preparing for recitals provides the student with a goal that includes a deadline and the reality of an eminent performance setting, which can greatly enhance the content and seriousness of many a practice session. Recitals are, in fact, an extraordinary taste of reality for young performers, with regards to how well they are progressing and how well they can actually perform at the moment. The numerous additional experiences gained from formulating, organizing, and administering all facets of a recital are also extremely valuable for a student's perspective and future in many aspects of the business of musical performance.

The most popular recital format is the pure solo recital, which usually involves a pianist to perform transcribed orchestral accompaniments, piano accompaniments, or as a chamber music colleague through the sonata repertoire. A full hour or more of such music requires a great deal from a young (or old) student, especially with regard to physical endurance and mental concentration. It is recommended that each student take every opportunity to perform in public, in front of other students, in classes, for friends and family gatherings, and at church services. Every opportunity possible should be taken to perform as a soloist. By creating small servings of what a full recital will become, it gets the body, the mind, and the spirit ready for the full course of a complete recital.

WHAT TO PREPARE

Planning such an event requires extensive thought, organization, and decision-making. For the typical solo recital, start with the selection of one very significant piece, perhaps a major concerto you have always enjoyed but never prepared or performed. The basic repertoire is a great place to start for such a work. If that chosen composition is from the romantic period (e.g., Strauss, Glière, Schumann, Czerny), then you might consider looking next for a work from the classical period (e.g., Mozart, Haydn, Beethoven), which would provide balance and contrast. Make note of the exact timings for these larger works, and then begin to find shorter baroque and/or contemporary works that might fill in the 45 to 65 minutes of music that is typical for most solo wind or brass recitals. This manner of selecting recital repertoire could be called the variety-show approach. The order of such a selection of works could be decided based upon the character and lengths of each of the pieces. However, you might also wish to start with the piece that feels most comfortable to play and end with the one that is either the lightest in style or that is most appropriate to your own strengths and abilities as a player. Chronological order (by date of composition) is also often interesting for an audience. Whatever you decide, it should be based on solid reasoning, artistic taste, and practical considerations all in balance. A recital with a plan is so much more interesting to prepare for as well as to attend.

Beyond this so-called variety-show design, there is a multitude of possibilities. Your imagination might be the only limitation here. Here are some ideas to get your thoughts rolling:

1. Contrasting pieces from the same historical period.

2. Contrasting works by composers from the same country.

3. Transcriptions of works for other instruments.

4. Compositions all of a lighter nature.

5. Contrasting works by female composers.

6. Single movement pieces interestingly grouped.

7. All or a large grouping of unaccompanied pieces.

8. Lecture recital based upon a research project.

9. All original works written by you or for you.

10. Works all based on folk, jazz, or ethnic cultures.

Chamber music added to a primarily solo recital or as a full recital plan is always well appreciated by the listeners because it opens the recital up to some of the greatest music ever written while it also provides both aural and visual variety. (With more people on the stage, there are also usually more people in the audience.) Of at least equal importance to the performer, intimate collaboration with other instrumentalists and/or singers through this music reaches the highest level of aesthetic communication available to the human species. Chamber music is a good thing! Though at the purely practical level it does take on many additional scheduling problems during the planning stages, it is (almost always) worth it.

As horn players, it is important to live with, learn, and perform the following: Brahms Trio, Op. 40; the Mozart Quintets, KV407 and KV452; the Britten *Canticle III*; the Beethoven Quintet, Op. 16, and Sextet, Op. 81b; Schubert's *Auf dem Strom* and Octet in F; the Nielsen Quintet, Op. 43; the Hindemith Sonata for four horns; and the Poulenc Sonata for brass trio and Sextet for wind quintet and piano. This will lay down the foundation for a professional level of musical competency in varied performance styles and heighten one's abilities to listen and spontaneously react to others. Cooperation and teamwork never reach such refined levels as in a well-prepared chamber music performance.

As you might expect, the decisions necessary in planning for a chamber recital are also quite numerous. Regarding repertoire, the previously mentioned pieces would obviously head a list of recommendations. Creating an hour's worth of music from that list would create a very special event. The following are a few more thoughts to take into consideration and to stimulate your own thinking and planning:

1. Become part of a working brass or woodwind quintet for multiple concerts.

2. Become part of a working violin, horn, piano trio (many fine works).

3. Become part of a working horn quartet (extensive new repertoire).

4. Choose a musician friend or friends you wish to work with and select repertoire that uses their instruments or voice types.

4. Choose a variety of timbres for the audience's enjoyment.

5. Choose from varied periods and use the horns and performance styles of those periods.

6. Prepare a recital of varied trios, quartets, or quintets.

7. Prepare a recital of horn duets, trios, and quartets.

8. Choose pieces for instruments that are not that familiar (e.g., harp, guitar).

9. Choose pieces requiring instrumentalists you wish to get to know.

10. Choose established ensembles with whom you wish to work, perhaps those being coached by someone from whom you wish to learn.

To continue at an even more practical level, it's recommended that you consider the following outline as a way of preparing for and creating these special moments in your musical life.

HOW TO PREPARE

1. **Begin to prepare the entire program three to four months in advance.**

   A. Choose the repertoire considering your abilities, needs, and preferences. Do this in conference with a mentor when possible. Have a plan or reason for the inclusion of every piece. Include basic repertoire as well as new works for you and for your audience.

   B. Consider a timing of 60 to 90 minutes maximum for the event (i.e., 45 o 65 minutes of actual music).

   C. Contact the musicians you wish to use immediately. Get the very best musicians you possibly can. Arrive at a mutual date and time for the recital. Request a firm commitment from all. Give each of them details in writing.

   D. Buy your own personal copies of all the music, make a photocopy of each part for safety only, destroy such copies after the recital, and distribute all original parts immediately. Plan rehearsal times as soon as possible and distribute the schedule in writing to all participants.

2. **Study the music (not just your part) thoroughly. Practice your own part in depth.**

   A. Listen to numerous recordings of these pieces and take notes of what you hear.

   B. Look for and study other editions of these works when possible, and take notes.

   C. Enjoy a special feeling for each of these pieces, growing with its familiarity.

3. **Practice performing, but don't just practice repeating. Begin performing in the practice room alone (while imagining the entire audience).**

   A. After your music has been fully learned a number of weeks before the recital, use your imagination to create the look and feel of the audience and the hall.

   B. Enter from the outside of your practice space, walk confidently to your music stand in front of a mirror (if possible), smile, bow, and perform complete run-throughs as often as possible. Count the rests, and hear the other part(s) in your mind.

   C. Bow, smile, acknowledge the other performers, and walk happily out of the room. All that you do is a part of the performance, so practice the performance. The actual recital will then be just another run-through for that audience as you have seen them so many times before.

4. **Begin full rehearsals as soon as possible and no later than 60 days in advance.**

   A. Schedule lessons and coachings with a mentor when appropriate.

   B. Plan informal performances of all pieces two or three weeks in advance of the recital.

   C. Tape-record your run-through rehearsals and informal performances several times, and then listen together with the other participants and talk about what you hear or would like to hear.

   D. Arrange early for a professional recording engineer to record your recital. Such tapes are invaluable information for your learning and growth as a performer, and live recordings when done exceptionally well are the best options for audition tapes in the future.

5. **Plan and prepare your printed program and publicity at least three weeks in advance.**

   A. Research all aspects of each piece and each composer for personal understanding and for eventual interesting program notes.

   B. Prepare an accurate and complete program with composers' full names, dates, opus numbers or dates of composition, and the names of all movements or sections.

   C. List all performers' names with their preferred spellings and their instruments.

D. Include in the printed program when appropriate balanced program notes for each piece, which will aid the audience in their enjoyment and understanding of the music. It is also appreciated when you include your own personal ideas and feelings about the recital. Under certain circumstances, verbal program notes are quite effective since they tend to break down the perceived distance between the audience and the performers.

E. Have the program printed on special paper. This shows respect for your audience. It is also true that recital programs are documents of your hard work. They should be saved since they will probably be referred to later in your career.

F. Publicize the event one to three weeks in advance. Create a clever, clear, concise, and colorful poster and post it in an appropriate place where your probable audience will notice it. Inform friends and family via e-mail, phone, post, and whatever works. They won't come if they don't know. Also, don't be reluctant to inform the local papers and public radio stations. Send them programs, posters, and a personal note. Such confidence in what you are doing is a good thing.

5. **Schedule a dress rehearsal in the hall during the week preceding the event including all participants. Plan to play through the pieces in concert order if possible.**

A. Decide seating and/or standing positions for each piece, considering both acoustics and appearance. Have someone listen from out in the audience to support your decisions.

B. Discuss all aspects of stage presence, including walking on, bowing, walking off, and returning to the stage. Practice all aspects thinking of the audience.

C. Discuss fully with all participants what specifically to wear. You should be dressed with respect for your audience, and your attire should be consistent in style with the other performers to avoid conflicting colors.

6. **Have a practice plan for the two days before and the day of the recital.** Stay consistent with what your body and embouchure are used to. Don't overdo or under-do. Know yourself and enjoy the anticipation, being proud of how well prepared you are.

7. **Plan all along to be relaxed, confident, focused, and enthusiastic.** Feel grateful for all that you can do and all of your blessed talents, and feel thankful for all the friends who will be attending your recital, wishing you your very best performance. Stay positive.

PERFORMANCE DAY

This is when the fun happens. This is when you get to share the music. Performing great music with others for others is a good thing. With all of the above information as your solid foundation, your confidence level should be quite high. Knowing you are prepared is powerful. With an intelligent and appropriate warm-up, the day should become focused on the music. Relish those special feelings you have developed for each piece. Sit quietly alone, and think them through note by note while breathing deeply and hearing in your mind's ear a successful performance. Enjoy yourself. Picture the audience enjoying the music and the performance.

Stay relaxed and focused on success. The language you use to talk to yourself and to others before and after the recital should be enthusiastic and positive. Talk to yourself with the language you would use to encourage and reward your very best friend for such efforts.

At the performance, stay focused on why you love this music, how wonderful it is to be performing with your friends, and what it is you wish to say musically. Your mind needs such substantive fuel to keep positive. Always breathe deeply through every moment of the event. Air is your body's fuel and the substance of life. Breathe life and love into your performance. Enjoy!

14. The Respond-able Teacher

These next two chapters are a grouping of thoughts in which I reverse the most common premise regarding the teacher/student relationship. The usual interpretation of this relationship is that the teacher is responsible for the imparting of knowledge to the student, and the respectful student is to respond to these directives, memorize them, and thus learn. I believe strongly that while teaching a person about musical performance the private instructor needs to develop a "respond-ability" to the timely needs of the student while imparting the appropriate knowledge. The student, in turn, must accept much of the responsibility for the actual learning by bringing all that he or she knows into each lesson.

To effectively teach another person is an important responsibility. The ability to respond to another person effectively is of vital importance to teaching. Listening, reacting, responding, and reforming our teaching tools with each student at each lesson reaches the most people and seems to be the most effective way to actually help them to continue their growth as performers and as self-fulfilled human beings.

As young beginning teachers, most of us found ourselves teaching as we were taught. Why? Because it was convenient and it worked, at least once. Now that we are the authorities, it is easy to assume that our own personal road to success is the best way to go. However, if we look back on our roads, we could surely identify many happy (and not so happy) accidents, coincidences, and chaotic events that helped us learn but had not been assigned, nor were they part of our teacher's plan. So if this early pattern of teacher impersonating is fully adopted and never questioned, then logically the only students who would benefit would be those with the same experiences, value systems, talent quotients, and intelligence as ourselves when we were their ages. If our students do not naturally fit this pattern, then we are requiring them to adjust constantly to our own personal master plan. We are limiting many necessary options both for them and for ourselves as growing, learning teachers. Of course, our students must learn to adjust and must learn to follow directives. Much of this can be done most effectively through emulation and imitation. So then let us take this one step beyond the obvious and while teaching, demonstrate our abilities to imitate, follow, and even adjust to and for our students. Said in another way, if I wish for them to learn to listen, react appropriately, respond, and reform their techniques, then I should openly demonstrate such abilities in my relationships with them during our lessons together.

It has often been demonstrated that the most important substantive learning is not generated from the materials being chosen. Real learning is much more abstract than that. If it were simply the perfect materials presented in a magical order that showed us the way, then we could learn all we needed from books. And in a similar light, to assume that to demonstrate a perfectly executed solo for a student in any way teaches him or her how to do the same is simplistic and largely incorrect. It is the process we teachers must teach to our students. The products (that is, polished performances) are readily available with each new recording and live performance. Obviously, these products are of vital importance for a student's perspective and inspiration, but do they actually teach?

Let us look deeper into the use of imitation as a mode of teaching. We teachers have within ourselves sufficient experiences to become fine lesson-giving improvisers. What we know and have experienced should allow us to respond to the correct and incorrect processes as well as the correct and less correct products of our students. If we wish for students to adjust to our ideas, we must learn how to adjust to theirs. If we expect them to learn to follow instructions, hints, or directives from us, we should take such cues, however subtle, from them and lead them by following their immediate needs into an effective and timely process of improvement. As an example, let us say that we wish for students to improve their tonal concept. To juxtapose our sound next to theirs and say, simply, "sound like that" is to ignore the process and to set up that lesson as a forum for failure. If, instead, we could empathize with their actual sound at that very moment, could feel for ourselves the manner in which they are producing that sound based on our experiences in the past, we could begin gradually to introduce them to a possible process for improvement. That process could be what we did, or what we would do under those circumstances if that were our sound. Begin by asking them the questions you would ask yourself if you were alone with this problem. Respond verbally to their attempts at a solution as you would respond to yourself if you thought those thoughts or made those particular sounds. Be with them, suffer their feeling of confusion, stimulate their problem-solving abilities, help them find their own way, and be ready to celebrate with them when they have finally arrived at their own solution, no matter how partial that solution might be.

The most important moments in our growth as performers come during those practice sessions when we are alone and very aware of exactly what is happening, when we are having strong feelings of optimism, feelings of emotional and physical strength, and the idealistic belief that we alone can solve the problems at hand, be they musical or physically developmental. So it is up to us, the teachers, to create an environment during each lesson for students to somehow find those characteristic problem-solving powers within themselves. It is up to us to help them experience some aspect of optimism, emotional and physical strength, and especially idealistic thoughts that they alone can solve their problems by creatively processing what they already know.

My three principal horn teachers—Jack Snider at the University of Nebraska, Philip Farkas at Indiana University, and Paul Ingraham at Yale University—helped me feel just such personal empowerment during and after numerous lessons. They helped me find my way, and they celebrated with me my successes. They even allowed me a certain self-indulgent attitude now and then at a time when I needed such power within myself to improve. Consequently, they made it seem as if I didn't need them all that much. How can I thank them enough?

To some extent, I guess I still do teach as I was taught. However, I've chosen to emulate my teachers' attitudes, not their words, personalities, or even all of the same written materials. I've instinctively chosen to incorporate into my teaching their love for the horn, their love of teaching people about music, and their intense interest in that one moment, lesson after lesson, when we were together trying to find my solutions to my problems.

As teachers, we can challenge ourselves to be actively reactive and to develop our abilities to spontaneously respond to each moment of discovery during each and every lesson. We should learn to read our students by listening and watching and asking them the questions they need to ask themselves. We must help all students find far-reaching answers to their most pressing questions.

I can imagine no loftier purpose in life than to be an active participant in the powerful and positive evolutionary process of learning. The art of spontaneous, improvisational teaching seems to be a most effective way to indulge in that purpose. Mr. Snider, Mr. Farkas, and Mr. Ingraham certainly dedicated themselves to this purpose many times over and, thankfully, I am one of the many recipients. To dedicate oneself to the continuation of such a process is a wonderful opportunity and an awesome responsibility. So let us all respond accordingly.

15. The Responsible Student

According to Pablo Casals in his book Joys and Sorrows, *just the fact that you have talent is no reason to be vain. You did nothing to acquire talent; it was given to you. What you do with that talent is most important. Continually work to develop and nurture it.*

And Gunther Schuller says in his book Horn Technique, *"Given an adequate talent, a player will only be as good as he wants to be."*

Both of the above statements put a great deal of personal responsibility on the individual student. This is as it should be, because that's the way it is!

While growing into maturity as performing musicians, we all have been tempted to look for shortcuts for the quickest ways to arrive at our lofty goals. We would like to believe that if we own the ''best'' brand of instrument, read all the "best" books, and study from the "best" teacher, we would soon become the "best" performer. What we often do is look outside of ourselves for that winning recipe for success while ignoring the long, strong look inside for our own personal answers.

"A man should learn to detect and watch that gleam of light which flashes across his mind from within, more than the lustre of the firmament of bards and sages." Ralph Waldo Emerson, *Self-Reliance*

We must learn to trust our own intuitions and our abilities to take all that we know and have experienced and put it together into those answers needed for each moment of learning. Learning is like eating a meal. While we are learning we meet people, hear music, read books, watch videos, go to lectures, and take lessons. All of these are good for us only if we fully digest that which is necessary for growth.

"As the human body does not live by the foods we eat, but by those we digest, similarly the human mind does not evolve by everything we read, but only by that which we mentally assimilate."[4] Edmond B. Szekely, *The Art of Study*

Long ago, the human species chose to learn to control and educate the mind and mental processes and leave the digestive system alone to continue on its own with no interference from our conscious manipulating. Evolutionarily speaking, that part of the body seems to be doing well for itself. Much of what we've done with our educational system, however, has tended to complicate as much as clarify our natural mental tendencies. If we could learn to listen to and trust our own inner voices (what we feel is true for us at any given moment), we could more quickly and thoroughly nourish the positive processes of learning, and we could better use our digested experiences for our own growth. We would be healthier and, consequently, happier students.

Now let's bring this much closer to home. Let's talk about taking lessons. If what Confucius said is true, "The greatest wisdom is to know what we know, and to know what we do not know," then we all need help from other sources to clarify the details. Private lessons are the single most effective way for one person to learn from another person, as long as the activity is founded on sharing information and perspectives and not on superficial role-playing (e.g., master and disciple). In the previous chapter, "The Respond-able Teacher," I suggested that the teacher's primary role is to respond to specific student needs and concerns, and mind-sets and manners of learning, and to work together with the student as a team toward the ultimate goal of learning how to learn.

"Learning is facilitated when the student participates responsibly in the learning process. When he chooses his own directions, helps to discover his own learning resources, formulates his own problems, decides his own course of action, lives with the consequences of each of these choices, then significant learning is maximized."[5] Carl Rogers, *Freedom to Learn*

This doesn't mean or assume that students already know everything they need to know. It means that they are responsible for finding out what they do know and what they do not know. They must become their own best teachers. Said in another way, let us do unto ourselves what we would have our teachers do unto us.

As a student, you should feel responsible to inform your private teacher about what has worked well for you regarding etudes, exercises, and warm-ups. This may require extensive thought and self-analysis, which is good. You should feel free and comfortable to inform the teacher as to what your perceived strengths are. This will take some objective thinking as well, but it is vitally important for you to have thought this through. It is equally important for you to believe in these strengths and base your growth and self-confidence upon them. You should also clearly communicate to your teacher your present goals for the near and distant future, as well as your plans for achieving these goals.

To go to your teacher having only discussed and demonstrated your weaknesses and worries gives a very shallow picture of all that should be known. It also leaves a concerned teacher too much room to jump in with experimental solutions that could waste time and perhaps cause harm. This may not be the fault of poor teaching. We teachers simply cannot be held responsible for not knowing what you have failed to tell us. Your "weaknesses" will certainly reveal themselves with little or no fanfare. However, your teacher does need to know what is bothering you most at any given lesson time. Such specific and timely information, along with the information shared at earlier lessons, should combine in a way that allows both the student and teacher to arrive at a viable solution to an urgent problem.

The responsible student feels full ownership for successes and mistakes and thoughtfully uses this most valuable information for the future. Whenever possible, the responsible student designs lessons around what seems most pressing, what is the most polished, what might contrast last week's lesson, or what could be a forum to discuss a topic of timely importance. Such lesson planning should intelligently relate primarily to short-term goals while always considering an overview of long-term goals. Materials presented at lessons should come from a much larger body of materials in preparation. A teacher can't possibly hear all that should be under way. However, it will soon become obvious to the teacher that a student is practicing a large cross-section of materials by the way any single piece of music is demonstrated.

Keeping track of all that you need to do to progress seems daunting. Now imagine what happens to a teacher of 15 to 20 students (or more), who finds him or herself feeling fully responsible for all aspects of their learning. The chances are that you, as one of those students, will possibly be shortchanged. Assignments and expectations will be by necessity abbreviated in one way or another. I'm sure this is not your hope or plan. So since this is your career, do all that you can to take the controls.

So, where do you start? I'm sure you already have. Look over how you practice. Has it improved your playing today or this past week? How? Why? Is your practicing organized, thoughtful, and varied? Do you have a plan for every aspect of your practicing? You must have a plan for each work, each session, each day, each week, each month, each year. Plan also to leave each practice session being able to do something better than when you began. That's one good basic plan.

What follows is another detailed basic practice plan that seems to have helped many of my more motivated students to take control over their own improvement:

1. Look over your selected study or composition and decide as best you can the composer's intentions both technically and musically. Take all the time you need.

2. Decide its value(s) for your technical and musical needs at present. Plan what you hope to accomplish through this work.

3. Slowly and carefully go through the entire work away from your horn. Sing it aloud a number of times, considering all accidentals, dynamics, articulations, breaths, musical ideas, and so on.

4. Now, with Nos. 1, 2, and 3 above in mind, read through the work very slowly with your horn. Don't miss a thing. Always produce a full and beautiful tone.

5. Mentally go back over the sections that seemed most problematic. Decide why. With your horn, practice these sections slowly until they become as fluent as the rest of the work.

6. Now repeat the entire work "perfectly" at this original slow tempo a number of times, always considering Nos. 1 and 2 above.

7. Begin gradually to increase the tempo using a metronome when practical. Increase the tempo only a few beats per second at each run-through. (Reference to a chromatic tuner might help.)

8. If not indicated, decide on a tempo that best suits the musical and technical characteristics of the work and decide upon new breath marks at this faster tempo. Then begin to polish.

9. After it is fully prepared, play it through several times "perfectly." Only at this point in your preparation can you actually begin to practice the art of performing. Up to this point you have been problem solving. Enjoy your achievement over and over again.

10. Take time now to review what you have accomplished and learned both technically and musically. Were your original perceptions and plans in No. 2 above appropriate to these eventual results? Will you change your approach next time? Have you discovered new needs requiring further study?

11. Now take the above work to a lesson, or not. It's your choice.

It is important to notice that we tend to "perfect" what we practice and how we practice. It is true that if we practice well, we perform well. The opposite is also true.

To keep track of all that you need to be working on is certainly overwhelming. So make a list, or use the list below as a point of departure. While you are considering such details, rate yourself for each aspect of concern using a numerical system, such as the following:

5-Excellent, 4-Good, 3-Average, 2-Problems, 1-Get to work!

1. Playing position/posture: standing and sitting

2. Fingerings: F horn, B♭ horn, and optional

3. Tuning: in general and extremes (use chromatic tuner)

4. Breathing: efficiency, control, capacity

5. Embouchure: mouthpiece placement, muscular focus, relationship to air, various ranges

6. Tonguing: clarity, fluency, variety, double, triple, flutter

7. Slurring: various intervals, various dynamics, register changes

8. Tone quality: centered resonance, consistency in all registers, varieties of timbre

9. Ranges: extremes, clear controlled sounds (high, middle, mid-low, low)

10. Dynamics: response, control, and intonation at all extremes and in all ranges

11. Accuracy: initial attacks at all dynamics, consistency hearing entrance notes and intervals

12. Endurance: ease of production at all levels of fatigue in all ranges

13. Concentration: ability to mentally focus for long periods

14. Lip trills: fluency, control at all dynamics, knowledge of all fingerings, also lip tremolos

15. Stopped horn: tonal control, responses, projection, F and B♭ fingerings

16. Muted horn: tonal control, responses, projection, noiseless manipulation of mute

17. Transpositions: E♭, E, D, C, G, B♭ basso, A, B, B♭ alto, C alto, A♭ , F♯, D♭ (approximate order of use)

18. Sight reading: bass clef, "old notation bass clef," key signatures, varied styles and periods, meter changes, complex rhythms

19. Vibrato: control in all ranges, varied styles and manners

20. Extended techniques: glissandi, vocalizations, half-valve techniques, quarter-tone fingerings, combinations

21. Hand horn: concepts, techniques

22. Jazz horn: concepts, techniques

23. Coordination: successfully combining above elements

24. Repertoire: knowing the basic solos, etudes, chamber music, technical studies, excerpts

25. Warm-up/maintenance session: progressive, daily routine incorporating much of the above, personally designed and modified over time

As you add to this extensive and all-important list and include your own personal objective ratings for each element, you will clearly see what needs the most work. Keep track of all your work and reactions to it in a journal or practice diary. Such a thoughtful postlude to your practice routine will reap surprising rewards over time. The specifics of your lessons should also be written down (transcribed from a tape or disc recording, whenever possible). Take the time to document your improvements, mistakes, impressions, hopes, frustrations, and successes. A practice/performance journal is highly recommended.

Another important element in taking control of your own learning while gaining valuable perspectives is the development of your own library of basic literature for the horn. How do you decide what is "basic" and what is "best"? It takes time—lots of time—but that's the point. The time spent searching for and listening to repertoire becomes your experiences, and it is only through experiences that you actually learn anything. Search through solo contest lists looking for the common pieces. Study discographies to see which solos are recorded most often by major soloists. Listen to as many recordings as you can find in the libraries or borrow them from colleagues. Keep accurate notes on your impressions and begin to purchase your own collection. Competitions for solo performances at the national and international levels will also tell a great deal about which works are considered important to our instrument. You should also ask your teacher and other teachers what materials they enjoy coaching and performing. Ask them which of those they find most lasting. Lasting power tells a great deal about the depth and quality of a work of art.

Excerpts from the orchestral repertoire must also be collected and studied for many reasons. It is very important that we all become fully aware of what the greatest composers think the horn does best. Excerpts are also the means to acquiring a job, from community orchestras to major professional orchestras. Teaching positions also assume an expertise in this repertoire. How do you know where to start? Attend orchestra concerts every chance you get. Listen to the composer's style and the way the horn is used with other instruments, and notice and remember the exposed solos. Keep notes on what you hear and learn. Notice what pieces appear most often on the season listings for various orchestras. Acquire excerpt books that have been recently published. (Arthur T. LaBar's *The Horn Player's Audition Handbook* and Richard Moore's *Anthology of French Horn Music* are fine publications for the excerpts most frequently requested at auditions in recent years; see Chapter 24.) Always listen to complete orchestral performances first. Know the music, and then learn the excerpts. After having studied the context and having listened to the entire composition a number of times, take the prepared excerpts to a qualified teacher or teachers for their input. Keep notes and look for common ground regarding tempos, articulations, dynamics, and stylistic ideas. Excerpts are the repertoire that you must assimilate to the point of memorization, especially if you plan to participate in professional auditions. If you really want to do it right, collect scores and all important horn parts available and do a thorough study. (Please see the chapter "Professional Orchestra Auditioning," Chapter 5, for more details.)

With regard to taking lessons, it is always helpful to "psyche-out" your teachers' personal/professional preferences. What do they like to teach or discuss or perform? What are their experiences? Know your teachers' résumés or ask about their professional activities. Take advantage of their strengths and always help them feel comfortable and enthusiastic during your lessons. These lessons are for your own good, and you might be surprised how much control you have over the chemistry between you and your teachers. This is not advocating a fabricated adulation; this is simply suggesting that you know as much as you can about a most important resource—your teacher. From such thoughtful research and acquired knowledge, you can better evaluate and understand what you are learning in that particular context we call private lessons.

If you ever find yourself in a learning situation where such independent thinking and personal work is discouraged, I suggest you try to deal with it by becoming as much of an observer as a participant. I have personally learned a great deal observing insecure, control-hungry teachers. Let me rephrase the earlier Confucian quote, "The greatest wisdom is to know what we need to know and to know what we do not need to know." If you have accepted responsibility for your own learning and have experienced the empowerment that level of acceptance brings to your sense of self-worth, then you will know best how to cope with, and not inherit, other people's problems.

Finally, be wary of a teacher/student relationship in which you have or are expected to have as your ultimate goal an imitation or emulation of your teacher's manner, horn, mouthpiece, musical preferences, professional experiences, etc.

> "There is a time in every man's education when he arrives at the conviction that envy is ignorance; that imitation is suicide." Ralph Waldo Emerson, *Self-Reliance*

This gentle warning applies to the "full package," not the important individual demonstrations by a well-meaning teacher that instill concepts and show what is possible. That type of imitation is an important tool for the teacher and can be an important resource for learning. My concern is for the students who are made to feel that they must be like someone else. You can't be! It is that simple. You will waste a large amount of your valuable time looking outside of yourself for what is already inside just waiting to be discovered. Believe deeply in what you can do, who you are, and what you are becoming. Pay a great deal of attention to your own musical passions, act on them, and always care.

> "Good and bad are but names very readily transferable to this or that; the only right is what is after a man's constitution; the only wrong is against it."

> "Nothing is at last sacred but the integrity of your own mind." Ralph Waldo Emerson, *Self-Reliance*

16. One Way to Teach

After having taught for many years, primarily at the college and advanced high school levels, I was invited to share my approach to teaching through an interview. That interview eventually became an article, and now that article becomes an important chapter in my book. It is difficult to explain my teaching, which over the years has evolved into a responsive rather than a prescriptive manner. Many of the particulars from which I draw my responses are easier to explain and are presented throughout this book.

One might describe my method of teaching as an unstructured structure. I have attempted to explain what I've done in the past by describing certain identifiable consistencies, however vague. Please refer to the chapter "The Respond-able Teacher" for further discussion.

After having taught for a short while, it became obvious that how I had been taught and what I had previously thought about teaching was not working for me as a teacher. I began to read a great deal from many disciplines and began to experiment with ideas that were primarily student-oriented. What soon developed was an approach in which I would teach people rather than teach a structured method with a planned sequence of literature requiring particular equipment. Each of those aspects of method certainly does constitute important considerations in the development of all musicians. However, most of my students seemed to need to be nurtured, encouraged, and informed more than they needed to be forced or led down a predetermined path to success, a path decided on by this one person with only one set of experiences. Though many of us teachers maintain an active and admirable playing career, is it best for us to assume that our students should do what we do as we have chosen to do it? Should imitation and adulation be their way? It has become quite obvious over the years that such an assumption, if taken at full value, is ill-advised, self-aggrandizing and, much more important, far too limiting for them.

I have chosen not to prescribe or indoctrinate, but instead, to consider my role to be a "primary resource" for students. Ultimately, the teacher should become obsolete, except perhaps as an occasional resource (maybe even a friend). Therefore, I purposely avoid the typical master/disciple relationship in all ways possible and try instead to respond to students' immediate needs rather than to prescribe a grand plan of study. Students tend to learn and remember those things that are important or have value to them at a given time. To be aware of all of this, a teacher must remain open to students' immediate concerns, lesson after lesson, rather than be too eager to administer some preordained master plan. A personal/professional relationship with the student is the key, to strive for communication as a helper rather than to be the perfect example or the primary motivator.

Of course, all students need goals and structure, but such important conclusions should be planned for and decided upon by the students themselves. When that happens, their plans become much more important. So I ask them the kinds of questions that might reveal a potential plan or at least a source of motivational direction. Through their answers, they set their own goals, and then I contribute what I might know that can help them find ways to reach those goals. During each of their lessons, notes are taken and kept in their files. Follow-ups on these annotated experiences, concerns, and plans occur when needed or appropriate. Such record keeping also helps me to observe patterns that allow me to ask better questions. Students do take themselves quite seriously and do honestly wish to improve. Sometimes they just don't quite know how.

I sincerely believe that all students do the best they can at all times. A teacher must be aware that there are a tremendous number of unknown aspects to students' lives and, thus, must give them the benefit of the doubt. Just because my students' priorities may not seem ideal (an ideal derived from my own value system and past choices) doesn't mean they aren't serious about their work. This fundamental belief becomes the foundation for mutual respect and substantive communication. Learning doesn't always seem to follow a logical progression of improvement. Most learning occurs in shifts—sudden insights, unexpected discoveries, and *ah-ha*'s. Understanding or at least accepting a student's erratic learning patterns allows a teacher to strike when a particular aspect is sparking or when a new awareness level is hot.

In short, I have chosen to teach *people*. The *subject* is the horn and all of its related materials and aspects. The horn is what brings us together and serves as the focus for our relationship. The *language* we try to understand or experience through these many and varied activities is *music*. The principal *objective* is to fully discover the student's particular abilities and most effective manners of learning and to make sure that the student realizes how to utilize this knowledge for *self-learning*.

To bring all of this about, I try to shift the responsibility of learning to the student as soon and in as many ways as possible. (Please see the chapter "The Responsible Student" for an in-depth discussion.) To begin our lessons together, I often give studentes a folder of etudes, excerpts, and duets covering the basic technical and musical requirements for a hornist, asking them to prepare these in whatever order they choose. Each week they bring in their chosen preparations. Upon listening, notes are made regarding all aspects of the performances and regarding the particular items chosen to be performed. This gives us time to get to know each other, and allows us to see better each student's strengths and weaknesses. It also demonstrates what students wish to show me about themselves.

Some students prepare only those examples that will sound most impressive, while avoiding their problems. Others will immediately bring in what they cannot seem to do or do not understand. Most, however, combine these two extremes. Thus, they are all immediately permitted many controlled choices while getting to work on a cross section of problems that helps them identify their own needs, perhaps for the first time. After an appropriate amount of time, we discuss together what has transpired, and together we plan a specific set of goals (e.g., a selection of appropriate materials) both for the short-term and the long-term. Of course, changes are inevitable, but from this exercise we can both know a great deal more about what needs to be done to create an effective structure for this individual. Another advantage for the student is that such an exercise delays the normal tendency for me to dive into the relationship by immediately teaching my favorite or most immediately effective lessons to impress the student with my own particular brilliance. Teachers have a tendency to want to impress the students too.

It has proven to be important that the studio environment where the lessons are taught be both physically and psychically comfortable. This involves a number of small touches. Number one is to place the student at the center of the conversational space. That space needs sufficient light (full-spectrum bulbs are best) and a comfortable chair with an adjustable stand so the student is facing the teacher's chair and desk. The student should also be between the teacher and the outside door. (This might seem unnecessary at the conscious level, so I consider it at the unconscious level for certain young students and accommodate.) Plants and warm colors always help create a comfortable mood. Wall hangings and knickknacks that emphasize the horn are preferable to those that emphasize the fame and prowess of the instructor. If the teacher always sits or stands at eye level with the student, if the teacher talks *with* rather than *to* the student, and if both the teacher and student feel free to tell each other what needs to be said for mutual growth and understanding, then we have a good chance for a successful learning relationship.

Throughout my teaching, I have consciously tried to emphasize the positive. It is often revealing to ask students what they do well on the horn, in other words, what their major strengths are. Frequently, they can't even think of what to say, or they find saying it very uncomfortable. Too much time is spent in our educational system focusing on what's wrong. (While I was growing up, all the marks on my papers were to acknowledge the errors. Little was ever said about the right answers; they were certainly never adorned with the bright red pencil.) Such an emphasis on the negative can bring students to the point where they are totally unaware of what is right with themselves or with their playing. Lessons, in turn, need not be a weekly appointment for fault finding. A positive outlook provides the foundation for significant learning. Our bodies and our minds grow with the best food and the best food for thought. I try to interpret all events in a lesson or performance as learning, which is our ultimate objective. Mistakes are not failures; they provide basic information we need if we wish to grow. If we set expectations for ourselves or for our students that are doomed to failure (e.g., If you don't win this audition, or if your solo performance gets a bad review, then you have failed!), then we are creating negative, demeaning, damaging goals. Expectations for each event in their musical lives should be communicated to students as a license to learn. A performance is not the final destination for all of their practicing, proving once and for all their worth as musicians. It is much more important than that. It is the concentrated context where they gain new and valuable information about themselves as performers. Everything they do should be openly represented as an opportunity to learn.

Consequently, students should spend much of their time observing and documenting in journals what works for them in practice, lessons, rehearsals, and performances. What doesn't work is important information that can and should be forgotten as soon as it is replaced by a positive solution. Looking back too often might cause students to lose sight of all that is ahead of them just waiting to be enjoyed. We must encourage all students to continue on, looking ahead and enjoying all the new solutions and abilities there to be discovered and incorporated.

To aid the student in developing these attitudes and approaches, I spend a great deal of time encouraging the discovery of various aspects of relaxation, both physical and mental. (See the chapter "Relaxation and the Performing Musician" for further discussion.) The physical sensations of heat and heaviness are important for the body and the mind. Calm and confident thoughts are also important for the mind and the body. They all work together to allow us to do our best. Deep breathing (and all that it involves) is central to all of the above, while it conveniently supplies the horn player with the necessary fuel for that beautiful, warm, confident tone.

Thoughts and/or spoken phrases such as "I have a warm, confident, beautiful tone," "I am enthusiastic," "I love what I am doing," "I feel calm and quiet," and "I am truly well prepared" are strong building blocks to be used by the positive student. These are called affirmations or autogenic phrases. When said often by a performer, they bring about desirable results. The antithesis is, unfortunately, more common to many of us: "My sound is weak and wobbly," "Why am I doing this to myself?" "I sure hope I don't get nervous," or "I wish I had just one more day to practice." We all know what these powerful thoughts can cause. Our society, however, seems to reinforce such negative self-talk and even considers it normal, while there is a tendency to denounce more positive thoughts, considering them to be conceited or self-centered. Centering on one's self is actually the idea behind learning. To play well, students must feel well, both mentally and physically. They must focus on the best, believe in the best, and expect the best of themselves.

If students can learn to know themselves, trust in their own special talents, truly enjoy their many practice sessions and performances, and even admire themselves as worthy individuals, only then will they make the most of their music and their musical lives. It is our responsibility as teachers to help to find the passages needed for each student to arrive at such levels of confidence.

This is not the easiest way to teach. The presentation of set patterns of learning, the use of established methods, incorporating an exact progression of materials, and the use of simple imitation ("do it like this") is the easiest way to teach. That way does actually work now and then depending largely on the flexibility, intelligence, talent, and all other experiences of each individual student. (That translates into a large number of qualifications.) The way I have chosen to teach works for me, so I will be the most comfortable and effective working this way. There is only one way to teach, and that is whatever way helps each student find his or her best way to learn. Each teacher must find his or her own way to do that. However, I do highly recommend letting each and every student's individuality help you to decide. Such a way keeps the act of teaching interesting, often stimulating, and sometimes just plain thrilling.

RECOMMENDED FURTHER READING

Ferguson, Marilyn, *The Aquarian Conspiracy*, J. P. Tarcher Inc., 1980. (Especially Chapter 9, "Flying and Seeing: New Ways to Learn")

Gardner, Howard, *Multiple Intelligences: The Theory in Practice*, Basic Books, 1993. (Based on his concept of individual competencies, multiple writings on the results of a decade of applications)

Kohn, Alfie, *No Contest: The Case Against Competition*, Houghton Mifflin Revised Edition, 1992. (Many powerful arguments on "Why we lose in our race to win.")

Montessori, Maria, *The Absorbent Mind*, Dell Publishing Co., 1967. (Based on her lectures regarding early education)

Palmer, Parker J., *The Courage to Teach: Exploring the Inner Landscape of a Teacher's Life*, Jossey-Bass Publishers, 1998. (A brilliant discussion on who is the self that does the teaching)

Rogers, Carl R., *Freedom to Learn*, Charles E. Merrill Publishing, 1969. (Based on 35 years of innovative thinking on educational processes)

Schwartz, Barry N. (ed.), *Affirmative Education*, A Spectrum Book, 1971. (Radical approaches to education by 18 authors)

Creativity and the Complete Musical Self

17. Derivative Etudes: Create Your Own

The next four chapters all focus on thoughts about the creative process, how it works, and how it can be used by performers to better their interpretive skills. Each was originally presented as a talk and discussion session focusing on the same subject while examining different objectives. The contents include creating personal etudes to solve performance problems, jazz and improvisation as a means of personal expression and for freeing up performance inhibitions, composing for the purpose of finding one's deepest musical thoughts and for learning to empathize with the great composers, and the art of thought and its applications toward the creative process through cadenza writing, etudes, improvisation, and composition. Since each was a separate presentation, there is cross-over and some repetition of ideas. These common threads constitute significant points worth repeating, so they have been left intact for reasons of completeness within their own particular contexts.

All students of music have learned to practice etudes and in most cases understand them to be a successful means to the end result of technical competency. There are also a few etudes that address musical awareness. During the earlier stages of development, this broad-based approach to growth is totally appropriate. However, after having reached a level of technical competency and musical maturity, which allows performance of the basic repertoire of the masters, this general shotgun approach doesn't seem to hit the mark very often. General etudes seem to lose their function as the most appropriate means to an end.

Once one reaches a level of musical seriousness where detailed problems require artistic solutions in addition to technical answers, it becomes necessary to examine the methods for improvement. One must delve deeper in the search for new ways to balance the craft with the art and the technician with the musician. What can one do to raise competency to the level of artistry?

For master composers to create a new work requires innumerable technical considerations, trials, and errors. Then for the successful communication of the piece, they are ultimately dependent upon the skills and insights of the performer. For the performer, technical abilities, trials and errors, and a dependency on the musical substance of the composer's creation are required for successful performances. The composer-performer connection forms a sophisticated symbiotic relationship.

It is universally understood that Mozart, Beethoven, and Brahms have lived up to their half of this relationship. So how then do performers balance out this relationship and create through sound a masterful performance of a masterful composition? Master the art of understanding. In other words, learn as much as possible about the art of compositional intent and then decide the best way to convey that intent to others through thought-filled performances.

In an attempt to improve the depth of understanding of a new composition, it is immediately obvious that the usual simple repetitious practicing is not enough. However, performers often indulge in such an approach exclusively while learning a solo or ensemble work. Repetitions do provide us the familiarity needed, but problem-filled repetitions only reinforce the problems. The point or actual intent of the piece may never be realized.

So, is a search for etudes necessary to help you solve these particular problems? This could take a great deal of time, and most etudes are too general in their design to help with such specifics. Instead, consider the etude concept or etude discipline and carry it to a more specific, focused level, one that will aim at and hit the specific targets needed—the other half of that symbiotic balance with those great composers. Perhaps in the process we might even develop a few new skills and build on our own self-respect as creative beings.

Create *solutions* for the challenges of a new piece before those challenges become *problems*. Derivative etudes could be defined as the performer's creation of a series of progressive studies built upon the specific difficulties and requirements, including both technical and musical, of a pre-existing work of music. The results could be a series of original etudes created by the performer with the hopeful end being a more insightful and masterful rendition of the chosen composition. This could also provide the creative performer (i.e., you!) with a greater understanding of the composition in question, a broadened musical maturity, an increased level of learning, and ultimately better performances.

To begin such a process, the performer must first decide, through a thorough and thoughtful examination, what are the actual technical challenges, aesthetic problems, and needed nuances inherent in the chosen composition. To adequately administer such an examination requires profound thoughtfulness and some actual empathy with the composer. Within this search, the performer must also consider his or her own strengths and weaknesses as they relate to the composition's design. This will include identifying technical requirements and personal capabilities initially, as well as one's own musical and interpretive expertise and stylistic experiences. To juxtapose what can be known or felt about the composer's wishes and intentions with one's own experiences and capacities as an artist helps to keep the performer on a practical and purposeful track. It helps to combine the aesthetic with the mundane. The music itself then becomes the teacher, as the performer strives to relate intimately with all that it has to offer both in challenges and rewards. This approach to musical study does indeed contrast with the usual meandering repetitions and run-throughs most common in the initial stages of preparing a new piece of music.

The actual details for such an approach vary as much as the differences in abilities and experiences from one person to the next. However, an effective way to begin could include the finding of a technically demanding section within the work followed by a creative analysis of why that section is difficult for you. You should simply sit and think about it for a while (for quite a while). Write down your thoughts as they come to you. Follow these new discoveries with a set of technical exercises based on the specific problems. Write them out. Develop these ideas as if you were creating a polished exercise book with your name on it for publication. All along you should be practicing these newly derived exercises on your horn, modifying them as you gain further perspectives. After a time, return to the original composition and decide what the composer was trying to do *musically* during this technically demanding section. Next, take your purely technical exercises and use them as the foundation for motives to compose a more extended concert etude. This etude should attempt to capture a concentrated and musically significant variation or multiple variations of the composer's original materials.

As you continue this process for the entire piece, try to be patient. If you have never done such a thorough study of a work, it will seem to take an inordinate amount of time away from your practicing. However, far more time is wasted trying to undo the misunderstandings and misinterpretations developed through mindless repetitions at the initial stages of learning.

For performers to be concerned with the identification of problems within a piece is obviously the most common trait of normal practice routines. However, to compose and to actually create personal musical solutions inspired and derived from the most masterful works for the instrument brings one a step closer to the great composers and to their problems, solutions, and, most important, their musical intentions. With this creatively earned closeness to the great works in the repertoire, you will ideally have also created a better balance in your symbiotic relationships with the masters.

18. Jazz and Horn and More

One major difference between studying and understanding jazz in contrast to classical music is that jazz is made up of individuals and their messages, while classical music is more concerned with established standards, traditions, and manners in which they are conveyed. The jazz musician is primarily concerned with a free and uncluttered expression of the present moment and of themselves, while the classical performer is responsible to the past and to the constant pressure to repeat that high level of perfection required by past traditions. Neither is better than the other, of course. They are just different. For musicians to be comfortable within both mindsets would certainly add greatly to their overall musical capacities. This chapter begins by presenting a brief history of the horn as a jazz instrument and then becomes an informal monologue about improvisation and the positive implications of developing such a creative skill.

"If you've got the feeling and if you've got the beat," according to jazz critic Nat Hentoff as he quotes one of Ellington's sidemen, "you can play jazz on anything. On a comb, on the bagpipes, on the kitchen table with some spoons. Of course, some of those strange instruments will give you a harder time than others. You just got to stick with it, long as it takes." Tom Varner, *Motion Stillness* album (LP), Soul Note SN1067, 1983 (Liner notes by Nat Hentoff).[6]

Throughout the history of jazz, the horn has been considered a less than significant voice. Not many horn players have stuck with it as long as it takes, but there have been a few. According to the foremost jazz historian and former horn player Gunther Schuller in the introduction to his book *Horn Technique* (second edition), the first French horn player to appear and record with a jazz ensemble was Jack Cave in 1939, on Artie Shaw's recording *Frenesi*. Cave went on to record with Pete Rugolo and Henry Mancini well into the 1960s, but never as a leader or improvising soloist. John Graas was perhaps the first to attract significant attention to the horn as a solo jazz instrument. Graas worked initially with the Claude Thornhill jazz orchestra and then moved on to perform (with Jack Cave) in Pete Rugolo's group, as well as with Shorty Rogers and Stan Kenton, among others. Graas began to lead his own groups in California and had a significant influence on the West Coast style of jazz writing through his prolific compositional output. He was actually one of the early third-stream composers, combining jazz and classical constructs. As a recorded performer, his improvisations were, at times, somewhat cumbersome and labored, but he worked with the best players of his time and was a significant pioneer on what at that time might as well have been a comb or a set of bagpipes as far as the jazz world was concerned.

The most significant and successful jazz horn player of this early period was Julius Watkins. Watkins was included in more than one hundred jazz albums from the 1940s until his death in 1977. He recorded and performed often with the who's who of the East Coast jazz scene. These included Miles Davis, Dizzy Gillespie, Thelonious Monk, Oscar Peterson, John Coltrane, Gil Evans, Charlie Mingus, and many recordings with the bassist Oscar Pettiford, to name only a few. Julius Watkins was the very first to reach out beyond the label of a French horn player playing jazz, to the reality of a jazz musician who just happens to play horn. He obviously had the feeling, he got the beat, and he stuck with it a lot longer than it took. For Watkins, the idiosyncracies or peculiarities of the horn were not so much an issue as they seem to have been for most of the classically trained hornists. He had music to express, and the horn just happened to be his chosen medium, his musical voice.

During this early period of jazz horn, others who became involved as sidemen included John Barrows, Gunther Schuller, James Buffington, Vince DeRosa, Earl Chapin, Paul Ingraham, Sandy Siegelstein, Junior Collins, Ray Alonge, and David Amram. Amram also performed as a leader and even wrote an early autobiography that describes his emergence upon the jazz scene. The book is titled *Vibrations: The Adventures and Musical Times of David Amram* and was published in 1968 by Macmillan. Here is a good-spirited, proud, and youthful rambling through Amram's first 35 years of life. David Amram is still very active as a composer and as a world music and jazz performer, conductor, and gregarious personality.

Another wonderfully sensitive jazz hornist who, like Amram, seems to bridge the gap between the earlier period and today is Willie Ruff. He has been performing for decades with the amazing jazz pianist Dwike Mitchell. The Mitchell/Ruff Duo, in which Ruff plays more bass than horn, has recorded numerous albums. Ruff, who has been a professor at Yale University for more than 20 years, has recently completed his autobiography titled *Call to Assembly*, published by Viking Press (now out in paperback). This is a wonderfully written rags-to-musical-riches story told by a great soul. As an improviser on horn, Willie Ruff never really cuts loose. He most frequently chooses to emphasize the melodic content and the "mojo" as he plays deep from within. Willie Ruff has a great deal to say and has been saying it for 50 years.

Though Ruff and Amram are still active, an obvious new crop of horn playing talent hit the jazz scene in the 1970s and early '80s. In the summer of 1971, I met a terrific horn player at the Berkshire Music Festival by the name of John Clark. He was spending most of his free time transcribing improvised solos by the great saxophonists such as John Coltrane and Charlie Parker. He was the first hornist I'd ever met who was so motivated towards jazz. It was actually quite exciting to hear him work. Then what seemed like just a few years later, Clark had produced his first jazz horn LP, *Song of Light*—a great album! Since then he has continued to record and be a dominant force in the jazz horn scene in New York City. He plays in an aggressive, confident, and fluent manner, making frequent use of synthesized sounds, reverb, and other electric toys to enhance the elements of jazz/rock fusion. John Clark often includes original songs on his albums that run the gamut from simply playful to powerful and angry.

Clark was joined in New York in the early 1980s by another powerhouse jazz musician (who just happened to play horn) named Tom Varner. Varner spent some time in Boston at the New England Conservatory, just like Clark had, and was also influenced by the third-stream department and their open-minded attitude toward jazz as an option even for horn players. With at least ten solo albums to his name as leader, Varner has reached a very high level of self-expression through his truly innovative improvisational style and through his prolific output as a most creative composer. Varner is a very exciting performer with a great wit and a strong sense of adventure when it comes to making alternative sounds on his horn.

Others who are performing jazz at the solo recording level include the incredibly facile Rick Todd (first horn in the L.A. Chamber Orchestra) and in New York City, Sharon Freeman, Vince Chancy, Alex Brofsky, Bobby Rouch, and Peter Gordon. Others around the country include Jeffrey Snedeker, Bill Hoyt, Adam Unsworth, Lydia Van Dreel, Kevin Frey, Sandi Green, and Marshall Sealy, to name a few. Thomas Bacon, from Houston, has produced a fun-loving CD titled *The Flip Side*, and Russia's Arkady Shilkloper has made a remarkably strong impression at recent International Horn Workshops and through his recordings. Others I've heard of but not actually heard perform include Claudio Pontiggia in Lausanne, Switzerland, and Martin Mayes in Torino, Italy. Perhaps jazz horn is becoming infectious. I do hope so.

Have you ever wished you could play jazz on your horn? But then why should you? You've already got enough to do with all that great orchestral music and Mozart and Strauss. Who needs it? Why make a fool of yourself? What's really in it for you, anyway? (How about some good, clean fun for a starter?)

Did you happen to notice that many of the jazz hornists mentioned were also composers? Each of those mentioned who were leaders, and most of those mentioned who were side-men, also improvise extensively. Improvisation is, to a great extent, a form of spontaneous composition. And both improvisation and composition involve the searching for and ultimately finding of the most intimate music we will ever get to perform or know as individuals. When musically trained individuals begin to invent or create even the smallest arrangement of notes and rhythms, they are calling forth a full spectrum of musical experiences and awarenesses. They finally get to use all of those years of study and listening and practicing. Even more important, they are beginning to investigate, through the abstraction of their own newly discovered music, what it is that they think and feel, deep down, and personal.

To improvise is to free one's self from the page to a large extent and to free one's self from the limitations of other people's ideas and other people's music, people you don't even know very well. However, such freedom is threatening, to say the least, or just plain scary for most of us. What if we mess up and somebody hears us? What if we improvise on the wrong pitches to a given chord and can't even tell? These are real fears.

The next question is, why jazz? Why not just learn to improvise in the style of Mozart or Brahms? That would be wonderful, but it would not be you. You have to do your own music, or it becomes simple mimicry, and you will again be limited by their notes, not stimulated by your own thoughts. Jazz is a great option because it is wide open. Jazz is a genre that makes plenty of room for you stylistically, is rooted in the human condition, and is a language that simply demands neither technical nor artistic perfection, at least not to the extreme that classical music does. All it really wants is sincerity, a sense of play, and inventiveness. Jazz is our universal form of urban folk music. The majority of us are city-dwellers, I would guess, which would clearly make jazz our folk music. It's who we are, it's where we come from to a certain extent. It's also fun, and it communicates. Jazz communicates probably better than any other language across cultures, races, and nationalities. Doesn't everybody love jazz in one form or another? If not, I believe it's because they haven't invested the necessary time to listen and gain a familiarity. Jazz is not better than all other music; it just obviously seems to claim a rather large musical territory involving human communication and the dissemination of pleasure. Pleasure comes from understanding, and understanding comes to those who open their minds and exercise their abilities to empathize with what they are hearing, and to empathize with the people actually creating the event. To empathize with creative people, to hear through their ears and think in the ways they think, takes some serious hands-on experiences. To more fully understand such spontaneous creativity as musical improvisation, and to derive greater pleasure from such creative events, participation in the processes is necessary.

So what am I saying? Let's all experience spontaneous composition! Let's all improvise. Why not? Why is this activity so difficult for us to do? In an attempt to answer that question, I read a paper at the 26th International Horn Symposium in Kansas City in 1994 titled "Compose Yourself" (which is now Chapter 19). One of the points made there, that I will also make here, involves the true-life reality of fear, the fear of sharing our own personal creativity. For some deep-seated reason, most of us are profoundly afraid of being wrong. We are afraid to create mistakes, especially in front of other people. When it comes to improvising, most of us experience the performer's worst nightmare of sounding stupid, under-prepared, or, worse yet, untalented altogether.

Each of us has a strong opinion of what constitutes great music. Most of us can also tell what is an effective improvisation. So why should we subject ourselves to the humiliation of creating inferior music? Why should we improvise what would most certainly be considered bad jazz? Why not? Who do you suppose is actually paying all that much attention? Where do you suppose all of those accomplished improvisers started? (My guess is that they started from wherever they were at the time.) To overcome this natural but unnecessary fear of sounding stupid, we will need to think differently about this mode of performing and also think differently about ourselves. We must think more about our potential as improvisers, while simply developing our understanding of the process of becoming, rather than how ultimately unbecoming the product might make us appear to others. Perhaps you noticed that the suggestion was to experience spontaneous composition and to improvise, not to learn how. Let's start by turning improvisation into a game of solitaire. The fun of the game, the private process, might just become all-consuming. (Playing solitaire when no one else is watching is often when one wins!) Follow the rules. Don't follow the rules. Just have fun. Play!

Jazz in particular is a great medium for us to use to exercise this process of improvisation, this process of spontaneous composition, this process of digging inside ourselves for our own music. To define jazz adequately is quite difficult, largely because it is a language that incorporates so much. Musical categories such as ragtime, swing, bebop, free-jazz, fusion, rock, Latin, new age, world music, third-stream, and even western classical music can be and have been considered jazz-oriented, jazz-influenced, or as Jazz with a capital *J*. If this is true, each of us should be able to find our own internal music somewhere within these varied styles.

Gunther Schuller in his book *Musings* writes the following:

> What makes jazz jazz is the basic fact that it is an inherently creative music . . . it is essentially an improvised music . . . it is generally couched in a rhythmic language based on a regular beat, modified by free rhythmic, often syncopated inflections, all with a specific feeling and linear conception we call "swing" and, . . . unlike many other musical traditions, both European and ethnic/non-western, [jazz is] a music based on the free unfettered expression of the individual . . . . This last [point] is perhaps the most radical and most important aspect of jazz and that which differentiates it so dramatically from most other forms of music-making.[7]

This is one very significant reason why jazz would be the logical medium for all of us to explore. It's a medium that is rooted in the expression of the individual, and we are each unique individuals. Jazz as a style of music also applauds creativity and sincerity along with this individuality. So do it for yourself and maybe only for yourself. Begin to create your own, individual, sincere songs for yourself. However, if (or when) it becomes appropriate to share this music of yours, be it improvised or composed, you will find that the jazz audiences are quite different from the classical audiences. They tend to listen for and care about hearing totally different elements or aspects of a performance. They seem to be more eager to hear what you, the performer, really mean. They listen more for what you have to say than how you say it or how perfectly you say it. In other words, jazz audiences seem to be more interested in who the performer is (as a real person) rather than how the performer does (as a polished artist.)

My first public, improvised jazz performance on the horn took place in Madison at the University where I teach (but only after I had received tenure). My dear colleague, Joan Wildman, a pianist/theorist/positive force, was pulling a few of us odd instrumentalists out of our classical closets: a harpsichordist/musicologist, a bassoonist, a violinist (with obvious gypsy-like genes), and a guy who just happened to play horn. This was the very first time I ever went out on a stage in front of a hall full of real people, all of whom bought tickets, with my horn in hand without having a solid plan as to what I was going to play. We had looked over the tunes during our one brief rehearsal a few hours before the concert. But for this performance, I hadn't practiced every note over and over, deciding the composer's intentions and how I would play each phrase with polish and finesse like I always try to do for a classical solo performance. I was given only a simple and vague outline of what we would do and more or less when. I was supposed to play on three of the selections spread out over the whole concert. The first solo came out not at all the way I had hoped it might. My mind was racing through every possible fear-filled phrase I could create: "Why on earth are you doing this? Do you realize you are making an absolute fool of yourself? Ah! Maybe the entire audience is thinking about going out after the concert for drinks so they aren't actually listening to this mess. The drummer, listen to the drummer, he sounds great! Why me, God?" By then I was done and the audience clapped. They were just being nice; I knew that. I stepped back and didn't really listen to the others; I just shook and tried to remember what I had just done. I couldn't. I couldn't actually remember much of anything.

The next tune came by, and so I decided to breathe deeper, which always helps, stand a little taller, look over at Joan a few times for a confidence-building smile or two, and then just go with the flow. During this one, I was actually semi-conscious. I even remember thinking of a few clever ideas and actually making them happen. However, I was still not as aware as during my usual over-rehearsed classical performances. The audience seemed to clap even a little harder this time, and that was nice.

The third song began, and I was actually starting to smile on my own. I figured it like this: "You've already done it to yourself, you've played the fool and they've all heard it, so what the heck, just have a good time!" So I had a good time. I had a really good time. We were romping! After my solo chorus, the audience clapped a lot. I looked out at them, and they smiled a lot. They appeared to be genuinely happy for me. Perhaps we had even communicated. It seemed as if they had totally forgotten all about my tragic first improvisation. Or had they? Maybe they did remember, and that's why they liked my third one so much more. (In fact, that third solo really wasn't all that incredible either.) I believe that the reason they were clapping with such enthusiasm came from a much deeper level of human understanding. They saw me suffering and watched me pull out of it on my own to a level of at least basic competency. They let me tell my story. They listened and identified with my experience. We had, in a manner of speaking, communicated.

I came away from that concert feeling a rush I had never felt before. I had taken a chance, I even came out somewhat unscathed (with only minor ego abrasions), and I had learned that improvisation could provide a whole new set of experiences for me that I could and did carry over into what I do as a classical musician, teacher, and guy who just happens to play horn. That evening I had begun to unfetter my individuality as a performer.

I have actually had similar feelings and "rushes" upon premiering an original composition. A composer and an improviser both share a large piece of themselves, a significant aspect of their individuality. One feels somewhat exposed to the world at a time like that. It is certainly not a private feeling when we reveal our inner selves. Emerson wrote in his essay *History*, "there is no history, only biography." I feel strongly that most effective original music (e.g., composition, improvisation) is primarily biographical. However, through music we communicate autobiographical information through abstract sounds rather than readily definable words. When one's inner self is out in the open, it is a comfort to realize that most of the people who are actually paying attention at all probably don't hear past the abstractions anyway.

So let's get back to the problem we all have, or have had, regarding the fear of sounding stupid, the feeling that keeps us from taking the necessary first steps toward composing or improvising. How do or did all of your favorite composers and jazz performers do it? How did they unfetter their inhibitions and release their musical individualities? Perhaps they gave themselves permission. Perhaps they released themselves from that powerful ego-centered self-image of having to be as good at everything in the field of music as they are at something. Many of us can perform on our instruments rather well. What happens so easily then is that we think that that level of competency is our identity as a musician, or even as a person, and we simply won't be caught dead doing anything less. Such self-imposed limitations quickly become a straight-jacket for any new learning. We get stuck. We feel a more powerful need to sustain our self-imposed musical image than we feel the need to grow and learn something new.

This unrealistic concept of perfection is pervasive in the classical music profession. Rationally we all know it is impossible, but the older we get and the more advanced we become the more we seem to be obsessed by the requirements of perfection. That requirement causes us to pull in our wings, limit the chances we take, become more conservative and, thus, stifle our experiences, the very experiences we need to keep growing. When Picasso wrote, "If you want to paint a perfect picture, first become perfect and then just paint naturally," he probably meant that since perfection is only a concept and is not actually possible by us simple mortals, let's eliminate the concept as a requirement and just paint, dance, perform, compose, or improvise naturally from within our own natures. Perfection is not who we are, and neither is the music we write or the solos we improvise or the pictures we paint. Those are simply things that we do. Those objects or sounds do come from within our own personal beings, but they manifest themselves only as something we are doing at that moment in time. A few moments later they will probably sound (or look) quite different. To bring all of this around to a common denominator, music is what we do; it's not who we are, so let's get out the paints and try some new colors. Give yourself permission to at least try to improvise for awhile. Take some time to write down a musical thought or two every day. It can just be something that you do, and it just might be a lot of fun. Take the fetters off. Just start. Begin, one pitch at a time.

Jazz is a worthy and welcoming musical genre for just such growth to occur. Give it a try. Listen to as much jazz (in whatever style appeals to you most at the moment) as often as you possibly can until the familiarity becomes a natural part of your thinking. You will find many others traveling the same road. They'll love to play along. If not exactly jazz, then find your own music. Open up the possibilities through your horn, through improvisation, and perhaps the eventual notation of those ideas. Keep a tape or a journal of motives and phrases and songs just for the fun of it. Take the fetters off. Just start. Begin one phrase at a time.

This is the way those great jazz horn players must have started. Like them, we can listen and play, just letting it happen, over and over again. Those artists have opened the doors, and we can benefit from their examples. Their recordings are not yet in all the stores, but they are available. It's worth the search. Let their music talk to you and help you believe. If you wish to read more about jazz in general, or even more specific ways to approach improvisation in a theoretical and organized fashion, I've included a suggested reading list that follows. Some of my students who have delved more deeply into jazz have done it by just going after it from their ears outward. Others have followed the formulas presented in the many successful how-to books and articles. Everyone is different, so any way that works, works.

One last thought: Don't waste your valuable creative powers evaluating all that you are doing as an active improviser (or composer, while composing). Being the judge while being the performer spoils the performance! Just do it. Such value judgments will be coming from a different space within your being. They will simply clutter the flow of inner ideas with unnecessary intellectual chatter. You don't need that information! Simply begin to play. Begin to write your own songs one at a time, and enjoy getting to know new aspects of your musical self. There is plenty of time to evaluate your actions after the song has ended and you've allowed the melody to linger for awhile.

SUGGESTED MATERIALS THAT RELATE TO THE FRENCH HORN IN PARTICULAR AND JAZZ IN GENERAL

Books and Articles About Jazz and the Horn

Agrell, Jeffrey, Reviews and Interviews of Individual Horn Players, *Brass Bulletin*.
   Bacon, Tom, Vol. 45
   Clevenger, Dale, Vol. 54
   Gordon, Peter, Vol. 50
   Todd, Rick, Vol. 68
   Varner, Tom, Vol. 47
   Watkins, Julius, Vol. 41

Agrell, Jeffrey and Kevin Frey, "Jazz Clinic" series, *The Horn Call, Journal of the International Horn Society* (beginning April 1986, including more than 17 separate articles on jazz, improvisation, and the horn).

Amram, David, *Vibrations: The Adventures and Musical Times of David Amram*, Macmillan, 1968.

Blake, Curtiss, compiled by, "Jazz Discography by Player," *The Horn Call, Journal of the International Horn Society*, October, 1982.

Ruff, Willie, *A Call to Assembly, the Autobiography of a Musical Storyteller*, Viking-Penguin, 1991.

Schaughency, Steve, "Learning Jazz Styles Through the Recordings of Julius Watkins," *The Horn Call, Journal of the International Horn Society*, November, 1996; February, 1997; November, 1997; February, 1998.

Varner, Tom, "Julius Watkins," *The Horn Call, Journal of the International Horn Society*, October, 1988.

_____, "Jazz Horn—Post Julius Watkins," *The Horn Call, Journal of the International Horn Society*, April, 1989.

Other, More General Readings on Jazz

Berliner, Paul, *Think Jazz, The Infinite Art of Improvisation*, University of Chicago Press, 1994.

Gioia, Ted, *The Imperfect Art: Reflections on Jazz and Modern Culture*, Oxford Press, 1988.

Hodeir, Andre, *Jazz, Its Evolution and Essence* (revised edition), Grove Press, 1979.

Kernfeld, Barry (ed.), *The New Grove Dictionary of Jazz*, St. Martin's Press, 1988–1994. (The most complete single volume on jazz available)

Meltzer, David (ed.), *Reading Jazz*, Mercury House, 1993. (A diverse anthology of writings on jazz by Igor Stravinsky, F. Scott Fitzgerald, Jean Cocteau, Norman Mailer, William Carlos Williams, Darius Milhaud, among many others)

Schuller, Gunther, *Musings: The Musical Worlds of Gunther Schuller, A Collection of His Writings*, Oxford Press, 1986.

Jazz Method Books (How-To)

Aebersold, Jamey, *Play-a-Long Book and Recording Sets* (CDs and cassettes).

Baker David, *A Creative Approach to Practicing Jazz*, Aebersold Jazz, Inc. 1994.

Baker, David, *Jazz Improvisation: A Comprehensive Method of Study for All Players*, Frangipani Press, 1983 (revised edition).

Clark, John, *Exercises for Jazz French Horn*, Hidden Meaning Music, 1993.

Coker, Jerry, *Complete Method for Improvisation*, Studio P/R, Warner Bros. Publications, 1980.

Russell, George, *The Lydian Chromatic Concept of Tonal Organization for Improvisation*, Concept Pub., 1959.

Coker, Jerry, *How to Practice Jazz*, Aebersold Jazz, Inc., 1990.

Coker, Jerry, Improvising Jazz, A Spectrum Book, Simon & Schuster, 1986.

Haerle, Dan, *The Jazz Language: A Theory Text for Jazz Composition and Improvisation*, Studio 224, Warner Bros. Publications, 1980.

A New Approach to Jazz Improvisation, P.O. Box 1244, New Albany, IN, 47150.

Recording Artists on French Horn (Among Others)

Julius Watkins, John Graas, David Amram, Willie Ruff, John Clark, Tom Varner, Rick Todd, Vincent Chancy, Alex Brofsky, Jerry Peel, Peter Gordon, Bobby Rouch, Arkady Shilkloper, Jeffrey Snedeker, Thomas Bacon (see discographies in *The Horn Call*, October 1982, April 1989)

19. Compose Yourself

What follows is a revised written version of a talk given in June of 1994 at the 26th International Horn Symposium held in Kansas City, Missouri. Consequently, the writing style is somewhat verbal and informal in its manner. The message is a strongly felt advocacy for all musicians to compose, not for what those compositions might do for the world of music, but for what experiencing the process will do for the composer.

The original reason for using this ambiguous title for my talk was to allow for a discussion of either achieving composure for the self—for you and for me—or to talk about the joys and advantages of musical composition for the performing student, teacher, and artist. As it turns out, both aspects will enter into this discussion.

However, my main point is to encourage every one of you to compose something from scratch, something that won't be graded, something that might never even be shared with another, or perhaps something to be played for a friend or even a friendly audience—your choice.

Upon discussing this with a friend, it was suggested that there might be those who would think I'm advocating composition simply because that's something I've enjoyed doing. I wondered, is it worth your time listening to someone talk about something they don't enjoy? Well, let me assure you that composition is something I do because I believe in its far-reaching musical importance, at least for me. It fills a space in my creative self that can be filled in no other way. It is a most significant part of what I will call the "triangle of musical wholeness":

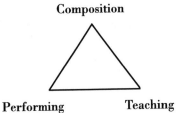

Composition

Performing   Teaching

One of the major elements in the world of musical performance during the twentieth century has been the emphasis on the classical music of the past, primarily of the eighteenth and nineteenth centuries. There are those among my colleagues who feel strongly that this music is somehow greater and more profound than the vast majority of what is being composed today. So for the sake of argument, let's assume that this is true. Let's consider what might be one of the most obvious differences. Think of the composers we most admire and tend to see programmed often, such as Bach, Mozart, Beethoven, and Brahms; if you are a pianist, Chopin and Liszt; if you are a violinist, Pagannini and Kreisler; if you are a horn player, Franz Strauss, Rossini, and Punto. What do these composers have in common? The most obvious is that they were all active performers, and most, I believe, were active teachers. Such versatility was expected of them as an assumed extension of their musical maturity. This "triangle of musical wholeness" was common to the vast majority of musicians at that time, not just the famous whose compositions have stayed with us.

In the twentieth century, which composers come to mind as exceptionally fun to perform and listen to and are consequently programmed often? My first thoughts include Benjamin Britten, Paul Hindemith, and Leonard Bernstein. These composers were all considered geniuses. Why? Because they functioned at the highest levels as performers, as educators, and as composers. This was not nearly so unusual 200 years ago. Why is it so exceptional today? I believe that it might just be because we specialize our ways and means of musical expression into smaller and smaller compartments so that we can compete. We have been led to believe that to become exceptionally good at anything, we must ignore everything else but that particular specialty.

Let's look at the three points of this "triangle of musical wholeness" more closely. The performer's primary job is to re-create through the wonders of sound the great compositional ideas of others. This is of course very important. Without performers, there would be no music. Thorough performers will study the scores, analyze the musical content both theoretically and historically, and, if so inclined and capable, put a twist of their own interpretation toward a polished and intelligently sensitive rendition of another's music.

The teacher's traditional job is to share knowledge with others and to find ways of encouraging students to love to learn and learn to do all that a performer must to interpret the music of the great composers. To accomplish all of this, a teacher must have a thorough background and working knowledge in music theory, music history, and educational psychology, as well as a good deal of experience as a performer. A few "street smarts" regarding the business of music also comes in handy.

The composer's primary activity focuses in a different direction from the other two. While performing and teaching primarily look outward for their necessary information and materials, the composer looks inside for what's going on musically. The information and materials used by composers are of a more personal, intimate nature when it finally comes down to doing the actual writing. The composer part of each of us has something to say that is a very personal synthesis of all those experiences we've had as performers and teachers. In addition, I believe what's even more exciting is that composing brings closer to our musical surfaces what we are as complete human beings. Our personal histories are all in there: how we played games when we were three years old or what we felt about our siblings, our grandmother, the loss of a loved one or a pet, the anger over the absurdities of war, how great it feels to ride a bike really fast or paddle a canoe very slowly across a pristine lake.

We are all musicians. That's our common language. Composition is a wonderful way to get inside and find out about ourselves and then, perhaps, share it in an abstract but effective and important way. This is our way to communicate fully in the deepest sense with others. Call it introspection or self-discovery or just another effective and delightful way for you to expand musically. It might even result in some personal composure as you grow into it.

So what difference should all of this make to the person who really only wants to perform? Let's consider the basic process a composer must undertake. First, a choice must be made from among the millions of possibilities what to compose and where to start. After that, decisions must be made regarding what to communicate and then how to go about it in the most effective way. Such problems are overwhelming to say the least. For a performing musician to start to solve even a few of these problems at whatever level possible is to begin to get closer to the great composers and their music—the very music that we want so much to understand and to perform well.

Musical composition is, aesthetically speaking, at the highest level of problem-posing/problem-solving that we humans can experience. Musical composition is truly a complicated and profound process. What we must realize and learn to believe is that the product is not the reason to indulge in the process, at least not initially. The product—a completed piece of music—is not all that vitally important. It is the process that teaches us what we need to know and what will make us more complete musicians, more competent performers, and more comprehensive teachers. It's not so much the result as it is the work we do and experiences we create for ourselves that is of value. It's not the destination, it's the journey that counts.

Why did I say the same thing in so many different ways just now? Because I believe strongly that here we have the primary reason that so many performing teacher-musicians avoid composing like the plague: the fear of creating a bad piece! It seems to me that the foundation for this rather universal fear is in part the result of a sickness prevalent in the classical music world: that all such music and musical activities must be judged and evaluated somehow. It must be decided whether they are "good" or "bad," acceptable or unacceptable. Did we get this tendency from our music schools or from our private teachers? How did they inherit these attitudes? Where do performers learn to tear down each other's work? Or even more appropriate to this discussion, where do we learn to tear down our own attempts at composition by raising the work of other composers to often distorted and lofty heights of greatness? Do all within your power to reject that tendency to evaluate. Simply let history decide if your first composition (that two-minute work for solo horn and tree branches) will pass the test of time for future generations of theorists to ponder. I encourage you to give it a try for the fun of it and for what you can learn from the experience about yourself and about the processes of composition.

A few years ago, I gave an assignment to all of my students. I asked them to write a piece of music. Whatever they decided to write was okay. And I wanted it to be performed near the end of the semester. (Now for all of you teachers who wish to unify your class of students, this is one way that works. It is called the "common enemy" technique.) I decided, however, that this assignment should be preceded by two other experiences that could help ready them for that final "fun-filled" event. First, I asked them to identify a playing problem that had plagued them for a long time, one they hadn't been able to solve yet. Then I asked them to devise or compose an etude or set of exercises to help solve that nagging problem and present their solutions/creations to each other at a class a few weeks later. This was the challenge of problem-posing/problem-solving housed within their own self-acknowledged playing deficiencies. The resultant class was, I felt, quite successful, especially in that they each became interested in the others' problems and solutions, and they seemed to have lost track of their own inhibitions and fears of exposing their own defects in public. I feel they also caught a good glimpse of their own capacities to solve some personal playing problems through compositional means. (See Chapter 17, "Derivative Etudes: Create Your Own," for more discussion of this concept.)

Later in the semester, I invited a guest professor from our faculty who is a highly motivated teacher and unique improvisational performer at the keyboards. Her name is Joan Wildman, and her class started at the beginning of that wonderful process of improvising in public ("public performance without a plan"), with the artistic ego left unprotected by extensive rehearsals. Such an activity is socially awkward to say the least. But after she had pairs of students converse through their horns by doing abstract questions and answers, by improvising phrases that explained what they did last summer, or by explaining what they wanted for dinner, we were on our way out of the fear. At a later class session, Joan had the students take a three-note phrase and play it one after another modifying it only a little. This was done again with two more three-note phrases. It gradually became apparent that the group was recomposing a popular jazz standard that was built on those simple three motives. (It was the song "All of Me.") The class had experienced the building of a composition, in this case a great tune, through the act of improvisation on their horns.

Finally, that fateful day arrived for my somewhat bemused group of horn students. It was time for their original, unrestricted compositions to be presented to each other. That particular class session was without a doubt one of the most incredible experiences of my teaching career. The students each presented a piece of themselves. No two compositions were at all alike, and each new piece openly demonstrated an honest, unique quality of sincere invention.

We teachers spend our years listening to students struggle with basic repertoire over and over again. That's an important part of our job, so we love it. However, most of the serious and at times insurmountable struggles are not the technical ones that are easy to identify. The difficult problems come from our simply not understanding the composer's intentions. How can we as performers understand a composer's intentions if we have never experienced such intentions of our own? At no time during the students' presentations of their own compositions was there any problem with the misinterpretation of the composer's intentions. That alone made it a special occasion.

I would now like to discuss what the students presented as the reasons or personal motivations for their compositions. You will immediately notice that most of these works tend to be sincere expressions of some small part of the creator's own biography. One student had a very young relative to whom she liked to sing a lullaby. This little melody was original to the student, so she decided to arrange it for three horns using basic block chords under the tune with some melodic development. Another student was touched by the beautiful explosion of springtime in Madison as it related to her love of the nature poetry of Walt Whitman. She called her piece "Songs of Seeds" and composed it for unaccompanied horn with poetry read by the player just before each movement.

A Native American legend that had played an important part in another student's past experiences became the program for a successful work for horn and piano. The death of a close family member was to be the inspiration for a piece by an older student. That piece never developed. It didn't flow. Instead, the composition for this fellow took a 180-degree turn and became a jazz tune about his neighborhood, which seemed rather like the 1950s to him. Another student found it rather easy to decide to write about canoeing on the boundary waters area of northern Minnesota. The ending came to her first, and then she developed it into a horn duet that flowed back and forth between the parts as if rowing calmly upon a clear lake.

One of my lesser-inhibited students went to the stage, slouched in his chair with legs reaching out straight, and explained that this was the way his highly improvisational piece came to him after a most tiring day. He glued his favorite ideas together and shared some of his introspective musical thoughts with us.

A few weeks before this session, one of my younger students was very frustrated about getting started. After giving her plenty of time to decide for herself, I suggested a few ways to begin. The one she found interesting was to take a piece of manuscript paper and a pencil and draw an arbitrary, wiggly line across the staff, then put some dots on that line, play them with her horn, and see what it sounded like. From that, she chose what worked. She eventually came up with a solo line of music that brought back other ideas she had had before. The result was a Bach-like perpetual melody that she said she wanted to expand upon.

Another very creative solution to the problem of this assignment was to turn the event of the assignment itself into a solo piece with narrator describing in story form the whole process of being given this assignment, being upset that it interrupted a perfectly good day, asking others to write the piece for her, and then eventually coming up with a rather delightful tune in the end. The title was "The Horn Player and Her Teacher," and she was actually a little afraid that this might offend me. Being creative, clever, and honest with a sense of humor is certainly not offensive to me. (This student went on to write two more compositions that she included in recitals.)

There was one student who didn't seem to have a piece ready. It happened rather mysteriously, so I let it go until we could have some time alone. It seems that her rather innocent initial intentions flowed full-force into a horn quartet based on the *dies irae* motive and became a musical working through of an important loss from a few years back. She simply wasn't ready to share this part of herself with her peers. However, the process she experienced dealing with such powerful emotions through musical composition changed her perspectives.

Allow me again to restate an earlier question: How does this activity of composing actually help a performer? From this assignment came one wonderful example. The last student composition performed in this class was by a young man who had begun as a composition major and changed to music education with a major in horn. His work was a full concerto with piano. He played his piece with great enthusiasm. He had completed the work earlier and had played it through many times. (When you write a piece of your very own, which you like, you tend to practice it quite often because it feels good.) What occurred at the following week's lesson is my point. This student found that the Dukas' *Villanelle* had become easier to play and a lot more fun. He suddenly knew what to do with it. Through his increased, enthusiastic practicing and the successful performance of his own piece, his love for playing had increased and he had brought together all we'd been talking about both technically and musically. In the case of this young man, I feel he's going to find his musical self from the inside out.

Through this composition assignment, my students had to care about what they wanted to say musically. They couldn't help but care about their own music. As you remember, one of them tried to decide what the poet Walt Whitman really meant and then found herself naturally translating that into what the poetry meant to her. Next, she had to decide how to put such a personal blend of thoughts and feelings into an abstract soundscape to make the poetry even more vivid for herself and for her audience. To finally decide to compose music to enhance the meaning of something of personal importance, such as a favorite poem, can become a major turning point in a performer's musical life. It is only then that one begins to gain true insight into the creative process and the remarkable sensations of creative intent felt by our greatest composers. It is then that we begin to understand.

It is impossible to fully understand another person's actions or intentions. But the more experiences we have had that are similar to another's, the closer we become. So what is most important to discover through one's own composing is that every aspect of a musical composition—every little nuance, pitch choice, articulation, dynamic, phrase length, or tessitura—chosen by a composer was for a very sincere and important reason. This might sound rather obvious, but let's think about the way we go about learning a new piece. If the composer labors over every detail, shouldn't we, out of respect, attempt to discover its depth of meaning? This great music is for us to discover, not just to use. We can grow as performers all along the way by empathizing with the creators of the music we play. The more similar are our experiences, the closer we can come to rendering our fellow composers' intentions.

Once a performer reaches a level of ability to play the advanced repertoire, does he or she have the right to ignore the composer's intentions? Is it appropriate to take those rather intimate and certainly personal thoughts and decisions from another human being and bend them to our own convenient preferences? Should we make Haydn sound like Strauss because we play the late Romantic style better or prefer it, even though Haydn could not possibly have meant it that way? When posed as such a loaded question, most of us would say, "Of course not!"

I believe strongly that if you experience even the ground levels of composition, you will develop an empathy for composers. You will care a little more about their message than before. You will understand their methods and be able to transfer that into new ways of blowing, tonguing, and singing on your horn.

If all of this is so important to us as performing musicians, why is it not a more integral part of our educational systems? Now that's a good question. Art, dance, theater, and even English majors base their curriculum on creativity. Can you imagine a graduating art student who has not yet created an original work of art or an English major who is not required to compose a story or poem? How is it then that one can get a doctorate in music performance without ever creating an original piece of performance music? We dabble with certain technical aspects of composition in theory classes but seem much less concerned with originality, creativity, and those problem-posing/problem-solving decisions that are so important to the actual act of original composition. Composition needs to become a more active part of our musical training, even if that means we do it on our own.

Have you noticed how the average person feels comfortable scribbling on a sketch pad to pass the time or dances with all kinds of physical gyrations simply because it's fun? Why don't we just pick up our horns and scribble some sounds or spontaneously dance with the sounds of our horns on an improvised rhythm? I'll bet it's because of the fear of sounding stupid. I think we all know too much. We can all tell what is great music and what is not, and we are probably right most of the time. So why create something that is inferior to the best we can imagine?

Why not? Do you scribble as well as Picasso or dance as well as Fred Astaire? Why should you compose as well as Brahms? You shouldn't because you are not a composer. So if you agree that you are not a composer, you should go right ahead and compose just as you might scribble or dance. The fear of writing a bad piece, of sounding stupid, or of simply creating an inferior product has just been eliminated. It is the process not the product that counts.

To paraphrase a famous quote I once heard: If you want to compose the perfect symphony, first become perfect and then just compose naturally. Stop evaluating, stop judging, and just start. Get some manuscript paper and a pencil. Don't tell anyone what you are doing or why. You don't even have to know yourself. Just start! Then feel free to toss what you've done and start over again—and again. Remember, it's the process that you are experiencing.

Take your horn into a dark room and play your feelings for awhile with no one around. Improvise in the style of the moment. It will help a great deal if you can think of your horn as your voice and not your nemesis. Blow it freely as if it were a folk instrument. As you become more comfortable, add a tape recorder to the room. Save the best thoughts and sounds. Transcribe the ones you like most and let it develop from there. Have fun without any deadlines or expectations. Don't even compare your last piece with your first one. Let them each stand alone. Each piece has its own life.

Obviously, the intent of this chapter was to encourage you to compose yourself. I've presented all of these ideas because I believe in them. For me, this activity helps keep the true musical spirit alive. The idealism that drew me into music originally needs to be refreshed now and again. This does it for me. It might for you as well. I do hope so.

20. So, What Do You Think? The Creative Spirit, Creative Process, and You

In this discussion, I will both expand upon and summarize many of the thoughts found in the preceding three chapters. However, here the emphasis is on the actual creative process and on general concepts of thinking for the student, the teacher, and the performer. This was originally a verbal presentation, so it remains somewhat conversational in its manner.

So *what* do you think? So what do *you* think? So what do you *think*? *So* whadoyouthink? Isn't it interesting how the actual meaning of a phrase can change with the simple shifting of an accent? But then, seriously, how does a string of words (or a series of pitches for that matter) actually acquire a meaning? Where does that meaning come from? Who creates that meaning? What do you think? My guess is that meaning can only come from what *you* have *decided* to *think* based on what you have experienced and what you understand to be true.

This may seem simplistic until you dig a bit deeper into the relevance and power of thought as teachers, performers, and students of great music. I wish to discuss the activity of thinking and especially of creative thinking: what it is, why it is so important to us, and what we can do about it and with it. I hope that by the time you have finished reading this chapter and have had a chance to think about your own personal power of thought, you will accept the challenge to compose a piece of music for yourself or to improvise an original song or variations on a favorite melody, to write a great new cadenza, or to create a terrific etude that can help you work through a technical problem. I want you to think about these things right after you've finished reading this chapter and for the rest of your life. To be creative is to be in contact with our own best thoughts. Why spend your time going only part of the way in this huge musical world you've chosen for yourself? Why specialize yourself into only a small set of musical experiences, closing off so much of your potential insights and abilities? Why just be a player who only performs or a teacher who only meets with students or a student who only does what he or she is told? Each and every one of us has the potential to do it all at one level or another. Be a student and practitioner of the creative process for yourself as a fully functioning and ultimately fully realized musician.

I'd like to organize this discussion around the three major components of its title: WHAT, YOU, and THINK.

Think

Let's begin with thought and thinking. Thought is our power. It is our greatest power. It is the one thing that the vast majority of us actually have any consistent control over. Thought is also where we are, where our being actually exists most of the time. So it is, consequently, our primary environment, our place of being. We exist within our own thoughts.

It has been frequently said by the greatest of philosophers and seers that nothing has ever existed that didn't begin as a thought. Such a statement as that has very important implications. For instance, by comparing the collected creation mythologies from the many cultures and religions of the world, we can recognize a surprisingly large number of similar elements. A greatly simplified synthesis suggests that life as we know it began as the Eternal Parent, the First Spirit resting in an unconscious, dreamless sleep, thinking of nothing. Then as the glimmer of thoughts formed, there was illumination, and then there was light and dark. As these and other pairs of opposites entered thought, the concepts sprang into being. Time also began; there was the past and the future. All of life, light, and the spirit of life came to be from the power of thought.

If this wonderful power of thought is the illumination, the stuff that initiates all of creation, then it also might be the substance of all creative acts. Our own creative powers as performers, teachers, students, and composers could quite easily be imagined as a mirror or as a parallel version of that very same power that originally created us and all that is around us. We have within us as individuals that same potential power to create, to be creative, to be creators. That power is housed in our thoughts, simply waiting to be made manifest by our actions upon them.

Every original, musical thought you have had that has remained unobserved, misunderstood, unstudied, or simply undeveloped may possibly have cost you a composition, a brilliant performance, or perhaps the improvement of an existing problem. Conversely, every original thought you have pondered, studied, understood, and acted upon has perhaps brought with it new knowledge and growth, not to mention a bit of pride and self-esteem. Thoughts are things. They can be observed, studied, developed, and acted upon. Thoughts are things. They can be ignored and left to decay into nothingness. We create our thoughts, they are our own, and we can improve our lives by understanding and feeling their fire, their energy, their illumination. The more we observe, consider, and define our thoughts as things, the more seriously we may treat them.

I was brought up and constantly encouraged to respect objects and the physical aspects of existence far more than those silly daydreams, or those "fleeting thoughts" that seemed to cross my mind arbitrarily. I was led to believe that since there was no measurable substance to such thoughts, I should not trouble myself to place any true or lasting value upon them. They were simply fanciful distortions, figments of my distracted imagination, useless hodgepodges of insubstantial chatter originating from nowhere in particular. Other thoughts, ideas, and facts that I was instructed to remember and even to memorize were based upon what I had been taught in school, read from assigned texts, or had been told by others wiser than me. As I look back now with the power of hindsight, most of what I must have considered as the truly important thoughts were simply a collection of random facts needed to pass the next set of exams. Does any of this seem familiar?

Without respect for our own personal thoughts, without respect for our own creative powers, we just might go through life looking to only external sources—to schools, teachers, computer programs or networks, books, repertoire, etudes—for all of the answers to all of our needs as performers, teachers, scholars, and human beings. That, I am convinced, would be a serious mistake. We would be relinquishing our only true power, the only thing we actually have any real control over in our lives—the vast power of personal thought.

As students, performers, and teachers, what can we do to make the most of our best thoughts? How can we develop those thoughts into a broadening of our musical powers of understanding? How can we think our way into becoming more complete musicians? I believe that through a thorough understanding of the creative process and its design, we can learn to use our best personal thoughts to grow through original actions.

The creative process, according to many researchers on this interesting subject (see especially Howard Gardner, Daniel Goleman, and D. N. Perkins), can be generally defined as following six progressive steps. First, we have to identify the problem, the need, or the wish that requires a creative solution. This step is called *identification*. Next, we must indulge in the multitudes of ways of studying that problem and researching all possible solutions. This step is often called *preparation*. Third, we experience the inevitable *frustration* that comes from the usual lack of a focused and easy answer. This is the point at which many of us give up on the creative process altogether, feeling that we are not capable of such a venture. Fourth, many of us will consequently distract ourselves with other activities or the lack of activities and allow the frustrations to incubate or to recede into the unconscious mind where additional work actually seems to take place. This is called the *incubation* period. Often, after such unfocused and unrewarding periods of instability, the creative person finally experiences that incredible moment of *ah-ha*, that feeling of *illumination*. (And then there was light!) This is the stage of the creative process that seems to get all of the glory and attention, that sudden feeling when we say, "I think I've got it!" However, that all-important moment is not yet a creative act in the fullest sense. What happens next is the diligent and conscientious hard work. This stage is called the *translation*, when one takes the thought and translates it into an action or an object. So to review, the six stages of the creative process are as follows: identification, preparation, frustration, incubation, illumination, and translation.

Another way to describe this process is that you've got a problem, you've figured out exactly what it is, but you can't quite solve it, which really bugs you; so instead of getting mad, you decide to forget about it, but it stews away in your subconscious. Then one day when you least expect it, you suddenly know the answer and decide to take action to solve the problem so you can get on with your life. Sound familiar? If so, consider yourself actively involved within the creative process. You are already a creative problem solver, at least now and then.

So what do you think? Could you apply this natural skill to, for instance, an original composition without experiencing the fear that it is beyond you? Could you apply this natural skill to solving a technical performance problem without the aid of a master teacher's guidance? Could it really be possible for each and every one of you to identify consciously your musical problems or needs and then create new and innovative musical solutions? Could you, by simply acknowledging that you have thoughts worth studying and developing, actually create new ways to interpret music? Of course you could! It's simply a matter of paying attention and observing those important and original thoughts, studying them from every angle, believing in yourself, and taking the time necessary to learn through trial and error how best to translate it all into sound.

When I was growing up in Lincoln, Nebraska, I was fortunate to be a student of the very special junior high school music teacher Kenneth Freese. He freely shared his simple yet intense love for music in all of its facets whenever I decided to stay after school and hang out in the band room. He encouraged me to learn to improvise on the string bass and the horn and to chord at the piano. Then he showed me how to write down the tunes that grew out of those chords. They were my tunes. I got comfortable with the creative process long before I could possibly have known how such music might be compared to Johannes Brahms or Duke Ellington. This wonderful man opened my eyes to the magical possibilities of my relationship with music. I vividly remember a response he gave me once when I came to him with a playing problem I was experiencing on my horn. "How will I ever play this *glissando* to a high A?" "You'll figure out a way. You always do." (And I did.)

An interesting parallel was one of my father's favorite phrases that has stuck with me as well. Often when I presented him with a problem of mine, he would generously respond, "You are just the guy who can do it." So all of you teachers be sure to share these important ideas about personal creativity and problem-solving with your youngest and oldest students by encouraging them to be creative and by showing them how to translate their own creative thoughts and tendencies into musically expedient solutions.

It is best, however, to do such teaching as the result of some hands-on experiences of your own. So if you have yet to exercise the creative process for yourself to the extent that I've been discussing, then do the process along with them. Students love to watch their teachers learning. It makes learning and growing seem like the most important goals for musical success, which, of course, they are. It is absolutely true that creativity is a natural attribute for all of us to one degree or another. The visible (and audible) results come from common folks who just decide to think a little harder, spend a little more time searching for their own answers, decide to be patient a little longer, and then have the confidence and capabilities to act when those moments of illumination begin to shine through.

You

Let me try to explain why I think all that I have been discussing is so important for young developing musicians and at least of equal, if not greater, importance for those of us who have spent many years as strictly performers and performance teachers. All music revolves around the compositions of the past right up until yesterday. Even jazz improvisation and aleatoric compositions to a great extent are based on composed songs or pre-established criteria by innovative composers. For us to communicate these ideas of others adequately, we must understand them. Working directly on the first performance of a new composition with the actual composer helps a great deal, but such an opportunity is rare. (However, take that opportunity every chance you get!) Then what about Mozart, Brahms, or Strauss? How can we communicate their messages or their musical ideas without any personal contact? Empathy is the key, and empathy is defined as the intellectual identification with or the vicarious experiences of the feelings, thoughts, or attitudes of another person. Simply stated, if we are empathetic, we can put ourselves in another person's shoes.

I am sure we all agree that musical performance is a form of communication. Then what is there to communicate but feelings, thoughts, and attitudes? And just whose feelings, thoughts, and attitudes are we wishing to communicate to our audiences? I would like to propose that our primary purpose as performers is to communicate our own feelings, thoughts, and attitudes about the feelings, thoughts, and attitudes of the composer. We have a very sophisticated symbiotic relationship here, don't we? We performers and composers need each other. Composers are ultimately dependent upon our skills and understanding. In turn, we are dependent upon the personal integrity and musical substance of the compositions being performed. Since the composers have, in most cases, already completed their job and produced the particular piece of music we wish to perform, it is up to us to apply our skills and understanding to what they meant in every detail. Our skills, craft, and technical abilities to perform on our instruments are being exercised constantly throughout practice sessions. It is our understanding of the music and its message that concerns me here. How can we understand or empathize with a composer if we have never fully experienced the thrills and tribulations of original composition? Looking at it from the other way around, how do we as performers tend to react to the compositions by the composers who have no understanding of the way our instruments work or sound? For me, that one thought makes a very strong point. Taking this just a little further, I would venture to guess that more composers have experienced high levels of performance than have most of us performers experienced the full processes of composition.

So if understanding is the key here, and we performers are charged with conveying this understanding to our audiences, we will have to find some effective way to develop a solid foundation for our empathy. Since we can't truly know anything outside of our own experiences, then we had better get to work on the actual activity of composing, be it through cadenzas, etudes, or original compositions. This exciting creative process when applied to musical composition is the stuff of our understanding of all composers and their feelings, their thoughts, and their attitudes.

That's just one of the most important reasons for applying the creative process to our musical growth. Another great reason is the incredible thrill of the actual experience while you are creating something of your own. Some psychologists call this "flow," others call it the "white moment," and still others call it "peak experiences." This is when everything clicks. This is when your skills and interests are so perfectly suited to the challenge at hand that you seem to lose all sense of self-consciousness. Your attention is so totally immersed, fascinated, and involved in what you are doing that the passing of time goes unnoticed. You become utterly lost in the present.

If you have yet to experience such a focused flow, please believe me that it is worth the journey. During such a time, all about you becomes timeless and selfless. You lose your sense of place entirely while you feel totally alive and full of vibrant energy. So not only do you develop a better understanding of and empathy for the great composers by experiencing some of what they have experienced through the creative process of personal composition, but you will also experience what seems like a warp in time!

Trust me that you can do this. (You'll figure out a way. You always do!) Go ahead and challenge yourself to a controlled and conscientious attempt at the creative process. You are the one who is sure to benefit since, let's face it, you are all you have to work with.

At this point in the discussion, I can sense a possible argument against the idea of musical creativity for all of us. We all know what great musical literature is when we hear it, and we all know that there are finely composed etudes and exercises already available. So why should we feel committed to write ones that probably won't be as good? What need is there for us to compose an original cadenza when we could easily copy our favorite one off a CD? Who needs more chamber music when Mozart, Brahms, and others have already written such great music for us? These are truly important questions but only if we are simply considering the product and its importance to the history of our instrument.

Let me ask you to consider this thought: If you were to create some new etudes, or a cadenza, or perhaps a solo for your instrument, who do you think would pay all that much attention to the details of your endeavors? I do not mean to be offensive, but I do wish for us to think about this as objectively as possible. In fact, such creative activities would initially be just between you and you. If you were to begin to experience the creative process through an original composition, that you would write in the privacy of your own space, who in fact would notice? Probably no one, unless you decided to share it with others. It is the process of doing that which I am advocating. Do it for yourself. Compose it only for yourself; that's really good enough. It's what you experience that's important. Then it's what you learn from thinking about what you have done that is the first reward. Next, it's what you have learned from your creative experience and how that relates to the next composition you plan to perform that becomes an additional reward.

To quote a phrase from one of my favorite thinkers, Ralph Waldo Emerson: "There comes a time in everyone's life when they arrive at the conviction that they must take themselves, for better or worse, as their only portion; that nothing good can come to them but through their own toil bestowed on that plot of ground which is given to them to till." I interpret that to mean that we had better get to work on what we have to work with or we just might wake up one day and find our own personal plot of ground to be all dried up.

What

Now it is time to become more specific about exactly what you can do to make this all-important, expanding turn toward a more creative work ethic and a more creative musical life. During the past few years, I have made assignments for my students at the University of Wisconsin in Madison that address many of the ideas I've been discussing. Each has had as its ultimate goal an act of creative thinking. Of all these assignments that I have forced them to endure, the least frightening has been the writing of their own original cadenzas. It probably seems most like a common theory assignment for which the limitations are all laid out and the traditions surrounding the specifics are rather well known. However, I do believe that cadenza writing is a wonderful place to start to develop a sense of confidence in one's own potential compositional capacities.

As a student, you should begin by relating the writing of a cadenza to the six stages of the creative process. Start by identifying the problem as the need for a cadenza that best represents your own capabilities and your musical feelings about the piece. You should then initiate preparations (stage two) by studying the traditions of cadenza writing and performance practice at the time of the piece's composition. In Mozart, for instance, you learn that a cadenza is to serve to ornament the fermata near the end of the movement, which then leads into the final coda. It should sound improvised (though it usually isn't). It should take into account what Mozart wrote harmonically, rhythmically, and of course melodically for both the solo voice and the orchestra. The limitations of the solo instrument of that period should also be considered as a matter of taste and artistic unity. The length of the movement should dictate the approximate proportions of the cadenza. This original cadenza should take on a harmonic, melodic, and technical shape of its own design, a mini-composition in its own right, without distracting from the actual piece.

These points, among others, should be part of the preparations. As a means to this end, many of my students extract into notation each individual motive from the entire movement and begin to work out their cadenzas as if they are puzzles by rearranging the ideas in clever and new orderings. This method often requires originally composed transitions to link the puzzle pieces together and make the overall cadenza more successful. Such a project certainly sets a stage for some creative musical arranging, if not actual original composing. However, working with the themes of a master like Mozart can be rather intimidating for some of my students. It was obvious that a few were still in that third stage of the creative process, the one called frustration, while they were presenting their cadenzas to the class. They had waited too long to get started. They apparently failed to understand the magnitude of the full creative process. Perhaps they thought it would be more like the numerous assignments that so often fill up their academic lives, those that require little or no original thought and can be crammed together the night before.

To make full use of the creative process in its complete six-part design requires an extensive amount of time and thought, even when applied to the creation of a rather short, derivative cadenza. After the difficult and tedious exercise of organizing your ideas, you should let it sit, come back to it now and then, and edit as it comes to you. Your subconscious will work for you if you have planted the right information and if you continue to care. When the appropriate amount of time (for you) has passed and the incubation period is over, it will all fall together, and you will ideally be able to say to yourself, "This is just right; I really enjoy playing my own cadenza and am proud to perform it in the context of a Mozart concerto. Though it may not be as grand as Mozart's music, it is as good as I can do right now." When you can say all of those things, then your cadenza is complete. Chances are that you will also be proud of what you have done, and I'm absolutely certain that you will understand the concerto, its style, and its compositional design much better than before you had worked creatively within it. You will have actually shared some themes with Mozart himself. That's the beginning of true empathy.

Another assignment I have used is a little more abstract and personal and thus requires more of the students at the stage-one level of the process. They are encouraged to create some derivative etudes. I define this exercise as the creation by the performer of a series of progressive studies built upon the specific difficulties and requirements of an existing work of music. (Please see the chapter "Derivative Etudes, Create Your Own" for further discussion.) I want them to identify a problem spot in a solo, chamber music, or orchestral piece that has been bothering them for a while. I ask them to sit for a long time and ponder the root or roots of the difficulty. Were the problems technical, artistic, conceptual? What playing weaknesses of theirs might be contributing to the problem? What have they always assumed about this particular problem? Take that thought and turn it around, or turn it inside out. Question all previous assumptions. Try to look at it for the first time all over again. I encourage them to write down their thoughts and reread them over and over in the following days. After such a thorough and creative identification has occurred, they can then begin to decide what can be extracted from the original piece and modified or developed. What could be used to make an effective set of exercises that when practiced frequently would help to solve the problem and fill the need?

During this preparation period, I suggest that they modify the exercises while the practicing continues, improving on the studies, as if a book of exercises with one's own name on it were being prepared for future publication. After having spent a period of time with these exercises, I suggest that they return to the original piece and consider its musical content thoroughly, then return to the content of their own original exercises, and, as a second stage, develop those materials into a more complete, extended etude of greater musical substance. This is not as easy to do, so here is where one might possibly experience greater frustration. However, after a period of incubation has occurred, the musical etude has been created, and the student has actually played through it and the exercises many times, the return to the original piece and its problem spots should seem much more familiar and much easier to perform. That is certainly the plan, and it works, especially for those who spend the time and energy appropriate for sincere, personal growth. One thing is obvious: Each of the students, because of this creative and thought-provoking exercise, has a much greater understanding of the piece in question and the composer's intentions. They also seem to have discovered some new tools for improvements that might be needed next time in a similar situation. There is also the sense of accomplishment in knowing that one can alone solve problems with a bit of creative thinking and persistence.

Now, what about creating our own personal music through improvisation? How does that work? What should be done? My suggestion is simple and to the point: Start! Put your horn to your face and just do it! Do something that is not found on a piece of music somewhere. Give yourself permission to try something new. Go off to a quiet room away from everyone, turn off the lights, sit back in a chair, and spill your soul into your horn. Don't be afraid of anything, expect nothing in particular, enjoy what happens for a while, and then stop when you start to get bored. I suggest that you don't stop when you simply get frustrated, but wait until you are truly bored. Do go back again soon and improvise some more, trying out new ideas or maybe redoing some of the old ideas from before if they still come to your mind. By doing this, I am certain that you will get to know your way around your instrument much better. While you improvise, notice what moods you go through and then, more important, how you choose to turn those feelings into sound. After it begins to feel more natural, bring in a tape recorder, turn it on, and forget about it. Just let it run. If after a session you remember having had an especially good time, listen to the tape for a while. If what you improvised seems to have lasting appeal for you, you may want to notate its contents on a piece of manuscript paper.

There is really nothing wrong with letting your original ideas last only as long as they last. That's the way it is with the vast majority of the musics of the world. Songs and chants are rendered and often improvised for all sorts of reasons and left only to the memories of those who were there. However, our commercial and our academic cultures seem to demand that we document and collect every possible event for posterity, for possible research projects, or for profit. Consequently, most of us have been conditioned to accept that value system. We feel compelled to collect tapes of all that we do as performers so that those moments will last forever. This attitude helps to make the act of improvisation seem less important, of a lesser value, or of no true lasting value at all. It's here and then it's gone.

Do you value casual conversation with your friends? Do you enjoy taking a walk with nowhere in mind to go? Do you enjoy telling and hearing stories? If you answered "yes" to any of these questions, let me suggest a situation as a second stage for developing your improvising skills. Invite one of your musical friends to your practice room and start to take a walk nowhere in particular through your instruments. Enter into musical conversations about nothing special. Make up some sounds to, with, and for each other. Musically respond to each other's ideas and sounds and moods of seriousness and silliness. Share your stories through abstract sounds. Loosen up. This could also be done with a larger group of compatible friends. However, I might suggest that you start with only one or two. Let it grow gradually. Keep it simple so you can focus on your own comfort factor and your own creative spirit. Such experiences can be life changing and thus don't need to be captured on tape to be of ultimate value.

If composition is important to you (and by now you know that I certainly think it should be), some of these improvisations could easily become the catalysts for new compositions. If you do find yourself repeating a particular melody or rhythm incessantly, perhaps you should tape it and transcribe it onto manuscript paper. It must be important to you for some reason, especially if you can't get it out of your mind. It could be the germ of a fine new composition. To notate it will also help you get it out on the table so that you can consciously develop it or so that you can simply save it and move on to other ideas, coming back to it later. Perhaps that particular idea once clarified will incubate in your subconscious for a while, eventually to illuminate a future masterpiece or at least a fun song.

I would like next to discuss in more detail the ultimate creative experience for classically trained musicians: what it is like to compose your own music from ground zero. (Please see the chapter "Compose Yourself" for further discussion.) First, let me share a couple of ideas as to why this particular musical activity is at once both compelling and repelling. What might be at the root of the fear and anxiety that accompanies original composition? One thought is that such an activity invades your privacy. It pierces your armor. It potentially reveals too much about you and what you think, what you feel and who you are, what you have experienced and what you know, and what you have to say and how you find yourself saying it. True, honest, original composition is all about you the composer. Digging deep down inside the one person you know the best, the one you are most responsible to protect from all dangers (including the invasion of privacy) seems somewhat threatening. When put that way, original composition also holds some pretty exciting possibilities for self-discovery. But do you want anyone to know all of those things about you? At these earlier stages in your expanding creative activities, you must remember to objectify and ask yourself over and over again, "Who is really paying all that much attention to my attempts at composition? Who else really cares enough to listen so carefully that they might actually be able to psychoanalyze my deepest thoughts and feelings?" Do not forget that composition can be about your working with and for yourself. All of this should also help to eliminate the more obvious fear of creating something that is inferior to what is known as great music. It is the activity not the commodity that should motivate us as serious and complete students of music. Worry about the critics after you start getting commissions from the major orchestras of the world.

Original composition does, however, require a certain optimism, a certain sense that you can solve your own problems, that you can rely on your own abilities, and that you can trust your instincts and intelligence. But don't forget that all of these requirements can be learned and developed along with your conscious effort to just do it. If it turns out in the end that a particular composition isn't all that you might have hoped it would be, just don't tell anybody. But do try again!

How does one start? This is the most challenging and unique part of creating an all-new piece of music. The way music and musical tastes have been going in these last few decades, almost anything that organizes sound has been considered music. That's just too many choices. When I have assigned my students to simply write a piece of music, with every aspect about it being their choice, many of them find this moment of identification to be the most difficult part. Many of them have no clue of what to do. After they have relaxed a little and start to forgive me for making such an outrageous assignment, most find themselves writing pieces that grow from within their own experiences. That's a great place to start! Look inside yourself, not outside like we normally do for answers. All of art, all of literature, and I believe all of the true and lasting music is autobiographical. It can't help but be. You can only know yourself. Your experiences are you, are unique to you, and are like no one else's. So when you tap into your own personal biography with your own personal creative spirit, chances are you just might have something rather unique to say.

Start with the smallest of ideas. Something you love is a great place to begin. Let's say you love being outdoors. How does that make you feel? Get into that feeling, that mood. Does this bring with it visual images, or does it re-create sounds in your memory? Go to your own instrument or to a piano and just begin to doodle around. Make some appropriate sounds. Was there ever a poet who made you feel as if you were experiencing the outdoors? What in particular do you enjoy most about being in touch with nature? Is it watching the birds? Seeing a hawk circling on the wind? What does a hawk circling on the wind sound like in your imagination? Can you find it on your instrument or on the piano? Keep trying. Keep listening to your own thoughts.

After a while you could search out that poetry you were thinking about and just read for a while, or you could go outside and look for that very hawk you've been imagining. If you find a special poem that gives you the feelings you have had watching that hawk, that symbol of unbridled freedom whose abilities you might envy in some way, maybe you should write a piece for voice based on that particular poem. With this decision made, you must then begin to think about song and singing and all that it requires. You have identified, and next you must prepare. Live with the words of the poem. Read them over and over for rhythm, sound, texture, and of course meaning. Read about hawks. Watch them move, and sit silently while you do. When anything grabs hold of you, even faintly, write it down or play it into a tape recorder. Sing through your thoughts. This is when the fun begins, when one thing leads into another and you begin to feel the flow. The flow of ideas comes and goes just as that hawk does on the wind. Everything begins to remind you of a hawk. You see hawks everywhere, and you become submerged and maybe even a little obsessed within your own creative spirit. Nothing is more important than setting that poem and sharing the wind and the clouds with that hawk, that wonderful symbol of freedom and flight, that beautiful, wild creature that has a life so unlike your own that you want to be that hawk.

This all sounds quite romantic doesn't it? That's because it is. Romantic is good, especially if it has developed from something you have realized you feel strongly about. It is actually quite thrilling. That very set of experiences I have just described was much like the beginnings of what has become a recent composition of mine entitled *A Place for Hawks* for voice, horn, and strings. By including the horn in this piece, I am able as a performer to fly like that hawk along with the singer. The whole experience causes me to feel musical nuances I have never felt before on my horn because I have created those moments to be that way. It has helped me connect both my playing and my composing with a wonderful Wisconsin poet named August Derleth, primarily because I have lived within his poetry. This new compositional experience has given me a much greater appreciation for and understanding of melody and words and the possibilities of vocal timbre. I have also thought more about the problems of string players, their bowings and finger patterns as well as their potentials for lushness and harmonic flow.

In other words, as a performer, I have experienced the full gamut of intentions of the composer because in this case I am the composer. This is the most important reason I can think of for each and every one of us who loves to perform other people's music to at least begin to dabble in composition. Live with composer problems for a while, and your depth of understanding and empathy for all of the great composers will inevitably come through your own performances as communication.

You are what you think. So what do you think? Everything you know has come only from your thoughts about your personal experiences. You simply can't know anything else. That's good! That's good enough! That's as good as it is going to get!

If you want to be a more well-rounded or a more complete musician, be sure to use the greatest power you have—that wonderful power of thought—to look at music from the inside out and the outside in. Use your creative spirit to carry you into new ways of seeing and hearing what music really means to you. Let that spirit, that creative spirit, carry you like the wind carries a hawk.

It's now up to you to finish what we have started here. The bulk of this discussion has centered around the three words, *what*, *you*, and *think*. What words have I left out of my original question? The words *do* and *so* rejoining the three words discussed can be rearranged into the statement, "So do what you think!" Create your own thoughts, collect them, combine them, trust them, allow them to incubate for a while. Let them flow through your music, creating new and wonderful places for your mind and your heart to be.

A READING LIST ON THE CREATIVE PROCESS AND MUSIC

Aaron Copland, *Music and Imagination*, Harvard University Press, 1980.
The six Charles Eliot Norton Lectures consisting of a "rather free improvisation on the general theme imagination plays in the art of music" for the listener, interpreter, and creator. Also, the manifestations of that imaginative mind.

Eloise Ristad, *A Soprano on Her Head*, Real People Press, 1982.
"Right-side-up reflections on life and other performances." A somewhat seriously funny and imaginative approach to the solving of performance problems by a very creative teacher and a delightful personality.

Anthony Storr, *Music and the Mind*, The Free Press, 1992.
How and why music evokes emotions in the listeners. The psychology of the creative process and the healing powers of the arts.

Peter Michael Hamel, *Through Music to the Self*, Element Books, 1976.
An expansive view of world music and its natural laws and seemingly magical properties by an active German composer, sociologist, and psychologist.

Ted Gioia, *The Imperfect Art*, Oxford University Press, 1988.
A wide-ranging aesthetic discussion on the art of jazz and improvisation as viewed within the full cultural environment of the twentieth century. Imperfection as art.

Derek Baily, *Improvisation, Its Nature and Practice in Music*, Da Capo Press, 1993.
A discussion of the nature of improvisation in all of its forms: baroque, contemporary, East Indian, flamenco, rock, "free," organ music, as well as jazz as a basis for all music-making.

Mildred Portney Chase, *Improvisation: Music From the Inside Out*, Creative Arts Book Company, 1988.
An idea-filled and inspirational book based "on the conviction that we are all born with the ability to improvise."

Paul F. Berliner, *Thinking in Jazz: The Infinite Art of Improvisation*, University of Chicago Press, 1994.
How musicians learn to improvise. The rigorous practice and thought and the complexities of "composing in the moment."

Daniel Goleman, Paul Kaufman, and Michael Ray, *The Creative Spirit*, Penguin Books, 1992.
A companion book to the PBS Television Series discusses how "creativity can be cultivated by anyone." Includes a series of practical exercises.

D. N. Perkins, *The Mind's Best Work*, Harvard University Press, 1981.
An exploration of the creative process in the arts, sciences, and everyday life, including creative episodes of Beethoven, Mozart, Picasso, and others.

Mihaly Csikszentmihalyi, *Flow: The Psychology of Optimal Experience*, Harper Perennial, 1990.
A study of the states of "optimal experience." Flow, a state of concentration so focused that it amounts to absolute absorption in an activity.

Howard Gardner, *Creating Minds*, Basic Books, 1993.
"An anatomy of creativity as seen through the lives of Freud, Einstein, Picasso, Stravinsky, Eliot, Graham, and Gandhi." Creative lives that shaped modern culture.

Howard Gardner, *Art, Mind, and Brain: A Cognitive Approach to Creativity*, Basic Books, 1982.
Explores all aspects of creativity from a child's song through a Mozart symphony, drawn from developmental, cognitive, and neuropsychology as well as philosophy.

Literature & Repertoire: The Means & the End

21. Solo Repertoire: The Basics and Beyond

Numerous review opportunities over the years have provided me with a broad perspective of many of the more recent publications available for solo horn. However, there is a need to mix the old with the new. The standard, or basic, repertoire is basic for a reason, and quite often that reason involves its musical quality. The progressing student needs to become familiar with these standard pieces for artistic as well as practical reasons. Much of this is great music, and we should know it. We also need to know what others before us have learned so we can all share in the jargon of being a horn player. Still, the individual in all of us requires that we find lesser-known works that we wish to make our own and, perhaps, present on our own unique recitals. This chapter will focus primarily on what I see as the basic repertoire, which is actually quite extensive for the horn. It will be supplemented by works I have discovered to be a fine complement to the basics and know to fill in gaps in the repertoire. Beyond this, I highly encourage each of you to search out your own special, new, and wonderful pieces. Encourage others to write for you, or simply write for yourself. It is through the solo repertoire that we develop our individuality as artists.

A number of years ago, William Robinson (at that time the professor of horn at Baylor University in Waco, Texas, an author, a performer, and one of the original founders and officers of the International Horn Society) sent out a questionnaire to many leading American horn teachers. In it he asked what materials they used and recommended for their students. From the 43 respondents, one could make a case for accepting the top-ranking solos as basic repertoire, at least within the United States. (Etudes were also included in this study, and you will find most of the top-ranking etude collections reviewed or mentioned in the chapter titled "Basic Etudes in Review.")

Percentages of usage were included in his tabulations, which I found to be a wonderful help, beginning with a 95 percent listing for the four concertos by Mozart (our finest repertoire!), down to 5 percent for the Rheinberger Sonata in E♭, Op. 178 (which I think is an exceptional Romantic period work). In the following discussion, the results of Robinson's survey are taken into consideration, with supplements to fill in the gaps. My discussions and listings of recommended repertoires are grouped within general periods or eras of composition. Each period will begin with the most popular or most basic of repertoire and move toward the lesser known. This manner of grouping is done for reasons of programming considerations and for the pedagogical purpose of encouraging all students to know what is basic. The Romantic and Classical periods are, without a doubt, the periods receiving the most attention, with the Baroque and contemporary needing the most encouragement.

The Baroque Period

The Baroque period, dating approximately from 1600 to 1750, is perhaps the most neglected era of music for today's advancing student horn players. The range requirement for the solo works written especially for the Baroque (clarino) horn is primarily within the top octave and periodically above the high C. This is simply because the overtones become diatonic at third space C, which allowed the composers conjunct options for melodic interest. At that time, horn players (who often doubled on trumpet) specialized in high horn performance while using small horns and mouthpieces. As performers, they were required to play only in the top two-and-one-half octaves. Today we focus our technique around the mid-range and have to administer three-and-a-half to four octaves. There is, however, a fair amount of Baroque literature that has been successfully transcribed for the horn centering on the mid-range. The stylistic differences, however, are quite significant. Thus, I encourage everyone to learn both the music originally written for horn in the clarino style and the many other Baroque transcriptions.

On the top of the list of clarino horn solos is the **Concerto in D** by **Georg Philip Telemann**. (In the Robinson list, this is the first Baroque work specifically for horn, and it ranks at only a 14 percent usage.) This work has been frequently recorded and provides the player with many of the typical clarino gestures without overly extreme high-range demands. Repeated note patterns, allowing for a player to utilize interesting articulation variety, a lyrical slow movement with typical dotted rhythms (recommended by some experts to be performed as a double dot), and repeated dance-like passages calling out for some original ornamentation appropriate to the period make this the best introduction to Baroque solo playing available. Note that many of the recordings of this work are literal renditions of the notes on the page and, if imitated by the student, will provide only a portion of the challenge and almost none of the musical value of learning a work so typical of the performance expectations of the period. Rising only to a high B, this work, though enduring, is accessible and can be a perfect passageway to the idiosyncrasies of Baroque performance practice.

Equally important are the **Concerto in E♭**, and the **Concerto in E♭, No. 2**, by **Christoph Förster**. Both are delightfully written, are not excessively high though demanding, are full of acrobatics and extended technically—active passages, numerous suggested ornaments (especially trills in No. 2), and have a great deal of melodic interest. The first of these has been recorded often, and the second, edited and made available by William Scharnberg, is lesser known but is equally enjoyable to perform. Appropriate opportunities for ornamentation are less obvious throughout these works, except for the final 16 measures of the first concerto where the Schirmer edition has written out Barry Tuckwell's recorded ornamental ideas. I encourage students to create their own ending in the style of the movement as would have been done in the period. (Don't ever pass up an opportunity to be appropriately creative!)

The **Concerto in D** by **Leopold Mozart** and the **Concerto in E♭** by **Jan Neruda** are two more concertos that have been available for some time but are not performed often enough, considering how delightful they are musically. One reason is that their range requirements are above high C. Also, trumpet players have for a long time considered the Neruda as one of their own.

Two other works of important historical worth include **Concerto in C**, *La Choisy*, by **Michel Corrette** and *Deux Divertissements* by **Jean-Joseph Mouret**, considered to be among the earliest horn concertos and earliest solos for horn with continuo. They are enjoyable to learn, would make an interesting addition to a recital program, and are recommended even though they may not satisfy your most sophisticated artistic needs.

In recent years, numerous Baroque period concertos have been rediscovered and published. The largest collection was found in a library at Dresden, with copies at Lund University in Sweden. Barry Tuckwell has recorded a number of these quite effectively on a modern instrument. Because of these discoveries, interest in early music horn performance practice has increased and has become available to us all through the scholarship and performances of such individuals as Thomas Heibert, Lowell Greer, Richard Seraphinoff, William Scharnberg, Mary Rasmussen, Claude Maury, Viola Roth, Ludwig Güttler, Hermann Baumann, and Peter Damm.

These new concertos written specifically for the Baroque horn and worth investigating (though they might not be as easy to find) are composed by **Johann Friedrich Fasch, Johann David Heinichen, Johann Matthias Sperger, Johann Georg Knechtel, Johann Joachim Quantz, Johann Gottlieb Graun, Carl Heinrich Graun, Christien August Röllig,** and **Johann Friedrich Reichardt**.

There are many fine transcriptions for the horn from the Baroque period, the styles of which are significantly different from the clarino horn. This too is good. The most popular are the **Six Suites for Solo Cello** by **Johann Sebastian Bach**. Three editions are readily available, and each differs regarding the articulations, breath markings, and even pitch choices when the original double-stops are not possible. Each has its strong points. The wisest way to learn these, however, is to purchase an urtext edition for the cello and create your own edition. These remarkable pieces lie on the low side and, thus, are a wonderful way to improve the mid-low range while experiencing some of the finest music ever written. Other works by Bach that work well on the horn include **Aria from the Third Suite** and **Sonata No. 2 in E♭**, originally for flute and continuo. The last two movements from the **Sonata for Flute Alone in A minor** also works beautifully when transposed to C basso. Other published transcriptions well worth the time and energy include **Sonata in G minor** by **G. F. Handel**, *Allegro Spiritoso* by **J. B. Senaillé**, **Sonata in G minor** by **H. Eccles**, and the **Sonatas in F, G minor, and D minor** by **Archangelo Corelli**.

The Classical Period

The Classical period, which dates roughly from 1750 to 1825, could easily be considered the Golden Age for the horn as a solo instrument. During this extraordinary time, Mozart, Beethoven, and Haydn recognized the unique qualities of the hand horn and were inspired by the virtuosic abilities of Thaddaus Steinmüller, Carl Türrschmidt, Giovanni Punto, and Ignaz Leitgeb, among others. During no other period in history has such a large percentage of the major composers contributed so significantly to the horn repertoire. For that reason alone, we should all study the hand horn to discover the musical and timbral reasons why.

The single most important body of work for the solo horn (from any period) is the **Concertos in E♭**, (K. 417) (No. 2), (K. 447) (No. 3), (K. 495) (No. 4), and the so-called **Concerto No. 1 in D**, (K. 412) by **Wolfgang Amadeus Mozart**. Written perhaps casually for a family friend named Ignaz Leitgeb, these truly remarkable masterpieces have been recorded scores of times, are published in numerous editions, and are included on all contest lists from middle school through international competitions. As one ages, the musical mastery of these great composers becomes even more meaningful and gratifying. Mozart, it appears, started seven horn concertos over his lifetime but fully completed only the first three in E♭. Hans Pizka compiled the complete available manuscripts and reproduced them in a text entitled *Mozart and the Horn*. With such details readily available, publishers have finally begun to treat these great works with more respect and less unnecessary editing. Be careful, however, of the editions you buy. The new Schirmer editions are well done. You should feel free to determine your own exact dynamics and to modify the articulations, always considering what Mozart did and did not include on the original horn parts and what he marked in the string parts for similar passages. He assumed the soloists of the time would take such liberties. Make sure that the parts you own are written for horn in E♭ or horn in D (for No. 1), not horn in F! One should always see the music of this period as the hand horn player saw it. This is also the most musical and enjoyable way to develop and practice your transposition skills.

The fact that these important compositions are introduced to young students as early as middle school and presented primarily as accessible contest repertoire often causes years of distorted opinions. Many of my incoming freshman students feel they are bored with these pieces and want nothing to do with them ever again. How to remedy this is a difficult question. Fine recordings help validate their worth and help students get the sound of the full orchestra in their ears, rather than a mere piano reduction using only some of the notes.

There are so many performance concerns to consider. I will list a few here: Tempos should be moderate, since fast in Mozart's time was the speed of a horse, not the speed of light or warp speed; emphasize gently but convincingly the first note in each measure within artistic reason; consider opera and the sounds of voices when interpreting a line, contrasting those vocal inflections with sudden juxtapositions of instrumental-like passages (for example, scales and arpeggiated figures) almost as if you are in a dialogue with yourself; make dynamic contrasts obvious but not violent or drastic (Mozart had his powerful ideas but within the context of classical proportions); and always create a beautiful sound. (Vibrato can be quite effective when used sparingly.)

Finally, let me encourage you to create your own cadenzas. Begin by listening to classical cadenzas (especially Mozart's) for other instruments, primarily wind, violin, and piano concertos, so that you might absorb the proper instincts as to a basic form and proportion. Next, write out each motive within that movement of your chosen concerto, including the orchestral parts and continuing through the entire horn part. These will become your building blocks. Separate these motives and begin to play through them in an improvisatory manner and in every possible ordering. Write down what works and begin to edit out what doesn't. After you have compiled what seems sensible, tape yourself and listen again the next day. Edit as needed until you find yourself feeling rather proud of your creation. (Further discussion on this subject can be found in Chapter 20.) Be sure that what you perform as a cadenza would have been possible and probable for the hand horn player of the period for reasons of musical logic and artistic taste. Also, consider more specifically what the composer considered appropriate for the horn in this context and don't overdo it. We can think in the chromaticism of Strauss, but Mozart never did. When preparing and performing Mozart, always think Mozart.

Ludwig van Beethoven wrote his **Sonata Op. 17** in 1800 for the most famous horn soloist in Europe, Giovanni Punto. Beethoven's purpose was to attract critical attention to a concert of original compositions shortly after his arrival in Vienna. The horn part was written the night before, and Beethoven improvised much of the piano part, notating it later and publishing it in 1801. Punto, being a *cor basse* player, was asked to play what was simply the most perfect example of what a solo hand horn player was expected to do at that time. I encourage this work first for any student beginning to discover the hand horn. The range is limited to a written G atop the treble clef staff, but it descends to the factitious tone of G on the bottom line of the bass clef. Typical second horn, or *cor basse*, figurations are spread throughout the work, which, as one might expect knowing its history, features the piano more than the horn. This also becomes a remarkable experience in chamber music, requiring the hornist to frequently adjust to the attack and decay characteristics of the piano. This work requires an exceptional pianist.

Two more important works by a major composer from this period are **Concerto No. 1 in D** and **Concerto No. 2 in D** by **Franz Joseph Haydn**. The second concerto ranks slightly higher in the aforementioned tabulations, perhaps because it is one of the finest works for the development and use of the mid-range and low registers. These works are thought to have been for first horn and second horn, respectively. The second concerto is primarily low, with many of the *cor basse* arpeggiated configurations. The first is primarily for high horn, rising often to the sixteenth harmonic (written C, sounding D) and infrequently to the written D, but with the unique inclusion of a repeated *cor basse* passage in the lyrical second movement. This was an extraordinary request for that period but was in response to the extraordinary performing abilities of Thaddaus Steinmüller for whom it was written.

The first concerto sounds the most like many of F. J. Haydn's compositions, full of lightness, humor, and clarity, requiring precise articulations and a relaxed fluency in the high range. The second was thought for a long time to have been composed by someone else, primarily because of its style, which is also delightfully fun but which seems almost Baroque at times. (It has since been officially declared, by H. Robbins Landon, to be a work by F. J. Haydn.) Cadenzas (create your own!) are required in all movements, except for the middle movement of the second concerto. This provides the performer with a wonderful opportunity to study these works more deeply while gaining a greater empathy with the composer. It is recommended again that you buy the cleanest edition possible for horn in D. (I presently prefer the Boosey & Hawkes edition.)

Franz Joseph's younger brother **Johann Michael Haydn** also wrote two concertos for horn, of which the **Concertino in D** has taken its place as repertoire and, consequently, been recorded a number of times. Similar in style to his brother's works, and of comparable musical value, the concertino finds its uniqueness in its rather unusual form. The first movement is a lovely and rather lengthy larghetto followed by a spirited and technically tricky allegro movement, both of which are in sonata form. The last movement is a minuet, requiring the horn only incidentally in the trio section. Though this unique work seems to have unjustifiably received less attention and fewer live performances than the concertos of Franz Joseph, it is attractive and a musically gratifying opus worthy of sincere attention.

Mozart again enters the tabulated list with his **Concert Rondo (K. 371)**. This single movement is believed to have been the third movement of yet another concerto. That concerto was never finished nor was the accompaniment for this particular rondo. Mozart completed only the horn part, so all published editions contain the editor's realization of an accompaniment (which opens up the possibility for each of us to enjoy our own additions or modifications). Only recently has it been discovered that there were 64 more measures in the middle of this work. Breitkopf, the new Schirmer, and Birdalone Music include this striking new find in their editions. This delightful, dance-like movement is unique in Mozart's concerto output in that it is not a stylized hunting horn chasse in 6/8, as are the four other rondo movements. It is actually more similar to the rondo movement of the Quintet (K. 407), with its technical acrobatics, and it requires an original cadenza.

The fragments of two incomplete concertos by Mozart have been compiled and serve as the inspiration for two sets of published realizations. The Concert Rondo (K. 371) is thought to have been the last movement of the **Concerto in E♭ (K. 370b)**. The other work, **Concerto in E (K. 494a)**, is drawn from only a few measures of an opening melody. Hermann Jeurisson and James Collarafi have completed these truly interesting, though much less significant, bits of horn history.

Next in popularity are two concertos by the lesser-known Bohemian composer Franz Anton Rössler, who published under the Italian name **Francesco Antonio Rosetti**. His many concertos are discussed at length by Christopher Leuba in Volume VIII, No. 2, of *The Horn Call: Journal of the International Horn Society*. Of these, the **Concerto No. 2 in B♭**, and the **Concerto in D minor** are the most popular, perhaps because they have been the most recorded. During his lifetime, Rosetti was considered by his peers as a composer comparable to Mozart and Haydn. His Concerto No. 2 is a delightful work with many memorable melodic passages and a few sparkling technical challenges, which help to draw attention to the hornist's virtuosity. In at least one of the most available editions, the exposition of the first movement can be easily cut without affecting the balance of thematic materials. Hermann Baumann's recording of this work is a fine way to learn of this composer. The compositional substance of these pieces is certainly less profound than those of Mozart, but they are entertaining and representative of a style of composition that we must be capable of administering. The D minor concerto is for me less satisfying musically than the E♭ and no more interesting than his many other concertos which, according to Horace Fitzpatrick, contributed much to the development of a melodic style for the instrument.

Franz Danzi, well known by wind players for his 12 convincing woodwind quintets, wrote three important works for solo horn, of which the **Sonata in E♭, Op. 28**, is the most popular. This is truly a charming, melodic three-movement work that features both the horn and piano. On the hand horn, it is more demanding than the Beethoven due to some of Danzi's less empathetic pitch choices, but this is of no consequence to the valved horn player. A remarkable recording by Barry Tuckwell with Vladimir Ashkenazy raised my admiration for this work. Danzi's other two works for horn, **Sonata Concertante, Op. 44**, and **Concerto in E**, are each worth the effort to learn and perform though they lack the spontaneity and youthful personality found in his earlier sonata.

Though **Carl Maria von Weber** is often thought of as one of the fathers of Romanticism, his music is well rooted in the Classical style, both harmonically and formally. His one significant contribution to the solo horn literature, the **Concertino in E, Op. 45**, first written in 1806 and revised in 1815, is a tour de force for either the hand horn player or the valved hornist. It is actually easier on the hand horn if one's technical abilities are comparable. The form of this multifaceted work is a typical theme and variations followed by a somewhat whimsical polacca. The athletic character of much of this work is well balanced by an operatic introduction and recitative-like cadenza variation. Included within this cadenza is the first notated use of multiphonics for the horn. The act of singing and playing simultaneously, causing chords of three, four, or more pitches (briefly discussed in Chapter 3, "Extending Techniques") was a trick often done by Punto and other virtuosi of the period. Weber's actual choice of pitches is not exact, but the harmonic implications and basic design should be emulated and made to match the performer's voice quality and range.

Learning the Weber was how and when I solidified my E horn transposition. There are many awkward passages to maneuver in that key, and the range becomes a factor as it races frequently above the staff, but E was the composer's choice of crook. After this energetic piece is worked out technically, most other awkward E horn passages will be a breeze. Thus, I recommend that my students buy an edition for E horn, not the one transposed to E♭.

Another important pair of works similar in style to the Weber, but this time in F, are the **Two Sonatas** by **Luigi Cherubini**. Though a rather cantankerous individual, Cherubini was widely respected as a master craftsman with Beethoven pronouncing him as one of the immortals. The label for these two unequal movements is somewhat misleading. They were originally for horn and strings though they work well with piano, and the first sonata is simply a short, introspective composition that serves most successfully as an introduction for the second sonata. The second is often performed without the first, standing alone as another rousing and rambunctious rondo.

A third in what could be thought of as a series of such works, including the Weber and Cherubini, is the **Prelude, Theme, and Variations** by **Gioacchino Rossini**. Composed a little later than the others, this admirable work is still in a classical style and deals with many of the same mannerisms, moods, operatic emulations, and acrobatic antics. There are editions of this work that have been abridged and are, thus, not recommended. If cuts are needed, the appropriate spots to avoid repetitions are obvious. The piece in its entirety is worth doing just as the composer intended it. The printed repetitions provide the opportunity for performers to build and intensify their interpretations, carrying this fun-filled piece to higher levels of excitement. This music is a pure delight and was actually meant for horn and piano (not orchestra). Consequently, it works even better than the above transcriptions. Rossini also composed an **Introduction and Allegro**, which is also effective but not as gregarious, charming, or memorable.

Two other works that did not appear on Robinson's list but are certainly of comparable worth are the **Sonata in F, Op.34*** by **Ferdinand Ries**, and **Sonata in E** by **Nicolaus von Krufft**. Ferdinand Ries was a piano student and eventually a biographer of Beethoven, while studying composition with Albrechtsberger. His close association with Beethoven is blatantly obvious in this exquisite imitation of the latter's Sonata, Op. 17. Written ten years after Beethoven's opus, Ries chose the same keys, and forms, indulged in some exact motivic emulation, and created similar musical relationships between the two instruments. This work is somewhat more substantial, lasting 24 minutes and, as with Beethoven, requiring a virtuosic pianist. Having recorded this sparkling work for Crystal Records with Karen Zaczek Hill, I never tire of its sincere yet gleeful character and felt as though I were performing another fine chamber music masterpiece by Beethoven.

The Nicolaus von Krufft Sonata is similar to many of the others and is thus important. The first modern publication of this work was for horn in F, but Birdalone Press has recently released it as it was originally published in 1836 in the key of E. This is a better key, especially for hand horn, the instrument upon which this work is receiving its recognition in live performances and on recordings.

The Romantic Period

The Romantic period, ranging from the early 1800s to the early 1900s, was dominated by large orchestral works in which the horn took its place of prominence as a solo voice. The music of Schumann, Wagner, Brahms, Bruckner, Strauss, Dvořák, Tchaikovsky, and Mahler just wouldn't be the same without the horn to blend the orchestral voices together and periodically stand out as the warm, strong, heroic voice of the period. Of these composers, only Strauss and Schumann wrote for the horn as a concerto voice. The horn as an instrument experienced wide variations of valve configurations and, consequently, the hornists as practitioners were all going through major transitions of historical importance. This didn't stop all of the Romantic composers, however. There are many fine works from this period that receive a great deal more attention from students and professional performers than any other single block of works. Perhaps it is because players also believe the horn to be that warm, strong, heroic voice, and we search out music to highlight such a fine reputation and dominant inclination.

The single most performed solo work from this period is, undoubtedly, the **Concerto No. 1 by Richard Strauss.** Written by the son of a great hornist of the time, this youthful, energetic, powerful, and intelligently formed composition exemplifies better than any other single work what the horn represents musically and what the hornists were capable of technically during the mid-Romantic period. Other concertos may be more demanding, but none are more musically successful. The work is tightly unified compositionally through the use of cyclic motivic development. Strauss obviously chose to emulate the accompanimental and somewhat the orchestrational style of Mozart while creating melodic materials reminiscent of Mendelssohn. He was only an 18-year-old student at the time (thus his emulations) but was soon to compose his remarkable orchestral tone poems, beginning with *Don Juan.* The first movement of this concerto is the most effective audition piece available, lasting five minutes and covering all major aspects of playing. This concerto is also the one work conductors wish to program whenever a solo opportunity presents itself for a hornist. This is true for most orchestras, but especially for those with lesser budgets that can't afford the time to learn and rehearse a Strauss tone poem. With this they can program a great work by Richard Strauss for a chamber-sized orchestra featuring a horn soloist and still have the time and money left to rehearse other pieces. Thus, hornists should all know this piece and have it at near ready throughout their careers.

Robert Schumann's **Adagio und Allegro, Op. 70,** was the first solo work by a major composer featuring the relatively recent technical developments of the valved horn. Written during a manic period of remarkable productivity (1849), Schumann created a nine-minute work that seriously challenges the abilities of performers to this day. Taking the hornist to extremes in range, lengths of phrases, musical expressiveness, and physical stamina, this piece can serve as a test for all. To understand and enjoy the profoundly musical interaction between the horn and piano, listen to recordings of Schumann *lieder* by such vocalists as Dietrich Fischer-Dieskau, Fritz Wunderlich, and Christa Ludwig. The musical content of this powerful work is beyond the proportions of a single horn and piano and will, consequently, always feel just out of reach. That is as it should be. Schumann stretches us. During that same year, he composed the Konzertstück für 4 Waldhörner, Op. 86, which stretched the hornists far beyond their normal limits. Today, we must meet these challenges. This is a major piece of our repertoire. I would, however, be remiss in not mentioning my firm belief as a musician that Op. 70, which was also published and is frequently performed as a work for cello and piano, sounds more appropriate in that context, especially in the adagio movement where breathing becomes a musically unfortunate problem for the hornist. Listen to both cello and horn recordings to truly learn this work.

Next on Robinson's list, but certainly not the next most frequently performed Romantic period work, is **Concerto No. 2 by Richard Strauss.** Written near the end of his life and thus incorporating many melodic, harmonic, and rhythmic reminiscences, this demanding work presents a fascinating reflection of Strauss's first concerto from 60 years earlier. Composed once again for chamber orchestra, also in the key of E♭ (this time requiring the hornist to transpose), both concertos are very similar formal designs, somewhat cyclic motivically, and have near identical range demands. The second concerto differs primarily in its accompanimental manner and harmonic language and in the technical fluidity required of the soloist. The first movement seems to have been composed more in the manner of a woodwind composition than one for a brass instrument. This is not a fault; it actually presents an exciting challenge, which is more than worth the effort. This is a strikingly exciting, remarkably rewarding tone-poem-like composition that features the "hero's voice" throughout.

A remarkable, single-movement song from this period that best captures the vocal lyricism, the resonant warmth, and the emotional depth of the horn is the **Nocturne, Op. 7,** by **Franz Strauss.** The father of Richard Strauss, Franz was Wagner's favorite hornist (though the two shared personal animosities). His affinity for the instrument is demonstrated throughout his rather substantial compositional output, but his compositional genius is nowhere as obvious as in the Nocturne. In recent years, this work has received frequent performances by trombonists, tubists, and flügelhorn players, and for all the right reasons. Audiences love this piece, and it sings with a naturalness quite uncommon to the horn repertoire. **Concerto, Op. 8,** by Franz Strauss soon followed the Nocturne and has enjoyed great popularity as well. This concerto follows the typical three-movement design with the outside movements sharing identical content while framing a truly beautiful slow middle movement. Here is an exceptionally good example of a fine piece of music, which can challenge but not discourage a younger player technically while it musically stimulates the more advanced performers and their audiences and gives the impression of being more difficult than it actually is. Franz Strauss's **Introduction, Theme and Variations, Op. 13,** ranked at ten percent in the tabulations and has many fun-filled moments and technical challenges, but it is clearly not as musically substantive as the earlier compositions. It is, however, a fine showpiece for a rising virtuoso to use as well as a work of fine art for a musician to render.

Morceau de Concert, Op. 94, by Camille Saint-Saëns is a three-movement work lasting only about nine minutes, during which technical fluidity and dexterity are challenged. A melodic stopped horn passage occurs, lyrical low-range passagework enhances the lovely and dramatic second movement, and the last movement moves through the three octaves to the high C while requiring some very rapid tonguing. The end result is actually a rather successful piece of music. The opening theme in the style of a French march sets a powerful tone and provides an effective pattern for the two contrasting variations that follow. The first movement also works well as an audition piece. Available for horn and orchestra (uniquely orchestrated for pairs of winds, three trombones, timpani, and strings), this compact concerto has also been transcribed a number of times for horn with band, which I have found serves such a performance opportunity remarkably well, much better than a Mozart or Strauss concerto.

The next Romantic work of note was actually composed in the early 1950s (published in 1953). **Reinhold Glière's Concerto for Horn and Orchestra, Op. 91**, has become a favorite Romantic concerto, especially since Hermann Baumann's recording of 1985. The inspiration for this virtuosic Russian opus was, according to the composer, the Tchaikovsky violin concerto. Such relationships are noted in its length of 24 minutes, its sweeping melodic lines, its powerful orchestral proportions (only barely realizable on the piano), its absolutely gorgeous second movement that reaches impassioned climactic moments, and its frolicking dance-like third movement that seems most to imitate Tchaikovsky's concerto. A lengthy cadenza is required in the 11-minute first movement, which I feel should be of the performer's creation. However, the International Music Company edition includes a cadenza by Valerie Polekh, the performer for whom this concerto was written. Use this as a set of ideas and as an example of the approximate proportions, and then go on from there to create a more melodically oriented cadenza that is more consistent with the composer's approach to the horn. This is a major, major work in our Romantic period repertoire, based purely on its style rather than its date. I recommend most seriously that you try to find a copy of the premiere recording of Polekh and the Bolshoi Theatre Orchestra conducted by the composer that appeared on a Classic Editions LP CE6 (later listed as 3001) to hear the true Russian way of interpreting this luscious composition. Listen not to imitate but just to understand.

There are a number of short single-movement Romantic works that are frequently performed as separate solos or brought together as sets. The most popular of these include **Richard Strauss's Andante, (1888)***; **Alexander Glazounov's Reverie, Op. 24**; **Reinhold Glière's Romance, Op. 35, No.6**; **Valse Triste, Op. 35, No. 7**; **Nocturne, Op. 35, No. 10**; **Intermezzo, Op. 35, No. 11**; **Camille Saint-Saëns's Romance, Op. 36**; and **Alexander Scriabin's Romance**. Here is a wealth of melodic beauty. Each of these is a musical gem. The Strauss was composed as a twenty-fifth wedding anniversary present dedicated to his father and rings true with a rich passion, requiring an accomplished pianist with a mutual sense of rubato. The Glazounov is a classic Russian melodic work of dramatic proportions, requiring an expanded range and resulting in great satisfaction for the performer and audience. Glière's Opus 35 is a collection of works devoted to many of the woodwind and brass instruments. The four for horn that are readily available are similar in mood and texture, with the Valse Triste being the most active with its large leaps and impetuous melodic undulations. The Valse Triste and the Romance both build to a cadenza-like release of tension before returning to their initial moods. Each of these four are musically compelling and group well as Nos. 6, 11, 10, and 7. Both the Saint-Saëns Romance and the Scriabin Romance are refined, alluring little works that are accessible to younger players and perfectly satisfying to the more advanced. It is easy to recommend playing any or all of these pieces for such occasions as weddings and church services. There is yet another Romance by Saint-Saëns published for both horn and cello, which is Op. 67. Although it is a rather beautiful piece, it seems to work more successfully for the cello.

Another lavishly beautiful work from France is the **Larghetto**, Op. posth., by **Emmanuel Chabrier**. This nine-minute, one-movement work literally shimmers with lush harmonies and graciously undulates between moments of calm loveliness and ardent fervor. This work sounds as if César Franck might have written it, and begins to suggest the colorful characteristics of what would become French Impressionism. Effectively composed for horn with orchestra, this enticing composition works quite well with the piano and should be performed often.

Gabriel Joseph Rheinberger's Sonata, Op. 178*, represents his only work for solo horn and stands alone as a major sonata from this period. Aside from the Schumann, all of the large Romantic period works I've discussed as basic were originally for horn and orchestra. The harmonic and formal structure of this three-movement work is actually quite classical, or Brahmsian, with its overall sound being perhaps more like a less impassioned Schumann. Rheinberger was a very prominent composer, scholar, and teacher of composition near the end of the nineteenth century. This remarkable sonata begins with a solid statement of the theme for horn alone and continues to share many wonderful themes evenly with an exceptionally well-written piano part. The stunning second movement contains some of the most persuasive melodic writing in all of horn literature. The final movement vigorously dances in a most lighthearted manner through open fifths and mutual syncopated patterns.

Another important virtuosic work for horn and piano, written in 1848 and left unpublished until 1973, is the **Andante e Polocca in E** by **Carl Czerny**. What great fun this piece is to learn and to perform. Most noted for his piano etudes, Czerny, a piano student of Beethoven's, was nicknamed "The Ink Pot" because of the many blackened notes he wrote and performed as a virtuoso pianist and prolific composer (including 861 numbered compositions). The Andante e Polocca, written more than 30 years after the valve was invented, was intended for the hand horn and represents some of the most advanced and demanding yet thoughtful hand horn writing in the literature. *Virtuosic* is the key word in describing both parts (valves or not). The musical impression, however, is one of great charm and elegance from the Andante and a rousingly good time as the performers dance through the thematically captivating Polacca.

Other composers worth investigating from the Romantic period include **Bellini**, **Blanc**, **Borodin**, **Dauprat**, **Duvernoy**, **Franz**, **Gallay**, **Goedicke**, **Gounod**, **Mercadante**, and **Reinecke**, among others. There is also a large number of fine transcriptions of works by many major composers often compiled in collections. Noteworthy are the three collections of Verne Reynolds that include compositions by **Schubert**, **Schumann**, **Liszt**, **Tchaikovsky**, **Strauss**, and **Brahms** and the numerous collections by Frøydis Wekre and Thomas Bacon.

The Modern Period

The modern period has produced a large number of solo works featuring the horn, many of which are fine compositions. I'll first discuss the most basic conservative works of the twentieth century. Lucky for us, solos with piano and unaccompanied solos have become a more frequent focus for composers and publishers in recent years. Also, there are many more performers finding numerous performance outlets providing composers and publishers greater reasons to produce. How a particular composition becomes basic repertoire from this point in history forward is largely a matter of opinion since we have less of a perspective as to what will pass the test of time regarding such works. With the Robinson tabulations in consideration, I would like to discuss those pieces as they relate to my experiences, that are most admired by my students, and that seem to appear more frequently on concerts and at workshops.

There can be no argument against the profound significance of the three solo works for horn by **Paul Hindemith**. His **Sonate in F** (1939) stands alone as the finest sonata for horn of the twentieth century for many reasons. In 1973, ten years after Hindemith's death, his colleagues at Yale University celebrated his life and musical output with a week of performances of his most representative music. Of all the sonatas written for all of the instruments, the faculty at Yale selected the horn sonata as his finest. Being privileged to perform for this event, my wife and I studied the work with Professor of Piano John Kirkpatrick, who had accompanied Hindemith as violist and had been his colleague since the 1940s. His animated enthusiasm for this work was infectious.

Important points that Kirkpatrick made during our sessions together included a recommendation to sincerely adhere to the mood and manner set by the tempo markings. All three movements are designated at approximately the same metronomic marking. These settings establish important musical parameters. To perform the first and last movements too quickly and the second movement too slowly seems to be the tendency for most students and many professionals. Hindemith has provided the contrasts desired through his compositional content. To assume that a genius such as Hindemith, who was a profoundly meticulous composer and teacher, would notate tempos that were not intended is presumptuous. There is great weight and power that can only be expressed at or near the tempos indicated for the outer movements and a flowing lyricism and momentum in the second movement that occurs only with a somewhat active tempo. You must not deviate more than four to eight metronomic markings from these indications. Then as you perform, be flexible. This music needs to breathe and must ebb and flow with the phrases. It is tempo indications that suggest both the attitude and the message of the musical content. Feel what he wants you to feel, and then feel what you feel.

Kirkpatrick also expressed his thought that to know Hindemith's music, one must relate its formal designs to Mozart and its musical substance to Brahms. To perform this sonata with a Mozartian clarity and precision and with a Brahmsian sound and musical depth raises this work to the level it truly deserves.

Hindemith's Concerto (1949) was composed for Dennis Brain and recorded by him with Hindemith conducting. There is no better way to study or to learn to love this work than by listening to that recording. The design of this 15-minute composition is truly unique. It begins with two miniature movements: the first is a sonatina with two themes and no development that marches through rapidly shifting meters; the second is a sprightly scherzo with a catchy melody thrown about with accent displacements. The third and most substantial movement is an expansive palindrome beginning with a disjunct, powerful, pleading melody that becomes progressively more aggressive. The central section is the most agitated, even violent moment, culminating in a most unusual recitative-like notated cadenza. Hindemith composed a nostalgic poem, included in the score in old German, suggesting that the sound of the horn calls forth a longing for the "half-forgotten," for the "long-departed . . . forebears," and provides "resurrection to these cherished phantoms." The rhythm (but not the actual words) of the German text is "recited" by the soloist through the notated music during this remarkable section. It is truly a work of genius. The piano reduction works well, if not great, but does require an accomplished and dexterous performer.

Sonate for Althorn in E♭ (1943)** by **Paul Hindemith** is yet another remarkable composition by this generous composer. As the rumor goes, Hindemith told John Barrows that he preferred this piece on the "French" horn to either the E♭ alto horn or the alto saxophone. Each of the four movements has a totally different character and feeling from the others and from his earlier Sonate. This piece was created for a lighter voice, requiring more of the woodwind characteristics of the horn than the brass. The last movement includes a verbal, poetic dialogue between the two performers. The part designated for the horn player describes, as he did later in his Concerto, the nostalgic thought that "the sounding of a horn to our busy souls" is "like a sonorous visit" from ages past. The pianist adds that it is our task "to grasp the lasting, calm, and meaningful" from "amid confusion, rush, and noise." Throughout this uncommonly inventive movement, the horn intones its expansive, melancholy line while the piano performs a perpetual rush of activity.

Hindemith never indicated whether these poems were to be read aloud, put in program notes, or simply used as inspiration. Any of the above or any combination can be effective. If you choose to read them aloud to the audience, take your verbal performance as seriously as your playing. Have others hear you in the hall and tape your verbal delivery for your own scrutiny. This can be quite effective and can add a special dimension to a recital.

One of the most popular works, and perhaps the most recorded, from the early twentieth century is *Villanelle* by **Paul Dukas**. In France, composers often write works requiring many of the technical capabilities of the horn for the conservatory juries, and Dukas wrote one of the finest. The name suggests a country scene, perhaps in southern Italy. The essence of folk melodies is present throughout. The entire opening section, repeated briefly before the final stretto, was meant to be performed without valve, as if on hand horn. I encourage students to learn it that way to understand what the composer actually wanted to hear. The resultant timbral relationships are important to understand as one interprets this section. Performing it in this manner is also quite interesting for the audiences, though it is not often done. The middle section, marked "stopped" in some editions, was meant to have been "echo horn" (lowering the pitch one half-step with the right hand, thus fingered as F♯ horn). The difference is quite important, with the echo horn projecting a more distant, less focused, and covered sound as opposed to the nasal, compressed quality of the stopped horn. This is one of our most playful and melodically memorable solos; it is both demanding and great fun.

Bernhard Heiden was a student of Paul Hindemith's in Germany in 1939, the year both composers wrote their sonatas for horn and piano. Heiden's **Sonata** (1939) was the first of a number of fine pieces for horn(s). His Concerto for Horn (1969), Five Canons for Two Horns (1971), Quartet for Horns (1981), and his Variations for Solo Tuba and Nine Horns (1974) are all very important repertoire, showing an affection for and a solid understanding of the instrument. The Sonata is immediately appealing though somewhat problematic from an interpretational perspective. While playing the first movement, you should feel free to let the tempo fluctuate. The first theme, and every time it returns, should be somewhat broader than the rest of the movement. Go with your instincts. The second movement is quite enigmatic. The A section is a rhapsodic and lovely yet halting little waltz. The B section suddenly finds the two players chasing each other with aggressive, punctuated eighth-note phrases over ten beats in 3/4 time. The return to the A section is enhanced by a convoluted piano line. The movement ends with what must be interpreted as a metrically loose, impassioned pleading from the horn. Very interesting! The last movement literally dances through mesmerizing metric changes and ends with a rapid rush.

Another popular French "jury piece" is ***En Foret*** by **Eugene Bozza**. This vigorous and enticing single-movement tone poem depicts a day in the forest, including the excitement of anticipation, a romp with rapid horses, hunting calls (literal quotes), monks chanting an actual Gloria from the Easter Mass, an animated encounter with a hunting party, a calm moment of love and contemplation, and the inevitable return to the impetuous spirit of the horses and the delirious excitement of the day. The natural harmonics are requested for the hunting calls, the chant should be notated for echo horn (but is not in some editions), and the beguiling muted melody can be effectively performed with flexible mute position, opening for the forte gestures and closing for the piano. There is a remarkable arrangement of this piece for horn and wind ensemble by Wayne Pegram from the department of music at Tennessee Tech University in Cookeville, Tennessee.

On September 1, 1957, Dennis Brain met his death in a tragic car accident. Shortly after this shocking event, **Francis Poulenc** composed his hauntingly poignant **Elegy for Horn and Piano** in memory of Dennis Brain. Though these eight minutes have been described by others as a tone poem depicting the event of Brain's auto accident, along with other detailed aspects of Brain's personality and career, I have found this work to be much more profound. As a composer who has experienced the death of a loved one, I know how music instinctively becomes a medium through which grief can be explored. Poulenc's Elegy follows the stages of grief with total commitment. He begins with the dead and empty calm of a 12-tone row, with no stability or point of rest, only disorientation. Next is the anger, uncontrolled and passionate. This all repeats itself at a lower pitch but no less impassioned. What follows is a calm winding downward with a sudden outburst, ending in a brief unsettled rest. He then writes a section of love-filled melodic fragments, the first beginning with a cry from the high A downward. Each loving melody (memory) rises up toward a climax and suddenly, before its time, comes to rest. Anger interferes with these contemplations, followed quickly by the tolling of the bells (spirituality) sounding with inordinate force and then stopping suddenly. At number 12, *très calme expressif*, the piano shimmers with a bittersweet simplicity. From this intimate moment, the Elegy evolves into gradual groping towards strength. A certain power enters both voices as they begin a repetitious search for something stable. This too is interrupted. The horn finds magic as it sings (stopped horn with vibrato) the first five measures of a deeply introspective melody, creating a brief moment of pure magic as another interruption and another beginning, this time seeming to promise some resolve. Twelve measures from the end we arrive at an emphatic V/I cadence, growing through *pp*, *mf*, *f*, to a three-octave C in *ff*. This moment of strength and stability is immediately interrupted by the horn line, another twelve-tone row, which winds its way down to sustain as the third within C major. This doesn't last either, as the introduction of a B♭ in the piano leaves us suspended within an unresolved dominant seventh chord. Thus ends this inspiring and solemn work of genius.

Gordon Jacob composed his **Concerto for Horn and Strings** for Dennis Brain in May of 1951. Brain frequently performed the work over the next few years but never formally recorded it. Soren Hermansson only recently made available on CD what has become one of the most popular concertos for horn from this century. Though this may not be a composition of profound musical depth, it is certainly one of great fun, especially the outside movements. They are both technically quite demanding of one's flexibility, endurance, and high range. The middle movement has its moments of beauty but comes across as somewhat inconsequential and a bit too repetitive. Rapid tonguing is a requirement for the stylish outer movements. Students could and have treated these as musically demanding articulation exercises. The piano reduction was prepared by the composer, but that does not make the rapid repeated notes in the last movement any easier. A facile and forgiving pianist is necessary.

From here on, ideas as to what might or should be considered basic or even important repertoire for horn and piano begin to differ wildly. I will continue with some anecdotal recommendations and listings, beginning with the more conservative twentieth-century repertoire. I again encourage you to enjoy your own search through and beyond these pieces into the many newer works for horn.

Jean Françaix's *Divertimento* is a scintillating and, if performed with the proper sense of humor, a very funny composition. There is a mocking, capricious attitude in the first movement, bridged by a very simple aria, then followed by what must be a musical rendition of the routine of a sophisticated circus clown.

In 1978 **Trygve Madsen** composed his **Sonata, Op. 24**, to commemorate the 150th anniversary of Franz Schubert's death. Written for Frøydis Ree Wekre, Schubert's melodic gifts and his tendencies toward repetition are emulated throughout. The last movement is a striking set of variations based on the slow movement of Schubert's last published work, the Piano Sonata No. 7, Op. 167.

Verne Reynolds has contributed so much to the brass and horn repertoire. I've not played or heard anything of his that I would not freely recommend. The two works for horn and piano that have been most obviously available for the longest time are his **Partita** (1964) and his **Sonata** (1971). Both are remarkable works and seem to frame well his composition style. Each is quite technically demanding but musically rewarding, and they differ primarily through harmonic language, with Sonata being much less tonal. (See also his *Fantasy-Etudes*, **Vol. V**.)

John Barrows (1913–1974), according to Alec Wilder, "possessed such exquisite taste in music as to cast a spiritual glow wherever and whenever he performed." This helps explain why there are so many inspired works for horn by Wilder, who wrote three sonatas and one suite, along with scores of chamber music including the horn, all for John Barrows. Of these, **Sonata No. 3** is most often performed; the **Suite** contains the most popular song and dance-like materials; **Sonata No. 2** is his most serious; and **Sonata No. 1** just might be his strongest, it being the very first piece he composed in a serious vein. Wilder's fame came first as a popular songwriter. If you listen to Barrows' recordings, you will know what Wilder meant. After Barrows' death, Wilder wrote a set of love songs that are also quite haunting.

In 1993, I composed *Song Suite in Jazz Style for Horn and Piano*, now available through Manduca Music Publishers. My goal was to write some beautiful and memorable melodies. Along the way, I selected five contrasting original songs and arranged them as if they were part of a Broadway musical or a set on a club date. The contrasting melodies ("Easy Going," a jazz waltz; "Quiet Tears," a Latin ballad; "Dream Scene," a modal perpetual motion; "All Alone," a love song; and "Blackened Blues," a down and funky blues) are all fully notated to sound like an alternatingly tightly arranged and partially improvised performance. The publication includes lead sheets of each song, including chord changes for those who might wish to improvise their own arrangements. These were meant to be enjoyed and are certainly unique within our repertoire.

Other well-seasoned multi-movement works that deserve special attention from this period include the sonatas for horn and piano by **Quincy Porter, Halsey Stevens, Leslie Bassett, Edith Borroff, Jane Vignery, Willy Hess, Charles Koechlin**, and **Peter Racine Fricker** and the concertos by **Henri Tomasi, Othmar Schoeck, Lars-Erik Larsson, Kurt Atterberg, David Amram, Alexander Goedicke, Frigyes Hidas, Jiri Pauer**, and **Alan Hovhaness**. Other effective single-movement compositions that deserve serious attention include works by **Nielsen, Seiber, Searle, Reger, Damase, Planel, Bozza, Schmidt, Vinter, Piantoni, Abbott, Nehlybel**, and **Kvandal**.

Let's now take a brief look at the more aggressive, newer, sometimes experimental compositions of the last 50 years. Please refer to the extensive chapter in which I review and discuss the many wonderful compositions written for Barry Tuckwell. Of those for horn with piano, I give special attention to **Sonata Notturna**[**] by Iain Hamilton, **Music for Horn and Piano**[**] by Thea Musgrave, and Richard Rodney Bennett's works **Sonata for Horn and Piano** and **Romances for Horn and Piano**. These are each highly successful works by important composers of this century.

Other works I have enjoyed and admired over the years include the following: *The Goddess Trilogy* by **John McCabe**; *Symbols* by **Zsolt Durko**; *Sonorities II* by **Walter Hartley**; *Three Colloquies* by **William Schuman**; *Capricci* by **Klement Slavicky**; *Lirizmi* by **Ivo Petric**; *Alpha* by **Jean-Michel Defaye**; *Songs of the Wolf* by **Andrea Clearfield**; *Sonata* by **Gunther Schuller**; *Deep Remembering* by **Dana Wilson**; *Sonata* by **Eric Ewazen**; and *Duet II* by **Christian Wolff**.

All of the above works were written or transcribed for horn with piano. There are a number of concertos, especially in recent years, that are important additions to our repertoire but would not be conducive to piano reductions. Again, please see the Tuckwell article and note especially the concertos by **Thea Musgrave, Don Banks, Oliver Knussen, Richard Rodney Bennett**, and **Gunther Schuller**. Schuller has also recently rereleased and recorded his **Concerto No. 1**, a work he composed as a teenager. Interesting comparisons can be made with his **Concerto No. 2**, written for Tuckwell over 30 years later. Other composers of note who have recently contributed works for solo horn with orchestra include **Ellen Taaffe Zwilich, Roberto Sierra, Daron Hagen, Bernhard Krol, Wolfgang Plagge, Trygve Madsen**, and **Hans-Georg Pflüger**.

Another concerto of unique importance is the tremendously effective, and extraordinarily demanding **Concerto for Horn and Wind Ensemble** by **Bruce Yurko** (available from Yurko Music, 1 Cobbler Court, Sewell, NJ 08080). There is no other work known to this writer that presents the horn so well amid the power of a large wind group. The horn ardently projects its own inherent strength and flexibility, contrasted by moments of both intimate and lavish beauty.

There are so very few works of substance for horn solo with a band or wind ensemble. The Yurko may very well be the best, but it is extraordinarily difficult. Two other works, recently composed, that are more readily accessible to both soloists and student bands, and are of notable musical substance are *Caduceus* by **Peter Schmalz** (published by Phoebus Publications) and **Concerto for Horn and Band** by **John Zdechlik** (published by the Neil A. Kjos Music Company). There are many transcriptions of various horn concertos with band, but of those in my experience, I would recommend the Saint-Saëns *Morceau de Concert*, and the Wayne Pegram arrangement of the Bozza *En Foret* mentioned above, since both program well and are musically satisfying.

Horn Alone

One additional solo outlet that needs to be discussed is the unaccompanied horn repertoire. There are many fine works in this genre, and the number increases each year. With a little creativity, a complete concert of such works could be devised. Endurance for both the audience and the performer is the major concern, but the variety is available.

As discussed before, the **Six Suites for Solo Cello** by **J. S. Bach** are quite popular with horn players, but they are less successful to perform than his **Sonata in A minor for Flute Alone** (the last two movements are best for horn). Breathing needs to be written into the music of this period, especially to allow for the proper flow that was desired and expected by the composers. Let me also recommend the unaccompanied works for flute by Telemann.

Within the Romantic period, the following work well as solos if programmed intelligently: **J. F. Gallay's** (Unmeasured) Preludes, Op. 27, (especially Nos. 23, 26, 27, 35, and 37); etudes Nos. 1 and 4 from **Johannes Brahms'** *10 Horn Studies*; the long call from the opera *Siegfried* by **Richard Wagner**; and **Gioacchino Rossini's** *Le Rendez-vous de Chasse* (transcribed by Hermann Baumann). Other fine concert etudes from the nineteenth century might also be considered.

Within recent years, a number of unaccompanied works could easily be considered basic repertoire. **Bernhard Krol's** *Laudatio*, written for Hermann Baumann, is a very provocative, lyrical, and spiritual piece and would rank near the top. *Horn Lokk* by **Sigurd Berge** is based on a Norwegian folk melody and on every variety of horn call from the most primitive to the most modern. This work was written for and made famous by Frøydis Ree Wekre. *Parable VIII*** by **Vincent Persichetti** also evokes some deep spiritual feelings and provides the soloist with numerous technical and interpretative challenges. This is an intelligent and substantive opus. The **Sonatine, Op. 39b***** by **Hans Erich Apostel** has been listed on international solo competitions largely because of its obvious worth as an excellent example of twelve-tone composition. Full of personality and charm this palindromic study is great fun to learn. *España* from the *Travel Sketches* by **Vitaly Buyanovski** has become a major tour de force for solo horn virtuosi. The flamenco dance and the Spanish folk song provide the substance for this very showy solo. A most poignant and compelling solo, the **Elegy***** by **Verne Reynolds**, written for and premiered by yours truly, is a work of subtle magic and great emotional depth. Many of the etudes from Verne Reynold's **48 Etudes** also work well as unaccompanied solos. (Consider especially Nos. 3, 44, and 18 as a set.) **Malcolm Arnold's Fantasy** and **Otto Ketting's Intrada** also are frequently performed and are both quite musically accessible, if somewhat less substantive than the others mentioned above.

Other more conservative solos that work well as occasional pieces or fillers in a recital include: *Cinq Pieces Poetiques* by **George Barboteu**; *Kaddish* by **Lev Kogan**; **12 Pieces for Solo Horn** by **Alec Wilder**; *Prolonged Shofar Variations* by **Yaacov Mishori**; *Partita* by **David Lyon**; *Kol Koreh* by **Joachim Stutschewsky**; **Romp for Solo Horn** by **Jeffrey Agrell**; and Stephen Gryc's *Reflections on a Southern Hymn*.

Solos that are more demanding technically, musically, and from the standpoint of interpretation include the following: *Miniatures* and *Colored Leaves* by **Pamela Marshall**; *Topango Variations* by **Stanley Friedman**; *Postcards* by **Anthony Plog**; and **Character Pieces for Solo Horn****, Reflections for Horn Alone, and **Elegy for Horn Alone** by **Douglas Hill**.

There are also a few pieces that are certainly worth the effort but are quite musically imposing and require a great deal of preparation. These include the following: *Around the Horn* by **Milton Babbitt**; *Sea Eagle* by **Peter Maxwell Davies**; *Alarme* by **Ake Hermanson**; *Glowing Embers* by **Mark Schultz**; **Sonata for Horn Solo, Op. 101***** by **Avram David**; and **Tryptych for Solo Horn** by **Martin Pearlman**. **Gunther Schuller's Studies for Unaccompanied Horn**, Nos. 12 & 8***, fit into this group as well and are quite effective as a set for solo horn.

Another very demanding solo of great importance became the sixth movement of a twelve-movement symphony titled *Des Canyons aux Étoiles* by **Olivier Messiaen**. The horn solo was written in 1971 as a eulogy for the young composer Guezec. Originally titled *Le Tombeau de J. P. Guezec*, this broad-sweeping spiritual communion became known within the symphonic context as *Appel Interstellaire*, or "Interstellar Call." The details of this multidimensional work were realized with the guidance of Daniel Bourgue, who later performed it numerous times as a solo and who assumed it would be published as such. This was never the case. In fact, Messiaen eventually decided it should not be played separate from the symphony. That is why one needs to find a copy of the score to the symphony to get a copy of the solo. Perhaps this magnificent meditation should be performed as one would the long call from the opera *Siegfried*—as an extended orchestral excerpt. To perform it as such would simply acknowledge the composer's original intent. This is such important, meaningful music, even if one never performs it. The technical, musical, and spiritual content deserves sincere and serious attention.

Jazz is a style of music that too many horn players have decided is out of their domain. The unaccompanied solo repertoire is a perfect medium through which one could attain some jazz chops. (If you are all by yourself, you might more readily loosen up and relax into the medium.) A published, unaccompanied solo that has worked well for my students is **David Amram's** *Theme and Variations for Monk*. Based on the basic twelve-bar blues changes, Amram, who is quite a successful jazz hornist himself, has written out some improvisations on an original melody in the style of Thelonious Monk. Monk had died shortly before Amram wrote this piece for me to premiere at the International Horn Workshop in Avignon, France in the summer of 1982. The publication has a few obvious mistakes, including added measures at the beginning of Variation IV turning twelve bars into fifteen (eliminate the first three measures), and has printed half-step rather than whole-step pitch bends, which ineffectively deviates from the blues scale and from the original manuscript. There are jazz-like sections in the solo horn works by Friedman and Wilder, listed previously, and a **Study in B♭ Blues for Horn** by **Waldo Campos**, which fit the range of the horn well and present many typical melodic be-bop patterns. If you are very ambitious, I recommend that you tackle *Bluefire Crown II* by **Les Thimmig**. This is an exuberant jazz tour de force for horn alone lasting nearly ten minutes (without cuts), which fully tests one's mental as well as physical endurance and ability to sustain a driving beat. This piece is available from the composer and from Turquoise Flame Music, School of Music, University of Wisconsin-Madison, WI 53706.

I have composed seven different jazz solos and compiled them into two sets entitled *Jazz Soliloquies* for Horn[**] and *Jazz Set* for Solo Horn[***]. These demanding works incorporate many extended techniques derived from both the jazz performance medium and the classical avant-garde (third-stream). They are meant to be fun to play and enjoyable to listen to, but they do demand a very strong sense of pulse over many complicated gestures, including vocalizations, quartet-tones, extreme range fluctuations, a myriad of glissandi, bends, doinks, smears, rips, and all manners of vibrato. The *Jazz Set*, which has been the easiest to purchase in recent years, is being performed more frequently to what I've been told is critical acclaim. The titles include "Blues-like," "Mixin'," and "Laid-back," in *Jazz Soliloquies*; and "Lost and Found," "Cute'n Sassy," "Lullaby Waltz," and "Fussin' for Emily" in *Jazz Set*.

[*](The Ries and Rheinberger Sonatas and the Strauss Andante were first recorded by Douglas and Karen Hill in 1976 and re-released in 1999 on Crystal Records, CD373.)

[**]The Hindemith *Sonate in E♭*, Hamilton *Sonata Notturna*, Musgrave *Music for Horn and Piano*, Persichetti *Parable VIII*, *Character Pieces for Solo Horn*, and "Laid-back" from *Jazz Soliloquies* for Horn, all appear on the newly reissued Crystal Records *The Modern Horn* CD670, Douglas Hill, horn, Karen Zaczek Hill, piano.

[***]The Reynolds *Elegy*, Apostel *Sonatine*, Op. 39b, David *Sonata for Horn Solo*, Op. 101, Schuller *Studies for Unaccompanied Horn*, Nos. XII and VIII, and Hill *Jazz Set* for Solo Horn all appear on *A Solo Voice*, GunMar Records GM2017D, Douglas Hill soloist.

SOLO HORN/PIANO REPERTOIRE

All of the following repertoire is recommended and grouped within general periods or eras of music for programming purposes. Each section is organized in the general order of preference of each composition's position within the basic repertoire, or as each relates to my opinion at the time of this writing. There is more literature of value coming out every year, and others are discussed in the previous chapter. This particular list should only be a point of reference from which to begin your own search and build a personal library.

Baroque Period
Telemann, G. P., Concerto in D Maj., Pegasus.
Förster, C., Concerto in E♭ (No. 1), Hofmeister.
Förster, C., Concerto in E♭ (No. 2), McCoy.
Corelli, A., Sonata in G min., Edition Musicus.
Mouret, J. J., Two Divertissements, Siècle Musical, Geneve.
Bach, J. S., Sonata in E♭ (No. 2), (Fl.), International.
Handel, G. F., Sonata in G min., AMP.
Corrette, M., Concerto, Heinrichshofen.
Neruda, J., Concerto, Billaudot.
Mozart, L., Concerto in D, KaWe.
Senaillé, J. B., Allegro Spiritoso, Southern.
Bach, J. S., Aria from 3rd Suite, Baron.

Classical Period
Mozart, W. A., Concertos 3, 2, 4, 1, Breitkopf.
Haydn, F. J., Concertos 1, 2 in D, Boosey.
Beethoven, Sonata Op. 17, Boosey.
Mozart, W. A., Concert Rondo, Breitkopf.
de Krufft, N., Sonata in E, Birdalone.
Danzi, F., Sonata in E♭, International.
Haydn, M., Concertino in D, Universal.
Rossetti, F. A., Concerto in E♭, International.
Ries, F., Sonata, Op. 34, Schott.
Cherubini, L., Two Sonatas, International.

Romantic Period
Strauss, R., Concerto No. 1, International.
Strauss, F., Nocturne, Op. 7, Universal.
Strauss, R., Andante (1888), Boosey.
Schumann, R., Adagio and Allegro, Boosey.
Saint-Saëns, C., Morceu de Concert, International.
Saint-Saëns, C., Romance, Op. 36, Belwin.
Strauss, R., Concerto No. 2, Boosey International.
Glière, R., Concerto, Op. 91, International.
Glière, R., Romance, Valse Triste, International.
Glière, R., Intermezzo, Nocturne, Leeds.
Glazounov, A., Reverie, Op. 24, Leeds.
Chabrier, E., Larghetto, Musica Rara.
Strauss, F., Concerto, Op. 8, Carl Fischer.
Weber, C. M. von, Concertino in E, Peters.
Rossini, G. A., Prelude, Theme & Variations.
Rheinberger, J., Sonata in E♭, Schott.
Czerny, C., Andante e Polacca, Doblinger.

Post Romantic/Conservative Modern

Dukas, P., Villanelle, International.

Françaix, J., Divertimento, Presser.

Bozza, E., En Foret, Leduc.

Madsen, T., Sonata Op. 24, Mussik Huset.

Scriabin, A., Romance, Belwin.

Françaix, J., Canon in Octave, International.

Vinter, G., Hunters Moon, Boosey.

Hovhaness, A., Artik (concerto), C. F. Peters.

Larsson, L. E., Concertino, Op. 45, Gehrman.

Planel, R., Caprice, Leduc.

Nielsen, C., Canto Serioso, Skandinavisk.

Wilder, A., Sonatas Nos. 1, 2 & 3, Margun.

Wilder, A., Suite, Margun.

Schoeck, O., Concerto, Op. 65, Boosey.

Piantoni, L., Air de Chasse, Leduc.

Damase, J. M., Berceuse, Leduc.

Modern

Hindemith, P., Sonate (1939), Schott.

Heiden, B., Sonata (1939), AMP.

Poulenc, F., Elegy, Chester.

Hindemith, P., Sonate for Althorn, Schott.

Jacob, G., Concerto, Galaxy.

Ewazen, E., Sonata, Southern.

Abbott, A., Alla Caccia, Arcadia Music Pub. Co.

Nelhybel, V., Scherzo Concertante, General.

Hindemith P., Concerto, Schott.

Vignery, J., Sonata, Op. 7, Brogneaux.

Reynolds, V., Partita, Southern.

Seiber, M., Notturno, Schott.

Koechlin, C., Sonata, Op. 70, Eschig.

Hill, D., Song Suite in Jazz Style, Manduca.

Kvandal, J., Introduction & Allegro, Norsk.

Tomasi, H., Concerto, Leduc.

Modern/Avant Garde

Musgrave, T., Music for Hn & Pno, Chester.

Hamilton, I., Sonata Notturna, Schott.

Hartley, W., Sonorities II, Presser.

Reynolds, V., Sonata, Southern.

McCabe, J., The Goddess Trilogy, Novello.

Durko, Z., Symbols, Ed. Musica Budapest.

Porter, Q., Sonata (1946), Robert King.

Schuman, W., Three Colloquies, Merion.

HORN ALONE
(listed alphabetically by composer)

Each of the following works is either briefly discussed or listed and categorized in the previous chapter. This is a rapidly growing repertoire for horn soloists and an effective way to develop one's artistry as an interpreter and a true solo performer.

Agrell, J., Romp for Solo Horn, Ed. Marc Reift.

Amram, D., Blues Variations for Monk, Peters.

Apostel, H. E., Sonatine, Universal.

Arnold, M., Fantasy for Horn, Faber.

Babbitt, M., Around the Horn, Southern.

Bach, J. S., Suites (for Cello), Southern.

Bach, J. S., Sonata in a min. (fl), Leduc.

Barboteu, G., Cinq Pieces Poetiques, Choudens.

Berge, S., Horn Lokk, Norsk.

Buyanovski, V., Travel Sketches, McCoy.

Friedman, S., Topango Variations, Seesaw.

Gallay, J., 40 Preludes, Op. 27, International.

Gryc, S., Reflections on a Southern Hymn, Robert King.

Hermanson, A., Alarme, AD Nordiska.

Hill, D., Reflections for Horn Alone, Manduca.

Hill, D., Elegy for Horn Alone, www.reallygoodmusic.com.

Hill, D., Character Pieces, www.reallygoodmusic.com.

Hill, D., Jazz Set for Solo Horn, Shawnee.

Hill, D., Jazz Soliloquies, www.reallygoodmusic.com.

Ketting, O., Intrada, Donemus.

Kogan, L., Kaddish, Israel B&W Pub.

Krol, B., Laudatio, Simrock.

Lyon, D., Partita, Schirmer.

Marshall, P., Miniatures, Seesaw.

Marshall, P., Colored Leaves, Spindrift Music Co.

Mishori, Y., Prolonged Shofar Variations, Israel B&W Pub.

Pearlman, M., Tryptych, IHS Press.

Persichetti, V., Parable VIII, Elkan Vogel.

Plog, A., Postcards, BIM.

Reynolds, V., Elegy, Carl Fischer.

Reynolds, V., 48 Etudes, Schirmer.

Rossini, G., Le Rendez-vous de Chasse, McCoy.

Schuller, G., Studies for Unaccompanied Horn, Oxford.

Schultz, M., Glowing Embers, JOMAR Press.

Stutschewsky, J., Kol Koreh, Israeli Music.

Thimmig, L., Bluefire Crown II, U.W. School of Music.

Wilder, A., 12 Pieces for Solo Horn, Shawnee.

22. Chamber Music: A Thorough Listing

It could easily be said that the most exhilarating musical experiences occur when mature performers participate in well-rehearsed chamber ensembles. Chamber music combines outlets for personal artistry, the need to adjust spontaneously to the musical impulses of others without the aid of a conductor, the inspiration felt from the musical gestures of others, and the opportunity to mutually interpret and perform some of our greatest composers' most significant compositions.

We horn players are fortunate! We have been included in a large body of celebrated chamber music compositions. The horn is also the only instrument included in two of the standard mixed-chamber ensemble groupings—the woodwind quintet and the brass quintet. Other secondary yet significant groupings that have attracted many composers include the violin/horn/piano trio; wind quartet (or quintet) with piano; brass quartet (two trumpets, horn, trombone); brass trio (trumpet, horn, trombone); horn quartet (also trio and duet); voice/horn and piano; horn with string quartet (string trio or string duo); wind octets, sextets, and mixed groupings with strings (i.e., violin, viola, cello, oboe, clarinet, horn, bassoon), etc!

In the following, I present a basic repertoire of 40 of the most significant chamber music works that include the horn. The choices have been made based on the quality of the works themselves, a mixture of ensemble groupings, and a cross-section of historical periods. The popularity factor as observed over 35 years of professional experience also entered into the selection and order.

Selecting a top-40 list was difficult to do! There is so much chamber music that is truly worthwhile for study and performance. Consequently, I follow this initial selection with a comprehensive list, grouped by ensemble, of the chamber music that through my experiences as a performer, teacher, and coach has proven to be of importance for one reason or another. Of these reasons, musical worth is the major consideration.

BASIC CHAMBER MUSIC REPERTOIRE FOR THE HORN
(Top 40 in a general order of significance)

Brahms, J., Trio, Op. 40 (vln, hn, pno), International.

Mozart, W. A., Quintet (K. 407) (hn, vln, 2va, vc), Peters.

Schubert, F., *Auf dem Strom* (sopr/ten, hn, pno), Breitkopf.

Britten, B., Serenade, Op. 31 (ten, hn, stgs), Boosey.

Beethoven, L. van, Sextet, Op. 81b (2hn, 2vn, va, vc), International.

Mozart, W. A., Quintet (K. 452) (ob, cl, hn, bsn, pno), Musica Rara.

Beethoven, L. van, Quintet, Op. 16 (ob, cl, hn, bsn, pno), Musica Rara.

Schubert, F., Octet in F (cl, hn, bsn, 2vn, va, vc, db), Eulenburg.

Nielsen, C., Quintet, Op. 43 (WWQ), Hansen.

Milhaud, D., *La Chimnée du Roi René* (WWQ), Southern.

Mozart, W. A., 12 Duos (K. 487) (2 hns.), McGinnis & Marx.

Beethoven, L. van, Septet, Op. 20 (cl, hn, bsn, vn, va, vc, db), International.

Poulenc, F., Sonata (trp, hn, trb), Chester.

Dvorak, A., Serenade in d min., Op 44 (2ob, 2cl, 3hn, 2bsn, vc, db), International.

Haydn, F. J., Divertimento a Tre (vn, hn, vc), Doblinger.

Hindemith, P., *Kleine Kammermusik*, Op. 24, No.2 (WWQ), Schott.

Berkeley, L., Trio, Op. 44 (vn, hn, pno), Chester.

Arnold, M., Quintet (BrQ), Patterson.

Hindemith, P., Sonata (4 hns), Schott

Bozza, E., Sonatine (BrQ), Leduc.

Reicha, A., Quintet, Op. 88, No. 2 (WWQ), Simrock.

Barber, S., *Summer Music* (WWQ), Schirmer.

Cooke, A., Nocturnes (sopr, hn, pno), Boosey.

Ewald, V., Quintet No. 1 (BrQ), Lyceum.

Scheidt, S., *Die Bankelsängerlieder* (BrQ), Cor.

Taffanel, C. P., Quintet pour Instruments a vent (WWQ), International.

Fine, I., Partita (WWQ), Boosey.

Scheidt, S., *Canzona Bergamasca* (BrQ), Philharmusica Corp.

Ibert, J., *Trois pieces breve* (WWQ), Leduc.

Harbison, J., Quintet for Winds (WWQ), AMP/Schirmer.

Ewald, V., Quintets No. 2 and 3 (BrQ), Schirmer.

Bach, Jan, *Laudes* (BrQ), Mentor.

Bach, Jan, 4 *Two-bit Contraptions* (fl, hn), Galaxy.

Janácek, L., Mládí (Youth Suite), (WWQ+bass cl), International.

Francaix, J., Quintet No. 1 (WWQ), Schott.

Cambini, G., Quintet No. 3 (WWQ), McGinnis & Marx.

Reicha, A., 10 Trios, Op. 82 (3 hns), KaWe.

Rossini, G., Le Rendez-vous de Chasse (4 hns), KaWe.

Tippett, M., Sonata (4 hns), Schott.

Tcherepnine, N., Six Pieces (4 hns), Editions Musicus.

COMPREHENSIVE CHAMBER MUSIC REPERTOIRE FOR THE HORN
Frequent Combinations
(*basic repertoire)
(listed in alphabetical order)

Horn, Violin, Piano
Brahms, J., Trio, Op. 40, International.*

Berkeley, L., Trio, Op. 44, Chester.*

Dussek, J. L., *Notturno Concertante*, Musica Rara.

Graun, K. H., Trio in D Major, McCoy (basso continuo).

Harbison, J., *Twilight Music*, AMP.

Ligeti, G., Trio, Schott.

Presser, W., *Rhapsody on a Peaceful Theme*, Presser.

Telemann, G. P., Concerto (arr. Leloir), KaWe.

Welcher, D., Partita (from composer).

Wyner, Y., Horn Trio, G.Schirmer.

Zelenka, I., Trio (12-tone), Editions Modern.

Horn, Voice, Piano
Schubert, F., *Auf dem Strom*, Breitkopf (tenor or soprano).*

Britten, B., Serenade, Op. 31, Boosey (tenor).*

Britten, B., *Canticle III*, Op. 55, Boosey (tenor).

Cooke, A., Nocturnes, Boosey (soprano).*

Bach, W. F., Aria, Tischer & Jagenberg (soprano).

Berlioz, H., *Le Jeune Patre Breton*, Op. 13 No.3, International (soprano).

Krol, B., *Horati de Vino Carmina*, Benjamin (soprano).

Lachner, F., 2 Songs, Musica Rara (soprano).

Lachner, F., *Die Seejungfern*, Musica Rara (tenor).

Lachner, F., *Notte Soave Delizia*, Musica Rara (alto).

Plog, A., *Aesop's Fables*, Southern (narrator).

Schuman, W., *The Young Dead Soldiers*, Presser (soprano).

Strauss, R., *Das Alphorn*, Boosey (soprano).

Horn, Miscellaneous, Piano

Beethoven, L. van, Quintet, Op. 16, Musica Rara (ob, cl, bsn).*

Dohnanyi, E., Sextet, Op. 37, Lengnick (cl, vn, vla, vc).

Ewazen, E., *Ballade*, Southern (fl).

Herzogenberg, H. von, Trio, Musica Rara (ob).

Kellaway, R., *Sonoro* and *Dance of the Ocean Breeze*, MS (tuba).

Mozart, W. A., Quintet (K. 452), Musica Rara (ob, cl, bsn).*

Reinecke, C., Trio in a minor, Op. 188, International (ob).

Reinecke, C., Trio in Bb, Op. 274, Western (cl).

Rochberg, G., Trio, Presser (cl).

Schuller, G., Romantic Sonata, G. Schirmer, (cl).

Stravinsky, I., Septet, (1953), Boosey Hawkes (cl, bsn, vn, va, vc).

Titl, A. E., Serenade, Molenaar (fl).

Tovey, D., Trio, Op. 8, Schott (cl).

Wilder, A., Suite, Margun (cl).

Wilder, A., Suite Nos. 1 and 2, G. Schirmer (tuba).

Horn with Strings

Amram, D., *Music from Marlboro*, Peters (vc).

Beethoven, L. van, Sextet, Op. 81b, International (2hn, 2vn, va, vc).*

Cherubini, L., Sonata No. 1 and 2, Sikorski (2vn, va, vc).*

Haydn, F. J., Divertimento a Tre, Doblinger (vn, vc).*

Heiden, B., Quintet (1952), AMP (2vn, va, vc).

Hill, D., *A Place for Hawks*, www.reallygoodmusic.com (voice, 2vn, va, vc, bass, or string orch.)

Krol, B., *Cantico*, Benjamin (2vn, va, vc).

Mozart, W. A., Quintet (K. 407), Peters (1vn, 2va, vc). *

Mozart, W. A., *A Musical Joke* (K. 522), International (2hn, 2vn, va, vc).

Reicha, A., Quintet, Op. 106, Musica Rara (2vn, va, vc).

Brass Trio

Beethoven, L. van, Trio, Op. 87, Robert King (trp, trb).

Hill, D., *Elegies and Variations* (1972), Manuscript (trp, trb).

Kirchner, L., *Fanfare*, AMP (2trp).

Nagel, R., Brass Trio No. 2, Mentor (trp, trb).

Pinkham, D., Brass Trio, Peters (trp, trb).

Poulenc, F., Sonata, Chester (trp, trb).*

Reynolds, V., Trio, G. Schirmer (trp, trb).

Reynolds, V., Trio, G. Schirmer (trb, tuba).

Running, A., *Aria and Allegro*, Shawnee (trp, trb).

Stevens, J., *Triangles*, Editions BIM (trb, tuba).

Brass Quartet

Bernstein, L., *Fanfare for Bima*, Boosey (trp, trb, tuba).

Hindemith, P., *Morgenmusik*, Schirmer (2trp (hn), trb, tuba).

Schuller, G., *Little Brass Music*, Mentor (trp, trb, tuba).*

Simon, A., Quartour, Robert King (2trp, trb).

Brass Quintet

Adson, J., *Masques & Anti masques*, Medici.

Arnold, M., Quintet, Patterson.*

Arutunian, A., *Armenian Scenes*, Editions BIM.

Bach, J. S., *Art of the Fugue* (Frackenpohl), Hal Leonard.

Bach, Jan, *Laudes*, Mentor.*

Bach, Jan, *Rounds and Dances*, Galaxy.

Bernstein, L., *West Side Story Suite* (Gale), Music Express.

Bozza, E., Sonatine, Leduc.

Calvert, M., *Suite from the Monteregian Hills*, Berandol.*

Cheetham, J., *A Brass Menagerie*, Mark Tezak.

Cheetham, J., Scherzo, Western.*

Dahl, I., *Music for Brass Instruments*, Warner Bros.

Dukas, P., Fanfare (La Péri), Presser.*

East, M., *Amavi*, Wimbledon.

Ends, J., *Three Salutations*, Accura.

Etler, A., Quintet, AMP.*

Ewald, V., Quintet No.1 (Symphony for Brass), Lyceum.*

Ewald, V., Quintets No. 2 & 3, G. Schirmer.*

Ewald, V., Quintet No. 4, Op. 8, Brass Ring Editions.*

Farnaby, G., *Fancies, Toyes, and Dreams*, Chester.*

Gershwin, G., *Selections from Porgy and Bess* (Gale), Musicians Pub.

Gregson, E., *Equal Dances*, Novello.

Harbison, J., *Christmas Vespers*, AMP.

Harbison, J., *Magnum Mysterium*, AMP.

Hill, D., *Intrada*, Manduca/PP Music.

Hill, D., *Timepieces*, www.reallygoodmusic.com.

Holborne, A., *Elizabethan Dance Suite*, G. Schirmer.*

Horovitz, J., *Music Hall Suite*, Novello.*

Husa, K., *Landscapes*, AMP.

Koetsier, J., *Kleiner Zirkusmarsch*, Op. 79A, Marc Reift.

Lovelock, W., Suite, Medici.

Lutoslawski, W., Mini Overture, Chester.

Peaslee, R., *Distant Dancing*, Margun.

Pilss, K., Scherzo 2, Robert King.

Praetorius, M., *9 Dances from Terpsichore*, Medici.

Reynolds, V., *Centone #s 1,2,4,5,9,10,11,12*, Southern.

Rieti, V., *Incisioni* (Engravings), General.

Rodgers, R., *Selections from The Sound of Music* (Gale), Musicians Pub.

Sampson, D., *Distant Voices*, Brass Ring Ed.

Sampson, D., *Morning Music*, The Brass Press.*

Scheidt, S., *Canzona Bergamasca*, Philharmusica, Corp.*

Scheidt, S., *Die Bankelsängerlieder*, Cor.*

Schuller, G., *Music for Brass Quintet*, AMP.

Stevens, J., *Fabrics*, Editions BIM.

Stevens, J., *Seasons*, Editions BIM.*

Stevens, J., *Urban Images*, Editions BIM.

Brass Quartet with Piano

Husa, K., Concerto, Leduc.

Reynolds, V., *Concertare IV*, Carl Fischer.

Horn with Winds

Bach, J., *4 Two-bit Contraptions*, Galaxy (fl).*
Beethoven, L. van, Quintet, (Op. posth.), Schott (ob, 3hn, bsn).
Handel, G. F., Sonata in D, Presser (2 cl).
Janácek, L., Mládí, (*Youth Suite*) International (ww quintet with bs cl).*

Woodwind Quintet

Arnold, M., *Three Shanties*, Patterson.
Barber, S., *Summer Music*, G. Schirmer.*
Barrows, J., March, G. Schirmer.
Barthe, A., *Passacaglia*, Rubank.
Beethoven, L. van, Quintet (from Sextet, Op. 71), Rubank.
Berio, L., *Opus Zoo*, Universal.
Blummer, Quintet in B♭, Op. 52, Zimmermann.
Bozza, E., Scherzo, Leduc.
Cambini, G., Quintets Nos. 1, 2, & 3, McGinnis & Marx.*
Carter, E., Quintet, AMP.
Chávez, C., *Soli No. 2*, Mills.
Dahl, I., *Allegro and Arioso*, McGinnis & Marx.
Danzi, F., Quintet in G minor, Op. 56, No. 2 (14 more), Leuckart.*
Etler, A., Quintets 1 & 2, AMP.*
Fine, I., *Partita*, Boosey.*
Foerster, J. B., Quintet, Hudebni Matice (a division of Supraphon).
Françaix, J., Quintets 1 & 2, Schott.*
Gebaur, F. R., 3 Quintets, McGinnis & Marx.
Harbison, J., Quintet for Winds, AMP.*
Heiden, B., Sinfonia, and Woodwind Quintet, AMP.
Henze, H. W., Quintet, Schott.
Hindemith, P., *Kleine Kammermusik*, Op. 24, No. 2, Schott.*
Ibert, J., *Trois pieces breve*, Leduc.*
Klughardt, A. F., Quintet in C, Op. 79, Zimmermann.
Lefebvre, C. E., Suite, Op. 57, Hamelle.
Ligeti, G., Six Bagatelles and 10 Stücke (1968), Schott.
Martinu, B., Quintet, Chester.
Milhaud, D., *La Chiminée du Roi René*, Southern.*
Nielsen, C., Quintet, Op. 43, Hansen.*
Perle, G., Quintet No.1, Presser; No. 2 & 3,Boelke-Bo-Mart, Inc.; No. 4, Galaxy.
Persichetti, V., *Pastorale*, G. Schirmer.
Pierné, G., *Pastorale*, Leduc.
Reicha, A., 24 Quintets, Simrock (Op. 88, No. 2).*
Riegger, W., Quintet, Ars Viva-Schott.
Schoenberg, A., Quintet, Universal.*
Schuller, G., Quintet (1958), Schott.
Schuller, G., Suite, McGinnis & Marx.
Taffanel, C.P., *Quintet pour Instruments à vent*, International (or Leduc).*
Villa-Lobos, H., Quintette en forme de Choros, Schott.
Wilder, A., Quintet No. 11, Kendor (11 more, see G. Schirmer).

Woodwinds with Piano

Beethoven, L. van, Quintet Op. 16, Musica Rara (ob, cl, bsn).
Casadesus, R., Sextet, Durand (fl, ob, cl, bsn).
Jacob, G., Sextet, Musica Rara (fl, ob, cl, bsn).
Mozart, W. A., Quintet K. 452, Musica Rara (ob, cl, bsn).
Poulenc, F., *Sextour*, Hansen* (fl, ob, cl, bsn).

Horn, Percussion
Hill, D., *Thoughtful Wanderings*, IHS Press (opt. with tape alone).
Reynolds, V., *Hornvibes* (vibraphone) Warner Bros.
Schultz, M., *Dragons in the Sky*, JOMAR Press (tape, percussion).

Horn, Organ
Albright, W., Romance, Peters.
Bach, J. S., *Arien und Chorale*, Heinrichshofen.
Bach, J. S., *Jesu, Joy of Man's Desiring*, McCoy.
Badings, H., *Canzona*, Donemus.
Faust, R., *Meditation*, Faust.
Faust, R., *Celebration*, Faust.
Krol, B., *Missa Muta*, Op. 55, Bote & Bock.*
Mouret, J. J., *Rondeau*, McCoy.
Pflüger, H. G., Concerto, Bote & Bock.
Read, G., *De Profundis*, Robert King.
Schmalz, P., *Processional and Recessional*, Phoebus Pub.

Horn, Harp
Chaussier, H., *Elegy*, McCoy.
Dauprat, L. F., Sonata in F, Chouden.
Dauprat, L. F., *Air Ecossais Varié*, Schonenberger, Paris.
Duvernoy, F., *Deuxieme Nocturne*, Richaut.
Koetsier, J., Sonata, Donemus.
Ravel, M., *Pavane*, Editions Musicus.

Varied Combinations
Beethoven, L. van, Septet, Op. 20, International (cl, bsn, hn, vn, va, vc, db).*
Dohnányi, E., Sextet, Op. 37, Lengnick (cl, hn, vn, va, vc, pno).
Fasch J. F., Sonata a 4, McCoy (ob, hn, vn, cont).
Hill, D., Scenes from Sand County, www.reallygoodmusic.com (narr.vn, va, vc, bass, fl, ob, cl, hn, bsn).
Ireland, J., Sextet, Augener (cl, hn, 2vn, va, vc).
Martinu, B., Quartetto, Panton (cl, hn, vc, little drum).
Nielsen, C., Serenata Invano, Masters (cl, hn, bsn, vc, db).
Schubert, F., Octet in F, Eulenburg (cl, bsn, 2vn, va, vc, db).*
Schuller, G., Trio, Op. 13, AMP (ob, va).
Strauss, R., *Till Eulenspiegel Einmal Anders*, Peters (cl, bsn, vn, db).

Horn, Tape
Hill, D., *Thoughtful Wanderings*, IHS Press (opt. with percussion).
Musgrave, T., *The Golden Echo*, Novello.
Schultz, M., *Dragons in the Sky*, Jomar (with percussion).

MULTIPLE HORNS IN CHAMBER MUSIC
(*basic repertoire)

Two Horns
Bach, J. S., 9 Duets (Ramm), Medici.
Barboteu, G., 4 Duos, Chouden.
Dauprat, L. F., 20 Duets (for Horns in different keys), McCoy.
Durko, Z., 8 Duos, Editions Musica Budapest.
Duvernoy, F., 20 Duets, Op. 3, International.
Gibbons, O., *Fantasia* (Baldwin), Philharmusica Corp.

Heiden, B., 5 Canons, AMP.*
Hill, D., 10 Pieces for Two Horns, Hornists Nest.*
Hill, D., 27 Rare Horn Duets, McCoy.
Hoss, W. (ed.), 60 Selected Duets, Southern.
Kopprasch, W., 8 Duets, International.*
Mozart, W. A., 12 Duos (K. 487), McGinnis & Marx.*
Nicolai, O., 3 Sonatas (Brockway), Kunzelman.*
Reynolds, V., *Calls*, Carl Fischer.*
Rimsky-Korsakov, N., Two Duets, Robert King.
Rossini, G., 5 Duets (Leloir), Masters.
Schubert, F., Five Duets (Goldman), Presser.
Schuller, G., Duets for Unaccompanied Horns, Oxford.*
Shaw, L., *Bipperies*, Hornists Nest.
Wilder, A., 22 Duets, G. Schirmer.

Two Horns with Piano
Beethoven, L. van, Sextet, Op 81b, Cor Pub.*
Fiala, J., Concerto in E♭, Musica Rara.
Haydn, F. J., Concerto (E♭), Pizka.*
Kuhlau, F., Concertino in F, International.
Mozart, L., Concerto in E♭, Musica Rara.
Rosetti, F. A., Concerto in E♭, International.
Schuller, G., *3 Hommages*, G. Schirmer.
Telemann, G. P., Suite in F Major, International.*
Vivaldi, A., Concerto in F Major P. 320, International.

Three Horns
Bach, J. S., 5 Trios (Shaw), and Trios Bk. 2 & 3, Hornists Nest.
Barrows, J., *La Chasse*, Hornists Nest.
Beethoven, L. van, Trio, Op. 87, Cor Pub.
Boismortier, J. S., Sonata (Shaw), Hornists Nest.
Dauprat, L. F., Grand Trio No. 1 & Grand Trio No. 2 (Meek), Billaudot.*
Fritchie, W. P., *Jazz Stylings*, Vols. 1 & 2, McCoy.
Gallay, J. F., Trio, Op. 24, Nos. 1, 2 & 3, KaWe.
Hill, D., 5 Pieces for Three Horns, Hornists Nest.
Hill, D., Trio Set, www.reallygoodmusic.com.
Mozart, W. A., Divertimento, No. 2 (Walshe), No. 4 (Hilfiger), Hornists Nest.
Reicha, A., 10 Trios Op.82, Suites 1, 2 & 3, KaWe.*
Scarlatti, D., Sonata XIII (Hill), McCoy.
Shaw, L., *Tripperies*, Hornists Nest.
Stich, W. (Punto), 20 Trios, KaWe.
Wekre, F., Fugue, McCoy.

Three Horns with Piano
Beethoven, L. van, Aria from Fidelio, No. 9, (Freiberg), Pizka.
Hanisch, A., Concerto, KaWe.
Telemann, G. P., Concerto, KaWe.

Three Horns in Chamber Music
Dvořák, A., Serenade in d minor, Op. 44, International (2ob, 2cl, 2bsn, vc, db).*
Beethoven, L. van, Quintet, Op. posth., Schott (ob, bsn).*

Four Horns

Bach, J. S., Gigue Fugue (Becknell), Hornists Nest.
Bach, J. S., Fugue in c minor, Hornists Nest.
Bassett, L., Music for Four Horns, Robert King.
Beethoven, L. van, *3 Equale*, Robert King.
Bozza, E., Suite, Leduc.*
Chávez, C., Sonata for 4 Horns, Mills.
Gallay, J. F., Grand Quartet, Op. 26, Pizka.*
Harris, A., Theme and Variations, Shawnee.
Haydn, F. J., 6 Horn Quartets (Reynolds), Ludwig.
Heiden, B., Quartet for Horns, AMP.*
Hidas, F., Chamber Music, Editions Musica Budapest.
Hill, D., *Shared Reflections*, Manduca/PP Music.
Hill, D., *Americana Variations*, www.reallygoodmusic.com.
Hindemith, P., Sonata, Schott.*
Koetsier, J., *5 Miniatures* (New Version), Editions BMI.
LeClaire, D., Quartet, Southern.
Lo Presti, R., Second Suite, Shawnee.
Mitushin, A., Concertino (Leuba), Southern.*
Molter, J. M., Symphony in C Major (Janetzky), Musica Rara.
Mozart, W. A., Overture to The Magic Flute, Hornists Nest.
Ravel/Debussy, *French Impressionists*, (2 vols.), Phoenix Music.
Reynolds, V., Short Suite for Four Horns, Robert King.
Rossini, G., *Le Rendez-vous de Chasse*, KaWe.*
Scharnberg, W., Ed., 19 Viennese Quartets for Horns, 2 Books, McCoy.
Schubert, F., Six Quartets (Reynolds), Southern.
Schumann, R., Six Quartets (Reynolds), Southern.
Shaw, L., *Fripperies* (8 Books of 4), Hornists Nest.*
Stanhope, D., *Cortettes* (humorous), Hornists Nest.
Tcherepnine, N., Six Pieces, Editions Musicus.*
Tippett, M., Sonata, Schott.*
Tomasi, H., Petite Suite for 4 Horns, Leduc.
Turner, K., Fanfare for Barcs & Quartet No. 1, Music Press Dist. (Neth.)
Turner, K., Quartet No. 2, Editions BMI.

Four Horns with Piano

Hübler, H., Concerto (Leloir), KaWe.
Rossini, G., *Le Rendezvous de Chasse* (Leloir), Billaudot.
Schumann, R., Konzertstück, Op. 86, International.*

Four Horns in Chamber Music

Doppler, F., *L'Oiseau des Bois* (Thomas), Southern (fl).
Schuller, G., Perpetuum Mobile, G. Schirmer (bsn).
Strauss, R., Till Eulenspiegels Blues (Haddad), Shawnee (bass, drms).
Wilder, A., Jazz Suite, G. Schirmer (hpschd, guitar, bass, drms).

Five Horns

Leitermeyer, F., 3 Studien, Doblinger.
Liszt, F., Melodic Alps Flowers (Jeurissen), McCoy (opt. alphorn solo).
Lo Presti, R., Fantasy, Israel Brass Woodwind Pub.
Schuller, G., Five Pieces for Five Horns, Margun.
Shaw, L., *Quipperies*, Vols. 1 & 2, Hornists Nest.
Turner, K., *Casbah of Tetouan*, Phoenix Music.

Six Horns

Bach, J. S., Allegro, Hornists Nest.

Beethoven, L. van, Sextet, Op. 81b, Baltimore Horn Club.

Dickow, R., *Midday Music*, Queen City.

Handel, G. F., 6 Pieces from The Water Music, Hornists Nest

Hervig, R., *Blue Horns*, Southern.

Kerkorian, G., Sextet, Hornists Nest.

Perrini, N., *Festival Fanfare*, Hornists Nest.

Telemann, G. P., *Tafelmusik Finale*, Baltimore Horn Club.

Winteregg, S. L., *Pastiche*, Hornists Nest.

(More than six horns is usually beyond chamber music. For larger horn ensembles refer to the catalogues from the Hornists Nest, Baltimore Horn Club, the Brass Players Guide sold by Robert King Music Co., Southern Music, Seesaw, Pizka Editions, etc.)

23. Basic Etudes in Review

Etudes, studies, and exercises (or whatever they may be called) often take up the bulk of a student's practice time. This can be quite beneficial at certain stages of development, especially if the etudes are chosen well and approached as a means to an end rather than as the final goal. The single most-important goal for today's horn players is versatility in both musical awareness and the complete technique of the instrument. Etudes can play a significant role in this process, especially if each practice session contains varied types of studies from different periods and playing styles. However, to devote one's etude practice only to the etudes of the nineteenth century, of which there are many fine collections, would be to go only part way. Students also need to pay close attention to all of the musical and technical challenges found within the great works of the twentieth-century composers.

It is impossible to present and discuss the varied contents of all the fine and available etude books. With more than 200 separate titles known to this writer alone, those discussed here can only serve to represent what is considered basic etude repertoire, supplemented by what an advancing player needs to develop versatility and a broad-based stylistic facility.

In the chapter "Solo Repertoire, The Basics and Beyond," I described the particulars of a questionnaire circulated by William Robinson that resulted in a tabulation of the most frequently assigned solos and etudes from 43 well-known American teachers. The etudes that ranked highly in those tabulations might be considered basic repertoire and are included below, among others.

Milan Yancich, *Method for French Horn*, (2 Vols.) Wind Music Inc., Rochester, New York.

In this collection of etudes, Yancich has organized both melodies and technical exercises to help the total beginner in both performance and basic music theory. The pace is somewhat slower than other beginning methods, but even many of those move far too rapidly for average younger players. He begins, as is typical, with the open tones in whole notes with whole rests but then also includes accent marks and dynamic indications. All of this is consistent with his concern for the immediate development of a clean and precise attack and release, and the need to listen closely to the quality of the tone. On a single page of explanations at the beginning of Volume I, Yancich discusses the tone with regard to the right hand position, the various types of attacks, and the care necessary for proper releases.

Throughout both books Yancich uses a unique device that makes these books quite appropriate for class horn, for example, educational techniques courses at the college level. Certain of the exercises can be combined and performed as quartets, trios, and duets. Scores for each of these ensemble possibilities are included near the end of the second volume.

As Yancich progresses and fills out the C major scale, the variation of dynamics plays an important role. Songs and recognizable melodies are soon added with the repeat sign, crescendo, ritard, and staccato indications. The theory begins with short studies on the basic six intervals and scale exercises. The book continues with a balanced exposure to performance problems and theoretical information embodied in the form of etudes.

By midpoint of Volume II, there are many sixteenth-note passages, varied dotted rhythms, a two-octave range from G below to G above the staff, and the inclusion of many familiar melodies. The key signatures by the end reach three sharps and three flats. Following the scores mentioned above, Yancich has included the major scales through six sharps and six flats, plus a short discussion, "Transposition," "The Use of the Double Horn," and "Muting" (i.e., stopped horn). This set of well-developed and effectively presented etudes could easily provide young students with a year or two of stimulation while establishing a strong musical and technical foundation.

Max P. Pottag and Nilo Hovey, *Pottag-Hovey Method for French Horn*, (2 Vols.) Belwin-Mills Publishing Corp./Warner Bros. Publications, Miami, Florida.

This set of studies has been around for a long time and has been quite popular. The major differences between this and Yancich's contribution is that this group progresses faster and further (through Grade II); there are no planned etude combinations for ensembles (but there are duets scattered throughout), and the second volume is more rigidly organized around keys. Each key is explored through scale studies mixed with tonal and melodic studies. At the end of Volume II, Pottag and Hovey discuss varied embellishments and include a few exercises requiring their use. These volumes could effectively supplement the Yancich books.

Maxime-Alphonse, *Deux Cents Etudes Nouvelles en Six Cahiers,* (6 Vols.) Alphonse Leduc, Paris, France.

These six books are graded as follows: Vol. 1, "70 Very Easy and Easy Studies"; Vol. 2, "40 Easy Studies"; Vol. 3, "40 Studies of Medium Difficulty"; Vol. 4, "20 Difficult Studies"; Vol. 5, "20 Very Difficult Studies"; and Vol. 6, "10 Grand New Melodic Studies for Virtuosity." Two of the special qualities of this extensive collection are the abundance of articulation suggestions and the use of many varied key signatures. From page one of the first Volume, the student needs to begin to distinguish between three different types of accents—staccato, non-staccato, and slurs—as well as three distinct dynamic levels arrived at both suddenly and gradually. Keys range from five flats through six sharps. However, the keys closest to written C major are the most frequently requested. The various keys are presented through both signatures and accidentals. All of this is in the first volume, so the published grading of "Very Easy and Easy Studies" should be interpreted accordingly.

These studies were first published in 1925 and are melodically typical of the late-nineteenth century. Each study has more substantial musical integrity and stylistic personality than most published etudes and is thus more enjoyable and challenging on many levels.

As you progress through the volumes, the demands for range increase, the length of exercises and the formal complexities of each study increase, the interval leaps widen, the rhythms become more complex, the tempos become more demanding, the articulations and their relationships to one another become a greater coordination problem, and additional techniques are introduced (i.e., stopped horn, lip and finger trills, traditional ornaments, etc.). Meter is also varied, with such compound meters as 15/8 being presented early in the third volume. There are no measure-by-measure meter variations, however. One interesting exclusion, even through Volume 6, is the near total lack of bass-clef writing. Each of the 200 studies is introduced by a short annotation or comment that discusses its primary purpose and suggests practice procedures. It is recommended that the student continue with this train of thinking and discover all of the problems left unmentioned in the printed notes before beginning to practice.

In Volume 6, you find extensive use of glissandi, cadenza-like passages, nearly unrestricted use of the top three octaves of the horn (c to c'''), very rapid harmonic fluctuations, and some flexibility demands that would more than challenge the virtuoso. It is Volume 5 that seems to be the most practical stopping-point for this style of harmonic and melodic writing. A performer capable of successfully executing Volume 5 should be adequately prepared for the orchestral and chamber music writing for horn of the late Romantic period. These books from Volume 1 through Volume 5 are truly basic repertoire and have been used extensively for generations.

Carl Kopprasch, *Sixty Selected Studies for French Horn,* (2 Vols.) Carl Fischer, LLC, New York, New York.

If there is any one set of etudes that all successful professional horn players have studied seriously during their development, it would be the famous Kopprasch etudes. These have been for a long time an important part of the other brass instrumentalists' repertoire as well through the form of transcriptions. There are a tremendous number of books that touch on similar problems and are also deeply rooted in the mid-nineteenth century style of etude writing, but Kopprasch seems to have best satisfied most horn players' needs for such a technical vocabulary and has done it without excess.

Unlike the etudes previously discussed, these don't actually follow the expected progression of increasing difficulty. After the first few pages of Volume 1, the studies seem to be placed with back-to-back contrasts in mind. Actually, some exercises in the first book are technically more difficult than most of those in Volume 2. Some of the more consistent problems addressed include the following: varied scale or arpeggiated patterns, primarily around the tonic, subdominant, and dominant tonalities of the few keys being explored; establishment of a given articulation pattern with little or no variation; and suggested variations of the original articulation patterns, which remain the constant throughout the re-execution of the study. Kopprasch also includes suggested transpositions for a number of the etudes: fingering facility etudes requiring precise and rapid tonguing; lip flexibility studies for rapid and at times very wide intervallic leaps; the performance problems of embellishments in slower etudes; a few warm and lyrical adagio studies; reading of ledger lines; and many excellent interval studies. These etudes are so basic that many advanced professionals never stop using them. Repeating many of them down an octave at a *f* to *ff* volume level provides one with a very effective low horn workout.

George Barboteu, *Lectures-Exercises Pour Cor*, *Études Classiques Pour Cor*, *Vingt Études Concertantes Pour Cor*, Editions Choudens, Paris, France.

George Barboteu, one of France's most recorded performers and past professor at the Paris Conservatory has composed 121 exercises that should certainly merit high standing among the standard etude repertoire for the horn. The primary reason, aside from the fine qualities of each study, is that they fulfill the need of presenting contemporary performance and reading problems to the young player before it is too late. They also carry the student into virtuosic situations that will be quite applicable to the chamber music, soloistic, and symphonic writing of many of this century's composers.

These books are prepared as a set of increasing difficulty, spanning the intermediate through virtuosic with some overlapping. "Lectures-Exercises Pour Cor" is a group of 80 studies that are short enough and within a limited-enough range to provide challenges while not exhausting a serious younger player. There are frequent and varied articulation indications and equally numerous dynamic requests. Stylistic suggestions also are abundant (e.g., *peasante e tenuto, dolce, dolce cantabile, molto expressivo tenuto, legato bien lie, joyeux*, etc.). Switching in and out of new notation bass clef is included throughout, as is the use of varied meters. As this book progresses, the use of stopped horn, cuivré, trills, and transpositions increase. The range also deviates from the usual middle C to G above the staff and stretches often to the high B♭, B, and C near the end of the book. This set of etudes effectively presents in capsule form numerous musical problems that often spring up unexpectedly when an inexperienced performer is first confronted with some of the newer music.

Barboteu has not only posed problems and provided solutions, but he has also composed some very enjoyable music. There are humorous elements interspersed throughout all of these books. This humor, along with many other unique musical moods and emotions, is certainly as important for a student to prepare as are the pure technical considerations found throughout most of the horn etude repertoire.

In the other two books, Barboteu precedes each study with brief instructions regarding its execution. Each of these etudes is nearly two pages long, quite an increase from the *Lectures-Exercises*. *Études Classiques* consists of the following: "study in difficult intonations, flexibility, opening of the middle register"; "study in line"; "study on muted notes"; "study in Romantic style"; "technical study"; "study of tone quality and flexibility"; "study of binary and ternary tonguing"; and a "study in virtuosity."

In his *Vingt Études Concertantes*, Barboteu treats many of the same problems but demands an even greater degree of facility from the performer. Throughout all three books, he never avoids the complexities that scales and arpeggios can present and seems always to work around tonal centers. Some of the more unique directions in Barboteu's *Vingt Études Concertantes* include the following: "interpretations to come as close as possible to the medieval style," "should exercise the eye of the interpreter." "difficult intonation, use of closed notes, mute, flutter tongue, large intervals in all the tessituras of the instrument"; "atmospheric study"; "music known as 'variety' and jazz"; and "some known horn effects and some discovered by the composer."

These three books make up a semblance of progression but with a desired second intermediate book apparently left unwritten. I have found these etudes to provide an enjoyable and meaningful foundation for exercising both the technical and musically stylistic challenges of twentieth-century horn writing.

Gunther Schuller, *Studies for Unaccompanied Horn*, Oxford University Press, London, England.

Gunther Schuller was a highly successful horn player, as first horn in the Cincinnati Symphony, followed by first horn in the Metropolitan Opera Orchestra, and as a frequently recorded jazz and commercial player in New York. As a composer, he was recently awarded the Pulitzer Prize. All advanced and advancing horn students should seriously study these etudes.

In these 13 studies, Gunther Schuller has covered most of the basic and traditional problems of playing, all within a logical contemporary musical framework. I often refer to these ingenious studies as "the twentieth-century Kopprasch" because they serve a similar function while addressing the actual performance requirements begun by Stravinsky, Schoenberg, and others. As a testament to their musical content, studies IV and XIII have been allowed as optional selections for performance at the International Competition for Horn in Munich, Germany—quite an honor for etudes! These 13 studies work on slurring, intervals, rapid tonguing, flexibility, articulation control, varied dynamics in all registers, rapid changes in tessitura, and the usual and unusual rhythmic shifts. Schuller has also presented us with reading problems and notational parallels (i.e., patterns in eighth-notes repeated in sixteenths); complex metric changes; many complicated rhythmic subdivisions (e.g., eighth-notes increasing to triplets, sixteenths, quintuplets, sextuplets, septuplets, and thirty-second notes, along with various combinations); and such effects as stopped horn, three-quarter-stopped (or echo-horn), glissandi from the echo-horn position to open, flutter tongue, and both fingered and lip trills.

Verne Reynolds, *48 Etudes for French Horn*, G. Schirmer, Inc., New York, New York.

When these studies were first published, they caused great turmoil among horn players, being referred to as totally impossible. However, after only a few years, it is said that Mr. Reynolds began receiving letters from high school and college students telling him how much they enjoyed working on them. Considering the actual difficulties presented, they would have needed to be very exceptional students to have done a truly thorough job, but the point is that it takes creative and courageous individuals such as Verne Reynolds (as it took a Richard Strauss in his day) to stretch the limits of horn playing.

"The Great 48," as they are referred to around Eastman School of Music where Mr. Reynolds taught for so many years, are a tightly organized group of fine compositions. The first 24 etudes are devoted to the intervals through the octave, alternating in contrasting styles and articulations. The next five are dedicated to the low register, and the next eight to the high range, with the following seven studies concentrating on varied metric changes. Etude 44 is an unmeasured work that can stand alone as one of the most exciting performance solos available for unaccompanied horn. Numbers 45 and 46 are double- and triple-note groupings, 47 deals with lip trills, and 48 is devoted to rapid alternations between open and stopped passages with added sudden dynamic complications. The deception inherent in the above description is that it oversimplifies the multiple challenges found in each and every etude. In the foreword to the book, Mr. Reynolds expresses his hope that these etudes contain sufficient intrinsic musical merit to warrant their inclusion into the solo horn literature, specifically Numbers 3, 6, 8, 10, 12, 16, 18, 30, and 44. I would add a few more to that list (22, 25, 26, 38, and 39) and encourage students to consider performing these fine compositions in recital even though they are labeled as etudes.

If range is a concern, be prepared for the full four octaves between pedal D and high D above the treble clef staff, perhaps all within the same etude. If any other of the basic technical problems are in a student's way, spend time first with Barboteu's books or the Schuller Studies. Learning the *48 Etudes for French Horn* should be one of the goals of every advanced student of horn. There may be other studies available that are as tough a mountain to climb, but the view—both musically and technically—just might prove to be less expansive or rewarding.

Joseph Singer, *Embouchure Building for French Horn*, Compiled by Richard Ballou, Belwin-Mills Publishing/Warner Bros. Publications, Miami, Florida.

Richard Ballou has compiled and edited these very basic and totally mechanical exercises which were devised and used by the teacher Joseph Singer, long-time associate principal horn in the New York Philharmonic. This collection of long tone studies, scales, arpeggios, and interval exercises are applicable to almost any level of ability beyond the beginner. The emphasis is on the development of embouchure strength, but also includes concerns for tonal control and flexibility throughout the entire range. Bass clef is presented in both the old and new notations mixed with ledger lines in many of the studies. Such reading problems aren't often found in the horn etude repertoire. These basic note patterns are ripe for transposition into all keys and could easily be the inspiration for writing simplified or intensified variations, depending on the student's abilities and needs.

Ward O. Fearn, *Exercises for Flexible Horn Playing*, Elkan-Vogel Co. Inc., Philadelphia, Pennsylvania.

Mr. Fearn, who served many years as second horn with the Philadelphia Orchestra and later as the professor of horn at the University of South Florida, has applied his extensive experience with both the middle-low register and the flexibility problems involving low horn harmonic lines in composing these twelve highly effective and useful exercises. Each study has its own musical personality, while providing a realistic challenge for the register of the horn that seems so problematic for many of us. The melodic design for many of these exercises is very enjoyable, which provides the students with the necessity to not only free up their sounds in that range but also to perform lyrically in an area of the horn that is often quite inflexible, stuffy, and uncentered.

Albin Frehse, *34 Etuden für Tiefes Horn*, Friedrich Hofmeister, Leipzig, Germany.

These etudes provide an extensive exposure to the low register with an abundance of old-notation bass clef. Varied key signatures (to six flats and five sharps), intervallic and rhythmic problems appropriate to early twentieth-century tonal writing, and rapid shifts between open and stopped horn all contribute to these worthwhile etudes. There is a strong need for horn students to thoroughly study low horn etude books. The basic solo, chamber, and orchestral repertoire require this range only sporadically, which is the point. Students must create the opportunity to develop a low-range facility, since it is not handed to them elsewhere. The Frehse etude book is highly recommended, but it is not as readily available as two additionally effective collections: *30 Spezial Etuden für Tiefes Horn*, in two volumes by H. Neuling; or the tuba transcriptions, *34 Characteristic Etudes for Low Horn Playing*, edited by Martin Hackleman.

J. F. Gallay, *40 Preludes for French Horn*, Op. 27, edited by James Chambers, International Music Co., New York, New York.

Of the many collected etude books by Gallay (eight opuses are known to this writer), the preludes, especially the last twenty, very successfully fill an important gap in horn etude literature. Students who have grown up with a rigid attachment to the metronome-like exactness of many etude books could benefit greatly from the last twenty unmeasured preludes. Note lengths are printed but are meant only to suggest a general rhythmic relationship, while the pulse and musical motion must be interpreted as if in a Romantic period cadenza. The majority of Gallay's etudes emphasize the uppermost octave and cor alto style, so there is a focus on high-range lyricism while frequently visiting high C. There is also the challenge to one's endurance. These etudes are highly recommended for the advancing student as a set of high-range studies, cadenza studies, lyrical studies, and, with many of them, as unaccompanied solos. (I have actually used two of them as encores, and Philip Farkas included four of them on his only solo recording.)

Domenico Ceccarossi, *Ecole Complete du Cor*, Vol. 2, Alphonse Leduc, Paris, France.

How often is it that students will say "I really have never been able to play stopped horn well," and how frequently do professional players grab their mutes when a passage for stopped horn or echo-horn comes up? With a thorough study of the second volume of Ceccarossi's *Complete Course for the Horn* in four volumes, hand muting of all kinds could become less fearful and more effective. This volume is exclusively dedicated to "exercises and studies on muffled, echo, and mixed sounds," with discussions of each technique at the beginning of the book. These studies could be helpful even for the early intermediate student—the earlier the better.

Julien Falk, *Vingt Etudes Atonales pour Cor*, Alphonse Leduc, Paris, France.

These twenty atonal studies present the most frequent technical demands that a player will face in today's technically advanced music. The hearing of intervals is the most completely tested problem, while many special effects such as glissandi, flutter tongue, stopped and echo horn, brassy, trills, grace notes, and varied articulations are all abundantly included. There are numerous unique metric signatures, as well as a few unmeasured studies. With no tonal centers providing the student with points of aural reference, these studies will challenge the advanced student with much needed ear training. The musical substance throughout these compositions is also worthy of note.

Daniel Bourgue, *Techni-Cor, Daily Exercises and Orchestral Excerpts* (5 Vols.), Gérard Billaudot, Paris, France.

Something new in the etude repertoire began in the late 1980s. Daniel Bourgue has combined written instructions with helpful diagrams in French, English, and Spanish (beginning with Volume 4), followed by basic exercises and directly applicable excerpts from the orchestral, chamber, and solo repertoire. Each volume addresses a specific category of technique, such as flexibility, staccato, articulations, synchronisms, and transpositions. He organizes each volume into six or seven sections, one for each day of the week's practice. Such a pace is surely appropriate for the advanced student of horn. The bulk of the material and the concept of design are quite creative and intelligently presented, successfully incorporating the means and the ends.

Robert Nagel, *Speed Studies*, Mentor Music Inc, Brookfield, Connecticut.

Though these studies were conceived for trumpet, they quite adequately fill an important gap in the etude repertoire for the horn. Many chromatic and often awkward patterns wind their way through the middle-low register far into the high, providing the fingers, the air, the tongue, and the embouchure with an extensive workout through many keys. It is suggested that the articulations be varied to include multiple tonguing patterns, which is an often neglected technique for the hornist. Major and minor modes are drilled, as are chromatic, whole tone, and mixed scale patterns. These are drill studies that require extensive mental and physical focus and stamina.

The Complete Horn Scale Book, Boosey & Hawkes, London, England.

This is the most basic, to-the-point presentation of scales and arpeggios I have seen. All keys are covered, major and minor notated over one, two, and three octaves, as are arpeggios, whole-tone scales beginning on each pitch, scales in thirds, dominant seventh chords, fully diminished arpeggios, and short exercises on varied broken intervals. This should become a basic reference book for all students confronted with juries and auditions. Memorization is recommended.

HORN ETUDES AND EXERCISES
(Listed in a selected order of importance and usefulness for the advanced high school/college level and beyond.)

Maxime-Alphonse, *200 Études* (Vols. 3–6), Leduc.
Kopprasch, C., *60 Selected Studies* (2 bks.), Fischer.
Fearn, W., *Exercises for Flexible Horn Playing*, Presser.
Gallay, J. F., *40 Préludes*, Op. 27, International.
Schuller, G., *Studies for Unaccompanied Horn*, Oxford.
Reynolds, V., *48 Études*, G. Schirmer.
Frehse, A., *34 Etuden für Tiefes Horn*, Hofmeister
Hackleman, M., *34 Characteristic Etudes for Low Horn*, Editions BIM.
Hackleman, M., *21 Characteristic Etudes for High Horn*, Editions BIM.
Shoemaker, J. R., G. Concone, *Legato Etudes*, Belwin.
Brophy, W., *Technical Studies*, Carl Fischer.
Barboteu, G., *Études Classiques*, Choudens.
Barboteu, G., *Vingt Études Concertantes*, Choudens.
Nagel, R., *Speed Studies* (trp), Mentor.
Falk, J., *20 Études Atonales*, Leduc.
Singer, J., *Embouchure Building*, Belwin.
Gallay, J. F., *12 Grand Caprices*, Op. 33, Leduc.
Franz, O., *Complete Method*, Fischer.
Brahms, J., *10 Horn Studies*, Henn.
Kling, H., *40 Characteristic Studies*, International.
Righini, P., *6 Studi Seriali*, Ricordi.
Gates, E., *Odd Meter Studies*, Sam Fox.
Neuling, H., *30 Spezial-Etuden* (low horn), Pro Musica.
Ceccarossi, D., *École Complete du Cor* (Vol. 2), Leduc.
Ceccarossi, D., *10 Caprices pour Cor*, Leduc.
Bourgue, D., *Techni-Cor* (5 Vols.), Billaudot.
Clark, J., *Exercises for Jazz French Horn*, Hidden Meaning Music.

Etudes and Exercises for the Earlier Levels
Hill, D., Froseth, J., *Introducing the French Horn*, GIA Publications.
Yancich, M., *Method for French Horn* (2 Vols.) Wind Music.
Pottag, M., and N. Hovey, *Method for French Horn* (2 Vols.) Belwin.
Goldstein, A., *First Book of Etudes* (2 Vols.), Cor.
Horner, A., *Primary Studies*, Elkan Vogel.
Tuckwell, B., *Fifty-First Exercises for Horn*, Oxford.
Maxime-Alphonse, *200 Études* (Vols. 1 and 2), Leduc.

24. Orchestral Excerpt Collections Reviewed

The following chapter consists of an updated and expanded article regarding the importance of excerpt study for all students of the horn, along with selected reviews of some of the most significant collections. If you wish to be a professional hornist, these excerpts are a most-important means to that end. Without a thorough knowledge of this repertoire, a hornist will have a much more difficult time trying to succeed as a performer and/or as a teacher. With knowledge of this repertoire, one experiences many of the reasons the horn is so popular with classical audiences. Excerpts are capsules of the finest music ever written for the instrument!

Orchestral excerpt books can provide the student of horn with a vast set of important musical experiences, perhaps more so than any other single source. However, some teachers neglect to expose their younger horn students to such a repertoire. Perhaps the only valid argument against using these experiences as teaching/learning tools is the simple truth that relatively few students of horn need to, or in some cases even wish to, prepare for professional auditions or for orchestral playing careers.

Professional preparation is, however, only one of a number of very important reasons for serious study of orchestral excerpts. Even the act of study itself is an idealistic goal that should not be discouraged. Where else can a horn player be so effectively exposed to the most profound melodic writing for the instrument than from the master orchestral composers? It is through the study of such excerpts that a student can develop stylistic vocabularies and a basic understanding of the stylistic evolution of western music, and the coloristic potentials of the horn. This first-hand experience of learning excerpts opens the door to a greater interest and more thorough knowledge of the finest of all instrumental music.

Practical and technical demands placed on horn players, which are often less clearly presented in etude books, are easily discovered in a succinct and frequently more musically rewarding manner in an excerpt context. This in no way is meant to downplay the importance of successful etude books, but only to point to the realization that most etudes are merely an attempted means toward the end, the results of which are more adequately presented through excerpt collections. More specifically, the study of excerpts is, perhaps, the most practical and valuable way for a student to learn the techniques of transposition. Students are not only confronted with the intellectual exercise of clef or interval shifts required for transposing, but also are made fully aware of the practical necessity for such abilities.

It is also realistic to assume that most students will participate in large ensembles while in school, and in community or professional groups after graduation. With this in mind, rehearsals and performances can be much more rewarding when the player has previous knowledge of, and the ability to successfully perform, certain solos. Internalized awareness of the great composers, including their styles and the compositions at hand, will also provide the player with more refined expectations and a greater understanding of the music in general.

For the student to gain the maximum results from excerpt practicing, the following suggestions are meant to help. Choose two or three contrasting compositions. Look (but don't play yet) through the chosen excerpts, carefully familiarizing yourself with their structure and obvious musical and technical demands. Before indulging in practice, find full scores of the selected compositions whenever possible and, together with the excerpt book, listen to all available recordings of the works being studied. It is important to listen to more than one interpretation. Compare the similarities in tempo, articulation, and breathing patterns (marking all such information in the excerpt book itself for future reference), and learn the sounds of all the other instruments, as well as the horn's place, within those varied timbres. Repeated listening is of vital importance, not only for the understanding of the particular horn excerpt's placement and degree of significance within the piece, but also for the student's exposure to the entire composition as a work of art of which the excerpt is only a small part. After gaining such awareness, the actual practicing, learning, and interpreting will be much more insightful and will have a greater impact upon the musical and technical development of the student. (Please see the chapter "Professional Orchestral Auditioning" for more detailed discussion.)

Reviews of Excerpt Books and Compilations

What follows is a compendium of brief reviews beginning with selected classic excerpt books (some of which are not readily available but are of great significance to the history of horn literature and worth researching), followed by a representative selection of the more contemporary compilations.

Max Pottag (ed.), *French Horn Passages*, 3 Vols., Belwin-Mills/Warner Bros. Publications, Miami, Florida, 1940.

Included in these volumes are many of the exposed passages from the orchestral literature of the eighteenth and nineteenth centuries, with an occasional reference to Baroque and early twentieth-century works. Of great interest is Volume 1, which includes the largest selection of the most famous horn solos gathered in one book. The extractions are left in their original keys and often include more than one horn part when it is of equal exposure. Pottag's Volume 1, the standard excerpt handbook for over 40 years, consists of excerpts from all of the Beethoven and Brahms symphonies, along with many of their smaller works and the most famous solos by Tchaikovsky, Wagner, and others. There are a large number of significant printing errors that should be corrected by the student through research into scores and recordings. (One legend is that Max Pottag, who was then second horn in the Chicago Symphony, compiled these passages, many of which are from obscure works of no practical use, from within his own memory and simply submitted them for publication.)

James Chambers (ed.), *Orchestral Excerpts for French Horn*, 7 Vols., International Music Co., New York, 1970.

Chambers' presentation of excerpts throughout all seven volumes is within the context of what is to be played before and after the major solo occurs, thus frequently pointing up the problems of endurance or sudden shifts of dynamics or range. These volumes also include lengthy quotes for the entire horn section, thereby providing potential ensemble practice material. Though a large portion of these volumes are dedicated to nineteenth-century literature, there is an ample representation of Mahler, Debussy, Stravinsky, and Prokofiev. Compiled by the principal horn in the New York Philharmonic, this set of books has, for nearly 30 years, served as a vital reference for aspiring orchestral hornists. Be aware that these volumes also contain many mistakes, including requests for incorrect transpositions, so always compare details with scores or actual parts.

James Chambers (ed.), *Richard Strauss—Orchestral Excerpts from Symphonic Works*, International Music Co., New York, 1968.

This book is quite similar to the Wipperich edition published earlier through International, which was perhaps one of the earliest of a number of more recent excerpt collections dedicated to a single composer. In this case, the composer is of maximum importance to the hornist because of his extensive influence on the instrument's musical development. Many of the solos presented in this book one can safely assume will be included at almost all professional auditions. The numerous ensemble sections represent some of the most demanding requirements placed upon the orchestral horn players in the nineteenth and early twentieth centuries. Consequently, this book deserves an extended amount of study. The many excerpts are extracted from *Don Juan, Death and Transfiguration, Till Eulenspiegel, Thus Spake Zarathustra, Don Quixote, Ein Heldenleben, Sinfonia Domestica,* and *Burlesque.*

James Chambers (ed.), *Richard Wagner—Orchestral Excerpts from Operas and Concert Works*, International Music Co., New York, 1966.

With this volume, I believe, Chambers began to publish his extensive and useful excerpt collections. Done in the same style as the Strauss and the seven-volume set mentioned above, Chambers focuses on Wagner, the first composer to truly feature the brasses, including the horn section. Many important passages, both technically and musically difficult, are quoted. Much less of this material is included on professional auditions in the United States than in Germany, but the technical and melodic materials presented are of great significance for any conscientious hornist.

Kurt Janetsky (ed.), *Bach Studien für Waldhorn*, 2 Vols., Friedrich Hofmeister, Leipzig, Germany, 1958.

This music, composed by the most significant of all Baroque composers, is a great way for a horn student to become familiar with what was expected of the horn players of that period. The other excerpt books only touch lightly upon the Baroque era, but in these volumes there is extensive space given to the most significant cantatas. Volume 2 also includes the two most frequently performed works of Bach, the Mass in B minor (BWV232) and the Brandenburg Concerto No. 1 (BWV1046). These excerpts could also serve as an excellent selection of studies for the high range and the very high clarino register. Nowhere in the standard horn etude repertoire does the student get access to the stylistic characteristics of the Baroque horn parts. These are important books and can be of great help.

Philip Farkas (ed.), *Orchestral Passages for the French Horn from the Modern French Repertoire*, Durand & Cie, Paris, 1958.

During the same period of time in which Farkas presented us with his major book *The Art of French Horn Playing*, he also collected and published an anthology that helps to round out the horn player's orchestral excerpt collection as it presents the technical and musical requirements unique to the French impressionists. Most of the major works by Debussy, Ravel, Saint-Saëns, Dukas, Ibert, D'Indy, Roussel, and Schmitt are included. The unique strength of this fine volume is the thoughtful perspectives Farkas shared regarding many of the passages, ranging from suggested tempo considerations to the renotation of ambiguous rhythms, practical translations from the French publications, and tutorial suggestions one can only receive from an erudite writer who was also a highly experienced orchestral artist.

Mason Jones (ed.), *20th Century Orchestral Studies*, G. Schirmer, Inc., New York, 1971.

This set of excerpts is one-of-a-kind. So little twentieth-century music has been excerpted largely because of copyright problems. However, here we find an exciting way for the horn student to become familiar with many of the divergent styles found in the twentieth century's orchestral music. Articulation requirements, interval ambiguities, and more complex rhythms are all well represented. Another very important attribute is Jones' annotations regarding each excerpt. Such insights and practical and artistic considerations, drawn from decades of experience as principal horn in the Philadelphia Orchestra, will truly add to a student's overall musical perceptions and understanding. More than half of the composers included are American, and large sections of the book are devoted to Stravinsky, Hindemith, Prokofiev, and Barber.

Richard Moore (ed.), *Operatic French Horn Passages*, Theodore Presser Co., Bryn Mawr, Pennsylvania, 1971.

This anthology of excerpts from 24 operas provides the student with a great number of lyrical (cantabile) passages and the complete gamut of transposition problems that are so much a part of operatic orchestrations. Well discussed in a forward by Gunther Schuller and a preface by Moore are uses for this collection and certain specific problems encountered in operatic horn playing. There is also a valuable glossary of terms and a short explanation of transpositions. Again, pertinent annotations are found that seem even more important and necessary for the preparation of operatic accompaniments than for straight symphonic music. The exposure to such composers as Verdi, Wagner, Mozart, Bellini, and Donizetti in their operatic contexts is quite interesting and extremely valuable for the ambitious student, especially if opera playing is a goal.

Richard Moore and Eugene Ettore (eds.), *Anthology of French Horn Music*, Mel Bay, Pacific, Missouri, 1986.

Richard Moore has followed his opera passages book with a very comprehensive selection of the most important excerpts drawn from the symphonic repertoire. Each composition has been selected from actual audition lists collected over a ten-year period. The omissions (acknowledged by the editors) such as Wagner, Bruckner, Mahler, Strauss, etc., can be rectified through the purchase of excerpt collections dedicated to each of them exclusively (see above Chambers' *Strauss* and *Wagner*). The strengths of this book are many. The table of contents lists each excerpt and delineates which quote is for which horn part (1st, 2nd, 3rd, or 4th). They have also included comments, sometimes rather extensive, for almost every excerpt to point out the hidden traps and make editorial suggestions. Dynamics and tempi, which are traditionally performed and accepted as musically appropriate but do not appear in the printed music, are published here within brackets.

Arthur LaBar (ed.), *Horn Player's Audition Handbook,* **Belwin Mills/Warner Bros. Publications, Miami, Florida. 1986.**

What Pottag's Volume 1 was for the aspiring orchestral horn player for over 40 years, Mr. LaBar's book has become for the present time. This is the one book to keep handy. It presents only the very basics as required at auditions. His choices were also largely inspired by compiled professional lists, and he includes some of the most basic Bruckner, Mahler, Strauss, and Wagner, as well as Bach, Beethoven, Brahms, Dvorak, Haydn, Mendelssohn, Mozart, Ravel, Saint-Saëns, Shostakovich, Schumann, Stravinsky, Tchaikovsky, and Weber. There are no annotations, but included is a glossary of somewhat confusing German (primarily) and a few French terms and phrases, which one might encounter in Mahler or Debussy. Although this book is arranged in alphabetical order for ease in finding each excerpt, a listing has also been included in the order of frequency of request on American orchestral auditions as determined in a survey by the International Horn Society.

Arthur LaBar (ed.), *Hornists Opera & Ballet Handbook,* **Phoenix Music Publications, 1995.**

LaBar returns with another very important, tightly organized, and extremely useful set of selected excerpts derived from pit orchestra audition lists from the United States, Canada, Germany, and Austria. This handbook is published in the Netherlands and includes the full text in French, German, and English. Much of this music is not as familiar to most horn students as is the traditional symphonic repertoire, which is a large part of its value. Consequently, it can serve as an introduction to many wonderful melodic and technical passages by composers such as Bellini, Berg, Bizet, Donizetti, Flotow, Gounod, Handel, Humperdinck, Lortzing, Prokofiev, Puccini, Stravinsky, and Verdi in addition to the more commonly excerpted, primarily orchestral composers. Many practical annotations by Howard T. Howard, principal horn in the Metropolitan Opera Orchestra, add additional depth to the quality of this fine publication.

Johannes Ritzkowsky, Alois Spachand, and C. F. Peters, *Orchester Probespiel (Test Pieces for Orchestral Auditions),* **Leipzig, Germany, 1992.**

The German Music Council, in collaboration with the German Union of Orchestras, has created a series of excerpt books for all orchestral instruments. The excerpts included are those most frequently requested for German and other European symphonic and operatic orchestra auditions. Such a selection is consistent with most of the American requirements (see lists included in the chapter "Professional Orchestra Auditioning"), plus the most obvious inclusion of important Wagner-Tuba excerpts from Bruckner, Strauss, and Wagner.

The most important aspect of this collection is the three CDs, which can be purchased separately and correspond directly to each well-selected and vitally important excerpt. Drawn from the complete editions by Deutsche Grammophon Gesellschaft, the student can hear the context of each and every excerpt. Many of the selections include a brief section of the orchestra leading up to the solo, and all provide a perspective of the level of exposure and the degree of importance for each excerpt. Though limited to only one particular recording, which is less desirable than hearing three or four renditions to compare tempos, interpretations, and recorded balances, this full set of materials is an absolute must for anyone interested in becoming a part of the orchestral performance profession.

There is simply no better way for horn players to truly know the potentials of their instrument, their role as a performer, and the artistic worth of the great compositions for large ensembles, than from actual participation in carefully prepared performances within such organizations. Excerpts obviously cannot substitute for this, but a thorough study of the excerpts in combination with extensive listening to recorded and live renditions of this all-important repertoire can serve as a vital component and basic foundation toward necessary fundamental skills and the development of a mature musical personality.

25. Horn Duets Reviewed

The original version of this set of extended reviews was published while I was a young teacher at the University of South Florida. It was obvious then, as it is now, that this literature deserves a great deal more attention than it usually receives. Duets are a wonderful and practical way for just two individuals to experience the challenges and joys of chamber music. They can serve as effective tools for teachers to share more than just words with their students. Duets can also help to build better section players by focusing on ensemble, intonation, blend, and articulation. And they are fun!

Duets Originally For Horns

Clifton Williams, Twenty-four Duo Studies, Southern Music Co., San Antonio, Texas.

Williams has composed some very compelling little pieces for the Grade II–III student. The harmonic language is tonally oriented, yet seconds, sevenths, and many open intervals provide a contemporary sound to which younger players need exposure. With only a very few exceptions, the parts remain in treble clef, and the first horn performs the melodic materials above the harmony. The rhythmic requirements are somewhat conservative, and the meters remain constant throughout each piece. The range extremes are G to b-flat", but the high b-flats are rare. There seems to be a general progression of difficulty in the ordering of these duos.

Williams suggests that a few of these pieces should be performed in various transpositions, at times to be played using only the notes of a given harmonic series (much in the style of the hunting horn). Such exposure might help some younger players to better understand the acoustical design of their horns. There are a number of especially effective duets that take on the character of folk dances, including the typical variety of accents and articulations.

One unique characteristic of this publication is that Williams uses a time signature with the number of beats above the actual note type (e.g., a 3 over a quarter note), rather than its equivalent number (3 over 4). As we get into the later duets, the leaps become greater, there is a more frequent use of clef change, and the span is wider between voices. One inconsistency is the use of the term "muted" and the symbol "+" simultaneously. Not until "Duo-Study XXII" do we see the word "stopped" and the "+" together.

These are excellent little pieces that could be used as studies by a teacher with a student as an introduction to some of the more basic contemporary aural and physical performance problems.

W. A. Mozart, Twelve Duos, (K. 487), Josef Marx (ed.), McGinnis & Marx, New York.

These twelve duets are a must for every advanced horn player (Grade IV–V). They are fun to play, lie well, are a delight for the listeners and the performers, and are Mozart!

The first half of this edition (one of many editions known to this writer) is devoted to a lengthy historical introduction (shown to be somewhat inaccurate in recent years) by Marx. In this introduction, he discusses not only the arguments related to the authenticity of these pieces as horn music (only a few are certainly for horn while the others are believed to have been for bassett horn), but also the problems and solutions of writing for the hand horn during the eighteenth century.

The duets themselves have been published in comfortable keys and have not been overedited to the point of stifling any originality on the player's parts. A few dynamics have been added, and the articulations while sparse are consistent with the few that Mozart wrote.

These pieces are in many ways more difficult to perform than are the concertos. The ranges include Horn I - c' to c''' (with some rather tricky technical passages in the top octave, typical of cor alto writing) and Horn II - F to f' (with a number of very large leaps into the lowest octave, typical of cor basse writing). The second horn part is almost entirely accompanimental and alternates between treble and bass clef. Aside from the obvious technical demands, the greatest challenge has to do with the transparency of each voice and the obvious musical significance of every note and phrase.

These duos are truly basic repertoire for hornists, and this edition works quite well unless you wish to play them on the hand horn or use them as transposition studies. (A facsimile is currently available through Thompson Editions, Inc., which would be more appropriate for hand-horn study and performance.)

Wilhelm Kopprasch, Eight Duets, (François ed.), International Music Co., New York.

Although these duets are great fun to play, endurance is a central challenge even within single pieces, and especially for Horn I. These are Grade V material because of the sudden changes in dynamics, articulations, and register; the preponderance of high range for Horn I and the middle low (the so called "break" range) for Horn II; and, most of all, the length of these pieces (and lack of rests for either part).

It should be noted that these duets are by Wilhelm, and the famous set of etudes *60 Selected Studies for French Horn* are by Carl Kopprasch. (Kopprasch did, however, write three duets, which are available through Southern Music Co.). The style of these pieces will be familiar to anyone who has played Kling, Belloli, Gallay, and other similar methods of the eighteenth and nineteenth centuries. The same basic technical demands focus on arpeggios, scales, and periodic chromatic embellishments. While almost all are written in the key of C, the exceptions are the key of F for Duet No. 8 and the trio section of No. 7 and C minor for No. 2. For modern hornists, self-prescribed transpositions would add yet another useful and logical dimension.

The form and character of the pieces do vary. The composer includes two sonata allegro movements, four simple ternary pieces (each with its own distinct personality), a theme with variations, a polonaise and trio, and a rondo movement. It appears that the Andante con Variazioni was not given a number, so one receives nine duets for the price of eight.

The range requirement for Horn I is e' (only two of them) to c''' (with many high c's). Horn I stays in the top octave throughout most of these works, even when playing an accompanimental role. This publication comes with two separate parts (so the right hand will not always know what the left hand is going to do next). Horn II must play from c to g'' and, more often than not, do the arpeggiated, cor basso, Alberti bass-like accompanimental figures.

N. Rimsky-Korsakov, Two Duets, Robert King Music Co., North Easton, Massachusetts.
Franz Schubert, 5 Duos für 2 Hörner in Es (Leloir ed.), N. Simrock, London.
Gioachino Rossini, 5 Duos für 2 Hörner in Es (Leloir ed.), N. Simrock, London.

These three sets of duets are all by major composers; and although perhaps not their most significant compositions, each is worth the time and effort to locate and learn.

Rimsky-Korsakov has written two short, simple, and delightful works. The first one is very similar to the horn calls of the eighteenth century, except that it uses a greater independence of line and a larger number of notes not in the expected natural harmonic series. The second piece employs a greater amount of chromatic movement than the first and sounds more in the style of the early nineteenth century fanfares and dances. (Range: c-g'', Grade III.)

Each of the 5 Duos by Schubert is in the tradition of the hunting horn. Leloir has provided a rather extensive number of articulations and dynamic variations, and he has changed some of the original unisons to continue the more usual horn-call harmonies. These are much less melodic than a horn player might expect from the composer of *Auf dem Strom*, but are delightfully fun, rewarding, and challenging nonetheless (and often quite soft in the high range). (Range: d'-b-flat'', Grade III, IV.)

Rossini's 5 Duos seem to capture much of this composer's personality. Structurally, these five pieces stand as a unit, with the middle duet (a pleasant Adagio non troppo in F) being flanked by two minuets (No. 4 being in a more traditional minuet form). These two minuets are in turn flanked by two march-like ternary movements. The outer four duos are all in B-flat. These are also highly edited by Leloir and, aside from a few brief static moments, are often quite musically satisfying. (Range: f-f'', Grade III.)

Alec Wilder, Twenty-two Duets for French Horn, G. Schirmer.

As was common with almost all of Alec Wilder's works for horn, the Twenty-Two Duets for French Horns was dedicated to the famous hornist John Barrows. In a forward by Mr. Barrows, there is a hint of their diversified character, which ranges from canonic writing to an exact unison, and from a serious introspective mood to a very outwardly humorous one. There is also a piece entitled "Blues" in the style that has endeared so many to the extensive horn music by Alec Wilder.

These duets are tonal and avoid complex rhythms and meter changes. There is great variation in dynamics, as well as a very wide range requirement: 1st horn from A (optional F') to c''', 2nd horn from A-flat to b''. An interesting inconsistency is his use of both old and new notation in the bass clef without any indication as to what was intended. (However, this only causes problems in sight-reading.)

A technique used to sustain both interest and endurance is the periodic exchange of roles between the horn parts, with second at times being higher than first. Wilder has also kept the pieces short enough so as not to tax endurance, yet in most cases long enough to justify possible performances. These duets are of a moderate difficulty, providing the players have substantial ranges. They would also be great fun as sight-reading for the more advanced college student.

Douglas Hill, Ten Pieces for Two Horns, The Hornists' Nest, Buffalo, New York, 1969.

In this group of short pieces, I have provided both players (Grade III–V) with primary and secondary roles. The varied styles and tempi are also meant to alleviate boredom. All of the pieces, however, share a similar harmonic vocabulary (tonally oriented) and make frequent use of the open intervals (P4 and P5) for intonation practice. There are titles for each piece ("Lament," "Hunt," "Dirge," etc.) meant primarily to set a mood or style of playing.

These duets are melodically oriented for the most part and periodically make use of metric changes. The most drastic of these multimetered pieces is the "Folk Dance," which is mathematically in 2/4 but has a number of changes (such as 3/8, 3/4, 3/8, 2/4) for the sake of a more accurate understanding of the intended accents. The "Dialogue" is in a very rapid 6/8, with a few 9/8 measures, which calls for some very tight ensemble work (with the parts often alternating each eighth-note causing a feeling of 3/4 with off-beats). There are also a number of slower song-like pieces, a march, a "Children's Song," and others. Contrasting character was an important plan in the compiling of these pieces.

The ranges remain in the middle to upper registers, with the extremes being e to b". These works were intended to provide both players with some moderate challenges and a satisfying experience for those who wish to listen. I have been told that they sound as if influenced by Bartok, Stravinsky, and Prokofiev, none of whom wrote duets for horns.

Douglas Hill (ed.), 27 Rare Horn Duets, McCoy Horn Library, Minneapolis, Minn.

These charming hunting horn duets were selected from three eighteenth-century publications housed in the Rare Books Library at Yale University in New Haven, Connecticut. Seven come from *Nouveau Manuel du Veneur*, 2nd Edition par Tellier; fourteen from *Les Fanfares des Equipages Francais* by Count Henri de LaPorte; and the last six from a British publication dated 1746, *The Compleat Tutor for the French Horn*. The selections were based on a cross section of the unique and the typical, with contrasting styles, familiar melodies, and melodic interest.

One will find melodies used by composers from Handel to Bozza, calls to the hunt, jigs, and water music. There are interesting ornamentations (including mordants, trills, and glissandi), unique notations left intact, and range requirements that are limited to two octaves up to the 16th partial (written high C).

These pieces would have been performed on hunting horns, using only the pitches available to such instruments without the hand for modification. All pieces are notated in the key of C major, as was typical, so other desired pitch levels or keys would have been realized by inserting different-length crooks. That makes these little gems perfect transposition studies for the modern hornists, and a fine opportunity for learning to love the sound of the harmonic series, "Nature's Scale." The eleventh harmonic (f") is frequently requested throughout, with the thirteenth (a") and fourteenth (b-flat") found in the later duets.

This is the music that set the foundation for what the horn does and how two horns are to be harmonized. Learning these typical melodic and harmonic patterns (which are still used by today's composers) and the inherent intonation problems add even more to the value of these delightful bits of history.

Bernhard Heiden, Five Canons for Two Horns, Associated Music Publishers, New York.

The first of these duets is an exact canon with a slight alteration near the end. It is in 6/8 with the canon at the quarter note, making the second voice quite syncopated. The voices enter at a perfect fifth, so some interesting relief from the busy contrapuntal movement comes in a passage of parallel thirds. The character is reserved and flowing, with a final burst of excitement in dynamics, range, and articulation, and quickly settling back into the final cadence.

The second canon is quite energetic, making extensive use of dynamic contrasts and periodic accents. It is primarily based on sixteenth-note activity, with sections of flowing eighth-note movement as contrast. This work is quite sectional, but the interval between the two parts remains at the major second within each section. Throughout, the lower voice leads.

Canon "III" is a very interesting work in Lento (quarter note = 52) in which the second voice follows the exact pitches and dynamics of the initial voice one half-note later. The staggered dynamic, crescendi, and cuivré indications, and the frequent minor second movement of the melodic materials, help to make this a strikingly mysterious duet. Heiden uses the stopped horn timbre very effectively from pp to f near the middle for contrast. He also employs quarter-tones that are approached by *glissandi* (bending the hand into the bell) and a "half-flatted" g' that is to be attacked fp (first and second valve on the F horn) on way to the normal g natural. All of this develops into a very hypnotic and enchanting work, both to perform and to hear.

"IV" is a canon at a perfect fifth, with the second voice an inversion of the initial theme entering one half note later. As in "II," there is an energetic primary theme (in this case dotted rhythms) with legato eighth-note movement for contrast. Incorporated are drastic dynamic variations, often quite sudden, and some uncomplicated meter changes. Canon IV in particular seems to have been greatly influenced by Paul Hindemith, who was Bernhard Heiden's teacher in the late 1930s and early 1940s.

As if to complete an arch form relationship among these five duos, Canon "V" is very similar in character to "I." This last canon is slower, however, and felt in seven (4/8 and 3/8 alternation) rather than six. The canonic procedures employed in "V" are also the most complex of the set, with each section seeming to employ its own devices and variations.

All of these five duets deserve the concentrated efforts of the advancing student (Grades IV–V), not only for their many musical merits, but also for the technical performance problems of harmonic complexity and complete independence of line.

Verne Reynolds, *Calls for Two Horns*, Carl Fischer, LLC, New York.

Calls for Two Horns is truly unparalleled in the repertoire and may easily be considered the most effective performance piece for recitals. It begins in an extended dialogue with each player located off-stage on opposite sides. Many of the melodic motives are introduced during these lengthy initial introspective recitations. Eventually, the second horn comes onto the stage and begins a much more rhythmically active section before being joined by the first horn. The two commence to chase each other melodically, coming together for moments of powerful unison. This middle section builds to a very exciting climax, followed by the return to the off-stage positions and a fading dialogue involving muted passages and an eventual dissolve into silence.

Due to the off-stage positioning, the intonation and ensemble present new challenges. Distance causes a projected lowering of pitch, so adjustments may need to be made. Though very few pitches are performed simultaneously while in the off-stage positions, the performers must listen and time their calls and responses in an effective and musical manner.

Gunther Schuller, Duets for Unaccompanied Horns, Oxford University Press, London, England.

In each of these four duets, Schuller has presented a different technical ensemble performance problem while composing some very effective music. In "I" the primary challenge is intonation. A pedal note (a constant b' being handed back and forth between the two voices) sets up many intonation problems: unisons and octaves, alternate matching of pitch, varied dynamics and articulations into the b', and frequently approaching the b' from opposite directions. As the piece progresses, the intervals from the b' get wider, yet the *molto legato* marking remains, which increases the musical and technical challenges.

"II" is a very rapid study in meter changes, with the constant sixteenth note at a suggested metronomic marking of 320 (i.e., quarter = 80). The meters range from 3/16 to 7/16 and from 2/8 to 4/8, with no regular pattern of change. This is only one of the difficulties. There are many different articulations and some very extensive intervallic leaps, with a few of two octaves or more. There is also the formidable difficulty of some very quick rhythmic alternations between the two voices. The range demands on the lower voice alone are three and one half octaves. All of this and the sudden unison sixteenths loudly rising to the b♭ make this exuberant duet a significant challenge for the very best of players.

"III" is obviously a study in various permutations of three against four in a slow tempo. This duet serves as an effective contrasting musical interlude within the set while it presents the performers with problems of range (E to a"), intervallic leaps similar to the other duets, and blending problems inherent with the rhythmic timing of the attacks.

The duet "IV" is very quick, but in this case the challenge is a chromatic arpeggiated perpetual motion in 6/8. The suggested tempo for the straight chromatic scales is less a problem than for the rapidly changing arpeggiated figures which make up most of the piece. Aside from a few staccato quarter-notes in the lower voice, this duet is primarily slurred, which adds to the difficulty of the many irregular and sudden harmonic shifts and drastic changes in direction.

Each of these pieces not only challenges highly developed hornists (Grade V) technically, but should also thoroughly satisfy them musically once they have spent the necessary rehearsal time to learn them well.

Claudio Spies, Times Two, *Boosey & Hawkes*, New York.

Times Two is a very potent and challenging atonal work in two movements. The structure is described through a riddle at the beginning: "For I. S. (Igor Stravinsky) at 86 in 68 from C. S. at 43 Times Two." Here is a composition written in 1968 for two voices in two movements, with the second movement being a nearly exact retrograde. The main differences are primarily articulations and dynamics, with Horn I also being asked to perform two stopped notes that were not a part of Horn II in the first movement.

As you might expect, the tempo is quarter note = 86 for both movements. There are a number of rhythmic intricacies, such as 4 over 3, 8 over 3, and 5 over 6 (with many related subdivisions), as well as the more frequently encountered syncopated problems in a 6/8 or 3/4 meter. The intervallic leaps both slurred and tongued in soft dynamics and the range (G to a#") may require some extra effort. This is one of the more musically successful works for two horns that incorporates the problems and potentials of atonality and complex rhythmic subdivisions. And for no other reasons than these, it deserves the conscientious attention of two equally advanced performers (Grade IV–V).

Everett Gates, Odd Meter Duets, Gate Music Co., New York.

These sixteen pieces were written "for all instruments in treble clef," so perhaps they don't belong under the heading of "Duets Originally for Horns"; but then, they are not exactly transcriptions either. They are, however, a most effective and challenging way for hornists to confront the many contemporary problems of uneven meters and the consequent rhythmic irregularities. Gates includes a discussion of many points concerning the content of these pieces and has made study suggestions at the front of the set. In the table of contents, he continues to explain certain structural characteristics and stylistic considerations for each piece. There is an abundance of five and seven beat meters, as well as the more common meters with less predictable inner accents.

Humor is definitely an element throughout this set of duets. The titles alone are chronically clever: "Aeolian Lament," "Seven to Go," "A Small Scale Development," "Billy Hill," "Ostinato Phrygiana," "Rumbalita," "Five Layer Cake," "Across the Border," "Tag-a-long," "Mixolydian Mixup," "Session at Seven," and "Chromatic Contrariness." Other titles are primarily descriptive: "Seventh Heaven" is in 7/4 and makes harmonic and melodic use of both major and minor 7ths; "Channel Five" is in 5/8, making use of five bar phrases; "Followup" is a strict canon; and "Heptonic Variations" consists of seven variations on a 7/4 theme, through seven keys, each in a different meter (1/4, 2/4, 3/4, etc.). Near the end of the book, Gates includes a few very interesting and historically significant examples of odd-metered excerpts from such composers as Handel and Tchaikovsky. The ranges are, of course, restricted by the oboe on the bottom, and the trumpet and horn on top. These pieces do, however, serve a very important rhythmic function, are in a category of their own, and are often musically enjoyable. (Grade III–IV.)

Lowell E. Shaw, Bipperies, Duets—Frippery Style, Hornists' Nest, Buffalo, New York.

Lowell Shaw has contributed some of the most fun available to horn ensemble enthusiasts through his thirty-two "Fripperies" for four horns. In the score for these duets he writes, "In response to an almost audible murmur of a clamor for duets from both of our Fripperies fans, The Hornists' Nest presents—BIPPERIES." Humor and jazz orientation are the keys to this set of nine light-hearted and varied pieces. He includes brief suggestions or considerations for each of the tunes, while asking for an overall lightness of style, *poco marcato* tonguing, and good rhythmic drive throughout.

The parts switch back and forth, providing an equality for the players as they frolic through such works as a jazz waltz, an impudent swing, two galloping chases, and a spooky tune with "a Halloween feeling." These are just plain fun and not too difficult. The range requirements are limited above the staff and more active in the middle low range (Lowell Shaw being a low horn specialist). The main challenge is the rhythmic trickery and jazz/pop styles of articulation. These fine pieces are well worth the effort and are appreciated by listeners. (Grade IV–V.)

Collected Duets (originals and transcriptions)

Max Pottag (ed.), Sixty French Horn Duets (2 Vols.), Belwin-Mills/Warner Bros. Publications, Miami, Florida.

Pottag has collected primarily original horn duets in these volumes. There is an abundance of works by C. T. Henning (1807–1865), from his "Instructive Duets," included in both volumes, and a number of duets by Oscar Franz (1843–1889) from his "100 Duets." The latter are largely found in Volume 2. The other inclusions are works by F. Duvernoy (1765–1838) from his "20 Duette," Gallay (1795–1864), and Poussey, two duo arrangements of the horn quartets found in Carl von Weber's *Der Freischtz* (in Volume 1), two arrangements of Schubert songs, one Mendelssohn arrangement, and a Mozart duet (not originally for horn). There are also a few folk song arrangements and some pieces not identified by composer.

The two volumes follow a pattern of progressive difficulty, with Volume 1 being Grade II–III, with the range of C to b♭"(though almost every piece is contained between g and g"), and Volume 2 covering the three octaves c to c"". Volume 2 also contains longer pieces and uses a greater number of turns, trills, grace notes, sixteenth- and thirty-second notes, causing most of the pieces to fall into Grade III or IV.

As one can tell by the list of composers, this is a collection of mostly nineteenth-century compositions, a period and style that seems to dominate the horn literature. Within that context, however, this collection is sufficiently varied and could be successfully used by teachers and their high school through younger college students, supplemented by Baroque period and twentieth-century works. These would also serve well as recreational reading materials for more advanced college and amateur hornists.

Wendell Hoss (ed.), 60 Selected Duets, Southern Music Co., San Antonio, Texas.

At the beginning of this diverse set of duets produced by the Los Angeles Horn Club, Hoss explains the many purposes of this volume:

> Primarily for the pleasure of the performers . . . to give practice in the various phases of horn technique and style: rhythm, attacks, slurs, intervals, and in the melodic use of scales and chords. Graduated from fairly easy to rather difficult . . . The earlier duets are planned for the beginning student, playing the upper line; with the instructor or a more advanced student playing the lower part.

To my knowledge (at the time of this writing), this is the most diversified collection of duets available. It starts from Grade I and develops through the level of Grade IV near the end. Throughout, most of the duets have a preliminary inscription that describes a style of playing ("with smooth legato style," "firm attack and solid tone," "strong bell-like attacks," etc.), a compositional technique being utilized ("use of chromatic scale," "exact imitation [canon]," "For practice in 5/4 time," "With sudden dynamic contrasts: f_{-p}," "In atonal style"), or for purposes of identification ("Three Songs for Christmas," "from the Eighth Symphony of Beethoven," and "from the Sixth Symphony of Tchaikovsky").

There are a few arrangements of traditional melodies ("Brother John," "Three Blind Mice," etc.), but most of the pieces were written by the contemporary composers Frank Allen Hubbell, George Hyde, Bernhard Kaun, Karl Kohn, Ronald LoPresti, Adolph Weiss, Mark Wessel, and Wendell Hoss. These men make interesting use of tonal harmonies (only Nos. 59 and 60 are atonal), with some intriguing rhythmic problems throughout. This set of duets could be a real asset, especially for a teacher with students of extremely varied abilities.

Oscar Franz, 100 Duets: Book 2, Sansone (ed.), Southern Music Co., San Antonio, Texas.

As mentioned previously, many of Oscar Franz's duets are included in the Pottag collection. My purpose in drawing attention to this second volume of Franz's 100 Duets is that the last half is devoted to the two-part inventions of J. S. Bach (though nowhere are they identified as such in the publication). The inventions are transcribed to avoid what would be exceedingly low second-horn parts if read directly from the original, and they are frequently transposed down to avoid the overabundance of the upper octave for Horn I. The two parts are published in separate books due to the extreme use of ledger lines in Horn II. The printing plates have the notes very close together, with the sixteenth-note and thirty-second note bars often running together, but it is still easier to read from these arrangements than from a piano score. A few suggested ornaments are included, but this edition is not as overedited as many Baroque-period publications. The opportunity for any musician to play Bach cannot be recommended highly enough. (Grade IV–V.)

H. Voxman (ed.), Selected Duets, (2 Vols.) Rubank/Hal Leonard Corp., Milwaukee, Wisconsin.

Here is another collection of duets that contains a very good cross-section of musical periods and styles from pre-Baroque to the twentieth century. Arranged in two volumes—Vol. 1 (easy-medium) and Vol. 2 (advanced)—these sets of duets are made up of both transcriptions or arrangements and selections from original horn duets by Mozart, Schubert, Gallay, Türrschmiedt, Kopprasch, Franz, Belloli, Jacqmin, and Winter. Other composers represented include Stamitz, Telemann, Bach, Handel, Purcell, Mendelssohn, Schumann, Fontana, Pohlmann, Vecchietti, Montclair, Weller, Fauconier, Devieux, Snow, Boismortier, Sambataro, and Pietzsch. I don't feel that the two volumes can be quite so easily classified as "easy-medium" and "advanced" since both volumes seem to cover a larger classification of abilities (Grade II, III, IV) and do quite successfully provide a wide degree of stylistic variation for the horn teacher who chooses to use duet literature for teaching.

Transcriptions

Orlando di Lasso, Twelve Duets, G. Smeltekop (trans.), MS Publications, Chicago, Illinois.

With this set of pieces, even the young player (Grade I, II) can get exposure to some sixteenth-century music. I have also found them to be enjoyable, as well as a real test of intonation, for any two horn players at any level of development.

All twelve pieces are written in 4/2 time, so there might be complications for some young performers to read a half-note pulse with dotted and double whole-notes. Each of the duets also has a suggested, half-note = 96. (Monotony might set in if all twelve were read in one sitting.) The written key signatures are C and G, and the ranges are held between c and e''. There is no bass clef used, so the extensive use of ledger lines in the second part may also provide a reading problem for the younger player. Doubly difficult is the published manuscript form, with the very small notes that are often crowded together. This set is an excellent introduction to the performance problems the hornist will confront in the many brass ensemble arrangements of Gabrielli and Pezel. Such problems include tuning the open intervals (P4, P5, P8), total independence of line, uneven phrase lengths, and the basic unimportance of the bar line as a point of reference.

Johann Schenk, Six Sonatas, Verne Reynolds (arr.), MCA Music, New York.

Johann Schenk (1656–1712), a virtuoso viola da gamba player, wrote these sonatas as a part of his Opus 8 *Le Nymphe di Rheno* for two solo gambas. Reynolds has extracted and arranged six of the original twelve sonatas, totaling 31 separate movements. The music itself is gratifying and sounds appropriate on horns. These are pieces, which in contrast to most of the available duet literature call for two equally developed players with balanced control of the top three octaves of their horns. Both players share the often beautiful, melodic materials, as well as the sudden extreme changes in register. Since the pieces are written almost entirely in the treble clef, both performers are confronted with an abundance of ledger lines. As would be expected from early Baroque music, there is an independence of line and in this case, frequently contrasting dynamic markings.

With the exception of Sonata IV these works are in sharp keys. I, III, and VI are in the written key of A, II is in G, and V is in D. This is mentioned because of its uniqueness in brass publications and, thus, the problems (or opportunities) it might present.

Because these were originally for string instruments, the horn players can expect longer phrases without built-in breaths, interval leaps of more than an octave (even within a fluid melodic line), and few pauses to rest the lip. The suggested ornaments are held to only half- and whole-step trills, however. Such challenges as these can only increase the horn player's technical and musical abilities. The ranges run from A to b'', and these pieces (depending on the movement in question) could be considered suitable for Grades III to V. To perform an entire sonata would require rather advanced players. These pieces, along with the Franz arrangements of Bach's two-part inventions, would add greatly to the development of the hornist's appreciation for the music of the Baroque and its stylistic performance problems.

J. S. Bach, Nine Duets for Horns, Eberhard Ramm (trans.), Medici Press, St. Cloud, Minnesota.

Assuming there can never be too much Bach, one needs to consider these nine dances transcribed from various simple keyboard pieces. If you were ever a young piano student, you will probably recognize a few of these simple yet profound keyboard compositions. Each of these dances is thoroughly edited by Ramm, including frequent articulation indications setting the style. Dynamics are indicated for each repetition, as are the ritards at the completion of the works. Mordants and trills are found throughout. The keys chosen are for the convenience of range, and the tempo indications are all quite specific. Such editing to appear in print may not be historically appropriate, but the choices are certainly musically accurate. Such information makes these duets a significant contribution to the understanding of the performance preferences of the Baroque period, which could be quite useful for young horn students.

Orlando Gibbons, *Fantasia*, David Baldwin (trans.), Autograph Editions, New York.

David Baldwin is another transcriber and composer who is dedicated to the increase of brass literature. His primary emphasis focuses on the trumpet and mixed brass ensembles, including this interesting single movement duet that is well worth investigating.

Fantasia recalls many of the rhythmic and harmonic problems found in the numerous Renaissance transcriptions for brass quintet and brass choir, and thus would be both good practice for such music and a supplement to it. Here is a very lively and highly imitative piece, with both staggered entrances and dynamic indications, as well as total rhythmic and melodic independence. The range is b♭ to a'', and both voices are expected to hold equal weight. If played at a brisk tempo, which would seem appropriate (no tempo suggestion is given), two facile players (perhaps Grade IV) would be needed. This publication is in a clearly legible manuscript with a minimum of added articulations and dynamic interpretations.

Duet Exercises

Verne Reynolds, Intonation Exercises for Two Horns, Wimbledon Music, California.

The one-hundred exercises included in this fine book are simple and intelligently practical. The basic pattern is for one voice to remain constant while the second voice eventually moves through all intervals from a unison to an octave. There is also a special emphasis on several versions of "horn fifths." The dynamics are left to the players and should be varied for obvious reasons. The printed range of G below middle C to G two octaves higher should also be transposed. Intonation problems above the staff and within the lower octave and a half should also be dealt with through these numerous interval relationships.

This is not "music" and would certainly not be performed, but they do serve the unquestionably important function of learning to truly hear the resonance of each and every interval while in the act of playing with another hornist. For two players to patiently work through a few of these studies, each session would make all of the other duets previously reviewed seem much more enjoyable.

26. New Music for and Because of Barry Tuckwell

In 1996, Johnny Pherigo, editor of The Horn Call: Journal of the International Horn Society, *invited me to write an article that would review the compositions written specifically for the soon-to-retire, world famous horn soloist Barry Tuckwell. A number of these wonderful compositions were favorites of mine already, so to learn of the others was a welcome opportunity. What follows is a revised version of the original, which was based upon an extensive interview with Maestro Tuckwell and a visual and, in most cases, aural review of each composition. The body of works discussed stands as representative of some of the finest solo horn writing of the late-twentieth century.*

Just over fifty years ago, a young Australian teenager named Malcolm Williamson and his buddy, a fellow horn player named Barry Tuckwell, decided that it would be a grand idea if Malcolm would write an original composition for Barry to play on his horn. Though the piece is lost, it could be said to have begun a legacy that includes at least 20 major compositions written specifically for this man who has become the world's most recognized and influential horn soloist. It would, however, be impossible to know all of the compositions that have been written because of Barry Tuckwell's inspirational technical prowess, adventurous performance aesthetic, and masterful musicianship.

The modern horn, which has been largely feared by contemporary composers and thus largely left out of this century's spotlight as a solo instrument, seems to have had an unusually significant life around this one particular Australian, British, and American French horn player. As early as 1962, Barry Tuckwell was the inspiration and stimulation for major works from such Australian, British, American, and French composers as Don Banks, Iain Hamilton, Thea Musgrave, Alun Hoddinott, Karl Kohn, Gunther Schuller, Richard Rodney Bennett, Robin Holloway, Jean-Michel Damase, David Gow, Paul Pritchard, and Oliver Knussen. It is this fine group of composers and their works for horn with orchestra, piano, and violin and piano, that I wish to present and discuss in this chapter. This body of work is both a significant indication of the strengths of Mr. Tuckwell's playing over the past thirty-five years, as well as a strong representation of the extensive compositional possibilities for the modern horn.

It was my pleasure to have had a lively and informative conversation with Barry Tuckwell on January 30, 1997, shortly after his formal retirement from the concerto circuit. We spent an hour and a-half discussing these twenty compositions and the problems of getting performances of modern music with orchestras. To quote Mr. Tuckwell, "It is actually the second performances that are the hardest to get. There used to be a gag that composers wanted the first performances done in Albert Hall (a notoriously live, echo-filled concert space in London) so that they could hear their pieces played more than once."

When asked which works he most often performed, Mr. Tuckwell explained that "the pieces most often performed were not necessarily the ones that should be most often performed. The decisions, certainly with regard to those works with orchestra, tend to rest with the management. My brother-in-law, the Earl of Harewood, so aptly noted that he had never heard me play the Strauss Second Horn Concerto. He says that this is the concerto that tends to be put down because the management crosses off the '2' and puts '1,' thereby saving an extra rehearsal."

Over the years, regardless of whether Mr. Tuckwell had wished to perform one of the more recent twentieth-century works written especially for him, or even one of the lesser-played though widely known basic horn solos, the orchestra management most often responded: "then if its not the Strauss 1, it's the Mozart Concerto . . . you know, the one in E♭ with the last movement in 6/8." (I found it quite interesting and somewhat reassuring that such a short-sighted and manipulative response not only happens to the rest of us.)

It was in 1962 that the Edinburgh Festival decided to commission a horn, violin, piano trio from **Don Banks**, an Australian-born British composer. Don Banks (1923–1980) moved to London in 1950, where he studied composition with Seiber, and later continued his studies with Babbitt, Dallapiccola, and Nono. His Australian roots remained strong throughout his life in Europe, most notably when he founded the Australian Music Association of London. Banks' **Horn Trio** was written especially for Barry Tuckwell, Brenton Langbein (violin), and Maureen Jones (piano), in part because they were all Australian-born performers. This is a three-movement work lasting approximately 15 minutes. The serial, atonal manner of composition, along with the frequent shifts and contrasts of energy, give it a somewhat intellectual bent, while the lyricism, found throughout with the emphasis on the descending minor second and the perfect fourth, provide a feeling of familiarity, long before the work reaches its completion. A few years after its composition and after numerous performances, the three for whom it was written recorded the Horn Trio along with the Sonata Notturna by Iain Hamilton (discussed later) for the British Council Series. However, that recording never received much circulation, so the original group of three recorded it again on a CD in 1987 for Ex Libris Verlag und Grammoclub, Zurich (#6059), a remarkably effective performance!

Tuckwell had met Banks at a film recording session for which Banks had composed the soundtrack. "Banks was a meticulous composer. He sent many letters about his plans and what he had in mind. After he died, back in Australia, he seemed to lose prominence as a composer." Tuckwell then lamented on how this so often happens to many of the finest composers.

Long before he died, **Don Banks** began to compose a piece for horn and piano. During its inception, he received a commission for a major work from the Peter Stuyvesant Foundation for the London Symphony. He quickly decided to transform this smaller work into his **Horn Concerto (1966)** for Barry Tuckwell, who was then solo horn in the London Symphony Orchestra. This exciting concerto, premiered by Tuckwell with Colin Davis conducting, quickly became a repertoire piece for Tuckwell and for the LSO, receiving many, many performances, including a tour of Australia. In 1974, Norman Del Mar conducted an exceptional recording of this work on Argo (ZRG 726), featuring Barry Tuckwell of course.

Scored for a very large orchestra, this eighteen-minute work begins with a unifying note-row, consisting largely of ascending minor seconds and tritones. The piece progresses through eight continuous sections of enthusiastic rhythmic complexities, notable orchestrational colorations, and astounding displays of flexibility, range, and interpretive prowess from this young soloist, who was just beginning his historic career. Both of these works by Banks are available from Schott & Co. Ltd., London.

The mid-1960s also saw the composition of two new and very effective works for horn and piano by the British and Scottish composers Iain Hamilton and Thea Musgrave. In 1965, **Iain Hamilton** (b. 1922) composed his **Sonata Notturna** for Barry Tuckwell and the noted pianist Margaret Kitchin. The high degree of structural design and proportion of this work could easily be attributed to Hamilton's having begun his adult life as an engineer. "In the precision of his writing you can see a strong mathematical mind. Even when it sounds aleatoric, it is all written out. Everything is all related."

With all of this formal structure, it might seem surprising how this highly effective three-movement sonata comes across as primarily a sensitive and dramatic dialogue. The reason is that this sonata was inspired by a brief quote from the French poet Baudelaire: "The sky / It closes slowly like an alcove / The impatient man changes into a wild beast." Hamilton uses a strict serial technique to portray these conflicts or polarities between the impatient man/beast and the suspended quiet of the night. This is truly an exceptional eight-and-one-half minute piece and should be studied and performed often. It does, however, require musically mature, sensitive, and flexible performers. The complexities require that both performers read from a score.

Iain Hamilton returned to the horn as a solo voice in 1970 with a commission from the London Sinfonietta, another group with which Tuckwell was affiliated. *Voyage for Horn and Chamber Orchestra* is an 18-minute piece created for Tuckwell, three winds, three brass, percussion, piano, and strings. This work is truly a tour de force for the solo voice, incorporating micro-tones, vocalizations, rhythmic glissandi, extensive amounts and extended sections of flutter-tongue, and numerous bravura sections, frequently stretching freely through a three and one-half octave range. There are many group improvisational sections and periodic multi-tempi sections. Tuckwell recalled that this piece "was done frequently. It almost became a repertoire piece for the group at the time." The difficulties in preparing the work did prompt Tuckwell to remember and remark, "The first couple of performances were rather hairy!"

An interesting parallel with Hamilton's earlier horn and piano piece is the derivative nature of its inspiration. Again, he goes to the poetry of Baudelaire and then also to Rimbaud as they both fantasize on the far-off places of the inner imagination made manifest by voyages upon the oceans and seas of the world. Hamilton also goes so far as to musically quote from La Mer and L'isle joyeuse by Debussy. A great recording was made of this work with Barry Tuckwell and the London Sinfonietta, David Atherton conducting, on CRI (SD 280). Schott publishes the Sonata Notturna while Voyage is published by Theodore Presser.

"I was invited to her basement apartment in London where we had some tea and scones, then sat down and played her new piece for horn and piano together. That was my introduction to Thea Musgrave." **Music for Horn and Piano (1967)** by **Thea Musgrave** was also written for Barry Tuckwell and Margaret Kitchin and became the first of many successful and challenging works by Musgrave that feature the horn. Born in Edinburgh, Scotland, in 1928, Thea Musgrave began as a student of medicine, but soon moved on to music, completing formal studies at the Paris Conservatory with Nadia Boulanger and Aaron Copland. She has taught, coached, and served on many European and American faculties, having emigrated to the United States in 1970. Music for Horn and Piano is a very dramatic, largely unmeasured, and gestural work that sounds and feels like a free dialogue. Two unlike timbres seem to blend as one, flowing into and out of each other's attacks, decays, and releases. The hornist reads from a part that includes extensive piano cues, suggesting the degree of simultaneity of attacks and releases. According to Tuckwell, "She spent a lot of time thinking about the practical side of performance which some composers don't do. So often you find it just doesn't work the way they wrote it. That is the thing about Thea, she is meticulous in how she writes."

In 1971, **Thea Musgrave** collaborated directly with Barry Tuckwell in the writing of her **Horn Concerto**, which Tuckwell calls "A work of major importance! It broke into a certain new territory and became one of the most effective pieces from the audience's point of view. It has an impact." As the story goes, Barry sent Thea a postcard from Tula, Mexico, with a picture of regional monoliths surrounding a central figure that Tuckwell quipped as being the horn section of the Tula Philharmonic. Such an image was all Musgrave needed to envision a work in which the horn section would eventually surround the soloist and the audience. The other brass then became a concertante group set against the rest of the orchestra. This work is scored for a medium-sized orchestra and makes wonderful use of the varied timbres of such an ensemble. This work is, in many ways, a study in orchestration and contemporary horn writing. Her use of extended techniques for the soloist (and others) is thoroughly knowledgeable and accurate. The quarter-tone scales, for instance, are beautifully notated and clear, and provide musically and technically memorable moments. The original recording, according to Tuckwell, "was done quadraphonically and should be rereleased as a surround-sound CD." I agree. That is the way this important composition was conceived and the way it works best. The premiere recording was produced in 1975 by the Decca Recording Co. (Headline 8) with Thea Musgrave conducting the Scottish National Orchestra, Barry Tuckwell, soloist.

One of Wales's most prominent composers is **Alun Hoddinott**, who was born in Bargoed, Glamorgan, in 1929. His development as a composer was greatly enhanced through his studies with Arthur Benjamin. Since those early years, his musical language has remained largely tonal, with intense chromaticism and subsequent complex harmonies. The Llandaff Festival commissioned him to compose his **Concerto Op. 65**, for horn and chamber orchestra (double winds, a large battery of percussion and strings) in 1969. In 1973, Barry Tuckwell recorded this 14-minute work with Andrew Davis conducting the Royal Philharmonic Orchestra, again for Decca Records (SXL6606). The percussion section takes on a large part of the responsibility with numerous pitched and unpitched instruments. In contrast, the solo line is primarily lyrical throughout this rather conservative, three-movement work. The opening melodic materials of the romanza weave their way to a climax and return to become thematic material for a rhythmic scherzo movement that further dances its way toward a dramatic cadenza for the horn, which is eventually rejoined with the orchestra in a quiet statement of the opening motive. "This is one of those pieces that never got performed often, however, I enjoyed recording it very much."

One of the more conservative pieces written for Tuckwell is the **Sonata for Horn and Piano, Op. 78, No. 2,** (1971) by **Alun Hoddinott**. "This was a piece that received many more performances than the concerto, because I controlled the input for my own solo recitals." Here, too, is a work published by the Oxford University Press. Premiered on August 28, 1971, by Barry Tuckwell and Margaret Kitchin at St. Donat's Castle, Wales, this piece is the result of a commission by the Vale of Glamorgan Festival. The traditional three-movement form begins around the tonal center G with lengthy and lyrical lines for the horn. The elegy-like second movement gives a strong impression of improvisational interplay between the voices. The final movement, "Presto," is a scherzo that dances jauntily along with a rather transparent accompaniment, concluding a satisfying and likable eleven-minute piece.

The first of the two Americans in this group of composers is the Austrian born **Karl Kohn** (b. 1926). Kohn immigrated to the United States in 1939 and began studies at the New York College of Music. After serving in the U.S. Army, he returned to study at Harvard with Walter Piston, Irving Fine, and Randall Thompson. In 1950, he began his professorship at Pomona College and Claremont Graduate School in California. It was there that Tuckwell and Kohn met. The three works written for Tuckwell began in 1971 with **Variations for Horn and**

Piano. Earlier, in 1967, Kohn had written *Encounters II* for horn and piano within a set of *Encounters I–VI* for various instruments with piano. Both of these works were published by Carl Fischer as a part of their Facsimile Edition series in 1972.

Variations is a demanding yet rewarding work lasting ten minutes and fifteen seconds. Tuckwell regarded Kohn as "one of the Boulez group" after working with him at summer festivals. He also "would love to have recorded it." A rather unique characteristic of this particular work is his request, "Move to position at narrow end of piano. Place bell of horn into direct contact with frame of piano harp." Playing in this position should "obtain sympathetic vibrations and maximum resonance" from the two instruments.

Karl Kohn continued with his **Trio for Violin, Horn and Piano** in 1972. Also published by Carl Fischer (and even dedicated to their 100th anniversary of publishing), this is another "very meticulously" written favorite of Tuckwell's. "I once was able to get a BBC broadcast of the Kohn Trio." This too is a work of great complexity, but "with no approximations." According to Tuckwell, Karl Kohn "knew exactly what he had written and knew when you had played what he'd written, and, by God, it had to be right." Though not as technically demanding as the *Variations*, there is still a great number of ensemble complexities, including free-sounding, unmeasured sections, which make this extensive 23-minute abstract piece a demanding challenge, but well worth the effort.

In 1974, Kohn approached Mr. Tuckwell and said, "Here, I've written a concerto for you." Tuckwell laments that he was never able to get an orchestra to perform it: The **Concerto for Horn and Orchestra**—scored for a chamber orchestra consisting of flute, oboe, clarinet, two bassoons, vibraphone, piano, and strings—appears to be a very demanding piece to prepare and perform. "As you can see from the score, it is like the Oliver Knussen piece, it requires very careful preparation." Perhaps here would be an opportunity for a striving talent on the horn to create a rewarding and significant premiere opportunity.

Thirty-two years after the talented 19-year-old first horn player in the Cincinnati Symphony, **Gunther Schuller** completed his Concerto No. 1 for Horn, conductor Mario di Bonaventura commissioned him to write a new concerto "on behalf of Barry Tuckwell." The result was the **Concerto No. 2 for Horn**, completed in 1976. It wasn't until 1978 that Tuckwell and Schuller were able to first perform this work together in Flint, Michigan. This is a work "for a huge orchestra . . . very expensive to produce. Most orchestra's budgets don't want to employ so many musicians." However, Tuckwell remembers "several performances . . . but not as many as I'd have liked, all with Gunther Schuller conducting." Though it never came to be, there was talk at one time of producing a recording with Tuckwell performing the concertos of Schuller, Bennett, and Knussen.

According to Schuller, the form of this concerto "is rather traditional, which makes it a novelty for a contemporary concerto." Schuller also admitted that the work is "a subtle tribute to the Strauss Concerto No.1 for horn. I've loved it, and played it often in my student days." Strauss was always "subliminally within the mentality of the piece." Though this piece is massive and demanding to the extreme in flexibility, strength, and range, the result for the audiences who might hear it performed well would be one of great respect for the power, lyricism, warmth, and color potentials of the horn.

"Who knows the horn's potentials better than Schuller?" is a phrase I have heard numerous times in the past. Having also performed Concerto No. 2 with Schuller conducting, I would say that Schuller's music is as demanding of horn players as he is demanding of himself as a creative being. He knows our potentials and has decided to stretch the envelope. That envelope is worth our time and study if we plan to help the horn advance as a viable solo instrument in the future.

One of the most extensive collaborations between Tuckwell and a prominent composer began in 1977 with the composition of *Actaeon* for Horn and Orchestra by the British born composer **Richard Rodney Bennett** (b.1936). According to Tuckwell, "This is a stupendous piece! The legend of Actaeon is readily identifiable. A vivid mood of the forest is set. You can even see in your mind when Actaeon is pursued by his own hounds and is torn apart. It is hair-raising and has had great impact on the audiences." This is one work that Tuckwell repeatedly said he wished he had formally recorded. However, "there was a live performance recording made at the International Horn Workshop held in Manchester, England."

Born in 1936 in Broadstairs, Kent, Richard Rodney Bennett did his formal compositional study with Lennox Berkeley and Howard Ferguson at the Royal Academy of Music in London, and in Paris with Pierre Boulez. He composed his first horn concerto in 1955–56, and has continued to compose prolifically in almost all genre imaginable, including extensive work for film, radio, and television productions. It is in this more popular mode of music that Bennett did the arranging for (and performed the keyboards on) a 1979 recording of songs: *A Sure Thing: Music of Jerome Kern*, with Barry Tuckwell rendering thirteen beautiful tunes over a small but lush chamber orchestra. These highly effective arrangements were written specifically for the recording session format and consequently are not available or even applicable for public performances.

According to Susan Bradshaw in her book *Contemporary Composers*, "no other composer has done more to develop the stylistic middle ground of twentieth century music or, incidentally, to encourage its listeners." One might describe Bennett's style as being neo-serial, which includes octaves, tonal chords, and emotionally expressive elements that stretch the listener's hearing, but does not exceed the limits of common experiences.

After *Actaeon*, in 1978, **Bennett** composed his **Sonata for Horn and Piano**. Within this twelve and one-half minute piece, the two performers wend their ways through six uninterrupted sections. Each performer has solo cadenzas, which serve to link the sections, and then they ultimately share a mutual cadenza movement followed by a brief statement of the opening "Declamato" materials to end the work. This metrically complex and technically demanding sonata (e.g., frequent stopped horn in the lower ranges) has often been publicly praised by Tuckwell as a major contribution to our repertoire. This is strong, intelligent, and challenging music, certainly worth our time. It is available from Novello and Co., Limited (Cat. No. 360001).

Tuckwell and **Bennett** performed the Sonata "so many times over the years that Richard said one day, I'm sick of the Sonata. I'll write another one." So in 1985, another twelve-minute piece was created for them to perform together. **Romances for Horn and Piano** was premiered in New York City in 1986, and has become another favorite for Barry Tuckwell. Somewhat more conservative and lyrical than the Sonata, the *Romances* are in four separate movements—Adagio, Allegretto, Presto, and Adagio, each having a definite musical association with the *Romances* of Robert Schumann. Tuckwell defines them as "dreamy." It seems, however, that such important music as this is not always made readily available. Published by Novello in 1990, these pieces are apparently out of print. Novello's catalog number for the *Romances* is 360002. Perhaps if we all ordered a copy, that might help the publisher to realize its importance.

Another little piece that should perhaps be mentioned shows the friendly relationship that has developed between Barry and Richard over the years. On Tuckwell's fiftieth birthday (April 28, 1981), **Richard Rodney Bennett** presented him with a one-minute frolic titled **"Happy Birthday to Who(m)?"** for Solo Horn. This is a clever little romp, based on the well-known Birthday Song, that weaves its light-hearted way through multi-meters and intrusive stopped-horn notes, builds to what seems a frustrated fall from an overly exuberant climactic high B, finally arrives at the triumphant naming of the "Who(m)," tagged by the much-needed final cadence. Though this piece exists only in manuscript, popular demand just might make this extremely happy little work an annual event for us all. Ask for it from Novello along with the *Romances*. That might just get it published.

Robin Holloway was born in Leamington Spa, England, in 1943, and was educated in Cambridge and Oxford, completing his Ph.D. in 1971 with a dissertation on Debussy and Wagner, which was later published in London in 1979. It is, perhaps, this deep love and affinity for the music of such late Romantic composers as Schumann, Strauss and Mahler, as well as Wagner and Debussy, that makes **Holloway's Horn Concerto, Op. 43** so very listenable. His contemporized stylistic mimicry of Straussian neo-classicism and Mahlerian rhythmic patterns, among numerous other derivative techniques so characteristic of his prolific output, makes Holloway's a strangely familiar, yet highly original voice. His Concerto is a three-movement work lasting 34 minutes. It wasn't until 1988 that the work was performed in its original design, with Tuckwell as soloist along with the Northern Sinfonia under Richard Hickox. It appears that the publisher Boosey & Hawkes convinced Holloway to break the work up into Op.43a and Op.43b, leaving the first movement, titled Sonata, as a separate piece. This was done because of its length, both for artistic reasons and with regards to the assumed stamina of the soloist. Tuckwell's feelings are that "you can't start with the second movement because the first movement is so relevant to what follows." This is a wonderful work that can be heard on a CD recorded in 1994 with Tuckwell and the Scottish Chamber Orchestra conducted by Matthias Bamert on Collins Classics (14392).

The famous Australian satirist Barry Humphries, whose characters Dame Edna Everidge and Sir Les Patterson are wildly popular in England, "is very well versed in the classical and symphonic repertoire. One day he approached me about commissioning a new work for horn and suggested **Jean-Michel Damase** (b.1928) because he liked his music." Thus, in 1985 a single movement **Rhapsodie pour Cor et Orchestre** was composed for horn solo, two each of the woodwinds, two trumpets, two trombones, four percussionists, harp, and strings. In contrast to the other pieces discussed so far, this is largely a linear, melodic piece. Damase asks for an unusual amount of muted passage work, which gives the solo line the effect of conversing with itself. As with so much of Damase's music, Tuckwell feels that this too, "is a lovely piece, really very nice." Since 1951, when Damase composed his delightful and evocative *Berceuse for Horn and Piano*, he has shown an unusual knack in writing well for the horn. He followed in 1956 with *Pavane Varie*, then in 1988 with *Aspects—5 Pieces for Horn and Piano* (student pieces). Since the Rhapsodie, he has composed and published another interesting work for horn and orchestra titled **Concerto**, which includes a piano reduction as does the Rhapsodie, both of which were published by Editions Henri Lemoine. Tuckwell informed me that he "performed the Damase only once at the premiere with the Royal Philharmonic. Again, it is the second performance that is the most difficult to get."

In 1988, another work based upon a mythological theme was created for Barry Tuckwell to perform. **Janus for Horn and Orchestra** was composed by **David Gow** through a commission by the Wyvern Theatre with funds provided by the Southern Arts Association of England. Gow was born in London in 1924, and has served as a Professor at the Universities of Oxford and London. Preceding this chamber concerto, he wrote a Sonata for Horn and Piano and a Quintet for Brass. *Janus*, according to Tuckwell, "was composed as a play/direct piece. This meant that the soloist was also expected to act as conductor. The first performance took place with the Bournemouth Sinfonietta in 1988. I've done it several times."

The inspiration and, thus, the concept behind the piece relates to the myth of Janus, who it is written was a god with two faces, one looking to the past and the other to the future. This was also thought to be the god of gates/doorways and entrances/exits. The soloist as conductor is the most obvious example of this dual perspective. Within the form of this single-movement work, there is a repetitious design of two contrasting moods and motions weaving back and forth throughout the opening and closing sections. These sections surround the larger and longer scherzando.

Paul Pritchard is an active freelance horn player, commercially successful arranger and composer, and the editor of and a contributing author to the truly fascinating and profoundly practical book, *The Business: The Essential Guide to Starting and Surviving as a Professional Horn Player*. "He's an old pal. Something like the Vince DeRosa of the London freelance scene." For the occasion of Barry Tuckwell's sixtieth birthday, Pritchard composed *Dreamtime for Solo Horn, Strings and Harp*, produced by Between the Ears Music in 1991. A sincere and loving little piece, this is an obvious gesture of friendship, which sings a gentle melody and would serve as a fine encore after one of the more highly complex works mentioned above.

The last major work to be composed for Barry Tuckwell and the last concerto he performed (with the Baltimore Symphony Orchestra on January 23 and 24, 1997) just before his formal retirement from solo touring was **Concerto for Horn and Orchestra** by **Oliver Knussen**. Born in Glasgow, Scotland in June 1952, Knussen studied composition with John Lambert and later with Gunther Schuller. His career began as the fifteen-year-old conductor of his own Symphony No. 1 and has gone on to include extensive and diversified compositions, numerous commissions and awards, college and major summer-festival teaching in Europe and abroad, conducting and guest conducting with many major orchestras (including the London Sinfonietta and the Philharmonia Orchestra) and administrative work, including co-artistic director of the Aldeburgh Festival.

Tuckwell has thoroughly enjoyed the numerous performances and also enjoyed recording *Ollie's Piece* on Deutsche Grammophon with the composer conducting the London Sinfonietta (#449572-2). "It works, and is actually easy to put together with a good orchestra; you might not think that to look at the score," Tuckwell went on to remember that his "best performance" was with David Zinman and the Zürich Symphony.

Based on a tape of a live performance, it is obvious that the orchestration for this uninterrupted, highly dramatic, and lushly lyrical composition allows the solo horn to dominate quite successfully. Many clever and fascinating dialogues occur, mostly between the solo horn and the winds, or with the other horns. Though the work is harmonically rather conservative, Knussen creates a great deal of tension and anticipation with a near-perpetual dissonant undercurrent. Both the extreme high and low registers of the horn are frequently requested, but always written to be heard without requiring excessive force from the soloist. Published by Faber, this concerto already seems to be of interest to other outstanding performers such as Gail Williams, who performed the work with the Chicago Symphony Orchestra during the spring of 1997.

It is my firm belief that it has taken this incredibly strong performer and distinguished musical gentleman named Barry Tuckwell to effectively convince the composers and performers around the world of what is actually possible on the horn. Now it is up to today's and tomorrow's active performers to become familiar with these new compositions, among other exciting and effective pieces of advanced horn writing. Through such study, a deeper understanding and appreciation for what else might be possible will develop and, thus, future performers will contribute to the continuing evolution of the horn's potentials.

These new insights might also provide us as players with the technical and musical knowledge necessary to better direct, inspire, and assist new and adventurous composers toward a greater and more active interest in the horn's potentials. Let's all go find our "Malcolm Williamsons" and help them learn from us while we learn their new music from them.

Barry Tuckwell, very early in our phone conversation, expressed his great sadness regarding Toru Takemitsu's death before composing his concerto for horn, which the International Horn Society had instigated. He felt strongly that such a loss should be a sign of what we need to do at the highest levels of encouragement: "The composers I would love to see write something for the horn would include Hans Werner Henze, Luciano Berio, György Ligeti, John Adams, Karlheinz Stockhausen, and John Harbison. I'm sure I'll think of others right after we hang up!"

Let us use this as a wake-up call to encourage our local symphonies, professional and amateur chamber ensembles, arts councils, and music clubs to support the creation of music that will bring the horn into the next century's spotlight as a more frequent and effective solo instrument. Let's help to perpetuate this remarkable legacy of fine new music written for and because of this important horn soloist, Barry Tuckwell.

27. Books and More Books

Over the years, I have reviewed numerous books about the horn because I love books and believe there are a large number of exceptionally good ones that are well worth reading, and many worth studying. Below are included all of the previously published reviews of the books about the horn that I have found helpful along with many new reviews and annotations.

Many of these books appear to be reiterations of the content of other publications. This could be considered as either an unnecessary redundancy or as a substantial reinforcement for those topics discussed. I prefer the latter description as it allows one to observe how the materials are stated and presented, usually resulting in a greater clarification, while drawing significant attention to the materials and topics that are important enough to be chosen by more than one author. Subtle variations and further illuminations can also be interesting to a receptive reader.

Pedagogy

Verne Reynolds, *The Horn Handbook*, Amadeus Press, Portland, Oregon, 1997.

Verne Reynolds has again created something very important. With the publication of *The Horn Handbook*, we are now all privileged to read and study the substantive insights of a person who, for the last four decades, has quietly been one of the most dominant, influential figures in the horn playing and teaching world.

Verne Reynolds was born in Lyons, Kansas in 1926, began his musical studies on the violin and piano, added horn at age thirteen, and continued through degrees in composition from the Cincinnati Conservatory and the University of Wisconsin followed by further study at the Royal College of Music in London. Reynolds followed all of this with a highly active and successful career in symphonic and chamber music performance (Cincinnati Symphony, Rochester Philharmonic, and the American Woodwind and Eastman Brass Quintets), and a most productive career in teaching (University of Wisconsin, Indiana University, and 36 years at the Eastman School of Music). Add to all of the above an extensive output as a composer and arranger for all genre of music.

Reynolds' depth of experience in so many fields of musical creativity can be felt throughout each insightful chapter. In the preface, he addresses the book to "anyone who is serious about playing the horn and to those who wish to organize their work habits. He seeks to make methodical those elements of playing that are calisthenic in nature, and to encourage study and analysis where historical, theoretical, or aesthetic considerations are important." Here is a book for those important years of serious, formal training. However, he emphasizes throughout the book his firm belief "that after the last lesson has been taken, we all face the necessity of becoming our own teachers." He encourages all "to continue growth toward becoming more complete musicians once the training years are passed and employment is obtained." He urges horn players "to search beyond the narrow path of their orchestral parts to discover the broad fields of great music that do not include our instrument." He also expresses his concern regarding a general "reluctance of horn players to reach out beyond their own playing to become active in the creation of superb new music for our instrument. The necessity for taking responsibility for the state of the literature should be a natural part of the musical development of all players."

This 254-page, beautifully bound hardback volume is divided into seven chapters with two epilogues. Chapter 1 is about "Practice" and thoroughly discusses the varied technical and, sometimes, psychological considerations necessary for a complete awareness of how and why things work. Reynolds' admonition that "the most productive word in the practice room is *why*," summarizes his consistent belief in the need for the student to know and grow through objective analysis and self-study. Aspects are discussed and many specific exercises are presented for such concerns as warm-ups, accuracy, breathing, embouchure formations (and changes), attacks, long tones, releases, tonguing speed, and slurring. He then continues with "the next link in our chain of practice experiences" by discussing large ensemble rehearsals as "an opportunity to practice performing at the highest standard." He also explains his thoughts on the dynamics of compatibility within a section and between oneself and the conductor. And this is just one of the many examples throughout this book of practical yet seldom discussed professional concerns that we all wish we could have come to grips with sooner in our careers. He ends this primary chapter with a truly insightful discussion of "the class lesson."

From Chapter 2, "Etudes," onward, Verne Reynolds presents to us for the first time in book form (to my knowledge) a comprehensive discussion of the basic repertoire for the horn, piece by piece. "The works chosen for discussion are those that are usually encountered for the first time during the high school and college years and continue to be studied and performed during the playing years." What we gain from this is literally dozens of clearly stated, highly effective lessons on our most significant literature.

The etudes discussed include Kopprasch (Volumes 1 and 2), Gallay (especially Op. 27 and Op. 32), and Maxime-Alphonse (Volumes 4, 5, and 6). Next, "given the enormous number of horn players now being trained, the ever-expanding technique required for contemporary works, and the noble desire of intelligent players to raise the standards of accomplishment," he recommends the etudes of Alain Weber and Charles Chaynes, and includes a thorough discussion of each of the *Vingt Etudes Concertantes* by George Barboteu; generous acknowledgements of teaching materials published and produced by James Decker, Gunther Schuller, Philip Farkas, and myself; and fourteen pages of discussion of each of his set of revolutionary etudes from the late 1950s (*48 Etudes*). This last inclusion is worth the price of the book alone.

In Chapter 3 "Playing With The Piano," Reynolds discusses the problems of performing with the fixed and uncompromising pitch and timbre of the piano. He shares thoughts on recitals, stage deportment, choosing of repertoire, and other elements of planning. Then he continues with more specific lessons on short works for horn and piano and unaccompanied works.

Chapter 4, "Sonatas With Piano," contains detailed discussions of the sonatas by Beethoven, Rheinberger, Hindemith, Heiden, Halsey Stevens, Quincy Porter, and Alec Wilder. Chapter 5 follows with discussions of the concertos of Mozart, Strauss, Glière, and Gordon Jacob. These discussions are, at times, profoundly substantive. Reynolds suggests a specific edition for reference and continues to illuminate at length those aspects important to each of the pieces. This can help us to understand their histories, appropriate performance practice considerations, significant compositional insights, the necessary and highly instructive technical directives, all toward the goal of a more informed and inspired performance.

The chapter "Chamber Music" devotes 22 pages to the discussion of the phenomenon of this most important genre of music. "In its highest form, chamber music is an effort among equals, in which each must make an equal effort." He devotes separate sections to the wind quintet and the brass quintet, and includes especially effective and insightful sections on the dynamics of the chamber music rehearsals and on intonation. Works discussed include the Mozart Quintet (K. 407), the Brahms Trio, Op. 40, the Lennox Berkeley Trio, Op. 44, and the Britten *Serenade* for Tenor Solo, Horn and Strings, Op. 31.

With Chapter 7, "Teaching The Horn," we enter into the private lesson venue as seen by the master teacher himself. Reynolds is remarkably candid and confident in his explanations concerning the myriad considerations necessary for the private teacher. This is a wonderfully original and thorough contribution to our learning as teachers and will provide many profound insights for the active student of horn regarding the complexities and concerns felt by their teachers. It is within this chapter that Reynolds gets very specific in his discussions of the orchestral excerpt repertoire and auditions.

Epilogues 1 and 2 complete this marvelous book with "26 Reminders," which are single, thought-provoking, and meaningful sentences, and a series of equally thought-provoking and meaningful questions that remind us of what is truly essential about the horn.

Verne Reynolds has composed for all horn players a new work of literary and pedagogical art. The language is clear, intelligent, and convincing. The content is insightful, important, and certainly necessary. The end result is original, personal, and often profound. *The Horn Handbook* by Verne Reynolds is beautifully balanced between idealism and realism, inspiration and exercise, subjectivity and objectivity, and manner and message. I recommend Verne Reynolds' new book without reservation and consider its publication of equal or greater importance than any other text of its kind.

Barry Tuckwell, Playing the Horn, *Oxford University Press*, London, England, 1978.

Little need be said regarding the ultimate historical importance of a method book by the famed virtuoso Barry Tuckwell. Fortunately for all of us, this collection of directives, opinions, and exercises is also an important addition to our literature.

Upon reading the table of contents, one sees the usual headings. One also might assume upon quickly leafing through the forty pages of material that there is little room for substantive new information. Slow down and read more carefully. There is a thread running through the entire text that is almost never seen in print, such as the following phrases:

"My whole approach to horn playing is to try to make it as simple as possible, cutting out all unnecessary physical activity."

"Remember that the conservation of energy is as important as muscular development." (regarding embouchure and stamina)

"Above all, breathing should be without exertion."

"Simply relax the abdominal muscles momentarily—to hesitate rather than to seize up." (regarding the release of a note)

He continues to remind the advancing student to undo those unnecessary muscular actions while acquiring new techniques and abilities.

Tuckwell addresses some interesting and less-frequently discussed problems such as posture with the bell off the leg and while standing and with the consequent right-hand position; the use of "Noo" in tonguing instead of "Too" to avoid tension and excess compression and the use of optional fingerings for tone color variety; lip and valve trills, intonation, and the avoidance of key action noise. He adds to that the use of the brass mute and some very interesting examples of a re-barring technique to aid in the practice of some selected complicated solo passages. These re-barring ideas are very interesting and quite useful.

Aside from a few excusable typographical errors, the apparent exclusion of some multiple-tonguing studies referred to in the text, and the photos of open and stopped positions of the right hand that were taken at an angle showing little if any difference, this publication has been done in a clear and exacting manner.

Tuckwell's astounding grasp of the subject and his equal ability to explain in so succinct a manner is periodically spiced with his subtle sense of humor, exemplified in the following statements:

"One can always be sure of one thing: nothing remains constant. Either there is progress or there is deterioration, mostly the latter."

"A good way of camouflaging a weak trill is to start very slowly, finish in a slow deliberate fashion as at the beginning, and incorporate a turn at the end. However dull this may sound, it is better than the disastrous mess that misguided over-enthusiasm will produce."

Barry Tuckwell and Oxford Press have also collaborated on *Fifty First Exercises for the Horn*—a progressive series of overtone studies on the F, E, E♭, D, and D♭ horns. This also is an interesting and useful book worth investigating.

William R. Brophy, *Technical Studies for Solving Special Problems on the Horn*, Carl Fischer, LLC., New York, New York, 1977.

William Brophy has composed, compiled, and written a very useful and significant supplement to our etude repertoire. As Mr. Brophy explains in his introduction, "The exercises . . . are typical of those which teachers have been scratching out for their students for many years . . . ." This statement is descriptive of the type of studies purely designed for technical ends; but it is overly modest in its tone, since much of the material is actually quite unique, and all of it is well presented and annotated by the author. Also from the introduction Mr. Brophy says that, "This book makes no attempt to duplicate the efforts of past writers for the horn. Conversely, the hope is that it will serve as an effective supplement to the standard works." This it does indeed!

Each new topic is treated with a short progression of individual studies, making it useful for the intermediate through advanced stages of study. The most unique contributions come in his chapters on pitch-bending exercises, aperture development in the low register, stopped horn exercises (well designed to foster accurate pitch, dynamic control, and lower ranges), and buzzing exercises. This chapter covers buzzing with and without the mouthpiece for the development of muscular control rather than mouthpiece pressure to control the embouchure and aperture. Mr. Brophy's chapter on buzzing is long overdue and contains some valuable insights and studies.

Other chapters involve discussions and exercises for low register, high register, lip trills, accuracy, rapid single and multiple tonguing, and a presentation of Arkadia Yegudkin's "New Beginning Exercises," which are studies for the development of secure initial attacks. This text is highly recommended.

Harry Berv, *A Creative Approach to the French Horn*, Chappell Music Co.

It is always a pleasure to find a method book that contributes high quality and new information. Harry Berv's *Creative Approach to the French Horn* does just that—and quite well. Berv states in the preface, "It is above all a practical guide; I feel it can greatly help the serious horn student, [be] useful to the instructor, [and] be of interest to the professional hornist who would like to compare his own concepts of playing and teaching with those of a colleague." Berv has aimed at a wide audience and, for the most part, has been right on target. The various chapters read as one might expect from a typical comprehensive method, but with some interesting additions, such as "Vibrato Technique" (very brief), "The Use of Mutes," "Moist Lip and Gold-Plated Rim," "Glissando," "Lips and Valve Trills," and (it's about time) "Terms Frequently Encountered in French Horn Parts." This final section also includes "General Music Terms and Directions," all in Italian, French, German, and English. A third section, "Musical Signs and Symbols," discusses musical abbreviations, a few articulation markings, ornaments, and other topics, but avoids delving into any contemporary notation, which is admittedly ambiguous territory.

At the end of some of the more problematic technical discussions (e.g., stopped horn, staccato, legato, slurred, trills), Berv includes some short original etudes and lists of recommended examples from standard etude repertoire, orchestral excerpts, and solo literature. Although there is an uneven depth of discussion in a few of the many topics included, it reads very well, contains needed new creative materials, and is recommended as a fine addition to all of our libraries.

Brian Frederiksen, *Arnold Jacobs: Song and Wind*, John Taylor (ed.), WindSong Press Limited, Gurnee, Illinois, 1996.

"When we combine song and wind, the musical message, song, is the principal element, comprising 85 percent of the consciousness. The remaining 15 percent is the application of the breath (wind) to fuel the vibration of the lips." One of this century's most influential teachers of both "song and wind" was inarguably Arnold Jacobs. He was best known as the tubist in the consistently phenomenal Chicago Symphony brass section from 1944 through 1988. Beyond his outstanding performance career, he also became one of the most highly respected authorities on the physiological requirements for artistic performance on wind instruments, especially for the brass family.

For many years, Brian Fredericksen served as Mr. Jacobs' assistant and has collected materials from many master classes, articles, interviews, past students, and colleagues. This book is full of anecdotal praise for all of the accomplishments and the vast influences rendered by Mr. Jacobs.

It is, however, the extensive and useful materials within the chapters titled "Teacher," "Physical Elements," "Mental Elements," "Performance," and part of the chapter on instruments that I recommend for all horn players and teachers. Through a thorough study of these nearly 80 pages of brilliant, insightful, helpful, and well-written lessons, we can all learn new ways to do what we need to do, both physiologically and philosophically, as performers and new ways to say it as teachers. This book compiles some of the most important philosophical principles, basic tenets, and quotations of Arnold Jacobs. That fact alone should explain why these chapters should be required reading for all wind-playing musicians.

Robert Weast, *Keys to Natural Performance for Brass Players*, McGinnis & Marks, New York, 1979.

Robert Weast, who has long been an active contributor to our growing knowledge about the many elements of brass playing, has written a remarkably fresh, innovative, creative, informative, and inspirational book. Throughout this tightly organized volume, he draws from the writings of brass pedagogy, philosophy, physiology, kinesiology, psychology, and perhaps some psychophysiology. He also uses some of what is found in *The Inner Game of Tennis* by Timothy Galwey and develops it, rather than simply rewording it as is the fad. The main premise of this treatise is stated in the preface, where Mr. Weast discusses the problems of defining the "natural player." He believes that the ideal "playing process lies outside the boundaries of language." "As the player becomes aware of musical values, he comes to know in an aural, nonverbal sense what he wants to sound like.

Players who possess a strong aural reference are able to will themselves to become something more than they already are. In this realm of the undefinable . . . the mind instructs the various technical parts of the playing system to nuance its every musical whim. But the parts function not one whit better than the stage of the mind's development."

Each chapter begins with a succinct statement of principle, such as the following:

"The playing process is controlled primarily by the subconscious mind. The conscious mind plays an attention-setting role and provides the stimulus to activate the learned motor responses."

"A quality, authentic sound and style is only possible to the player possessing a mental reference or memory of good playing by others."

"Playing concepts and techniques are more easily comprehended when one can relate these to experiences in other areas." (analogies)

The stated principle is then followed by a "Supporting Statement" drawn from the literature of the aforementioned disciplines, "Commentary," which is where the ideas develop for the brass player's specific needs, a statement of "Converse" for contrast, an "Example" of a specific activity that displays the problem in reality, an "Analogy," which illustrates and expands the implications of the principle being discussed, and then an explanation of the "Procedure" to use in helping to develop the necessary awarenesses and abilities through some well constructed exercises presented in both treble and bass clefs.

It would be easy enough to continue on about this fine book, but it is hoped that by now one can see that the *Keys to Natural Performance for Brass Players* is profoundly unique, timely, and a must for those interested in their own growth or the growth of their students toward confident, competent, and intelligent musicianship and performances.

Philip Farkas, *The Art of Brass Playing*, Wind Music, Inc., Rochester, New York, 1962.

The Art of French Horn Playing, published in 1956, has been for 40 years one of the standard texts for horn study throughout the world, and it is assumed that the reader owns a copy or is at least fully aware of its existence, content, and ultimate importance. Farkas' subsequent brass book, *The Art of Brass Playing* has been translated into at least ten languages, but has been less well known, at least in the United States. Written with the assistance of Nancy Fako, Farkas covers the basic physiological aspects of brass playing in the same logically organized and thorough manner as his previous book. The inclusion of numerous diagrams and photographs of important points being made, along with 36 photographs from three angles of the embouchures of the members of the Chicago Symphony brass section, adds greatly to this full discussion of the similarities and differences of performing on the various brass instruments. This should be the standard text for teachers of multiple brass.

Philip Farkas, *A Photographic Study of 40 Virtuoso Horn Players' Embouchures*, Wind Music, Inc., Rochester, New York, 1970.

This is a unique and potentially useful book, focusing on the characteristics of successful embouchures. Farkas' fascination with embouchure settings throughout his life prompted this collection of photos of the famous players of the day, two sets of orchestra players (from London and Stockholm) and a few younger, recently employed players. His introduction explains important and useful ways to consider these photographs as each player buzzes a high C, a third space C, and the C below middle C. Each is described by age, gender, height, weight, and lip density, as well as performing status, primary performance medium, and position. Each one's playing is then subjectively evaluated for its facility, tone, range strength, articulation strengths, tonguing speed, and dynamic control. The players' horn and mouthpiece types are also listed. Beside each picture, an approximate direction of the air stream for each buzzed pitch level is sketched. The strength of such a study rests in the reader's thorough and open-minded search for consistencies and relationships, rather than for specific solutions.

Philip Farkas, *The Art of Musicianship*, Wind Music Publications, Rochester, New York, 1976.

Farkas dedicated his final published book "to those musicians who are the performers. It is devoted to the desire to help these performers bring the music to life—to fill the air with the most beautiful vibrations possible." Within this text, Farkas does not discuss the specific techniques of playing the horn, but rather explores the nebulous realms of musical phrasing, dynamics, tempi, rhythms, articulations, expression marks, intonation, and ensemble playing. He also includes three especially unique and useful chapters on the psychology of getting along with colleagues and conductors, how to act and react within an ensemble, and ways of confronting nervousness and stage fright. This is a very wise book. It reaches out beyond the horn and the brass instruments and speaks to all musicians. It also reaches far inside its author and shares many important personal feelings and beliefs, all enclosed within Phil Farkas's typical humility and very special candor.

Gunther Schuller, *Horn Technique* (2nd ed.), Oxford University Press, Oxford, England, 1992.

Originally published in 1962, this compact 137-page volume contains great wisdom for horn players regarding the "technical problems not only in a technical sense, but in musical terms as well. As in all things in life, there is a direct proportion between a given result and the efforts necessary to obtain that result." Mr. Schuller brilliantly provides necessary information on "The Instrument and the Mouthpiece," "Tone Production," "Warm-up and other basic exercises," "Legato tonguing," "Staccato," "Miscellaneous aspects" (including muting, trills, vibrato, and an understandable discussion with graphs of the tonal spectrum of the horn), and "The Art of Practicing." The most unique information appears in the section titled, "Some Notes for Composers and Conductors." He also includes a repertoire list of nearly 50 pages, updated to 1992, with a strong emphasis on chamber music, including horn. This should also be considered a standard text for all horn students and teachers.

Frøydis Ree Wekre, *Thoughts on Playing the Horn . . . Well*, Norhornpress, Kjelsasv. 51e, N-0488 Oslo, Norway, 1994.

Frøydis Ree Wekre is one of the most effective horn teachers and clinicians in the world today. Her message is to-the-point and full of practical power, and her manner is overflowing with great charisma and universal humor. Her new book on playing the horn well is a perfect example of her relaxed and confident manner and is full of conversational substance. She writes about warming up, practicing, facial muscles, breathing, dynamics, intonation, memorizing, endurance, extremes, mental health and mental preparation, and includes a very intelligent and useful section on being your own teacher. She considers these issues from many angles and through many disciplines, and shares her beliefs in such a way that one can't help but feel that she is talking directly to the reader. This is truly a generous, creative, and helpful book.

Milan Yancich, *A Practical Guide to French Horn Playing*, Wind Music, Inc., Rochester, New York, 1971.

Milan Yancich shares many effective and, in some cases, unusual ideas and exercises used in his own development as a terrifically versatile hornist, and in his years as a teacher at the Eastman School. Special attention is given to warm-ups, re-warm-ups, preconcert warm-ups, long tones and tonal placement, multiple tonguing, and lip trills. The exercises included in these sections alone make this a special book for horn students and teachers. He fills out the content with considerations, suggestions, and exercises in posture, breathing, articulation, range, endurance, care of the lip, mouthpieces, performing skills, muting, and pianissimo playing. Here too are the best written-out exercises for the actual development (not just the exercising) of a lip trill known to me.

Douglas Hill and James Froseth, *Introducing the French Horn, The Individualized Instructor Series*, GIA Publications, Chicago, Illinois, 1976.

This beginning method book for the horn was the first of a successful series for all band instruments headed by James Froseth, professor of music education at the University of Michigan. The complete set of books is organized around a format usable for class groupings. However, there is a great deal of compact and practical information for the beginning student that is applicable to a private setting or even for self-teaching. What is still rather unique about this useful primer is the many informative photographs of elementary-school students. These

11-year-old children (one boy and one girl) were taught the exact posture, lip settings, mouthpiece positions, hand positions, tuning procedures, emptying of slides, and the basic steps of maintenance for the camera. They were not (yet) horn students and, therefore, had nothing to unlearn. (Many of these photos are included in Chapter 1 of this text and used by permission of the publisher.) Practice is discussed with helpful graphs and suggestions for parents and teachers, along with brief and to-the-point presentations of instrument care, posture, breathing control, embouchure, mouthpiece placement, articulation, instrument position, tone quality, tuning, rhythm, musical technique, and a well-illustrated section on instrument maintenance (including a very clear set of diagrams showing how to change a string). The text ends with an innovative fingering chart that descends from clearly notated open notes, thus demonstrating how the horn's valves actually lower the pitches. A short sound recording was included to help demonstrate a good tone.

Pedagogy/History Mix

Barry Tuckwell, *Horn*, Yehudi Menuhin Music Guides, Macdonald and Co., London, England, 1983. (Available through the International Horn Society)

Within 200 pages, Barry Tuckwell presents an overview of the horn, its history (made interesting), its construction and physical characteristics, its most significant composers, many of its most important performers of the past, and some insightful advice for young performers and their teachers, all within an entertaining and readable context. His perspectives gained from having been the principal horn and president of the London Symphony Orchestra, the world's leading soloist and recording artist, the first president of the International Horn Society, and now a successful conductor, a fine teacher and quite accomplished writer, leads me to recommend this book without reservation to everyone from the young and interested student to the teacher, the professional performer, and the general reading public.

Robin Gregory, *The Horn*, Faber and Faber, London, England, 1969.

Subtitled "A Comprehensive Guide to the Modern Instrument & Its Music," Gregory has provided us with just that. He devotes 180 pages to four large sections: "The Instrument," "The Player," "The Instrument and the Player," "The Instrument in Concert." This covers the historical, acoustical, and mechanical evolution of the horn, the physiological aspects of the embouchure and breathing, basic technical problems (including posture, articulation, trills, tremolos, glissandi, chords, notation, transpositions, and style), and the horn in both orchestra and chamber-music settings. The last 224 pages are devoted to one of the most comprehensive lists of horn repertoire available. The fact that this list is somewhat dated (and inaccurate) is a problem inherent to many other bibliographies. The value is in the massive amount of stimuli for further research.

History

Kurt Janetzky and Bernhard Brüchle, *The Horn*, James Chater (trans.), Amadeus Press, Portland, Oregon, 1988.

The Horn was originally published in 1977, only one year after the publication of Brüchle's and Janetzky's magnum opus, *A Pictorial History of the Horn* (see below). However, this wonderfully written, compact, 120-page overview of the history of the horn from its earliest origins to the horns and hornists of today presents many new photographs and effective drawings, along with a great deal more dialogue, as it tells the story of the horn. Brief biographies of important historical performers are included from the time of Count Anton von Sporck until the present, along with insightful discussions of the composers most interested in the horn over time. Acoustical idiosyncrasies and innovations receive special attention throughout this fine book. It is available as separate publications in German, French, and English.

Bernhard Brüchle and Kurt Janetzky, *A Pictorial History of the Horn*, Cecilia Baumann (trans.), Hans Schneider, Tutzing, Germany, 1976.

This book is a major tome and a one-of-a-kind publication for the horn student, professional, and enthusiast. In 300 beautifully produced, glossy pages, one finds nearly 300 illustrations and 17 colored plates, which alone give the reader a full visual perspective of the evolution of the horn from the conch shell to the

Paxman triple horn. The intermittent text, in both German and English, helps to explain the illustrations and includes numerous actual accounts and excerpts from the letters of important composers, performers, and from publications drawn from a variety of historical periods. Facsimile manuscripts, musical examples, and insightful dialogue all add to this magnificent publication! (Search in fine music libraries for this exceptional book.)

R. Morley-Pegge, *The French Horn* (2nd ed.), Ernest Benn Ltd., London, England, 1973.

Since 1960, *The French Horn* by Reginald Morley-Pegge has been the standard historical text for anyone interested in the horn. It is written in a very natural, readable style and contains numerous musical examples, illustrations, and photographs of horns from various collections throughout Europe. The evolution of the horn is the foundation for all inclusions. Morley-Pegge elaborates on this basic story with profound insights into acoustics, performance practices, and specific techniques from all of the various historical periods. Also included are notational considerations for each era, 27 pages of biographical sketches of distinguished hornists of the past, an extensively annotated historical list of horn makers, and a lengthy bibliography from as far back as the seventeenth century. All of this is interspersed with a running comparison of the parallel developments between France and Germany from the British perspective. He also includes representative examples of repertoire from the earlier periods of horn writing. This is the horn history book from which most others have drawn.

Horace Fitzpatrick, *The Horn and Horn Playing and the Austro-Bohemian tradition from 1680 to 1830*, Oxford University Press, London, England, 1970.

Ten years after the publication of R. Morley-Pegge's broad-based book *The French Horn*, Fitzpatrick published his scholarly, in-depth study of a limited but vitally important period and place in the development of the natural horn and its playing traditions. The Austrian traditions, which remain a standard of sound so many even today wish to attain, began with the highly influential Bohemian school of players during the late-seventeenth century. Count Anton von Sporck, upon traveling through Paris, heard the hunting horn and found it so agreeable that he caused two men from his retinue to be instructed in the art of playing it, which they shortly brought to the highest degree of perfection and upon their return to Bohemia taught others. Great details are shared regarding this important story, including the various types of instruments and mouthpieces, the specifics of the evolution of performance practices, and biographical sketches of the leading players through four generations. The text is copiously footnoted. There are numerous historically significant photographs and illustrations, a recording of 26 excerpts from Handel through Weber that were performed on various period horns, an informative glossary of terms, and an extensive bibliography.

Hans Pizka (ed.), *Mozart and the Horn*, Hans Pizka Editions, Kirchheim, Germany, 1980.

Pizka has compiled all of the known manuscripts for the horn by Wolfgang Amadeus Mozart and produced a facsimile collection with his own annotations. To see these great works in their original manuscript (including the varied colors) is quite fascinating, enlightening, and inspirational. Some additional discussion on the hand horn and on cadenzas (including written versions from various famous horn players) adds to the intended educational value. Regardless of some significant printing errors, simply having an opportunity to study Mozart's actual script is worth the price of this publication.

Reference

Mary Kihslinger (ed.), *Solos for Horn and Piano*, 5715 Windgate Dr., Toledo, Ohio 43615.

Mary Kihslinger compiled this very helpful list of solos in 1994 (in consultation with 18 colleagues and 15 publishers) with a special emphasis on the most successful pieces for earlier level students. Each entry is assigned to one of four categories, including those suitable for beginners, suitable for second-year or intermediate students, suitable for high-school or more advanced junior-high students, and suitable for the more advanced player. Each listing also includes the range, timing, publisher, and a helpful annotation. There is a ten-page section listing the available solo collections for horn and piano, including, when appropriate, the titles and composers of each piece. Kihslinger takes it one step further and provides the reader with an unusually helpful section titled "Music for Special Use," in which she separates the listed materials into the following categories for programming purposes or special teaching situations: church music, processional music, Christmas music, twentieth-century music, nationalistic works from various cultures, songs for developing a legato style, works with a jazzy or popular flavor, works about the hunt, beginner solos, and intermediate solos. She concludes her booklet with a convenient list of the publishers and their addresses.

Paul G. Anderson (ed.), *Brass Solo and Study Material, Music Guide* (1984) and *Brass Ensemble Music Guide* (1985), The Instrumentalist Company, Northfield, Illinois.

For those interested in the vast literature for all brass instruments (initially compiled in the late 1970s and updated in 1985), you would do well to acquire these volumes. Paul Anderson made use of his astounding organizational skills with the help of a computer center in compiling all possible information on the available materials from nearly 400 of the world's music publishers.

Perhaps the most valuable volume for the performing hornist, who is not teaching the other brass instruments, would be the Brass Ensemble Music Guide. The title of this compilation is misleading, as it suggests only "brass ensemble" repertoire. This is far from the total picture. The book catalogues titles in the following sections: "Two-part Music," "Three-part Music," "Music With Ten or More Parts," and "Additional Brass Ensemble Categories," and then re-catalogues the entire collection of titles in a "Composers Index." Within the sections, Anderson has organized the titles into many subcategories such as the following: 3 horns, 3 mixed brass (brass—perc.), 3 parts horn—woodwind, 3 parts brass—woodwind, 3 parts horns—keyboard, 3 parts miscellaneous—keyboard, 3 parts wind(s)—strings(s), 3 parts brass miscellaneous.

These specific categories are adjusted as is appropriate for the various repertoires, but the above should give you an idea of the dimensions of this volume. Brass with electronics, organ, voices(s), wind ensemble/band, orchestra, harp, and others are also presented. The first volume includes the teaching materials (e.g., etudes, excerpts, methods, and technical studies) and solo repertoire (e.g., concertos, sonatas, solos with band, orchestra, piano accompaniment, and unaccompanied solos) for all of the brasses along with a composers index.

Bernhard Brüchle, *Horn Bibliographie*, (3 Vols.) Heinrichshofe Verlag, Wilhelmshaven, Germany, 1970, 1975, 1983.

Mr. Brüchle's three-volume publication, devoted almost entirely to the performance literature for the horn, is certainly the most comprehensive and authoritative bibliographic reference available to date. The first volume was published in 1970, the second in 1975, and the third in 1983, making these texts somewhat dated. There are a few duplications among these volumes, but far less than one might expect. Every conceivable combination including the horn is listed within these 860-plus pages. The first volume concludes with a small collection of black-and-white photos of horns and art work that pertain to the horn, and the third adds an index of books, articles, magazines, publishing houses, libraries, collections, and music information centers.

Each of the three volumes has a thorough index of composer's names and includes many of their dates as well. It is this list that I tend to refer to often for spellings and birth and death dates while preparing programs. An added attraction is that each of the volumes is periodically adorned with interesting line drawings of horns and related materials, which make fine images for posters. These are very useful volumes for many reasons.

Michael Meckna, *Twentieth-Century Brass Soloists, Bio-Critical Sourcebooks on Musical Performance*, Greenwood Press, Westport, Connecticut, 1994.

This is the "first attempt by any musicologist to assign appropriate value to the artistry of brass instrumentalists selected on the basis of their recordings and solo appearances." The 250-page book is presented as brief biographical discussions with an emphasis on the solo recordings of each selected individual (from two to five pages each), including 49 trumpeters, 20 hornists, 18 trombonists, and 13 tuba players. The interesting selection of hornists includes Aubrey Brain, Dennis Brain, John Barrows, Meir Rimon, Philip Farkas, Domenico Ceccarossi, Alan Civil, James Stagliano, and Vitali Bujanovsky from the past; and Barry Tuckwell, Hermann Baumann, Georges Barboteu, Peter Damm, Ifor James, Ib Lansky-Otto, Frøydis Ree Wekre, Thomas Bacon, Mason Jones, Lowell Greer, and Douglas Hill from the current generations. The list is as intriguing for who it leaves out as it is for who it includes. Selected photos of a few of the soloists, and a selected discography for each is included.

Hans Pizka (ed.), *Hornisten Lexikon*, Hans Pizka Editions, Kirchheim, Germany, 1986.

In this extensive encyclopedic volume, Hans Pizka has brought together thousands of facts, photographs, graphs, trivia, information, memorabilia, data, opinions, experiences, knowledge, and suppositions regarding the horn and horn players from around the world (with a strong emphasis on Germany and Austria). This is a great browsing book for the stimulation of ideas and further study, but it includes enough subjectivity and errors that care should be taken when considering some of the details as authoritative.

Acoustics

Richard Merewether, *The Horn, the Horn...*, Paxman Musical Instruments, Ltd., London, England, 1978.

For many years, Richard Merewether was the primary horn designer for the Paxman Company, which provided him with longstanding concerns and an active involvement with many of the problems discussed in this substantive little book. This association also tends to give him an understandable commercial slant in many of his specific references.

This is basically a book on horn design, including measurements, metals, construction problems, valve systems, maintenance, and acoustics. The factual materials are extensive, important, and exceptionally well phrased. The uses of the right hand in the bell are discussed from an acoustical and intelligible point of view. The various designs of horn types and valve systems (e.g., full double, compensating double, full triple, compensating triple, dual-bore double descant, etc.) are presented in very clear diagrams, and there is also a very informative discussion about the Wagner tuba.

Much of the acoustical information is, of course, not new, but it is explained in such a manner as to be most accessible to the layperson. The "Harmonic Series" chapter alone is as clear an explanation as this reviewer has seen.

There are negative inferences made toward other authorities with other perspectives and toward other attitudes and styles. However, the extent and quality of information that one finds packed solidly into this small, 54-page book is an important and significant contribution to the performers', teachers', and students' knowledge of the horn as an entity in itself.

Willi Aebi, *The Horn and Its Inner Acoustics*, Schilke Music Products, Inc., Melrose Park, Illinois, 1970.

Though much has been written since the publication of the two articles included in Willi Aebi's booklet on horn acoustics, the historical importance of this initial study specifically addressing the horn is worthy of note. Though Mr. Aebi, who was an amateur hornist and acoustician from Switzerland, did get rather technical at times, this study could be described as user-friendly for those of us unaccustomed to such jargon. Both articles discuss the inner acoustics of the horn, and there is some crossover information between the two. The second section of the text, however, is actually a transcription of the lecture presentation by Dr. Aebi at the International Horn Workshop held in Tallahassee, Florida, in 1970. It reads with a more relaxed, verbal flow. There are graphs, all in German, but he did include a separate page of translations for the more technical terminology.

Christopher Leuba, *A Study of Musical Intonation*, Prospect Publications, Seattle, Washington, 1993.

The problems of intonation have not changed since this original and thorough study was written in 1962. However, ways of telling what pitches we are actually producing on our horns have changed. The chromatic tuner has revolutionized our abilities as players to receive instant information regarding pitch. The problem that still remains is our knowledge of what specifics work in which circumstances. The chromatic tuner can only inform you of your place on one specific scale—that of equal temperament—and that scale is not the only one we need to know about. There is so much involved in sounding in tune that goes beyond being in tune. Mr. Leuba's 25-page booklet can help to sort out some of those problems; the rest is up to us. The content is largely addressed to any instrumentalist, while freely using periodic examples from the horn repertoire.

Biography

Stephen Petitt, *Dennis Brain—A Biography*, Robert Hale Pub., London, England, 1976.

Written almost 20 years after Dennis Brain met his untimely death, this official biography discusses this extraordinary man's important life, especially the hectic professional side. The book begins "With an Appreciation by Benjamin Britten . . . penned in the autumn of 1957 in memory of an artist for whom he felt a deep respect and affection and with whom he so often collaborated." A number of other eulogies are included in Chapter 10, appropriately labeled, "Aftermath—Still Falls the Rain."

Large portions of the initial chapters are devoted to the horn playing careers of A. E. Brain, Dennis's grandfather (born in 1860), his uncle Alfred, and his father Aubrey. These careers are discussed along with the development and demise of numerous orchestras and orchestral societies in the London area. Alfred's move to the United States in 1922, first to New York and then to Los Angeles, is discussed as an important turning point for both Alfred's and Aubrey's careers.

The book's emphasis on the professional and musical lives rather than on the private life continues as Dennis enters the scene in 1921. Chapter 4, "Schooldays and Royal Academy," follows Dennis through piano and organ lessons, horn lessons with his father, his BBC debut as second horn in the Brandenburg Concerto No. 1, and his numerous awards in horn, piano, aural training, and conducting.

The coming of World War II found Dennis and many of his lifelong friends from the Academy in the RAF Central Band and Symphony Orchestra. From the early 1940s until his death in 1957, Petitt follows Dennis Brain's very active performing life. The many orchestras and chamber groups, the solo engagements, the recording sessions, the tours of Europe and the United States, the radio and television shows, the many collaborations with composers on new works for solo horn, and the development of his own orchestra that he conducted (and which occupied much of his time and interest toward the end of his life), are all discussed—at times, job by job. His personal life is revealed only through short anecdotes from his friends and colleagues, and through the inclusion of some interesting family-related photographs.

At the end of the book, there is an intriguing discussion and evaluation of Brain's style and technique. "In Dennis's hands, the horn became an instrument to be respected and enjoyed. Respected, because he raised the obscure classics by Mozart and Haydn from rare novelties to best sellers and then went on to draw inspired new works from many of the important composers of the day. Enjoyed, because his utter reliability enabled audiences to relax in his presence, savoring the true artistic expression that arises only from absolute mastery."

An appendix is then added, which includes a complete discography of the recordings by Alfred and Aubrey Brain, as well as the extensive list of official and unofficial recordings of Dennis Brain, numbering 128!

Many of us feel that it took a Casals, Rampal, Segovia, or André to bring attention and respect to their instruments. We owe it to ourselves as horn players to know as much as we can about Dennis Brain, the first to bring the valved horn into world prominence as a legitimate and respected solo instrument. This book, supplemented by his numerous recordings, is a fine addition to such knowledge.

Nancy Jordan Fako, *Philip Farkas & His Horn*, Crescent Park Music Publications, Elmhurst, Illinois, 1998.

The subtitle, "A Happy, Worthwhile Life," describes quite well the tone of this extensive and thorough biography of one of this century's most prominent and influential masters of the horn. This book is not a "dry academic document. . . . rather it is the story of the life of a warm, friendly, sociable, compassionate man who happened to have been blessed with enormous curiosity and an incredible drive to excel." Nancy Fako was a student, lifelong friend, and both musical and literary colleague of Farkas, and has created a wonderful 300-page document of fascinating details, from his childhood in Chicago until his death on December 21, 1992, in Bloomington, Indiana, his home for over thirty years. Through the many written records, the reader experiences glimpses of his extraordinary symphonic career, his equally extraordinary teaching career, his prolific writings, and his importance as the designer of Holton's "Farkas Model" horns. His family life is generously woven throughout this very readable tribute to a wonderful man.

Willie Ruff, *A Call to Assembly: The Autobiography of a Musical Storyteller*, Viking/Penguin Press, New York, 1991.

Willie Ruff is an exceptionally versatile man. Throughout his 60-plus years, he has been a jazz horn player, a bass player, a recording artist, a film maker, an impresario, a professor, a composer, an arranger, a linguist, and a writer. His autobiography, published in 1991, reads like a group of interrelated short stories, and each story is fascinating. Willie Ruff was born on Labor Day in 1931, in Sheffield, Alabama, where his musical beginnings included Mrs. Nance and her solo bass drum at the Sanctified Church.

Willie Ruff's boyhood during the depression was not easy, but it was sprinkled with many warm and touching moments. The drums were first, then the piano, followed by an open and active mind and heart to all things musical. The army came early; at age fourteen, he became a private. While in the army he was introduced to the horn and the string bass, and to his life long friend and jazz playing colleague, the pianist Dwike Mitchell.

Ruff moved on to study music at Yale University where Paul Hindemith's magnetic personality and genius expanded his musical perspectives. After having studied off and on for years with Abe Kniaz, Ruff's horn playing reached the level of an invitation from Erich Leinsdorf to join the Buffalo Philharmonic or the Tel Aviv Philharmonic. It was just then that the Lionel Hampton band, with his army buddy Dwike Mitchell at the piano, offered him a job playing horn and bass. He chose the jazz world, which brought him in contact with all the jazz greats of the mid-twentieth century.

The Mitchell/Ruff Duo, with Ruff alternating between the horn and bass, became a highly successful ensemble, gigging all over the country, specializing in young audiences, recording as a duo and with such artists as Dizzy Gillespie, touring throughout the world. Their Russian, Brazilian, and Chinese tours are full of fascination. But Willie Ruff doesn't just go along for the ride; his commitment is to spread the great story of jazz and the black music traditions to everyone who will listen. He learned the languages of the countries he visited and later added the skills of a documentary film maker to his active and creative life. He later returned to Yale University and became a professor of music.

There are so many engaging stories included in this fascinating autobiography. One learns to love this man, who appears to use every gift, every talent, every experience, and every moment of the day to learn, explore, and share himself and his music with whoever might listen.

Milan Yancich, *An Orchestra Musicians Odyssey, A View from the Rear*, Wind Music Inc., Rochester, New York, 1995.

Harold Meek, *Horn and Conductor, Reminiscences of a Practitioner with a Few Words of Advice*, University of Rochester Press, Rochester, New York, 1997.

These two recent autobiographical sojourns present, each in their own way, an entire era of orchestral playing from the perspective of two highly experienced orchestral performers. They both contain candidly expressed anecdotes about many of the famous conductors of the mid-twentieth century. These stories are, in many cases, part of the mythological fabric of their particular mid-century generation.

Meek's reminiscences include brief thoughts on different makes of horns and the changes that the horn has undergone, but most of its 115 pages are filled with personal stories regarding life in an orchestra, notably the Boston Symphony. He also includes an extended section in which the problems of 37 major orchestral horn excerpts are presented with anecdotal advice and solutions drawn from his own experiences and from his interpretations of numerous recordings.

Milan Yancich shares, with strikingly candid honesty, his observations, strong opinions, major and minor frustrations, and successes as he moves through his musical life as a performer in school, military bands, show bands, and orchestras such as the Rochester Philharmonic, the Cleveland Symphony Orchestra, and the Chicago Symphony. Throughout this 350-page, highly personal odyssey, he includes many short chapters discussing his thoughts about and memories of noted conductors, musical heroes, performance experiences, and fellow performers.

Miscellaneous

Douglas Hill, *Extended Techniques for the Horn: A Practical Handbook for Students, Performers and Composers*, Studio 224 (2nd ed.), Warner Bros. Publications, Miami, Florida, 1996.

This one-of-a-kind text (and recording) was written to fill a gap and to stimulate interest in the horn as a modern musical voice. The often simplistic horn parts being written by composers interested in the horn and the lack of horn parts by almost all other twentieth-century composers prompted Hill to investigate first what had been done and then investigate what could be done on the horn, regarding those extraordinary sounds described as extended techniques, sometimes referred to as special effects. The content is presented in a graph-like format for quick and easy reference, including the name of the technique, its notation, the sound effect it causes, the techniques necessary to produce it, and a subjective and helpful section of comments about its effectiveness and practicality. Original musical examples are also included and performed by the author on an accompanying 30-minute CD (since sound is what it is all about). The chapter titles include "Range," "Mutes," "Hand Muting," "Tonguing/Articulations," "Trills/Tremolos," "Glissandos," "Half-Valved Effects," "Varied Timbral Potentials," "Vibrato," "Quarter-tones," "Vocalizations," "Air Sounds," "Mouthpiece Effects," "Miscellaneous," and "Combinations" (of all of the above). The impact on composers since its original publication in 1983 has been significant, if not overwhelming, and many hornists are now much more comfortable with the unique potentials of this most versatile of all instruments.

Miroslav Hosek, *The Woodwind Quintet*, Bernard Brüchle Edition, Grünwald, Germany, 1979.

Miroslav Hosek's hardbound and artfully prepared book is primarily a bibliography and discography of over 3000 published and unpublished wind quintets. To add to the interest and uniqueness of this volume, there is a short essay on "The Origin of the Woodwind Quintet," which is informative though brief. There is also an essay on "Acoustics and Performance" by Mojmir Dostal, which delves into room acoustics and the relationship to the quintet's composite "unit of intensity." He continues to discuss seating arrangements, room size and reverberation, recording problems, and the individual properties of the five instruments' sound spectra and formants, rising up and dying away of the tones, and directional properties at various amplitudes.

Also included are portraits of some of the important early composers of quintet music and facsimiles of isolated pages of original quintet manuscripts and publications. An interesting inclusion is the international list of names, addresses, and varied personnel of many of the world's active quintets at that time. Other lists included are music with quintet in combination with other instruments through full orchestra, publishers with addresses, libraries and information centers, and a bibliography of sources for this particular text.

No such book can remain complete or accurate once it is published, so it was good to read in the foreword that it was meant as a beginning to be continued in a supplemental volume. This present text is, however, a special reference book for all interested wind music performers, coaches, and music libraries.

Daniel Bourgue, *Conversations About the Horn*, Nancy Fako (trans.), International Music Diffusion, Paris, France, 1996.

This is a collection of twelve brilliant lectures on subjects ranging from the French hunting horn, hand horn, Wagner tuba, and alphorn, through horn acoustics, transposition, pedagogy, interpretation, respiration, relaxation, and Mozart. Also included are insightful articles on Messiaen and his *Interstellar Call*, "The Horn Among the Woodwinds," a substantial list of repertoire, three French poems with horn overtones, and an interestingly diversified bibliography. The English translation reads quite beautifully thanks to Nancy Jordan Fako.

David M. Kaslow, *Living Dangerously with the Horn*, Birdalone Books, Bloomington, Indiana, 1996.

Subtitled "Thoughts on Life and Art," Kaslow has written a unique study on artistry from both the emotional/aesthetic as well as the practical perspectives. Included are discussions on contemporary concepts of health and healthcare, fearlessness as it relates to performance and auditioning, the strength of the individual within personal and professional relationships, and the many traps and necessities of perfectionism. The extensive bibliography demonstrates the scope of his broad-based and contemporary thought processes.

Paul Pritchard (ed.), *The Business, The Essential Guide To Starting and Surviving as a Professional Horn Player,* **self-produced, London, England, 1992.**

This unique and helpful book begins with brief introductory and complimentary notes from Andre Previn, Barry Tuckwell, and Vladimir Ashkenazy. The book begins by stating, "At college, technical prowess alone may have been sufficient to ensure your success, but now you are going to find that there are many other things to be taken into consideration." Five of the leading British hornists share their insights in the essays, "Your First Professional Symphonic Date" (Jeffrey Bryant), "Opera and Ballet" (Julian Baker), "The Horn in the Studio" (John Pigniguy), "Solo Performance and Chamber Music" (Frank Lloyd), and "General Freelance Work" (Paul Pritchard). This little book is full of very useful and practical information, insights, and stories, which apply to all professionals on either side of the ocean.

Stuart Edward Dunkel, *The Audition Process, Anxiety Management and Coping Strategies,* **Juilliard Performance Guides No. 3, Pendragon Press, Stuyvesant, New York, 1990.**

Though this is not a book directed at horn players in particular, it is, however, a book of great importance to anyone preparing to be a professional orchestral player or a professional performer of any kind. It deals directly with the realities of the music business, the specific physiological adaptations to audition stresses, ways to develop coping strategies while preparing for auditions (including diet, drugs, relaxation techniques, humor, autogenic phrases, etc.), and suggested successful attitudes and outlooks for auditioning. This is an important handbook that directly addresses these questions and provides some of the most effective answers. These are issues most of us would prefer not to think about and solutions that might require major changes in how we see ourselves as individual human beings. However, because auditioning stress is not a natural act for any of us, these issues require serious thought and investigation.

Afterthoughts: A Call to Action

During the 1970s, I was a music and book reviewer for both *Brass World Magazine* and *The Horn Call*. Through those experiences—along with my 30 years of college teaching, 40 years of performing, 25 years of workshop attendance, and perpetual reading about the horn—I have noticed some unfulfilled needs for literature, teaching materials, research, and gadgets. What follows are some of these observations and suggestions, which could use the attentions of some ambitious and talented teachers, inventors, composers, performers, horn aficionados, or the ever-searching, project-oriented graduate students.

Much of the readily available Baroque and Classical solo repertoire for the horn is poorly edited. No piano or violin teacher in the world would tolerate what we are asked to accept as justifiable editions of much of our basic repertoire. What we need are urtext editions, or at least clean publications that distinguish between the composer's markings and the editor's suggestions. A few publishers have begun this, for which I am grateful. All of our basic repertoire, however, should be made accurate and clear, and the publishers and distributing houses need to know that this is what we want and need. When students buy the least expensive (which are often the most frequently stocked) editions with no understanding of this problem, questionable phrasing, problematic ornamentation, inappropriate cadenzas, and wrong notes are perpetuated from one generation to another.

Another area that needs to be addressed is the Baroque clarino style of articulation and phrasing. Even advanced horn students have had little access to this important period of music and its unique performance problems. Because most young performers can't play fluently in the high register where actual Baroque melodic clarino writing exists, etudes should be created to introduce the style without the demands of extreme range. This would contribute more to the player's awareness of the appropriate cor alto/cor basso styles of writing than learning the Baroque style from the usual string transcriptions, such as the Corelli sonatas or Bach cello suites.

There needs to be some way to make the horn a more attractive choice of instrument for the elementary-level student. Perhaps MTV needs to be approached with videotapes of some rockin' horn players. There are such players who are actively involved in the jazz medium such as John Clark, Tom Varner, and Vince Chancy in New York City, and Arkady Shilkloper in Moscow.

At the early elementary level of learning, I am unaware of any materials or methods that truly help beginning students to find or hear their first notes. This is a major problem for the elementary- and middle-school level band directors. Extended work with chromatic tuners as feedback machines might help. How about some creative exercises involving the matching of pitches or the hearing of intervals?

Nothing in the current, readily available teaching literature, to my knowledge, actually starts at the beginning and truly *teaches* transposition. At present, most students learn by rote, playing through excerpts or complicated etudes in different keys, or they buy the transposition books that simply progress through various keys every other measure. However, to do those well, one must already be able to transpose. The understanding of key signature relationships, intervals, and clefs, along with the use of simple deductive reasoning, could all be covered in a progressive series of thoughtful studies.

It would also be helpful to have more progressive studies for younger students of modern musical and technical problems, such as multi-meters, unexpected intervals, unique notation, and some of the more basic extended techniques like flutter-tongue, half-valve, stopped horn, echo horn, vocalizations, various glissandi, and quarter-tones. These ear-stretching, mind-expanding musical challenges should be confronted long before a player has arrived in college, or before they have developed a too-conservative, close-minded opinion about such important musical gestures and techniques.

As far as new solo repertoire and frequent inclusion in contemporary chamber music compositions is concerned, the horn still lags behind the other brass instruments in popularity. Many modern composers have avoided the instrument out of fear of its reputed difficulty. Its reputation as the most difficult instrument to play tends to lead to lower expectations from everyone. This, along with the fact that many fine performers prefer to spend all of their time with the abundant literature of the eighteenth and nineteenth centuries, has caused many composers to become disinterested. During the past couple of decades, however, this trend seems to have shifted a little, thanks to new commissions, contests, and recorded performances by a few of the talented and visible performers. Every performer should continue this trend by encouraging composers to write and by being willing to perform such works. Better yet, we horn players should write for the horn. Composers might notice and take the hint and learn about what our capabilities and preferences are. Our instrument's future may depend upon it.

We now have some fine new excerpt books for the orchestral and operatic repertoire. Many are clear, accurate and, in a few cases, intelligently annotated by experienced performers. I know of no source, however, for difficult passages from chamber music in general or from the standard ensembles such as brass or woodwind quintets. There are also no collections of excerpts for the basic band and wind ensemble repertoire. I realize that there are always problems associated with copyrights for recent compositions, but similar problems have been overcome for the orchestral repertoire. All one has to do is ask for the permissions or go to the publishers who own the copyrights and ask them to publish the excerpts as a form of advertisement. Mason Jones did this with G. Schirmer for his "20th Century Orchestral Studies" collection.

Research projects that seem worthwhile and interesting could include the following: an English language study of the Scandinavian Lur, Etruscan cornu, Roman buccina, or the Russian horn bands; a thorough study on the problems and solutions for recording the horn well; Antonin Dvořák's writing for the horn; the horn and other composers of interest, such as Stravinsky, Hindemith, Musgrave, Richard Rodney Bennett, Verne Reynolds, Gunther Schuller, and others; extended biographical studies of such hornists as Bruno Jaenicke, Max Hess, Alfred Brain, or Anton Horner in the United States; or further back, Ignaz Leitgeb, Carl Türrschmidt, Giovanni Puzzi, the Lewy brothers, Franz Strauss, Friedrich Gumpert, to name a few.

There is a need, now that the International Horn Society's Advisory Council of 1997 voted to stop the publication of the *Horn Call Annual* (which was its only scholarly, refereed publication), for someone to create such a venue to encourage, collect, and make available to interested readers and libraries the finest thinking and research on the horn. Scholars interested in the horn, who are increasing in number every year, need the outlet and encouragement to continue to contribute to our learning. If the International Horn Society continues to feel that such a separate publication is not within its domain, then we must look elsewhere. But it should be done.

Developing chamber-music skills is crucial to a musician's growth. Chamber music is the perfect opportunity for students to heighten listening abilities, develop creativity and stylistic awareness, refine their sense of empathy and teamwork with other musicians, and generally grow as musical personalities. These same skills enhance a performer's ability to succeed in a large ensemble, such as a symphony orchestra or band. It would be wonderful if more schools and colleges developed their chamber-music programs as carefully as they have cultivated their bands and orchestras. In most cases this has not happened because of the problems of balancing the abilities, personalities, and time commitments of the many students and faculty involved. But if it could become a greater musical priority, the benefits would, I believe strongly, far outweigh the difficulties.

Some creative inventor should come up with a silent, spring-loaded mute exchanger for those times that the performer, while standing, doesn't wish to go through the visually distracting, and sometimes aurally distracting, activity of grabbing for a mute at a musically subtle moment. We could also use a portable, adjustable, lightweight reflector with a wood veneer (not lucite) to be positioned behind our bells at those times when we are placed in front of curtains, people's bodies, or an open space. How about a floating hand guard for the left hand, so that those who need or desire the lack of constant contact with the metal will not have to inhibit the free vibration of the mouthpipe and the bell-tail? I've also wondered whether it would be possible to have a constant (silent) sucking device, similar to the ones used by dentists for the eradication of moisture, to be attached to the first turn of the mouthpipe at the opening of a water-key. This could eliminate the constant dumping of the condensed moisture. The moisture could be collected into a bag for other purposes at a later time. Perhaps I should stop here and leave the inventing to others.

Regardless of all of the above concerns and ideas, I have a strong feeling that the turn of the century has truly become the best of times for horn players. There are many opportunities to hear the great performers on recordings, in live concerts, and at horn workshops. More outstanding craftsmen than ever are raising the quality of horn construction and modification. Factory-made instruments are also improving in quality and consistency. A great deal of previously unknown literature from the past is being uncovered and made available for study and performance. The horn has made strong inroads into popular music, especially jazz. The quality of teaching horn has improved by leaps and bounds due largely to the availability of information and the generational evolution of new teachers who have studied with the many outstanding teachers of the mid-twentieth century. The International Horn Society has opened new lines of communication and exchange around the world with its publications, workshops, grants, commissions, and composition contests. And the electronic tools now available have made self-recording easier and much better, self-tuning is now more effective and efficient, practice mutes are now almost silent to the neighborhood, and the internet chat lines give vent to those who wish to share the most recent information, opinions, and gossip.

There is always room for improvement and growth, but all it takes is a few talented people with concern, plans, and the enthusiasm to follow through. It takes people who want to make a contribution, who want to make things better. We are all a part of this wonderful period of growth. Let's all contribute what we can; let's all try to make a difference.

KEY TO MUSIC PUBLISHERS

Accura Music (USA)

AMP
Associated Music Publishers
(see Hal Leonard)

Arcadia Music Publishing Co.
London, England

Augener (UK)
(see ECS Publishing)

Baltimore Horn Club (USA)

Belwin-Mills Publishing Corp.
(see Warner Bros. Publications)

Benjamin
Anton J. Benjamin (Germany)
(see Theodore Presser Co.)

Berandol (Canada)
(see Magnamusic Distributors)

Billaudot
Editions Billaudot (France)
(see Theodore Presser Co.)

BIM
Editions BIM (Switzerland)

Birdalone Books
Bloomington, IN (USA)

Boelke-Bomart Inc.
Hillsdale, NY (USA)

Boston Music Company
Boston, MA (USA)

Boosey & Hawkes, Inc.
New York, NY (USA)

Bote & Bock (Germany)
(see Boosey & Hawkes)

Bourne Company
New York, NY (USA)

Brass Press
Clearwater, FL (USA)

Brass Ring Editions (USA)

Breitkopf & Härtel
Leipzig, Germany
Weisbaden, Germany

Brodt Music Publications
Charlotte, NC (USA)

Brogneauz
Editions Musicales Brogneaux (Belgium)

J. W. Chester Music (UK)
(see Music Sales Corporation)

Choudens (France)
(see Theodore Presser)

Cor Publishing Co. (USA)

Doblinger
Ludwig Doblinger (Germany)

Donemus (Holland)
(see Theodore Presser)

Durand S.A. (France)
(see Theodore Presser)

ECS Publishing
Boston, MA (USA)

Henri Elkan Music Publishing Co.
New York, NY (USA)

Elkan-Vogel, Inc.
(see Theodore Presser)

Elkin Music International, Inc.
Fort Lauderdale, FL (USA)

Eschig
Editions Max Eschig (France)

Edition Eulenberg (Switzerland)

Faber Music, Ltd. (UK)
(see Hal Leonard or Boosey & Hawkes)

Randall Faust (USA)

Carl Fischer, LLC.
New York, NY (USA)

Sam Fox Music Co.
(see Plymouth Music Company)

Galaxy Music Corp.
(see ECS Publishing)

General Music Publishing
(see Boston Music Company)

Gehrman
Carl Gehrmans Musikverlag (Sweden)

Hansen
Edition Wilhelm Hansen (Germany)
(see Shawnee Press)

Heinrichshofen Edition (Germany)
(see C. F. Peters)

Editions Henn (Switzerland)

Hofmeister
Friedrich Hofmeister Musikverlag
Leipzig, Germany
(see Elkin Music)

Hamelle et Cie (France)
(see Robert King or Theodore Presser)

Hidden Meaning Music
New York, NY (USA)

The Hornists' Nest (USA)

International Horn Society Press (USA)

International Music Company
(see Bourne Company)

Israel Brass & Woodwind Publications (Israel)
(see Robert King Music Sales)

Israeli Music Publications (Israel)
(see Theodore Presser)

Jomar Press
Austin, TX (USA)

Ka We
Editions Ka We (Germany)

Kendor Music Co.
Delevan, NY (USA)

Robert King Music Company
Robert King Music Sales, Inc.
North Easton, MA (USA)

Kunzelman
Edition Kunzelman (Switzerland)
(see C. F. Peters)

Leduc
Alphonse Leduc et Cie (France)
(see Robert King Music Sales, Inc.)

Leeds
(see Warner Bros. Publications)

Alfred Lengnick & Company LTD (UK)
(see Elkin Music)

Hal Leonard Corp.
Milwaukee, WI (USA)

Leuckart
F. E. C. Leuchart
(see Hal Leonard)

Lyceum Press (USA)

Magnamusic Distributors
Sharon, CT (USA)

Manduca Music Publications
Portland, ME (USA)

Margun Music
Margun/Gunmar Music, Inc.
Newton Centre, MA (USA)

Masters Music Publications, Inc.
Boca Raton, FL (USA)

MCA Music
Universal Music Group
(see Warner Bros. Publications)

McCoy Horn Library
Minneapolis, MN (USA)

McGinnis & Marx Music Publishers
New York, NY (USA)

Medici Press
St. Cloud, MN (USA)

Mentor Music, Inc.
Brookfield, CT (USA)

Merion Music Inc.
(see Theodore Presser)

Mills
(see Warner Bros. Publications)

Editions Modern (USA)

Molenaar Muziekcentrale
(see Henri Elkan Music Publishing Co.)

Ms Publications
Chicago, IL (USA)

Music Sales Corporation
New York, NY (USA)

Editio Musica Budapest (Hungary)
(see Boosey & Hawkes or Theodore Presser)

Musica Rara (France)

Musicians Publications
Trenton, NJ (USA)

Edition Musicus, Inc.
Stamford, CT (USA)
Music Express (USA)

Mussik Huset A/S (Germany)

New World Enterprises of Montrose, Inc.
Montrose, NY (USA)

Norsk Musikforlaget (Norway)

AD Nordiska Musikforlaget (Sweden)

Novello (England)
(see Music Sales and Shawnee Press)

Oxford University Press
New York, NY (USA)

Panton
(see New World Enterprises of Montrose, Inc.)

Patterson
(see Carl Fischer)

Pegasus (Germany)
Pelikan Musikverlag
Zurich, Switzerland
(see Magnamusic Distributors)

C. F. Peters Corp.
(Edition Peters, Germany, UK)
New York, NY (USA)

Philharmusica Corporation (USA)

Phoebus Publications
Oshkosh, WI (USA)

Phoenix Publications (Netherlands)

Pizka
Edition Hans Pizka (Germany)

Plymouth Music Company, Inc.
Fort Lauderdale, FL (USA)

PP Music
(see Manduca Music)

Prague-Hudebni Matice
a division of Editio Supraphon
(see New World Enterprises of Montrose, Inc.)

Presser
Theodore Presser Company
King of Pressia, PA (USA)

Pro Art Publications
(see Warner Bros. Publications)

Pro Musica Verlag (Germany)

Queen City Brass Publications
(see Manduca Music)

Editions Marc Reift (Switzerland)

G. Ricordi & Co. (Italy)
(see Hal Leonard)

Rubank
(see Hal Leonard Corp.)

G. Schirmer, Inc.
New York, NY (USA)
(see Hal Leonard or Music Sales)

Schonenberger
Paris, France

Schott Music
European American Music
(see Warner Bros. Publications)

Seesaw Music Corp.
New York, NY (USA)

Shawnee Press Inc.
Delaware Water Gap, PA (USA)

Siècle Musical
Geneva, Switzerland

Sikorski (Italy)
(see Hal Leonard)

N. Simrock (UK)
(see Theodore Presser)

Skandinavisk Musikforlag (Denmark)

Southern Music Company
San Antonio, TX (USA)

Spindrift Music Co.
Lexington, MA (USA)

Studio P/R
(see Warner Bros. Publications)

Mark Teezak (Germany)

Tischer & Jagenberg (Germany)

Universal Edition
(see Warner Bros. Publications)

University of Wisconsin School of Music
Madison, WI (USA)

Warner Bros. Publications
Miami, FL (USA)

Western International Music (USA)

Wimbledon Music Company (USA)

Zimmerman
Wilhelm Zimmerman (Germany)

Index

Applause

"Professor Hill's book is, in my opinion, the most important detailed analysis of horn-playing technique since that written by Philip Farkas. Having written my own method on horn playing, I am acutely aware of the difficulties an author has in presenting his/her thoughts in an understandable and clear style. Professor Hill has done this very successfully. The work is original and is well researched. The author has basically presented a treatise on horn-playing technique, which, if studied carefully, would be of great benefit to all students, professionals, and amateurs." Barry Tuckwell, international soloist, recording artist, conductor, author

"This is a book that we as performers and teachers of this wonderful instrument have been waiting for. I am sure that it will be recognized as the definitive benchmark, working tool for as long as there are people interested in making music on this instrument. Congratulations to Doug. I doubt that anyone could have done it better." Arthur David Krehbiel, 1st horn, San Francisco Symphony; San Francisco Conservatory (retired); Music Academy of the West

"This is a book to which horn players will return, time and again, for information about techniques, performance, teaching, creativity, and all areas of horn literature. It is written with a refreshing economy of words, resulting in an appealing way of getting right to the point. Douglas Hill has given us a book for 21st-century horn playing." Verne Reynolds, professor emeritus, Eastman School of Music; composer; author of *The Horn Handbook*

"It is obvious after reading *Collected Thoughts* that the author is an experienced and dedicated teacher. Hill's approach is one of extreme positiveness and encouragement, and he covers a wider variety of subjects than can be found in any other single book currently on the market. Douglas Hill's new work is an important addition to the field of teaching and learning and should be welcomed by students and teachers alike." Norman Schweikert, Chicago Symphony; professor of horn, Northwestern University (retired)

"In this book, Douglas Hill shows us what it means to be a whole musician. It encourages and empowers individuals to take active roles and responsibilities in their own education and life, leading to lifelong learning and enjoyment of music. The balance of 'big-picture' issues with specific details and strategies is outstanding, and the repertoire and reading lists alone are worth the price. Douglas Hill doesn't just cause us to think 'outside the box,' but he also shows us why and how the 'box' could be bigger." Jeffrey Snedeker, professor of music, Central Washington University; editor of *The Horn Call, Journal of the International Horn Society*

"Hill has long been a member of that small elite group of musicians who are superbly gifted as both teachers and performers. What makes Mr. Hill unique among them, as his new book so richly documents, is the stunning breadth of these interests combined with his eloquent reflection on every aspect of horn playing and musicianship. I know of no other book that treats in depth so many topics (few of which are covered elsewhere in books or articles on horn). It's all there—and more. Hill's interest in finely tuned personal teaching makes each article both a source of well-organized information as well as a passionate exhortation to put it into practice. Students will find here a complete road map through the tangled thicket of horn mastery, one that will guide, comfort, and inspire at every step in development. No horn teacher can ignore this book. Even professional players will find themselves muttering, 'Hmmm, maybe I should try that' more times than they thought possible. In short, Douglas Hill's *Collected Thoughts* is a refreshing read and a gold mine of horn lore. It is an indispensable book for all horn players. Period." Jeffrey Agrell, associate principal horn, Lucerne Symphony; composer; teacher, University of Iowa; horn editor for *The Brass Bulletin*

" I found Douglas Hill's new book *Collected Thoughts* thoroughly inspirational, educational, and most enlightening to read and study. Full of great hints and ideas for students and teachers of all ages, full of wisdom and useful information, this is a very welcome must for every horn player's library." Frødis Ree Wekre, international soloist; recording artist; author; professor at Norwegian State Academy of Music; past president of the International Horn Society

"Professor Hill's *Collected Thoughts* fills a unique place among the finest horn tutors with a holistic approach that encompasses technique, psychology, philosophy, creativity, and a positively contagious love of all things related to the horn. His book is the summation of a lifetime of experiences of one of the horn's greatest Renaissance men. Learn from this thoughtful teacher, performer, and composer. Read it, study it, and apply the wisdom from these pages." Randy C. Gardner, former 2nd horn, Philadelphia Orchestra; professor of horn, Cincinnati College-Conservatory

"Douglas Hill's passion for the horn, its sound, its technique, and its repertoire; for learning, creativity, and for teaching; and the power, communication, and value of music is abundantly evident on every page of this treatise. His words inspire the reader to self-improvement. His book is a resource I know I will use throughout the rest of my teaching career, returning to specific subjects for my own inspiration and referring students to sections particularly relevant to their present needs. Doug is meticulously careful to choose words that promote a relaxed and positive concept of horn playing, concepts apart form others' whose emphases are often on what to do rather than how to conceptualize. His writing is always personal and conversational, inviting the reader to respond with thoughtfulness and creativity. The overwhelming theme of the book is self-improvement: the art of becoming the best player, student, teacher, and musician that we can be. Doug Hill has presented all of us with a rare and generous gift." Kristin Thelander, professor of music-horn, University of Iowa; past vice president of the International Horn Society

"Douglas Hill is an intelligent, talented, and erudite musician and scholar who has already donated his talents to the music world through compositions, recordings, and performances; with time as president of the International Horn Society; through his many excellent students; and with his prose, including many articles and his remarkably clear book *Extended Techniques for the Horn*, arguably the best resource of its kind for any instrument. In this most recent book, Professor Hill creates a safe and supportive environment, similar to what he offers in person, as he integrates his knowledge into a comprehensive and clear passage. His writing is expert, confident, and encouraging; the tone is unfailingly positive and the mood generous as he shares his far-ranging and solid knowledge of playing and teaching. I discovered many suggestions and projects for improving my own playing, and I find myself reading excerpts to my students already to clarify points I am trying to make. This book will support a lifetime of playing music on the horn. Thank you!" Jean Rife, recording artist, horn instructor, chamber music coach, Yoga for Musicians, New England Conservatory and MIT

"Douglas Hill's latest book *Collected Thoughts* provides convincing documentation for why he is considered the epitome of the university horn professor and one of the most respected horn teachers and players in the United States today. Doug is not merely a 'horn jock;' he is a thinking, feeling, creating artist and human being. These qualities come out most sublimely in the book's sections on 'The Process of Teaching and Learning' and 'Creativity and the Complete Musical Self.' These twelve chapters offer valuable insights on artistry and creativity for all musicians, not just horn players. This book is full of information and inspiration from beginning to end. It is a must-have for serious horn students and teachers and should be in every music library." Johnny Pherigo, professor of music (horn), Western Michigan University; past editor of *The Horn Call*

"Thanks to his vast and diverse experiences, Douglas Hill is able to present this extremely important document that is all-encompassing. The in-depth coverage of every aspect of playing is articulate and concise. The section concerning literature and repertoire is comprehensive and of exceptional value." Michael Hatfield, past principal horn, Cincinnati Symphony; professor of horn, chair of brass department, Indiana University School of Music

"Douglas Hill, a superb horn teacher, has brought his intensity and integrity to bear on the many knotty aspects of horn pedagogy. Here is the most comprehensive compilation to date encompassing technical basics and the musical essentials for beautiful horn performances. This book provides a needed integrated summary of the basic details of tone production through necessary personal disciplines to annotated resources for horn students and teachers. Here is a book that brings to light the very heart, soul, and spirit of horn playing. It is a prized resource for all serious students of the horn." Paul Mansur, dean emeritus, School of Arts and Letters, S.E. Oklahoma State University; past editor, *The Horn Call*

"I thoroughly enjoyed reading your book. I thought the introduction to each chapter (in italics) was so helpful. It was interesting to read your explanations and reasons for including each chapter and the background of your experience with the subject under discussion. I felt as though you shared your whole life of musical and teaching experiences with your readers, and that is an incredible wealth of material. I loved the chapter on jazz and the one titled 'Compose Yourself,' where you encourage creative, original thinking and experimentation. The stories about your junior high music teacher and your father were especially memorable. Your chapters on repertoire are probably the finest descriptive comments and suggestions I have ever seen. I was amazed by your descriptive language. It is a superb reference section. Thanks for sharing it with me!" Nancy Becknell, emeritus professor of horn, University of Wisconsin-Madison; past officer, International Horn Society